REVIEW   1

WITHDRAWN

Editorial Board

REVIEW

Volume 1 1979

Edited by

James O. Hoge and
James L. W. West III

University Press of Virginia
Charlottesville

Contents

Contents

Preface

Review publishes review essays and reviews of scholarly work in English and American language and literature. We solicit rigorous and expansive essays which appraise, in detail and with meticulous care, the quality and value of the books under examination. No restrictions are placed on the length of a review: contributors are urged to write broadly about the current state of affairs in an entire field of literary scholarship as well as about the perceptiveness, accuracy, usefulness, and usability of a particular work or group of works. *Review* will avoid publishing brief or impressionistic or less-than-wholly-serious essays. We regard reviewing as important work requiring special talents, and we mean, frankly and boldly, to engender a reassessment of the nature and purpose of scholarly reviewing.

As a series devoted entirely to academic reviews, *Review* must be unique. With the partial exception of the *Review of English Studies,* there is nothing else like it. Few current journals, in fact, give much space or attention to the reviews they do publish. Nearly all scholarly journals place severe limits on the length of their reviews. Reviewers are routinely instructed to limit their comments to 400-750 words. Editors tend to reserve diligent scrutiny for articles and to direct reviews to the book review editor and, of course, to the back of the issue, where they are printed in reduced type to emphasize their insignificance. Perhaps as a consequence, scholarly reviewing is in a sorry state, having found the level of that low regard in which it has come to be held.

Why does such a situation exist? Why is it that one reads so many reviews that are brief and inconclusive, so many that fail to make any sort of firm statement either to praise or to blame, so many that are bland, or formulaic, or just plain badly written? Of course, the second-class treatment accorded reviews by most journals is one explanation. But clearly there is a reason behind that reason: the intellectual community, centered in the university, does not take reviewing seriously. Academicians receive little credit for doing reviews no matter how excellent those reviews may be; members of our profession are therefore, in effect, encouraged *not* to write reviews. This attitude ignores the fact that reviewing is a skill, even an art, demanding specific abilities—some of them quite different from the talents needed to do original research. This attitude also reveals a serious failure to comprehend the high value of a thoroughly tough-minded review. Such a review calls the author's or the editor's hand as nothing else can. It discourages imprecise scholarship and half-baked or repetitive criticism, along with the shoddy standards they reflect. And it helps to reward the careful and incisive writer and to promote the continuation of his good work. Could it not be that the dearth of painstaking reviews partly explains the mediocrity of much that sees print these days?

Each spring, *Review* will publish examinations of a considerable number of scholarly books: critical studies, literary biographies, textual editions, bibliographies, reference works, and volumes on book collecting and printing history. We even intend occasionally to review other journals. Some reviews will treat only a single book; others will deal with several related works. It will of course be impossible for *Review* to print notices of all scholarly works, in all fields, that appear during a given publishing season or year. *Review* will aim, rather, for representative coverage of literary genres and periods in a variety of scholarly disciplines. Some notices will be "timely," appearing shortly after publication of the book or books under review, but others may well appear several years after publication of the works they treat. In this way, *Review* authors will be able to take into account—and to comment on—the initial reception that works of scholarship have received.

All reviews are assigned to contributors by the editors. Acting on the advice of our editorial board, we have attempted to match scholarly works with reviewers who are qualified to examine them. And we have chosen reviewers from all ranks of the profession. We have enlisted "name" contributors who are experienced authorities in their fields, but we have also actively sought out talented younger scholars. We should make it clear that the reviewers' manuscripts are not automatically accepted for publication. All manuscripts are read by both editors and in addition by one or more members of the editorial board. Comments and suggestions for revision are then sent to contributors. Every review in this first volume has been revised, at our request, at least once after initial submission. Some revisions have been minor, others quite thoroughgoing. Regrettably, several reviews have been rejected even after extensive revision. In all cases, the editors have attempted to protect authors of scholarly works from capricious or unsubstantiated statements, but by the same token we have in no instance discouraged a reviewer from speaking his mind. We welcome commentary generated by our reviews and will publish such commentary if publication is warranted.

Review offers the scholarly community a new forum exclusively for reviews—a place, previously unavailable, to publish treatments that are both lengthy and exacting. We hope, we trust, that *Review* will stimulate new interest and activity in scholarly reviewing. We hope also that the appearance of *Review* will encourage editors of academic journals to expand their review coverage and to relax their length restrictions. Perhaps *Review* can thereby help to foster prudence, conscientious preparation, and forethought in the writing and publishing of scholarly work.

We are indebted to numerous persons for assistance in launching this first volume of *Review*. We should like particularly to thank John D. Wilson, Wolter J. Fabrycky, William C. Havard, Henry H. Bauer, Thomas E. Gilmer, Jr., Arthur M. Eastman, and Hilbert H. Campbell for their active interest and cooperation. We are also grateful to Walker Cowen, Gerald Trett, Linda Hamme, Ann H. Eastman, A. J. Colaianne, and Robert L. Entzminger for advice and suggestions. Finally, we owe special thanks to Leota Williams for her diligence, accuracy, and good humor.

JAMES O. HOGE
JAMES L. W. WEST III

REVIEW 1

Johnson on the Couch

John H. Middendorf

W. Jackson Bate. *Samuel Johnson*. New York: Harcourt Brace Jovanovich, 1977. xxii, 646 pp.

The epigraph to W. Jackson Bate's latest work on Samuel Johnson is attributed to Pythagoras: "What is your warrant for valuing any part of my experience and rejecting the rest? . . . If I had done so, you would never have heard my name." The epigraph points to Bate's intention to examine Johnson from every side—the man, the writer, the writing, both public and private. As other reviewers have pointed out, this places Bate's book in a tradition which began in 1785, the year after Johnson's death, with memoirs by Tyers, Shaw, and others—including Boswell's *Tour to the Hebrides*—and which has been carried down to our own time by, most notably, Krutch in 1944 and Wain in 1975.

The difficulties facing a modern scholar with such ambition are enormous, perhaps more so with Johnson than with any other literary figure, for by now a mountain of information and criticism has accumulated, and to reach its summit one encounters obstacles as formidable as any faced by Johnson's Hermit of Teneriffe. In one volume the known facts of the life can hardly be presented exhaustively (consider simply the work of A. L. Reade and James L. Clifford for the first thirty years alone), nor can the writings be given the careful analysis and interpretation that they merit. Choices must be made, perspectives established, decisions of focus and direction reached. For having succeeded as well as he has, Bate deserves the highest credit. We are not surprised to see that he has done his job well; we are surprised to see that he has done it at all.

One objection to the book, hinted at by earlier critics, should, I think, be laid to rest at the outset: Given the present advanced state of Johnsonian scholarship, what need to add to its bulk?

The obvious answer is that a man has a history of meaning just as surely as a book does; and every responsible attempt, like Bate's, to add to that history should be welcomed. The essential Johnson known to his contemporaries is not in every particular the essential Johnson known to us. The crucial question is not, Is there a need for another book on Johnson? but rather, Is there a need for another book on Johnson of this sort?—designed, as it is, for what Johnson would call the common reader. To this I must give a less confident answer.

The two best full-length lives and critiques in the past thirty-five years have been those by Krutch and Wain. Krutch has in important ways been superseded by Wain, but will Wain be superseded by Bate? No doubt Bate's name and reputation as a Johnsonian scholar will carry the day, but I am not entirely convinced they should. Both Bate's and Wain's portraits are notable for their generous, deeply felt understanding of Johnson's tortured humanity. But Wain's is presented with the stylistic touch and awareness of narrative form of a novelist-poet who not only knows Johnson but also knows his audience and keeps it steadily before his eyes. The result is a responsible and moving introduction to Johnson that cannot fail to grip the common reader for whom it is designed. Bate's fails to come through consistently with the same force, for he has not always faced up to the question of audience. Willy-nilly, he appears to have kept one eye on the common reader, one on the scholar. The result is a kind of squint-eyed study that cannot entirely satisfy either. In saying this, I realize that my assumption about the common reader is contradicted by the testimony of countless reviewers (in the popular press and elsewhere) and judges who have acclaimed the book. Perhaps that acclaim raised my expectations too high.

A simple illustration of the problem may be seen in Bate's handling of the famous Wilkes dinner so adroitly set up by Boswell. Bate uses it to help establish Johnson's concern for "good manners." He skillfully abridges the story to one paragraph, but in the process, inevitably, the narrative movement, the dramatic tension, and much of the sly irony of Boswell's account are lost. To be sure, the scholarly reader will have been reminded again of Boswell's account and will derive renewed pleasure from the memory, but he will have been given no new information or interpretation. The common reader, to whom the event may not be familiar, will have missed out on one of literature's most delicious moments, and if he *has* heard something about it, may well wonder what all the fuss is about. One can understand Bate's dilemma here: a life and critique of Johnson cannot *not* include the Wilkes story, for the common reader *should* know it; but it cannot be dwelt upon, for the scholar *already* knows it. Krutch, incidentally, compromises: he abridges the story and quotes the interchange in which Boswell is twitted and Johnson and Wilkes good-humoredly jab at each other's moral reputations. Wain knows a masterpiece when he sees one, and simply refers his reader to Boswell.

In any event, the fact is that when I first picked up Wain's book, I found myself swept along, heedless of occasional inaccuracies, not as convinced as he was that all moral standards disappeared with the eighteenth century, yet always impatient to keep moving. Wain made me into a common reader. In reading Bate—perhaps partly because of the demands of this review, but only partly—I found myself pausing to question details, wondering why this was included here, that omitted there. The scholarship took over, demanded attention and evaluation. Johnson always remained up front—how could he not?—but I missed the sense of being intimately in his presence as he lived out his life in his eighteenth-century world—the kind of sense awakened by Wain's book or by Clifford's less ambitious, more scholarly, more concentratedly biographical, and hence more densely textured *Young Sam Johnson*. Wain's book is an act of love, done with experienced spontaneity. Bate's is an act of love, performed more by rule.

Putting aside for a moment Bate's main concern—the psychology of Johnson—there can be no doubt that the traditional Johnson is here vividly presented, given a full share of attention: Johnson's uncompromising honesty and insistence on seeing things as they really are; his intellectual and conversational aggressiveness; his vile melancholy; his fear of insanity; his guilt-induced indolence; his courage, often verging upon foolhardiness and even self-destructiveness; his compassion and generosity, extended with never a moral price attached; his capacity for self-ridicule and horseplay; his humor. Indeed, Bate's chapter on this last is excellent, a long-needed corrective to Boswell's limited appreciation of this dominant yet elusive side of Johnson's makeup. The explanation of Johnson's cosmic laughter over Langton's will is exactly right.

At the center of this traditional view Bate finds what he calls Johnson's "essentialism," a term he uses less in its educational or philosophical senses than as a loose equivalent of realism, with dashes of empiricism and pragmatism. Essentialism is Johnson's "scorn of (or more often . . . oblivion to) . . . artificial distinctions and complaint (in Johnson's phrase, 'imagination operating on luxury')" (p. 212). It is "the 'stability' of concrete experience, the 'putting to use' of moral experience, so that we [can] learn 'how to live' " (p. 217). Johnson's "hunger for essentialism" is coupled with his "disdain for 'the local and temporary' " (p. 294). Essentialism is "the secret of [Johnson's] common sense" (p. 497), and it is at the root of his attraction to Shakespeare, who, like Johnson, " 'caught his ideas from the living world' " (p. 402). Certainly it is this quality of the traditional Johnson, call it by whatever name—his impatience with cant; his insistence upon cutting through to the heart of the matter, whether an idea or an institution; his refusal to be dazzled by the clothes of the world; his alertness to our infinite capacity for self-deception—that brings us back again and again to Johnson. Bate is quite right to point to it as the prime reason why Johnson continues to earn our admiration and love.

Bate divides his work into four main parts: "The Formative Years" (through Oxford); "The Years of Trial and Obscurity" (to the mid 1740s); "In the Middle of the Way: The Moral Pilgrimage" (to the mid-1760's); "The Johnson of Legend." The first chapter of Part I stresses Johnson's early illnesses and physical disabilities; the first of Part II his breakdown and despair after his departure from Oxford; the first of Part III his uncertainty of direction and his marital problems; the first of Part IV his approaching breakdown, religious struggles, and fear of insanity. Clearly Bate sees Johnson's life as a continuing struggle with the demons within, as a "moving parable" of a life begun and lived as radically wretched but lived heroically, punctuated by major periods of psychological anguish and near collapse. From the outset, his central concern with Johnson's psychology establishes for him the importance of Johnson's writing and provides him with a critical methodology. Indeed, his psychological reading of Johnson reflects an identification so close that at times it surfaces. This is particularly apparent when he is writing of the crises of Johnson's middle years. Occasionally he feels so at home in Johnson's thoughts and feelings that he is encouraged to reconstruct them. One small example, from early in the book. Speaking of the probable complex of Johnson's feelings during his first weeks at Oxford, Bate writes: "He would have to begin working in earnest. It might be some reassurance to know that he could make up, in speed and ready presence of mind, for lack of industry. But any solace this gave was very temporary. Nor did it, even temporarily, go very far except as the applause of others helped to dislodge—or distract him from—the sterner judgment of himself within his own mind—" (p. 91). The shift from the tentativeness of *would* and *might be* to the definiteness of *gave* and *did*, from conjecture to fact, not only points to the dangers and temptations of the scholarly enterprise, but suggests, as well, a kind of merging of identities. Mrs. Thrale once exasperatedly asked Johnson, "Will anybody's mind bear this eternal microscope that you place upon your own so?" One senses that Bate understands this side of Johnson better than most.

Bate's close identification with Johnson, his obvious admiration, works both for and against his book. Certainly a biographer's high regard for his subject is a sine qua non. But it must not interfere with sober appraisal and precise judgment. This is particularly true in a study of Johnson, whom Bate himself eloquently recognizes as needing no champions. We wish, then, that he had refrained from exaggerated claims. On p. 9 Johnson is "quicker to find excuses for human nature than almost any other major moralist"; on p. 78 Johnson's ability to get at the "quintessence" of things, combined with "readiness of mind . . . was ultimately to prove unequaled, or at least unexcelled, not only in his own century but also in the entire history of verbal intelligence as far as we know it"; on p. 83 we are told that Johnson wrote about the "treacheries and futility of argument with as much insight as any writer on human nature has ever shown"; on p. 209, "no major writer—above all, no major critic of literature—has equaled [Johnson's] . . . direct knowledge of what we might call the underworld of publishing and writing"; on p. 297 Johnson's courage is "unrivaled"; on p. 300, "as in no other classical moralist, we have a profound anticipation of what was to be the wide-scale nineteenth- and twentieth-century discovery about the mind that went on from the major Romantics down through the clinical exploration of the unconscious that follows Freud." As a Johnsonian enthusiast myself, I find no great difficulty in accepting statements like these. Johnson's knowledge of Grub Street probably *was* what Bate claims for it, and "unrivaled" need not be taken in its purest sense. But seeing these judgments in print, I also find myself asking whether their extravagance might not in subtle ways diminish Johnson and undermine our confidence in the portrait we are given. Less seriously, I find myself engaging in a kind of guessing game. Who *are* the winners in the hierarchy of major moralists? Just what *is* the "entire history of verbal intelligence as far as we know it"? Who *are* the other "writers on human nature" that Johnson equaled? In a book as massive as Bate's, examples of overkill like these I have quoted do not appear on every page. Bate's insistent psychologizing, however, allows him frequently to become uncritical in less obvious ways.

He sees Johnson as both enslaved and pushed to greatness by his "fierce and exacting sense of self-demand—for which Freud gave the now-common term 'superego'—with its remorseless capacity, in some natures, to punish the self through a crippling sense of guilt and through the resulting anxieties, paralysis, and psychosomatic illness that guilt, grown habitual and strongly enough felt, begins to sprout" (p. 121). Although presented in different terms, this view of the deeply divided Johnson goes back at least as far as Bertrand Bronson's *Johnson Agonistes* in

1944 and later Bate's own *Achievement of Samuel Johnson* in 1955. It is the latter which provides the essential outlines of the portrait of Johnson here considerably—and at times, it must be said, repetitiously—elaborated. To these outlines we can have no great objection, and not to admire the richness and subtlety of detail with which they are filled would be absurd. But even though Bate is in no way an out-and-out Freudian—for example, he has little to say about the sexual aspects of Johnson's relationships with his mother and Tetty—his psychological assumptions imply a kind of objectivity and finality that is difficult to achieve and maintain and that perhaps should not even be among the highest priorities sought by the literary biographer. Here again, I sense that Bate has been pulled two ways. Quite frankly, I think he is at his best when he has set his formal psychological notions aside and relied mainly on his literary imagination and critical sensibility. His account of Johnson's earliest years at school, for example, is told with a subtle understanding and narrative speed and force that owe little or nothing to theory but much to the kind of insight that results from a lifetime's immersion in literature. Similarly with influential relationships like those with Cornelius Ford and Mrs. Thrale. Both entered Johnson's life at crucial periods and helped him to discover priorities and set directions. Bate speculates more boldly than Clifford about the role played by Ford in suggesting new possibilities to the youthful Johnson. And he handles the sensational suggestions of masochism openly, soberly, tactfully. Both the Ford and Thrale relationships are convincing precisely because Bate's literary imagination had an abundance of evidence to work with and because it worked largely unencumbered by the burden of psychological theory.

Others among Bate's accounts, less successful, may well be so because the shadow of that theory—and the need to preserve the picture it helped to create?—has come between the author and his subject. A few examples. When Johnson was at Stourbridge school, Boswell tells us he "was much enamoured of Olivia Lloyd, a young quaker, to whom he wrote a copy of verses, which I have not been able to recover."[1] Clifford, in *Young Sam*

Johnson, simply says: "When Mrs. Cornelius Ford's niece, Olivia Lloyd, came to visit, he addressed verses to the attractive Quaker maid, two years his senior."[2] Bate quotes Boswell, adds details of her family and accomplishments from A. L. Reade and others, and continues: "Nothing, of course, came of the attachment. Probably nothing could have come of it, given the circumstances, even if they had loved each other for a few years. In any case, the close of this magical year at Stourbridge . . ." (p. 59). But we have no evidence of an "attachment," with its implications of mutuality, and the suggestions of "this magical year" carry us uncomfortably close to a kind of sentimental breathlessness for which there is only the barest justification. Again:—At Oxford Johnson briefly kept a diary. Its first entry: "I bid farewell to sloth, being resolved henceforth not to listen to her syren strains." "He is not," Bate comments, "as is sometimes thought, merely resolving to snatch the opportunity to finish a few books while he would still be at Oxford. He is understandably beginning to feel something close to despair" (p. 105). Knowing Johnson's lifelong battle with indolence, few would read this entry as a mere resolve to "snatch the opportunity"; but this aside, can the entry by itself carry the weight of Bate's interpretation? Again:—In 1733, when Johnson left Hector's lodgings and moved into his own, Bate speculates that he did so "probably [because] he was beginning to be afraid of himself, and to feel that he was sinking back into the state he was in before he came. If this were so, he would dread inflicting himself on others" (p. 136). Now this may have been so. But could it not just as reasonably be supposed that Johnson had gained enough assurance at Hector's to want to set out on his own? His subsequent relapse could then have been the result of a mistaken confidence and not recessarily of an anticipated downward course. Again:—Bate quite correctly praises Johnson's affectionate care for his black servant Frank Barber and recounts his efforts to bring about Barber's release from the navy after he had run away and enlisted. From the evidence we have, Barber began his adventure at sea on 7 July 1758. Johnson opened the campaign for his release no later than 16 March 1759 and followed this with a letter of appeal dated 9 November 1759.

Bate collapses the two latter dates: "In 1759 the worried Johnson, at the cost of some embarrassment [the need to call on Wilkes's influence and intervention], tried to get Frank released" (p. 326). My objection is only to the "worried Johnson." No doubt Johnson *was* worried, but the expression implies a degree of concern belied by the seven-to-eight-month delay between Frank's departure and Johnson's initial effort to effect his release (a release, incidentally, which Boswell tells us was "without any wish of his own"). Bate's admiration of Johnson's compassionate concern has here resulted in a distortion and perhaps prevented his asking an obvious, and quite interesting, question. Why *did* Johnson delay? The answer is probably very simple: He had more important things on his mind. But then this, in turn, may tell us something about Johnson's feelings for Barber. One final example. In 1762, just after Johnson had received his pension, Reynolds suggested a holiday trip to his native Devon. In his detailed account of this trip, which began in August of that year, Clifford tells us that in "the late summer of 1762 Johnson was in an unusually happy frame of mind" and gives reasons for so believing.[3] In Bate's version, Johnson "for some time . . . had plainly been far from happy. Reynolds, in fact, was becoming seriously worried about his state of mind . . . . He may have hoped that this trip would . . . help jolt or entice him out of himself and into a more hopeful state of mind" (p. 356). The apparent lack of evidence for Reynolds's concern is worrisome, especially since Bate is often at pains to tell us how adept Johnson was in concealing his state of mind.

I mention these few examples only to suggest the pervasiveness, and sometimes protectiveness, of Bate's psychologizing, and its tendency from time to time to limit his responsiveness to evidence or to encourage unwarranted interpretations or a special kind of selectivity.

On the larger matters of Johnson's political convictions and his understanding of what we today call the human condition, Bate's psychological digging yields ore, but it is ore of sometimes doubtful value. After a discussion (following Greene) of eighteenth-century Whiggism and Toryism and of Johnson's

brand of Toryism in particular, he tells us that Johnson's
"intellectual conviction of the need for protective order and
settlement is constantly being prodded—sometimes given
passionate, even explosive, urgency—by his lifelong struggle to
control his own rebellious nature, and to pull himself into
clarity and balance" (p. 198). No doubt this is true. We ignore
the psychological component of belief at our own peril, and
Johnson's belief was charged by the energies that found their
source in his inner turmoil. But in his consideration of
Johnson's politics Bate's interest is less in the belief than in the
component. He writes of the first accurately and sensibly, but
dutifully; of the second with zest and a noticeable picking up of
pace. Similarly, on "the condition of man," Johnson "traces the
inevitable 'doom of man' to inward and psychological causes.
He emphasized, as was common all the way back to the author
of Ecclesiastes, man's incapacity to be filled, to be long satisfied
with anything" (p. 281). Again true. My concern is with the
overall impression. Too often Bate's recognition of Johnson's
fascination—paralleled by his own—with "inward and
psychological causes" has a tendency to drain his subject's
political and religious thinking of its intellectual and moral
content. And ironically this tendency, in turn, has the larger
effect of reducing Johnson to the very kind of predetermined
mechanism which Bate so eloquently and *rightly* insists that
Johnson's life and career denied and were devoted to denying. "I
will be conquered; I will not capitulate" is Johnson's immortal
endorsement of freedom.

Strangely, after all the dissection, Johnson remains a puzzle.
Why, given his early sense of his own immense intellectual
powers and of his own grievous physical handicaps, did he not
simply give up from the beginning? To answer, with Bate, that
he was kept afloat by his insistent sense of self-demand is to push
the question aside. Why, on his visit to Langton, did he take that
marvelous roll down the hill? It was a time, we are told, when he
"was, in fact, rapidly entering a psychological crisis in which all
that he had most dreaded in his past seemed at last to be catching
up with him." Is it enough to add, "But no one would have
guessed it. He was watching himself very carefully" (p. 366).

Perhaps. But the hilarious vigor of that roll suggests something more than an explosion of self-protective energies. Just as Johnson must have picked himself up at the bottom of the hill and grinned his way back to his friends at the top, so too, in my mind's eye, I can see him springing up from his analyst's couch, still very much a mystery.

Readers familiar with Bate's *Achievement of Samuel Johnson* will, in *Samuel Johnson*, encounter essentially the same literary judgments. There is a fine analysis of the early poems as anticipations of the later; and the *Vanity of Human Wishes*, as in the earlier work, serves as a key to the prose. For all the major works we are given details of publication and informative evaluations, though *Rasselas* and the *Journey* receive less attention than they deserve. Particularly in view of Bate's awareness of the need to correct old views of Johnson the talker and to stress the writings, we wish that the limitations of form had not prevented him from going very far beyond his previous criticism and from making greater use of the impressive work of recent scholars with interests less biographical than historical and critical, who have done much to clarify Johnson's place in the intellectual context of his time.

In recent years there has been a lively debate about the value of Boswell's *Life*.[4] Indirectly, and inadvertently, Bate's book makes its contribution to the debate, not only by attempting—like others before it—to give suitable attention to Johnson's early years, about which Boswell knew and wrote comparatively little, but also by drawing upon material now available in the Geoffrey Scott edition and in the superbly edited Yale volumes of the Boswell papers. On some half dozen or so occasions, Boswell's omissions in order to keep his image of Johnson safe become glaringly apparent. Bate also supplies informed correctives to persistent misunderstandings and exaggerations of, for example, Johnson's use of opium.

The mention of Boswell suggests a summing up. *Samuel Johnson* is an impressive performance in its imaginative synthesis of the biographical materials that began to build up around the figure of Johnson long before his death and that have been added to most noticeably during our own century. But though it alerts the reader to the skewness of Boswell, *Samuel Johnson* gives us a skewness of its own. Instead of the Great Cham talking his way through life we have a modern sufferer of existential *angst*. Johnson was both—and more.

Notes

1. *Life of Johnson*, ed. G. B. Hill, revised and enlarged by L. F. Powell (Oxford: Clarendon Press, 1934), I, 92.

2. *Young Sam Johnson* (New York: McGraw-Hill, 1955), p. 91.

3. "Johnson's Trip to Devon in 1762," in *Eighteenth-Century Studies in Honor of Donald F. Hyde*, ed. W. H. Bond (New York: Grolier Club, 1970), p. 5.

4. For the latest commentary on this matter, see Donald Greene, "'Tis a Pretty Book, Mr. Boswell, But—," *Georgia Review*, 32 (1978), 17-43.

Bowers Does Fielding

Don L. Cook

Martin C. Battestin, ed. *Joseph Andrews*. Middletown, Conn.: Wesleyan University Press, 1967. xlvii, 389 pp.

Henry Knight Miller, ed. *Miscellanies by Henry Fielding, Esq; Volume One*. Middletown, Conn.: Wesleyan University Press, 1972. lv, 289 pp.

W. B. Coley, ed. *The Jacobite's Journal and Related Writings*. Middletown, Conn.: Wesleyan University Press, 1975. lxxxix, 515 pp.

Fredson Bowers, Textual Editor; Martin C. Battestin, Introduction and Commentary. *The History of Tom Jones A Foundling*. 2 vols. Middletown, Conn.: Wesleyan University Press, 1975. lxxxiv, 1080 pp., plus one map and six plates.

NOTE: All volumes are printed at the University Press, Oxford, by Vivian Ridler, printer to the university. They are issued in England with the imprint "Oxford: at the Clarendon Press," and are bound in various blue and black cloths. Volumes bearing the Wesleyan University imprint are bound in more sturdy scarlet cloth with deep red labels stamped in gold. Dust jackets are uniform and bear the names "Oxford" and "Wesleyan" on the spine and between them the combined logos of the two presses.

The presence of Fredson Bowers in scholarly editing has become so pervasive that one must acknowledge the justice of the phrase "the ubiquitous Bowers." From Marlowe, Shakespeare, and Dekker through Fielding and Hawthorne to James, Crane, and Dewey, he has spanned centuries, continents, and disciplines to figure variously as sole editor, chief editor, series editor, textual editor, and consulting editor. The power of his advice and the influence of his example are evident in numerous volumes and series that do not bear his name. He has even been known to decline acknowledgment in volumes whose editors he has assisted. The majesty with which he presides and the confidence with which he occupies whole new domains have inspired responses as intense as they are diverse. The annual ukase in *Studies in Bibliography* along with the several collections of his lectures and essays and his textual introductions provide a running commentary on the state of the art of editing and the text for the Greg-Bowers school. To review a Bowers edition, especially outside of one's field of literary expertise, offers an interesting opportunity to observe the Bowers method and manner in operation.

One must begin by saying that the volumes produced so far in the Wesleyan Edition of the Works of Henry Fielding leave no doubt about this being the new standard edition. It may in time be superseded, but one finds it difficult to imagine that very many references and significances remain to be elucidated. The annotation for each volume is unstinted and identifies the persons, events, quotations, and concepts that must be understood if the texts are to make full sense to the modern reader. We are given bibliographic guidance to Fielding's reading and to the scholarhip on the issues and ideas discussed in, or raised by, the books. The annotations also supply fascinating lore about such diverse topics as hoop skirts, prize fighters, the argot of whores and criminals, the Eaton Latin Grammar, the entertainments of London, the decline of the English woolen industry, and the operation and misapplication of English law. Surely few authors provide a more severe test of recondite research and erudition. Fielding's involvement in politics, theater, polemical journalism, law, and the administration of justice connected him with every level of society and every issue of public life. His reading and his memory were prodigious, if not always precise, and everything he did, saw, read, and *was* seems to have found its way into his writing. While eighteenth-century specialists may lament that Professor Battestin's annotations occasionally milk the text for support for his particular interpretation of Fielding as a Christian humanist, most readers will simply be grateful for the enormous amount of detective work the editors have done and for their succinct and occasionally witty manner of presenting the results.

The general introduction to each volume presents the biographical and historical facts that bear on the composition of the work. Surprisingly little can be asserted with confidence about Fielding's private life, but the editors have used documents shrewdly and inference cautiously to fill in some blanks and to correct misimpressions, most notably about composition dates and publishing histories. It seems likely that when the Wesleyan Edition is complete there will be need for another biography of Fielding that incorporates this new data and corrects past errors. The precise size of the Wesleyan Edition is as yet uncertain because it is difficult to determine in advance how many volumes will be required to accommodate Fielding's dramatic works. But surely the edition will exceed ten volumes; four titles in five hard-cover volumes plus one paperback reprint, *Tom Jones*, have been issued to date. The delay between the initial volume (*Joseph Andrews*, 1967) and the spate of volumes in the mid-seventies (*Miscellanies*, 1972; *The Jacobite's Journal* and *Tom Jones*, both 1975) suggests a quickening pace which one hopes the edition has both the financial support and the administrative coherence to sustain.

Anyone familiar with contemporary editing would recognize this as a Bowers edition, even though the only volumes that bear Bowers's name on the title page are the two containing *Tom Jones* (a single volume in paperback) where we read "the text edited by Fredson Bowers." The other title pages announce that the volumes were edited variously by Martin Battestin, W. B. Coley, and Henry Knight Miller, but in each case Bowers signs the textual introduction. In *The Jacobite's Journal* and *Joseph Andrews* he is given that credit in the table of contents as well. In the textual introduction to *Joseph Andrews* Bowers makes specific and repeated reference to what Professor Battestin has done with the text. Similarly, Bowers's textual introduction to *Miscellanies* states that "Dr. Miller has made a few alterations to remove patent error" (p. liii). The textual introduction to *The Jacobite's Journal* makes no mention of Professor Coley by name except as having collated particular copies. We are not told how the credit for the establishment of that text ought to be distributed between Professors Bowers and Coley, though the theory is clearly Bowers's.

I raise this point for two reasons, one practical and the other philosophical. Practically, it is useful to have a clear record of responsibility for editorial work. The application of textual theory to a particular set of variant texts is exacting and taxing work. Unless it is done with an accuracy well beyond that required in most critical and scholarly publishing, the result is not a purified text but a newly corrupted text. No edition is entirely without error in printing or editing, but textual editors aspire toward an error-free text for every word and mark of which they can offer a logical justification. In *Tom Jones* we know from the title page that any errors in the general introduction and the commentary are attributable to Martin C. Battestin, while any errors in the text, in the textual introduction, and in the textual apparatus and appendixes lie at the door of Fredson Bowers. But if we find errors in the text or apparatus of *The Jacobite's Journal*, to whom do we complain, or conversely, when we find none, whom do we congratulate? In none of the volumes do we find any information about the measures taken to maintain accuracy in the text and apparatus after it went to the printer. The scrupulous accuracy of the textual editor is the foundation of the reliable text, and a reputation for accuracy is too difficult to acquire and retain to be either lightly ascribed or carelessly squandered.

The larger issue turns on the question of what it means to *edit* a book. In the context of literary scholarship it is generally understood that editing means the establishment of a text by the study of its history and variants and the "perfection" of one rationally selected form of that text by the substitution of variants from other forms and the correction of errors discovered by the editor. The resulting edited text may then be published with or without annotation and commentary on the meaning and importance of the contents, but preferably with at least an explanation of the choice of the base text and a record of the alterations it has undergone. Most modern editions consciously avoid interpretation of the edited text on the assumption that it is the editor's job to prepare a reliable text of the document and the critic's job to interpret it. But the historian who edits is likely to see his duty as the elucidation of the contents of a document. He would certainly not consciously advocate careless transcription of documents, but he is likely to assume that mere transcription is a mechanical chore that involves few choices and only minor skills. This may sometimes be true for modern documents of which only one typewritten form exists. Happy the annotator whose editorial chores are so easily accomplished. But even when dealing with older documents that may exist in several holograph copies, the historical editor's assumption tends to be that the real editing consists of throwing light on the document through annotation. One can understand this emphasis. In terms of the time involved and the intellectual stimulation experienced, the annotation of Jefferson's unpublished letters undoubtedly engages the scholarly mind more pleasantly than does their transcription. But at its worst this attitude has led to distressingly casual and unreliable presentation of "edited" documents (including private letters, journals, diaries, and unpublished works and drafts) of both literary and political figures. Editions continue to appear in which the transcription has apparently been assigned to a typist or, as reported in one case, typed by a secretary from the editor's tape-recorded reading. One is shocked to find editors who are shocked at the suggestion that the edited texts of letters should be checked against manuscript, not just against microfilm. I think it is time that we at least acknowledge that editing means different things to different editors and specify exactly who has done exactly what in preparing the text and seeing it through the press.

The textual problems involved in these Fielding volumes are, with one exception, quite simple. The exception is *Tom Jones*, and I will treat that title last. For *Joseph Andrews* no prepublication form survives, so the first edition is taken as copy-text. The only comprehensive revision by Fielding was for the second edition. He slightly revised a copy of the second edition for the third, and of the third for the fourth. The fifth edition, the last in Fielding's lifetime, bears no variants from the fourth except those attributable to compositorial error. The explanation of the estalishment of a critical text follows the classic lines of Greg-Bowers copy-text theory, with the separation of authority for substantive variants from the authority for accidentals. Using the first edition as matrix and assuming that the accidentals of that text, being closest to the holograph manuscript and probably unrevised in detail by the author, are the most authoritative available, the editor introduces into the first-edition text those substantive variants in subsequent editions that he judges to be authorial. While the theory is unexceptionable, the description of its application suggests two weakness that have occasionally been observed in Bowers's editions. The first is a wholesale application of theory to details that might better be considered individually. The other is a mercifully transparent example of a kind of circular reasoning that turns up in several of Bowers's textual introductions, most noticeably in the Virginia Edition of Stephen Crane.

The wholesale application is suggested by this statement: "Since the critical editor acts as a judge in this editorial winnowing of evidence, it is proper to say that in *Joseph Andrews* all substantive variants in the second edition have been presumed to be innocent unless the editor to his satisfaction could prove them guilty as printer's corruption" (p. xlii). Now it may be that a skeptical testing of each second-edition substantive variant would result in exactly the same decisions that this advocacy procedure produces, but the tone of expediencey in this explanation of procedure is troubling, the more so when combined with the circularity of this passage: "Since so many [altered readings] are manifestly authorial, the 'indifferent' variant is more likely to be the author's, too, than a compositorial corruption. This *would be especially true if* Fielding had read proof on the sheets of the second edition, although we have *no evidence to support even speculation* in this matter" (p. xlii; the italics are mine). Thus the fact that such evidence would be useful, if it existed, becomes the occasion for "insupportable" speculation, which becomes, if not logical proof, at least psychological support for a premise that the absent evidence would have suggested, had it existed. One wishes the editor had simply applied to *all* of the variants the "more stringent test of authority" that is reserved for the variants "in the third and, especially, in the fourth edition."

Miscellanies is the first of two volumes that will contain Fielding's original three-volume publication. In this first volume only two items, the poetic essay *Of True Greatness* and the satiric essay *Some Papers Proper to be Read before the R—l Society*, were published prior to their appearance in the 1743 first edition. No authorially revised edition was published during Fielding's lifetime. Consequently, the editing has consisted almost entirely of the insertion into the first edition text of eight substantives and forty accidentals, almost all on the authority of the present editor. As in all of these volumes, the stated policy of emendations sounds very conservative, and the editors deny any intention "to achieve an unnatural consistency in spelling, capitalization, or punctuation" (p. liii). But in practice the emendation of accidentals seems occasionally to value regularity above authenticity of text. In a number of places punctuation is added on the authority of the editor when the meaning is perfectly clear without the change. I refer not to the substitution of question marks for periods in clearly interrogative sentences nor to the supplying of the missing half of sets of quotation marks, but to the insertion of commas in series, the repositioning of commas and parentheses, and the occasional substitution of one style for another when quotations are inserted. As the textual introduction to *Joseph Andrews* explains, "These changes have been made cautiously and in some small part with the convenience of the reader in view when marked anomalies might have distracted the attention" (p. xliii). In spite of the intended effect of "cautiously," "small part," and "marked anomalies," I think these departures from the ideal of an unmodernized text are unfortunate. The editor invokes that insidious argument from "reader's convenience" (meaning reader's incompetence) to justify the editorial "improvement" of the author's admittedly imperfect text. The most frequent readers of these critical editions will surely be scholars well-read in the eighteenth century and capable of sorting out minor confusions of syntax in the unemended copy-text. One cannot but wonder at times whether a comma is added at the end of a line of verse because the editor felt the comma would dispel the reader's confusion or because the editor feared his volume might be credited with a typographical error if the copy-text line were left unpunctuated. The use of "stet" entries in the list of emendations is also suggestive of this anxiety. There is something slightly ludicrous about supposing that a reader capable of finding his way through the two-and-one-half-page bibliographical description of the first edition of *Tom Jones* will be confused because in the copy-text the asterisk indicating Fielding's footnote to the phrase "the* well-wooded Forest of *Hampshire*" appears before "well-wooded" instead of after "Forest" as emended for the Wesleyan Edition.

The Jacobite's Journal and Related Writings is a synthetic volume in the sense that Fielding never brought the contents together in a volume as he did in *Miscellanies*. *The Jacobite's Journal* was the third of Fielding's four essay periodicals, and it began publication on Saturday, 5 December 1747. This four-page weekly continued publication through forty-nine numbers to its final appearance on 5 November 1748. From each number Professor Coley has edited Fielding's essays, separating out and reproducing in a forty-two-page appendix the items that Fielding reprinted from other newspapers, either as serious news or as objects of satire. Authorship of some of the edited essays remains doubtful, but they are all presented here, thus increasing from two to forty-nine the number of *Journal* issues available in modern editions. The volume also contains two related pieces, *A Proper Answer To A Late Scurrilous Libel . . .* and *A Dialogue Between A Gentleman From London . . . And An Honest Alderman of the Country Party*. Each of these appeared in only one authorial edition before inclusion in this volume. But there are a few variants because a reimpression of *A Proper Answer* shows a minor alteration on the title page, and minor variants among copies of *A Dialogue* resulted from alterations during a single press run. There is no problem of identifying variants as authorial or compositorial nor of choosing between early and late authorial variants. Only in *A Dialogue* is there any source of emendation other than the present editor. For this one piece the list of emendations records the variants among the *states* of the text, "a" through "e," and draws emendations from them.

It is somewhat surprising to find that even with this extremely simple textual history to work with, the apparatus records 74 emendations of substantives and 295 emendations of accidentals, all but 22 made for the first time by the present editor. These substantial lists are evidence of both the carelessness of journal and pamphlet printing in the late 1740s and of the generous emendation policy of this edition. One cannot argue with most of the substantive emendations, usually involving the removal of duplicated words or the replacement of a nonsensical word with one that suits the context. But one may wonder why it is *necessary* to substitute the singular "Aprehension" for the plural in the phrase "the dreadful Aprehensions which prevailed in every Mind" (273.22). The singular may be better, but the plural makes good sense and has the virtue, not to mention the authority, of appearing in the copy-text. One hopes that in future printings the emendation at 232.16 will be clarified so that we may know which "of" in that line has been added and that the entry listed at 358.6 will be changed to 358.5. The four-page list of emendations of accidentals provides mostly regularizations that smooth the text for the modern reader whether he needs this sort of assistance or not. For instance, the capitalization of nouns is made uniform. I suppose the reader has to accept the inauthentic smoothness imposed by the editor and console himself with the report of roughness provided by the lists. One might have thrown into the balance the exemption from charges of typographical errors that the editors thus seek, except that the lists themselves inevitably generate misprints, such as 41.5 instead of 41.15 and "86.19 However,] W;~ₐa-b" where the edition reads "However∧" and makes perfectly good sense doing so.

Whether it is desirable or not, the manipulation (inevitably tending toward modernization) of punctuation, capitals, and italics is a tricky business. It places on the shoulders of the editor the responsiblity for interpreting the writer's meaning, a responsibility that tends to expand toward improving the writer's writing. For instance, the editor changes the italics in one passage (42.5 Prussia] W; *Prussia a*+) to produce the particular emphasis in "have since talked of *Exterminating the*

King of Prussia." The change reinforces the parallel between
"Exterminating the King" and "healing the Differences" in the
next line. But is the rhetorical device the author's or the editor's?
Four lines farther on we find "the king of *Prussia* being
exterminated," and a note on the same page contains a
quotation from Fielding refering to "Vengance against the King
of *Prussia.*" The emendation at 42.5 does achieve an emphasis
on "King" rather than on "Prussia," though the emphatic
preposition dangles there rather vestigially, but is the means of
emphasis, or even the emphasis, Fielding's? We can't know. I
would prefer the copy-text to the editorial enhancement.

In a review of *The Jacobite's Journal* and *Tom Jones*,
Fredrick W. Hilles wonders "what is really gained by preserving
the conventions of an eighteenth-century printing house."[1]
Martin Battestin provided the sensible answer some years ago:
some of the meaning, and more than we might expect, derives
from the interplay of punctuation, capitals, italics, and the other
flexible accidentals of eighteenth-century prose.[2] I heartily
endorse Professor Battestin's view, but I should like to add two
comments. First, if we are going to preserve this indicator of
meaning, let's preserve all of it and not impose a modern
decorum foreign to the vagaries of eighteenth-century
publication. Second, Professor Hilles's remark suggests the view
that "un-modernization" is a kind of decorative effect *added* by
the editor to create a schmaltzy nostalgia. He likens it to naming
a candy store Ye Olde Sweete Shoppe. But a moment's reflection
will lead us to realize that the eighteenth-century accidentals are
not a decorative final coating added to the text, like the
sprayed-on "distressed surface" of phony antiques. The
accidentals are authentic, there to begin with, and if the
Wesleyan Edition errs, it is not in the application of artificial
rusticity to the text but in the regularization toward what
Bowers refers to as "an unnatural consistency in spelling,
capitalization, or punctuation" (*Miscellanies*, p. liii).

One of the recurring pleasures of examining Fredson Bowers's
editorial work is the opportunity to observe, and try to follow,
the ingenious textual sleuthing by which he wrests from his
documents more evidence than ordinary mortals are wont to

discover. *Tom Jones* provides that opportunity. The classic textual problem in the Fielding canon is how to account for the reintroduction into the fourth edition of *Tom Jones* of a section in Book VIII, Chapter 14, that had appeared in the first and second edition but had been revised and shortened in the third edition. Except for this section, the text of the fourth edition clearly derives from the third with general revisions by Fielding, but this passage in the Man of the Hill's story harks back to the longer first-edition version. Various hypotheses have been offered to account for the insertion of an apparently rejected passage from the first edition into the printer's copy for the fourth. It was even suggested that a Jacobite or Catholic printer deleted the Man of the Hill's brief but fierce anti-Catholic tirade and substituted the longer, milder version from the first edition. Bowers proposes the less colorful but more plausible hypothesis that Fielding yielded to ire while the third edition was in the press and inserted the intemperate attack on Catholics, but, when he read it again during his revision of the third edition for use as printer's copy for the fourth, he reconsidered and reinstated the milder first-edition passage. This hypothesis depends on the likelihood that when Fielding noticed the intemperate passage in the book he was revising, instead of crossing it out or rewriting it, he removed the offending pages, took from a spare copy of the first edition the parallel pages, and, without correcting the errata that had been corrected in the second and third editions, inserted these first-edition pages into the third edition and then resumed his revisions. The five-page explanation in the textual introduction marshals impressive bibliographic evidence and delights one with its demonstration of the way in which details of physical bibliography can be made to yield up the secrets of composition. But the explanation is based on the assumption that the chronology of publication was also the chronology of composition, and it is on this assumption that Bowers's hypothesis runs aground. More recently, Hugh Amory has demonstrated very convincingly that the short, intemperate passage in the third edition derives not from a revision of the second edition, but from the original version, printed for the first edition but canceled before

publication.[3] At least one set of sheets for the first edition,
containing these canceled pages (sheet 0 of Volume III), were
evidently folded and retained intact. The first edition with
cancellanses was entered in the Stationers' Register on 3
February 1749. The second edition, set from the first, was rushed
into print by the end of February, and a third edition was
released to the public on 11 April. Fielding made no overall
revisions for the second or third editions. In the rush of
publishing three editions totaling 10,000 copies in so short a
time, a (perhaps the?) copy of the first edition containing the
cancellanda was apparently used as printer's copy for the third
edition. This hypothesis accommodates the details of
bibliography cited by Bowers and is further supported by
watermark and headline evidence discovered by Amory. The
clincher is Amory's discovery, in a Harvard University copy of
the first edition, of offset from the canceled p. 234 on the facing
p. 235 of Volume III. Read in a mirror, the offset parallels but
does not match the text on the p. 234 presently bound into the
book. The simplest hypothesis then, and the one that best
accommodates all of the evidence, is that Fielding wrote the
short, hot denunciation of Catholics for the first edition but
during the printing of the book substituted the longer, milder
passage. The substitution necessitated the resetting of sheet 0 of
Volume III, which is indeed crowded into sparsely leaded pages
with more lines per page than adjacent gatherings carry.
Somehow a copy of the first edition that contained *canceled*
pages got used as setting copy for the third edition, and when
Fielding discovered the fact during his preparation of the fourth
edition, he had to cancel the passage a second time.

The story is worth relating for its own interest, but I have
another purpose in telling it here. That is to suggest that
Fredson Bowers's employment of the arcane formulae of
bibliographic description, his inductive leaps and deductive
inferences, and his massive demonstrations and reconstructions
are dazzling, and I use the term in awareness of its ambiguities.
His is without doubt one of the most seminal and interesting
minds at work in American scholarship. He has shown us the
power of a simple idea applied with imagination and daring.

He has taught us how to solve many editorial puzzles, and we are grateful.

But if gratitude and just admiration are not to become uncritical adulation, we must examine the results of his work by the same mundane standards with which we evaluate our own. However brilliant the detective work, are the details, the text, and the apparatus accurate? A reviewer, even a CSE inspector, cannot recollate all the variant texts and reedit the volume as a quality check, but a sampling of *Tom Jones* suggests that there is less precision here than meets the eye. For instance, a comparison of the bibliographic description of the first edition (pp. 1050-52) against a copy of the first edition in the Lilly Library, Indiana University (shelf mark PR 3454.T6 vault), reveals the following differences:

In Volume III the H gathering is not repeated; the collation should read, in part, "C-G^{12} H^{12} ($\pm$H8, 9, 10) I-L^{12}."

In Volume IV, leaf B^2 is not a cancellan.

The collation of Volume V should read "N^{12} ($\pm$N8)" not "N^{12} ($\pm$N2)."

While there may be some variants among copies (the Lilly copy has the 313 variant in Volume III listed by Bowers but not the turned figures on 264, Volume IV), the Lilly copy agrees in all the details I have listed with the collation provided by Hugh Amory.

In Bowers's description of contents, Volume VI ends with Book XVIII, Chapter 12. There are actually thirteen chapters.

In the press figures the following are omitted: Vol. I, 36-2; Vol. III, 228-1; Vol. IV, 135-3, 285-2 (and 183-2 should read 283-2); Vol. V, 111-1; Vol. VI, 284-1.

In the notes Volume IV B(B2) is indeed signed "B2," but it is not a cancellan as the notation indicates. N(N2) is not signed "Vol. V," but N(N8) is.

Does it matter? It does not change a word in the text, but the elaborate description is part of the editor's credentials. Not all editions include such a detailed bibliographic description, and its inclusion here is part of the demonstration of scholarly expertise.

Turning to the apparatus, I will not argue again with the regularization nor cavil over certain unexplained conventions of notation (137.17 Neighbors] i.e., Neighbors' in the emendations list, for instance). One finally figures them out. But why, after the entry "*48.5; 50.30 Miss] W; Mrs. I-IV" and a thirty-five-line textual note, do we find twelve entries below "55.20, 27, 29; 56.4, 16, 27; 57.6, 22 Miss] W; Mrs. I-IV"? The single entry at 41.6 took care of the "ₐtill] W; 'till I-IV" changes for the whole novel. Since the text reads "Hiding-places:" what are we to infer from the emendation "47.18 -places] W;~. I-IV"? Since the text reads "Vice" what do we infer from "60.5 Vice,] W; ~ₐ I-IV"? What is the logic of "*246.28 this] IV; these I-III" which refers us to the textual note "246.28 this many Years] For authority of the IV 'this' for I-III 'these', see the IV alteration at 342.9," which reads "342.9 this] IV; these I-III"? Where is the textual note signaled by "*257.2 it] IV; *omit* I-III"? There are eighteen more pages of emendation lists. Most of the errors may be called typos or clerical slips; they are none the less flaws in the work published over the editor's name.

The paperback reprint carries a preface acknowledging some misprints and oversights in the first hardback printing. The changes in the paperback are listed, it says, on p. 987. Actually they are on p. 991. There are seventy-nine of them, and if you enter them in your hardcover edition, the first two lines on p. 840 will no longer read "I'd have you to know I have got more Wisdom," but instead, "I'd have you to know I have a got more Wisdom." Who says editors have no sense of humor?

What does all this add up to? Is the Wesleyan Fielding a bad edition that needs to be redone? Certainly not. It is the standard edition now and is likely to remain so. It provides first-class annotation for a text that is more reliable than any other available. If you don't like the emendations made in the copy-text, you can consult the appendixes and restore most of the original readings. But it is not unflawed, and the flaws derive partly from carelessness in preparation and partly from policies that generate flaws. Because the editors regularize the accidentals, they create more opportunities for error than a less-emended copy-text would offer, and *Tom Jones* is at least carelessly proofread. The tedious multiple readings of proof against printer's copy, against copy-text, against the variant forms of the text, and against the apparatus is, admittedly, a trial. The five proofreadings once prescribed by the Center for Editions of American Authors are not the perfect number for every text. But from eye-straining experience I can testify that, while the number of errors diminishes with each reading, the errors persist much longer than does the intellectual challenge of the task. The volumes edited by Fredson Bowers have almost always been intellectually challenging. They have extended the range of inquiry into the process of composition and publication. His volumes almost always contain more ingenious application of detail than one finds elsewhere. But they also contain more errors than they ought. The final volume of the Virginia Edition of Stephen Crane contains a nine-page errata to the nine previous volumes. The first reprint of *Tom Jones* contains a list of seventy-nine corrections, introduces at least one more error, and misses many others. Bowers does not conceal his errors, and he gracefully acknowledges corrections. But how pleasant and beneficial it would be if an errata in the last volume of the Fielding edition were unnecessary. Those of us who admire his work as a textual theorist would be much heartened if the originality and insight of his investigations were wedded to elegant simplicity and scrupulous accuracy in the preparation of texts.

Notes

1. "Fielding Unmodernized," *Yale Review*, 65 (1975), 133.

2. "Fielding's Novels and the Wesleyan Edition: Some Principles and Problems," in *Editing Eighteenth Century Novels*, ed. G. E. Bentley, Jr. (Toronto: Hakkert, 1975), pp. 9-30.

3. "*Tom Jones* Plus and Minus: Towards a Practical Edition," *Harvard Library Bulletin*, 25 (January 1977), 101-13.

Brooks on Faulkner: The End of the Long View

Thomas L. McHaney

Cleanth Brooks. *William Faulkner: Toward Yoknapatawpha and Beyond*. New Haven: Yale University Press, 1978. xviii, 445 pp.

Cleanth Brooks is well known as an interpreter of William Faulkner, and his *William Faulkner: The Yoknapatawpha Country* (1963) has stood the test of time as an introduction to Faulkner's South and a guide through his mythical country. Brooks promised a sequel in which he would consider the fiction lying outside the "Yoknapatawpha County cycle" and discuss Faulkner's growth as an artist—"his beginnings, the forging of his style, and the working out of the special fictional techniques associated with his name."[1] He planned to "examine some of the earlier drafts" of Faulkner's novels and to study the implications of Faulkner's revisions for both style and structure. *William Faulkner: Toward Yoknapatawpha and Beyond* is the promised sequel, though it has not fulfilled all the intentions expressed in 1963.

Toward Yoknapatawpha and Beyond contains critical essays on Faulkner's apprentice writing and the non-Yoknapatawpha novels: *Soldiers' Pay, Mosquitoes, Pylon, The Wild Palms*, and *A Fable*. It also includes commentary upon some, but not all, of the unpublished poetry and fiction preserved in different manuscript collections. The book concludes with an essay entitled "Faulkner on Time and History," which does not attempt to sum up Faulkner or reveal the figure in his carpet. As appendixes Brooks prints two essays in which he returns to the novel that fascinates him most, *Absalom, Absalom!*, and one on affinities between Faulkner and Yeats. A mass of peripheral information and speculation appears in the notes, which are often miniature essays. Here are chronologies, analyses of

Faulkner's literary borrowing, discussions of characters, names, titles, and themes, and information about the literal background to the fiction. The notes are not confined to non-Yoknapatawpha material, and thus they supplement the notes in the previous volume. The general index includes entries for characters, but the citations are not descriptive and do not constitute the kind of "character index" provided in the earlier volume, nor are they complete.

Without intending to hold Brooks's feet to the fire for work he never intended to perform, it is still proper to point out what *Toward Yoknapatawpha and Beyond* does not contain. Though it touches most of the subjects he promised, it does not discuss a significant portion of Faulkner's manuscripts and typescripts, nor does it provide anything like a full consideration of the short stories and story collections, the essays, the motion picture writing, nor the interviews. It also does not substantially address the process of revision or the development of Faulkner's style. And though Brooks gives an outline by which the chapters of his two books may be interwoven to make a chronological overview of Faulkner's career, the resulting arrangement would not provide a full critical treatment. No one, of course, is likely to say the last word on Faulkner. We do not expect that. And Brooks's view, which will certainly still be important as Faulkner continues to be read, will have its future. But his view, for all its importance, has a number of limitations and a few mysteries which bear examination. Before taking up the book at hand, we will profit by looking at the evolution of Brooks's criticism of Faulkner and some of its peculiarities.

Identification of Brooks as Faulkner critic is now so strong, especially in academic circles, because of Brooks's essays, textbooks, lectures, and guest professorships, that it may surprise some to learn that he had little to say about Faulkner during the years when the latter's reputation might have benefited most from the intelligent and sympathetic readings which Brooks, at his best, provides. Unless I am mistaken, the critic first discussed Faulkner in a 1942 *Saturday Review* essay, "What Deep South Literature Needs,"[2] in which he laments the national habit of accepting southern fantasy as merciless realism and describes Faulkner as a tragedian, concluding that what southern literature needs most is readers who are more intelligent. In 1943 he and Robert Penn Warren continued trying to create such readers by publishing the sequel to their famous poetry textbook. In *Understanding Fiction* they explicated "A Rose for Emily" (inadvertently beginning, one might lament, the endless anthologizing and critical reading of that overworked tale). The importance of "community" in their criticism of the story seems to reveal Brooks's hand, but *Understanding Fiction* did not mark the beginning of more work on Faulkner. Between the early 1940s, when Faulkner's reputation was at its nadir, and the awarding of the Nobel Prize, when the reputation soared on its own, Brooks apparently wrote nothing else on him.

This is not to lay blame at Brooks's door. He was busy with other critical concerns. But one is puzzled to discover that the *Southern Review*, which he and Warren founded at Louisiana State University in 1935, ignored Faulkner in its literary essays and—of only two Faulkner books reviewed during the journal's first lifetime—permitted one of his greatest novels to be grossly misinterpreted. During its eight-year lifespan, 1935-1942, and while it was discovering and encouraging one of Faulkner's champions, Eudora Welty, the *Southern Review* did not review *Pylon* (1935), *The Unvanquished* (1938), *The Wild Palms* (1939), or *Go Down, Moses* (1942). Henry Nash Smith did consider *Absalom, Absalom!* in a compendium review of current fiction, showing sympathy but not much perception regarding the love-hate relationship he transferred from Quentin to Faulkner.[3] But Donald Stanford, who is current co-editor of the *Southern Review*, began his passing treatment of *The Hamlet* in another mass review by calling it "Faulkner's latest explosion in a cesspool, with a plethora of attempted rape, seduction, murder, and sodomy." Stanford ended after two paragraphs with the assertion, doubtless hopeful, that the scene depicting Ike Snopes and the cow was "the climax of Faulkner's literary career."[4]

The situation at the *Southern Review* may indicate inner complexities there, for Warren did take issue with Stanford's evaluation, mentioning neither reviewer nor journal by name, in the pages of the *Kenyon Review*.[5] Lack of attention to Faulkner may also reflect the degree to which he was without honor in his own land; nationally as well as regionally, even in his greatest decade, Faulkner had been assigned to the "cult of cruelty," and even a tough, philosophical southern realist like Ellen Glasgow could not discern the "blood and irony" or the morality she demanded through the panels of Faulkner's disturbing portraits. But to judge by the brief early responses and the fine later readings, we may be reasonably sure that Brooks knew or was learning what to make of Faulkner's incest, murder, miscegenation, and stock-diddling. Why then did he not develop a criticism to interpret Faulkner to his own country? Why does his major criticism of Faulkner wait until after 1951, after the Mississippian had been canonized in Stockholm?

The answers I offer are only speculation, but I think they may explain why Brooks eventually developed the criticism he has constructed, why he imposed the two-volume division into Yoknapatawpha writing and non-Yoknapatawpha, and why he chose a thematic arrangement for his first volume but a chronological order for the second. A consideration of these characteristics, in turn, reveals to us why the work studied in the second volume is put at a disadvantage and why Brooks has not created a holistic view of Faulkner.

To a greater extent than his friends Warren and Allen Tate, Brooks has chosen a typically academic career. He has devoted himself to a specialty, the criticism of poetry, and explored its history, theory, and practical application. He moved from the South to Yale and worked within the curriculum of his time, a curriculum that had little room for Faulkner until he won the Nobel Prize. The background of his work on Faulkner includes the Agrarianism of Warren, Tate, and John Crowe Ransom;[6] practical formalist criticism and the intensive reading in poetry of his scholarly specialty; an apparently pleasant exile in the urban East, where Faulkner would need a good bit of glossing, and a simultaneous nostalgia for the idealized South of his earlier years; and, perhaps corollary to close reading and the need to evangelize a new criticism, the development of a rhetorical style that makes Brooks not only a good writer but also a shrewd one.[7]

The combined effect of these interests and abilities is readily apparent in what I take to be Brooks's first two essays on Faulkner (excluding the brief general article in *Saturday Review*, cited above, and *Understanding Fiction*): "*Absalom, Absalom!* The Definition of Innocence" (*Sewanee Review*, Autumn 1951) and "Notes on Faulkner's 'Light in August' " (*Harvard Advocate*, November 1951). He argues in the first that Sutpen is not a traditional man, never embraces the tradition as he might have (thereby becoming an aristocrat), and remains outside the "community" except for his friendship with General Compson. Nineteenth-century southern society was sufficiently fluid to accept Sutpen, he writes, but Sutpen in his innocence believed he could shape the world to his own purposes, and so he adopted only as much of the tradition as served his immediate goals, doing that with what Brooks sees as cold abstraction. He remained an outsider by choice, although not upon any principle of isolation; he simply had no time for amenities. Sutpen's position vis-à-vis the community, Brooks concludes, reveals his tragic flaw and explains the innocence regarding human nature and the human community that provokes his tragedy. Twelve years later, and with only a few additions, this essay became the first half of Brooks's chapter on *Absalom, Absalom!* in *The Yoknapatawpha Country*, and phrases from it recur, now twenty-seven years later, in *Toward Yoknapatawpha and Beyond*. The other 1951 essay, on *Light in August*, goes even further to emphasize the power of community in Faulkner's fiction. Brooks argues that the main actors in that novel are defined by being outsiders, a condition that reflects not upon the community but upon themselves; they are, he believes, exiles by circumstance or choice who cannot "perform" their natures and become fully human.

This crucial dependence upon community as a touchstone is carried forward from Brooks's first essays to both his volumes on Faulkner, where it appears to some extent in the criticism of each work, but, more importantly, where it also provides much of the basis for Brooks's introduction, in the first volume, to

Faulkner's real and fictional worlds. *The Yoknapatawpha
Country*, as noted, is not chronologically but thematically
arranged. It begins with three chapters that lay out Brooks's
conception of Faulkner territory and then takes up *Light in
August* first of all the novels. Emphasizing community again,
Brooks spells out for the modern reader what he believes the
modern reader himself cannot easily perceive:

Community is the powerful though invisible force that quietly exerts
itself in so much of Faulkner's work. It is the circumambient
atmosphere, the essential ether of Faulkner's fiction. *But for many a
reader, the community is indeed invisible and quite imperceptible:* it
exerts no pressure on him at all—and lacking any awareness of this
force, he may miss the meaning of the work. Such readers find *Light in
August* quite baffling simply because they are unaware of the force of
community that pervades it and thus miss the clue to its central
structure.[8]

What is the reader to do who is baffled not so much by the
structure of *Light in August* as by the idealistic version of
community Brooks offers? To be sure, when he writes about "A
Rose for Emily," *Light in August,* or *Absalom, Absalom!*
Brooks admits, in a rhetorical concession, that unpleasant or
erring behavior exists in Jefferson, Mississippi, but he never
relents in his insistence upon community as a citadel of value, a
preserve of tradition, and a mark against which modern
alienation is quickly measured. While in other respects arguing
rightly against the southern typicality of events in Faulkner's
fiction—Miss Emily's behavior, for example—he upholds the
uniqueness of the stable, wholesome rural Southern
community.

One cannot disagree with Brooks about the extent to which
Christmas and Sutpen are outsiders. Each is a walking
metaphor for the confusion of value or identity that causes or
results from alienation. But are their fates dependent upon the
rural southern setting? To assume that this is true is to imply
that Faulkner has mistakenly omitted a necessary ingredient of
his fiction, for he has not depicted the places where their
tragedies occur as ideals. He more than hints the opposite,
unless we assume that he has failed to portray the community

according to his own wishes. Why is General Compson Sutpen's friend? Merely because it is necessary to the story? Are his values the same as those of the porch-sitters and night-riders whom Sutpen faces down before and after the Civil War? Sutpen is not the only underbred man in Jefferson. His family, despite isolation and without ever becoming part of the community, demonstrate, through Judith and Clytie, commendable human virtues, while the Coldfields variously fail. The Jefferson of *Light in August* is multifaceted, but more often vicious than not. The point is that Faulkner's "postage stamp" of north Mississippi contains a small town where much of his fiction takes place, and the fate of the individual in that fiction is always thrown into relief against a general background. But the individual, not the community, was what concerned Faulkner most. It is a mistake to assume that Faulkner took a crucial aspect of his fiction so much for granted that someone must always interpret it to us.

Faulkner was a traditional man, but the role was not altogether natural to him; like any intellectual, he had to choose it, to restore or perhaps even to create for the first time a life which his immediate forebears—father and grandfather, at least, and perhaps his intellectual great-grandfather, too—had *not* lived. The recent biographical reminiscence by Faulkner's stepson Malcolm Franklin indicates the extent to which Faulkner created and maintained a traditional ménage on the outskirts of Oxford, Mississippi, with some of the same fierce abstraction and even a bit of the inhumanity Brooks attributes to Sutpen.[9] Faulkner named his estate Rowan Oak out of Frazer's *The Golden Bough*. It would take too long to sum up his relationship to the community he lived beside, or his views of it, but from what we now know about his life, we can see that his attitude was often dark. To enjoy tradition, in the modern world, he had to create it. Brooks would be right to argue that the modern world, even in Oxford, Mississippi, is one thing, but that the nineteenth-century South was something else. He is correct when he points out how fully recent historians such as C. Vann Woodward and Eugene Genovese prove the validity of Faulkner's imagination, especially upon the topics of slavery

and race. But exactly what is Faulkner's fictional community?
First, it is a reflection of the time and place he lived in himself.
Relatively little of Faulkner's fiction is actually set in the past.[10]
Even when writing about the past, Faulkner loaded his work
with modernist images and ideas, and, just as Hawthorne and
Melville had done in their time, he could see the beginnings of
what we call modern alienation and loss of value and social
breakdown in nineteenth-century society. The force of
community is a power in Hawthorne's world, but hardly
idealized. For Melville, the ship and its crew become a powerful
metaphor for his contemporary community, and he judges it
harshly. Closer to home for Faulkner is the southern small-town
world of Mark Twain. Each of these nineteenth-century
examples of community seems no better than the worst aliens,
isolatoes, or religious hypocrites in them, and they often create
intolerable conditions for other, even well-meaning, men and
women. Such, I believe, is the case in Faulkner's fiction.
Jefferson is complex, varied; it is a culture, but it is also, at least
sometimes, a metaphor for the human condition. If Brooks must
interpret it to us, he limits Faulkner and reveals himself.
Faulkner has not left anything out.

   In *Toward Yoknapatawpha and Beyond,* Brooks reiterates
points he has argued before, but he must criticize fiction that he
excluded from his first book because it was not set in the
"community." The result is predictable, though Brooks has
retreated somewhat from a stronger position he took several
years ago in a lecture on *The Wild Palms.* The view he
maintained then is instructive:

   Most of you . . . regard Faulkner's great novels as those in which he
dealt in one way or another with the community that is to be found in
the hill towns of northern Mississippi. Yet some of Faulkner's most
interesting novels have settings other than those of Yoknapatawpha
County, and involve characters who either have broken away from the
values of that culture of else have never belonged to it. *Pylon* and *The
Wild Palms* . . . are representative instances. The loss of community
has all sorts of distressing consequences. Among them is the
disturbance of the sexual code and the concept of love.[11]

Charlotte and Harry's doomed attempt to follow the "ancient erotic heresy of the West," chivalric love, is intended as a gesture in the face of a world where love has disappeared, Brooks says, but the attempt is complicated rather than aided by a permissive society—that is, the world outside Yoknapatawpha—which provides few of the obstacles that give piquancy to the concept of romance. City folk, he in effect argues, don't have a chance. "Sophisticated rationality sees through most obstacles," while present-day " 'hygienic' society, when confronted with obstacles, is quick to call in the family physician, the marriage counselor, or the psychiatrist." The "older world—with its concrete relationships, its close family ties, its sharp polarizations of good and evil—provided a realm in which romantic love could exist and in which men and women could stake everything in giving themselves up to love."[12]

Brooks seems now to have modified his view of *The Wild Palms*, but he does not let up on the concept of community. Harry and Charlotte, he sees, do meet obstacles even in a permissive society, but he argues that they are rebelling against the traditional middle-class "crass" society. Since this is not Yoknapatawpha, they are not opposing a "community" but a "civilization so far gone in its worship of respectability that it takes public relations seriously and can acquire its preferences and aversions from an advertising agency" (p. 219). The rhetoric of this jeremiad—is the device catachresis?—is apparent. We have slipped out of Faulkner into a latter-day Spengler who has dragged his own symbols into the novel: first marriage counselors and psychiatrists, then PR men and ad agencies.

We can observe a similar process of condemnation in his judgment of the characters and events—through implicit condemnation of the setting—of *Pylon*. In the earlier lecture he cites the Reporter's comment upon the mechanical lives of the barnstormers. "It ain't adultery; you can't anymore imagine two of them making love than you can two of them airplanes back . . . in the hanger, coupled."[13] This statement expresses the rootlessness, the alienation of the flyers, a condition, according to Brooks, made more bleak still by the setting outside of Yoknapatawpha. In *Toward Yoknapatawpha and Beyond*, he wonders whether Faulkner would have "found an advantage in making Dr. Shumann a Jefferson physician and Roger, his son, a Yoknapatawpha boy"—touching base, at least, with THE community. He decides that Faulkner does not create the Yoknapatawpha connection because he "probably wanted to depict an alienation deeper still" (p. 203). This is a left-handed compliment that emphasizes the differences between Brooks's specially defined community and the rest of the world.

The decision to divide Faulkner's work into two sets of novels is even more problematical than the preceding examples indicate. *Soldiers' Pay* is, for all practical purposes, set into a Yoknapatawpha by any other name, although admittedly the conception is still embryonic; but the name Charlestown, Georgia, which the town in that novel bears, has not fooled anyone. Yet Brooks believes that "except for the Negroes," it "might just as well have been Charlestown, New Hampshire, or Charlestown, Indiana" (p. 99), because Faulkner had not really discovered "community" when he wrote it. The novel, of course, suffers.

It seems to me that in all this Brooks is arguing either backwards or circularly. He is not isolating the real factors that make some of the non-Yoknapatawpha novels less great than some of the Yoknapatawpha novels. He is overemphasizing an element of Faulkner's fiction because of personal views. Granted that the impersonality of the two flyers' flipping a coin to determine a child's paternity is chilling, is it so much different from the card game in *Go Down, Moses,* where two traditional "aristocrats" from the Yoknapatawpha community use the romantic hopes of a sister and a black half brother as stakes? The midwestern community into which the half-naked Laverne parachutes does not seem so different from the ones we see in *Sanctuary,* "Dry September," *Light in August,* or *Intruder in the Dust.* The reporter's snap judgment upon bloodless, mechanical aviators seems belied by the novel's events and the suffering, struggling, erring lives they lead. Ironically, his lust to be with them and the "art" he makes of their experiences contradict his flip image. If, as one could do, we multiplied examples from the fiction to illustrate the conflict between

individual and communty, we would find, I believe, that
Faulkner sympathizes with the individual, in Yoknapatawpha
or outside it. He prefers the single inexhaustible voice, even
when it is quarreling, to the voice of the majority, even when the
majority represents his most typical social sphere, Yoknapatawpha. Communal rituals in Faulkner do not contribute to one's
hopes for mankind; individual acts do. The purging of the
scapegoat does not restore the community to wholeness, though
it is memorable; what is memorable is the revelation of the
immutable persistence of a vivid human gesture.

His emphasis upon community as an ideal does not make
Brooks wholly unsympathetic to the non-Yoknapatawpha
novels, though, in fact, it is often hard for anyone to be
sympathetic to the work which is the principal subject matter of
Toward Yoknapatawpha and Beyond. But one feels that
Brooks's sympathies represent a mild moral condescension,
since for him the Yoknapatawpha setting cuts two ways: it
provides rich physical and spritual background, and its absence
creates bleakness, fragmentation, and rootlessness among the
characters who have no standards to live by or rebel against. If
Brooks had written a single grand book on Faulkner, taking all
the work chronologically, he might have achieved a better
balance, even if he had only used the non-Yoknapatawpha
works to explain what Faulkner was exploring between the acts,
so to speak, of his so-called cycle. As stated above, the
chronological arrangement he has provided at the end of
Toward Yoknapatawpha and Beyond, whereby one might use
razor and glue to construct such a book, would not make for
unity.

The non-Yoknapatawpha books can never be as great, for
Brooks, as those set in the county. Perhaps this is a valid
judgment, though different critics have developed strong
positions for *The Wild Palms* and *A Fable,* and the French think
highly of *Pylon.* Future criticism may find reasons for positive
unanimity about these three books, at least. One limitation of
the nearly exclusive non-Yoknapatawpha content of Brooks's
current study, of course, is that these three books are thrown
together with the apprentice writing, creating a kind of guilt, or

diminution, by association. The early works do fail of greatness,
and their failure, Brooks argues in part, is explained by
Faulkner's failure, at the time they were written, to understand
his "community" and the aesthetic uses to which it could be
put.

Of *Soldiers' Pay*, he writes, Faulkner is still "so deeply
immersed in the customs and folkways of his own society that it
doesn't occur to him there is anything special about them" (p.
98). In *Mosquitoes* he was still groping toward a "truth that was
true for Lafayette County, Mississippi, and yet also true for the
world at large" (p. 149), but leaning too far toward the universal
and abstract. Brooks's insight is valuable, but he carries the
implications of this argument too far by conceiving that the
resolution of the local and the universal was Faulkner's
discovery of the idealized north Mississippi community which
maintained values lost—now everywhere lost, one assumes—to
the rest of the modern Western world. I am not sure how
Faulkner came to balance his sense of place with his artistic
ambitions, his knowledge of north Mississippi with his
sophisticated aesthetic, or his native and circumambient
language with the late nineteenth- and early twentieth-century
poetry and prose he had been reading. It was clearly more than
stumbling into possession of his "postage stamp of native soil."
It did have to do with perceiving Yoknapatawpha as metaphor,
in the sense of returning to the place where he had started and
knowing that place for the first time, to borrow from Eliot. But
what does the metaphor stand for? Isn't it the human condition?
And what is the human condition in the universe according to
Faulkner? Brooks would say, "community"? Perhaps. I would
say diversity, complexity, a tendency for abstraction to oppose
action, and a right smart helping of alienation like that
Faulkner must have felt from the moment he sensed his
difference from those around him. Children and women in his
novels are called upon to straighten out a lot of damn
foolishness that the adult males and the community support.
The domestic sphere, which Ann Douglas describes in *The
Feminization of American Culture*, whose members are allowed
"virility" and active roles only in holy causes, must subvert the

community and the larger social and political orders. Women and children in Faulkner's works transcend the mores and moral values of community: they accept illegitimacy, prostitution, racial ambiguity, poverty, hard luck, and many other things that are harshly judged by the community, perhaps simply because in our culture they are set outside the social order. Such characters give us perspective upon community as Faulkner employs it, a topic there is not space to explore here to the point of defining what it is, exactly, though I believe we can say what it is not—an ideal order.

In a recent published conversation between Brooks and Robert Penn Warren, Warren asks about the importance of community in Brooks's thinking. He replies, "I think the problem of community affects us in every way—politically, sociologically, psychologically . . . the writer needs a community and is deeply affected when all sense of community is lacking." He goes on to talk about the crisis in Western civilization and to say that Faulkner retained the sense of community: "Faulkner still had a grasp on nature. He knew and loved the wilderness. He was part of a traditional society. He also had a grasp on history—history had visibly shaped the community; it entered into the fabric of the family. One of the many things that held the community together was the heritage of service in the Civil War and the experience of common disasters as part of the outcome of the war."[14] Here he makes community a broad word embracing the human unity he finds lacking in the modern world; he makes Faulkner a traditional man. While there is truth in both these views, neither acknowledges the reality of Faulkner's situation or his artistic personality. What they do express, it is more likely, is Brooks's situation and point of view. He grew up in a border state, a region of white yeoman farmers with none of the complexities dramatized in stories like "That Evening Sun" or "Dry September" or *Light in August*. He agrees on many points with the Nashville Agrarians and their kin, including the acceptance of rural southern life as a traditional ideal and the distrust of world-cities. His teaching career at Yale may have made it necessary to gloss Faulkner's world for the would-be eastern sophisticate, probably over-emphatically. He also legitimately tackled the sociological simplifications of critics who employ Faulkner's fiction to "explain" the South according to their own world views. But he himself lacks a full sense of cultural relativity, and he indulges in a grand oversimplification of Faulkner and his settings. We have seen what he says about *Soldiers' Pay* and *Mosquitoes*; the extension of that view is to find *Pylon* bleak beyond endurance because it does not touch Yoknapatawpha and to read *The Wild Palms* as a critique of the values of the world-city, in its major plot, with a half step back into Yoknapatawpha, as if to keep a foundation, in "Old Man." Brooks might have made a similar point about *A Fable*, but he doesn't because he does not discuss the horse-stealing episode (or even index its characters), which would seem to have affinities with the world of Yoknapatawpha. He can see *A Fable* only as the play of ideas, personified abstractions.

We do not have to be blind idolators of Faulkner to desire more critical insight into the three major non-Yoknapatawpha novels, especially *A Fable*, which Brooks slights the most. In an essay on Faulkner's British reception several years ago,[15] he noted the paradoxical nature of many early reviews of Faulkner's greatest works: reviewers acknowledged the sheer impact of the novels and then went on to denigrate style and subject as if that were not what had created the force to which they had responded. Faulkner's unconventionality had put them off, and, if the style and structure were odd, the book had to be odd, too. Brooks may have made a similar misconception of *A Fable*, which perceptive and independent critics like Delmore Schwartz, Heinrich Straumann, and Olga Vickery, for example, have admired. In his criticism of *Pylon* and *The Wild Palms*, where he has moderated earlier opinions, he seems to respond to fairly recent sympathetic readings, but with Faulkner's most enigmatic and possibly his most ambitious novel he seems not to have done so. Thus, while he writes of the way *Pylon* is counterweighted by *Absalom, Absalom!*, the composition of which its own making interrupted, he does not link *Requiem for a Nun* and *A Fable*, as he might have.

Brooks's achievement remains undisputed, and his readings of Faulkner, even when minimal, are helpful or provocative. He has laid out much to absorb in this new book. His knowledge and love of poetry help him to extend our view of Faulkner as poet. In *The Yoknapatawpha Country* he wrote of Faulkner as "nature poet." In *Toward Yoknapatawpha and Beyond* he enlarges our knowledge and appreciation of Faulkner's sources and his affinities with nineteenth- and twentieth-century poets; he leads us from the early experiments in verse to the great poetical passages in *The Hamlet* and *Go Down, Moses*. He identifies what is important—and also what is wrong—in the early prose sketches, showing how they foreshadow later themes and characters but suffer from the intended newspaper audience. His readings of the first two novels give them their due, and he puzzles intelligently over the lapses in diction, characterization, and plot that reduce them in any general estimation; on *Mosquitoes* he is particularly good. Anyone interested in Faulkner, or in American letters, must read Brooks's book, though no one will find in it all they need to comprehend Faulkner in part or as a whole. The concluding essay is, as noted, not a summing up. "Faulkner on Time and History" is, like the book, a bit fragmented, something of an argument against those who feel that the philosophy of Henri Bergson might provide some insight into Faulkner's conception of time. It is another argument for the position that Faulkner is old-fashioned and southern.

This book has been a long time coming, and we know the fate of long-awaited books. It may be, to apply to Brooks's study a point of view sometimes applied to *A Fable,* that the book has taken a long time because he is no longer compelled by the material. The first volume on Faulkner had some of the qualities of a labor of love. It was not only Faulkner who received the author's affection but also the South, specially defined. This South lacking, the second volume reveals some of the signs of being an obligation fulfilled. It is not the big book one would have wanted, and it has already been noted that the principle of division, in the first place, probably worked against the creation of such a big book.

There are still riches. More than that, there is the opportunity to engage oneself, as supporter or adversary, with a wise and generous and well-informed mind. Thanks to Brooks, we know and understand more about the early Faulkner than we did before this new book appeared. To understand the later writings and the career as a whole, we will have to work harder and longer. Brooks, at his best, has set a standard for that.

Notes

1. *William Faulkner: The Yoknapatawpha Country* (New Haven: Yale Univ. Press, 1963), p. ix.

2. *Saturday Review*, 19 September 1942, p. 8.

3. Henry Smith, "Notes on Recent Novels," *Southern Review*, 2 (1937), 577-93.

4. Don Stanford, *"The Beloved Returns* and Other Recent Fiction," *Southern Review*, 6 (1941), 619-20.

5. Robert Penn Warren, "The Snopes World," *Kenyon Review*, 3 (1941), 253-57.

6. See the first number of the *Southern Review*, for example, where Herbert Agar attacks the world-city and Rupert Vance writes on Agrarianism.

7. Brooks's use of rhetorical devices, to demolish adversaries or to sidestep critical issues or approaches of which he disapproves, is worth a study of its own. Synchoresis (a concession to gain sympathy as prelude to a tirade) and paraleipsis (claiming to forego a possible argument while in effect making it) are particularly in evidence.

8. *The Yoknapatawpha Country*, pp. 52-53, my emphasis.

9. *Bitterweeds: Life with William Faulkner at Rowan Oak* (Irving, Texas: Society for the Study of Traditional Culture, 1977).

10. The point is made by James B. Meriwether, "Faulkner's 'Mississippi,' " *Mississippi Quarterly*, 25, Supplement (Summer 1972), 15.

11. "The Tradition of Romantic Love and *The Wild Palms,*" *Mississippi Quarterly*, 25 (Summer 1972), 266.

12. *Ibid.*, pp. 273-74.

13. *Ibid.*, p. 266.

14. Robert Penn Warren, "A Conversation with Cleanth Brooks," *The Possibilities of Order: Cleanth Brooks and His Work*, ed. Lewis P. Simpson (Baton Rouge: Louisiana State Univ. Press, 1976), pp. 58, 59, 63-64. See also Brooks's lecture, "The Sense of Community in Yoknapatawpha Fiction," *Studies in English* (Univ. of Mississippi), 15 (1978), 3-18.

15. "The British Reception of Faulkner's Work," *William Faulkner: Prevailing Verities and World Literature*, ed. W. T. Zyla and Wendell Aycock (Lubbock, Texas: Interdepartmental Committee on Comparative Literature, Texas Tech, 1973), pp. 41-55.

This Will Never Do

Richard D. Altick

Margaret C. Patterson: *Literary Research Guide: An Evaluative, Annotated Bibliography of Important Reference Books and Periodicals on American and English Literature, of the Most Useful Sources for Research in Other National Literatures, and of More than 300 Reference Books in Literature-Related Subject Areas.* Detroit: Gale Research Company, 1976. xlii, 385 pp.

" 'Exceptionally useful . . . Best . . . Absolutely first-rate . . . Indispensable' ": thus ran the heading of the full page devoted to Patterson's *Literary Research Guide* in the 1977 Gale catalogue, followed in the body of the advertisement by more substantial excerpts from the reviews. The publisher was not playing the familiar game of selective quotation. As reference to the originals proves, these plaudits from notices in, respectively, *RQ (Reference Quarterly), Names,* the *American Reference Books Annual,* and the *Library Journal* fairly represent the reviewers' estimate of the book. That this not unambitious reference work-cum-textbook evoked such praise from supposedly knowledgeable and responsible reviewers suggests either that they did not examine it closely or that the standards by which bibliographical guides of this kind are judged nowadays have sunk out of sight. The *Literary Research Guide* is a bad book, and in light of the reception it has had, some space in a journal called *Review* may well be devoted to particularizing its defects, not with the futile intention of belatedly reversing the verdict but in the hope that this case study may prompt a reconsideration of library-oriented reviewers' competence to judge books designed for students of literature.

Patterson's purpose, as stated in the section of the introduction captioned "Vehicle and Tenor," is to serve a wide public: "the student—whether undergraduate, graduate, or professor—who

wants to be a self-educating individual," more specifically
"English or education undergraduates," enrollees in "both
English and library science graduate courses," and "teachers
involved in independent projects." The book is conceived of as
being at once a reference-room item, "a convenient desk-source
for quick reference when recommending books to students," and
a guide for original research, in short a *vade mecum* for all
seasons.

Of course, such a sweeping conception of the book's potential
clientele neglects the fact that each of the audiences mentioned
has its own peculiar requirements in research guides. A
sophomore will scarcely have the occasion or the will to cope
with the British Museum catalogue or Wells's *Manual of the
Writings in Middle English,* nor can a doctoral candidate be
expected to find much use for the all too numerous
bibliographies, hastily and uncritically prepared, which have
been issued in recent years by certain publishers to the library
trade who are avid for a piece of the reference department's
budget. Patterson fails to recognize that many items which one
group can use to advantage are worthless to another. In her
listings, as evidently in her reviewers' minds, no discrimination is
made between the monuments of scholarly bibliography and
literary history on the one hand and elementary ready-reference
tools on the other.

Granted that the once noble word *research* has been
increasingly debased over the years, one still is depressed to find it
used here in the sense of merely "looking something up"("IF
YOU (1) have a short, *easy* question, (2) need only a *little*
information, and/or (3) have a *limited* amount of time, THEN
YOU probably have a one-step research problem"), or, possibly
even worse, in the sense of desperately beating the bushes for a
topic that can be worked up into a paper for a course in English
Lit. Notwithstanding the repeated allusions to graduate students
and "professors," "research" is here regarded as a brief exercise
mainly performed in front of an undergraduate library's reference
shelves. Although the standard tools of professional literary
scholarship are well represented in this volume, the preponder-
ance of works cited are of the kind which serve such occasional

purposes, not because of any apparent principle of selection but simply because there are more of them.

The first test of a bibliographical work is its factual accuracy. In this volume there are relatively few conspicuous errors: the almost inescapable *Finnegan's Wake*, with the uncanonical apostrophe, occurs twice, and there is mention of a Dickens character named Mrs. Haversham. An occasional misfortune, such as misspelling a name in the course of indicating its correct pronunciation—"Magdelen College (maudlin)"—calls for commiseration rather than censure. Misreading of notes may account for Patterson's statement that the Library of Congress contains "at last count . . . about 72,000,000 volumes" and for her assumption that the *Wellesley Index to Victorian Periodicals* will index *all* of the "12,500 nineteenth-century periodicals [which] have been discovered so far." Her inference, from this faulty premise, that "this ambitious project will be many years in the making" constitutes one of her few understatements.

The *STC* does not, as she says, give copyright dates (this is not an error for dates of entry in the Stationers' Register, which she also mentions), and the Center for Editions of American Authors was not concerned with "authors whose texts have been corrupted through *careless scholarship*" (italics supplied). Patterson confuses "supplement" with "fascicle" and uses the phrase "in progress" both correctly (= in active process of publication) and incorrectly (= in preparation). In the "fine" glossary (the adjective is *RQ*'s) there are at least a half dozen flawed entries, typified by the definition of "bibliographical ghost" as "A title or name which never existed and which is included by some bibliographers in their publications as a deterrent to wholesale copying by other bibliographers." The interpretation of "signature" is not consistent in the three entries in which it occurs, and the statement that the Public Record Office contains "numerous . . . primary sources which scholars must consult when they are striving for authoritative literary and textual criticism" conveys not even a hazy notion of what the P.R.O. is.

The single feature of *Literary Research Guide* which was most original at the time it was published was its copious

annotations. (Since then, this feature has also been adopted,
much more successfully, in Robert C. Schweik and Dieter
Riesner's *Reference Sources in English and American
Literature: An Annotated Bibliography* [New York: W. W.
Norton & Co., 1977]). "Every book," Patterson writes in her
introduction, "has been scrutinized for strong points and weak
points, unique contributions, clarity, and authority. Long
evaluative annotations are provided for those books that,
because of their complexity or importance, seem to warrant the
space; short annotations point out the major features of the
others. All annotations [the "all" is a gross overstatement]
include problems and questions from literature to illustrate how
the student can best utilize the time, knowledge, and wisdom
that other scholars have contributed to their special field. They
are meant to spark the imagination of the reader, to show him
how he can use the reference material to make himself a better
writer and scholar."

Waiving for the moment the concluding logic, this avowal of
principles can hardly be faulted. But the principles have not
been translated into practice. This is not a critical bibliography;
it is, on the contrary, a lamentably uncritical one. Patterson has,
indeed, "scrutinized" every book mentioned. There is, however,
little evidence that she has brought to this scrutiny much
experience in scholarly (as opposed to reference-room) research.
Many of the practical uses she postulates for the items described
will raise the eyebrows of persons having a closer acquaintance
with them. *Poole's Index,* she says, "holds a wealth of
possibilities. Students might be interested in working with the
serial versions of *Great Expectations,* the contemporary review
[*sic*] of Hardy's *Tess* or an article on Hardy's women, the total
range of nineteenth-century periodical literature dealing with
Shelley, or the fact that Byron's *Manfred* received no critical
attention at all in the periodicals." Among the "possibilities for
extended research" offered by the *Wellesley Index* is
"examination of the technique used by authors when they
prepared serial installments of their novels." Most of the
projects Patterson suggests are no doubt practicable, but in
many instances they cannot much benefit from the works with
which she specifically associates them. Sometimes, however, her

invention fails and she comes close to throwing in the sponge. Of *Palmer's Index* to the London *Times* the best she can say is that it "undoubtedly contains invaluable information which should be researched. Entries can be found, for instance, that lead to contemporary reactions to Byron's death in 1824 and to Henry James's birthday celebrations."

There is seldom any intimation that one reference tool differs markedly in scope, reliability, or structure from others with which it might most pertinently be compared. Only in the case of one or two already well publicized sitting ducks, such as Block's *English Novel*, is any warning given of possible undependability. In literally scores of instances one expects, at the very least, judicious warnings of obsolescence, incompleteness, limitations of scope not indicated in titles, and—above all—lack of authority. It is incredible that Chauncey Sanders's *Introduction to Research in English Literary History* (1952) should be recommended as "an excellent basic work. . .[which] should be on the required reading list"; actually, it should never have been published in the first place. The novice student is not warned of the *CBEL*'s manifold weaknesses, and the assertion that the new edition is a "total revision" is wide of the mark. Nothing is said of the quite limited usefulness of *The Year's Work in English Studies*—that its coverage is erratic and the comments are too brief and perfunctory to be of much aid. No indication is given that the usefulness of Malclès' *Les Sources du travail bibliographique* (1950-58) is now much vitiated by age; it was never much good for bibliographical work in English and American literature anyway. The would-be user of Baker's *History of the English Novel* ("a basic, authoritative study") is not told that it is mostly a discursive collection of descriptions and synopses with little if any critical or scholarly value. The notorious bias of C. S. Lewis's volume in the *Oxford History of English Literature* goes unmentioned.

Indications of a work's standing among knowledgeable scholars, though they are easily available in reviews and elsewhere, are never offered. Qualitative considerations of this kind are restricted to the frequent assurance that this or that book has been written or compiled by "noted authorities."

(Publishers, too, are trusted beyond their deserts: the annotation
for a book presumably received too late for examination reads,
"The publisher is known for his excellent bibliographies, so
this should be good—it is certainly needed.") Patterson does not
seem cognizant of the basic axiom in scholarship which holds
that a work produced by an authority, or a whole syndicate of
them, for that matter, is not *necessarily* authoritative. Instead,
she is awed by the trappings of erudition. Of a recent volume
chosen to illustrate the Early English Text Society publications
she says, without apparent irony, "The extent of the scholarship
involved is proved by noting that of the 170 total pages, 61 are
devoted to an introduction and bibliography and 58 to notes and
glossary." Not a word as to whether the "scholarship" so
extensively manifested is good scholarship. The pervasive
noncritical spirit is illustrated another way in the comment on
James Thorpe's handbook, *Literary Scholarship:* "Thorpe is an
expert in problems of research, an author of many respected
publications, and an experienced lecturer-teacher-librarian.
Students should consider and accept his advice." One imagines
that Thorpe himself would be the first to refuse to endorse such
a forthright devaluation of critical independence.

Of the several "strong points and weak points" for which each
item was inspected, nothing can be said about "unique
contributions" because it is not clear what "unique
contributions" are. As for "clarity," which supposedly refers to
prose style, while tastes differ it is more than a little baffling to
find Patterson warning that the Baugh *Literary History of
England* is "not easy reading" yet at the same time praising
Chambers's *Elizabethan Stage* as "readable as well as valuable"
(in addition to being "fun browsing"). One could name dozens
of books listed in *Literary Research Guide* which are less easy
reading than, say, George Sherburn's unsurpassed treatment of
eighteenth-century literature in the Baugh volume.

Patterson's assertion that the length of her annotations is
directly proportional to the "complexity or importance" of the
book described is simply not true. Hundreds of works that
neither require nor deserve more than a succinct sentence or two
are overannotated, while a number of complex and important
ones are inadequately dealt with. The British Museum

catalogue, that most formidable of tools to the neophyte, is dismissed with a single bare sentence; no guidance whatsoever is offered to the student opening it for the first time. The problem of the successive cut-off dates which complicate the use of Sabin goes unmentioned, as does the tricky organization of Wells's *Manual* and its nine supplements, portions of which must be used for several more years pending the completion of the revision. ("Unmanageable," says Patterson, without saying why.)

Side by side with these recurrent lost opportunities to be of valuable service to the student exist trivial annotations almost without number. Once again, Patterson's intention is defensible: she wishes to illustrate the nature of a given work by sampling its contents—purposeful browsing is what it ideally amounts to. Unfortunately, however, the luck of the dip too often results in flotsam that either obscures the book's basic character and practical value or has nothing to do with them. Thus, most of the note describing Neil Ker's *Catalogue of Manuscripts Containing Anglo-Saxon* reports the author's introductory summary of scribal procedures and the fate of manuscripts in medieval times—the background, not the substance, of Ker's compilation. Under the entry for the *Seventeenth-Century News* we learn that Wigglesworth's *Day of Doom* was "a 1662 best-seller that was purchased by a larger percentage of the population than any other book in our history except the Bible—required reading for children on Calvinism." Under the periodical *New York Theatre Critics' Reviews:* "Students of contemporary drama—or professors who plan to go to the MLA conference in New York—may be interested in reading that Clive Barnes thought Paul Sills' *Story Theatre* was 'great, unequivocally great,' that Walter Ker applauded John Gielgud and Ralph Richardson in *Home,* and that praise of *A Little Night Music* was unanimous." The extended commentary on the *Wellesley Index* reveals that "one of the few women who did not use a pseudonym in this prim Victorian era was, believe it or not, one Jane Sexey." (Suppressed, oddly enough, is the fact that Jane's sole claim to a place in the *Wellesley Index* is the fact that she wrote for *Macmillan's Magazine* a novel called *A Slip in the Fens.*)

The bulk of the book is further increased—and room for genuinely informative commentary thereby reduced—by annotation that is not only pointless but empty and gratuitous. Of the *Penguin Guide to English Literature:* "In the preface the editor states that he tried to answer the questions of why, where, what, and which." Of Paetow's *Guide to the Study of Medieval History:* "The work has not been surpassed in excellence." Of De Ricci's *Census of Medieval and Renaissance Manuscripts in the United States and Canada:* "After stating that the present location of many MSS is unknown, the editor expresses his hope that his volume will call attention to that fact and that scholars will assist in the continuing search." Of Stratman et al., *Restoration and Eighteenth Century Research: A Bibliographical Guide:* "This is a most welcome addition which will bring research time down to a minimum." Of Abrams's *The Mirror and the Lamp:* "As Abrams manipulates [*sic!*] his theories and premises, he touches upon Aristotle, Johnson, Hazlitt, Mill, Nature, Metaphor, Imagination—a well-orchestrated medley of subjects important to the literature student." Of Ehrsam's *Bibliographies of Twelve Victorian Authors:* "Anyone making a study of literary criticism or Victorian society would surely benefit by using this source." Of Greene's *The Age of Exuberance:* "Readable—perfect for the supplementary reading list in that Survey of English Literature course." Of the *New CBEL:* "The serious student would be wise to know this one thoroughly." Of Kuntz's *Poetry Explication,* the *Explicator Cyclopedia,* etc.: "Every student and every teacher should use these sources regularly." Of Coleman's *Epic and Romance Criticism:* "The students who have waited a long time for this one will certainly be pleased with the scope." Of Cline and Baker's *Index to Criticisms of British and American Poetry:* "Teachers who want their students to cultivate good habits of research will require them to use this source."

These examples are sufficient to demonstrate how inane many of Patterson's "evaluative" comments are. As several also suggest, the comments are not infrequently cryptic, and almost unremittingly chatty. The remark in the introduction to the effect that application to reference books maketh a better writer and scholar is typical of many such infelicities of either thought or expression, and sometimes both. One encounters sheer bad writing, as in this sentence about *Baker's Biographical Dictionary of Musicians:* "The editor's introduction chronicles the tedious circumlocutions which he had to pursue to extract elusive and often embarrassing facts on the personages." Slipshod writing, imperfect knowledge, and erratic reasoning combine in this general observation on the practical use of abstracts and indexes:

It is possible, for instance, to trace the entry for any author or any subject down through the years, noting type of research, facets, trends, growth and fading of popularity, branching of knowledge. This can be summarized and analyzed to produce important conclusions on trends of literary style, criticism, and influence of external pressures on authors—social, cultural, religious, and political. John Cleland, for example, was avoided for decades until mid-twentieth century sophisticates could accept *Fanny Hill,* and nineteenth-century Victorian criticism of Byron was predominantly biographical and, therefore, quite naturally derogatory.

The function and limitations of indexes in particular are rather cloudily understood. "Clever researchers," Patterson says of Fisher's *Medieval Literature of Western Europe,* "will make good use of the index of proper names, for it is a clue to the activity of both primary and secondary authors." In a similar vein, she says of Jordan's MLA bibliography of English romantic poets: "Index of editors and critical authors only. An index of all proper names mentioned in the text would have permitted the student to locate a wealth of material on the interaction of people and ideas throughout the whole era." Apropos of the next item, the Houtchens' companion volume on the other romantic poets and the romantic essayists, we have: "Every student should read this review of research before embarking on the study of the Romantic period, for it selects the best critics, editors, and titles, shows the relationship between all the literary personages of the early nineteenth century, and, in addition, is pleasant reading. The proper name index provides access to all the important people mentioned in the text."

Off-the-cuff dicta and capsule homilies seem dropped into the text without regard for their appropriateness to the place where they land or, indeed, for their intrinsic sense. The annotation for

Adelman and Dworkin's *The Contemporary Novel* reads, in part: "Time-savers like this are the best possible argument for scheduling methods of research courses and for encouraging the habit of research. Students who don't know of the existence of these gold mines are handicapped before they begin." The following is not the best summary judgment ever made of the scholarly activity exemplified in Bowers's *Principles of Bibliographical Description:* "What begins as a science—recording the physical make-up of a book—results in a true art, for the facts are then used as a basis for authoritative textual criticism, the accumulation of valuable library holdings, and the study of literary and publishing history. Not for the dilettante, however—only the scholar with time, patience, and the desire to be *sure.*" John Carter's *ABC for Book-Collectors,* too, has been more usefully characterized elsewhere. Patterson's note says, *in toto:* "Simple enough for the beginner, but the unusual clarity, good humor, and liberally illustrated definitions will reinforce even the most advanced scholar's knowledge that research *must* be careful and *can* be pleasant." Frye's *The Educated Imagination* provokes this thought: "We have to show students how to approach the great philosophers—Shakespeare, Pushkin, Lincoln, Gandhi—because they speak only if we listen, and they speak in a very quiet voice." Two pages farther on, the note on Watson's *The Study of Literature* reads, again *in toto:* "A word to the wise is sufficient. Students *need* to consider Watson's premise that literature must be studied in the context of its time, that every author *does* have a purpose, and that the 'relevant' only confirms existing values whereas we, as educators, are obliged to cultivate judgment by comparison." Shapiro and Beum's *A Prosody Handbook* elicits this *cri de coeur:* "Would that all professors of literature could read this—why do so many of them teach a poem as if it were an essay?"

But the most impressive of all the characteristics of this unusual bibliographical guide is the fearful joy which Patterson strives ceaselessly to impart to her readers. Her enthusiasm is incorrigible if not necessarily catching. The encomia—"superb," "indispensable," "invaluable," "outstanding," "most satisfy-ing," "a work of art in itself" (this of *The Year's Work in Modern*

Language Studies)—strow her pages thick as autumnal leaves on the brooks in Vallombrosa. If she can find nothing else to admire, she falls back on the format: "particularly imaginative and attractive," she says of one periodical, "with wide inner margins and large pages for comfortable reading." More than a little of the time her praise seems either misapplied or excessive. "An astonishing gem of scholarship," she says of one item, "which started out as a dissertation, was abandoned, and then ended up as one of the most complete and helpful bibliographies that has [*sic*] ever been devised." Donald K. Fry's *Beowulf and The Fight at Finnsburh: A Bibliography* has never been acclaimed more warmly. However liberal Patterson is with her tributes, neither Greg nor Pollard and Redgrave nor Wing nor Evans is rated quite *that* high. Still, there are enough happy words and phrases to go round, even if superlatives must be repeated. Both the *MLA International Bibliography* and the *Annual Bibliography of English Language and Literature* are said to be "the most comprehensive" works of their kind, and it is only by scrutinizing the phraseology carefully that one discovers that both works are entitled to the distinction because the former covers scholarship "in literally hundreds of countries all over the world" (hyperbole knows no bounds) and the latter is restricted to work "written originally in English in the U.S., Great Britain, and twenty-two other countries."

A favorite way of bestowing praise is to recommend a given work for purchase, somewhat in the way that so-called "collector's items" are hawked in present-day advertising. If these best-buy ratings are to be taken literally and not simply as alternative rhetoric for expressing enthusiasm, the student's shelf would include these items, among others: *Webster's New Dictionary of Synonyms* ("The purist, the linguist, the conscientious professor, the careful writer should own this one"), Gates's *Guide to the Use of Books and Libraries* ("The best possible source . . . belongs on the desk of every student who wants to become a self-educating individual"), the *Princeton Encyclopedia of Poetry and Poetics* ("absolutely indispensable"), two histories of English literature (Daiches's *Critical History*—a quite debatable choice—and Day's three paperback volumes, the latter as preparation for M.A. and Ph.D. examinations), *Webster's New Collegiate Dictionary* ("Buy it—you can't go wrong here"), Benét's *Reader's Encyclopedia* ("a one-volume substitute for the nine Oxford Companions"), and *Roget's International Thesaurus* ("the wisest purchase . . . the best possible way to increase one's vocabulary and to sharpen style and meaning"). And one more, the *MLA Style Sheet:* "Much to their dismay," writes Patterson, "English literature students will have to own and find their way around in this one. Once the basic facts of footnoting, spacing, punctuation, and form of bibliographies and quotations are mastered, however, the typing becomes easier, the research quicker, the awareness of other scholars' errors keener, and the confidence surer. Students will benefit—in accuracy, efficiency, and scholarship."

The sheer audacity of Patterson's non sequiturs commands admiration. More irritating than breathtaking, however, is her indomitable tone of flip familiarity. As several of the samples already given reveal, she sells reference works like breakfast cereals or household remedies. "If you're at all interested in literature," she proclaims, "you'll want this one around the house"—"this one" being Gassner and Quinn's *Reader's Encyclopedia of World Drama*. Elsewhere the tone is that of a publisher's blurb: "One of the few reference books that have sparkle, warmth, and a really good idea in every line" (Deutsch's *Poetry Handbook*); "This is a memorable book—a thoughtful, helpful book" (C. S. Lewis's *Allegory of Love*). Sometimes Patterson is cute ("This"—Nicoll's *English Drama 1900-1930*— "is an essential research tool that would seem to be the gold tassel on Professor Nicoll's already well-established cap"); sometimes she is brightly with-it (of Watt's Goldentree bibliography of the British novel from Scott to Hardy: "Because of the recent copyright date, Victorian literature students should give prime time to this accumulation of research on eighty novelists"; of the *American Poetry Review:* "A really fine, modern mag").

This bibliographical pitchmanship evidently is the kind of thing Patterson means when she says that her annotations are "meant to spark the imagination of the reader." One must doubt that her compulsive mateyness will have any such effect upon any reader intelligent or sensitive enough to be interested in "literary

research" in the first place. A merry reference tool is a new
phenomenon in the world of learning, and it is not a particularly
requisite one. Out of the juvenile *Zeitgeist* of the present moment
which insists that anything to be taken seriously or even soberly is
automatically "boring" comes the fun-and-games approach to
learning, a grotesque reference-room vivacity resting on the
premise that to succeed—with undergraduates, graduates,
grizzled "professors," "self-educating individuals" at large—a
bibliography must, God save the mark, be entertaining. To the
extent to which he was unwittingly responsible for propagating
the notion that "Research Can Be Fun" (even though he also took
pains to stress that it involves hard-won knowledge, rigorous
thinking, controlled imagination, and not a little sheer
drudgery), the author of *The Scholar Adventurers* and *The Art of
Literary Research* has a good deal to answer for.

But a graver question of responsibility remains. Of the
reviewers who mentioned the annotations, only one, in *Booklist*,
found them in any way unsatisfactory: "inconsistent in quality
and size. . .in turn brief and perfunctory, lengthy and rhapsodic,
straightforward, or facetious." The *Reference Book Review*,
more typically, said flatly that they "tell the reader what he wants
to know . . . . [They] should be mentioned, not merely for their
evaluative qualities, but also for the aid they offer in choosing a
reference work to suit a particular purpose . . . . Such
annotations cut down considerably on the time one must devote
to finding a reliable source." Other reviewers described them,
without elaboration, as "adequate" *(RQ)*, "detailed, evaluative,
and infused with examples and cross references" *(Library
Journal)*, "critical as well as descriptive" *(Wilson Library
Bulletin)*, and "thorough and critical" *(Choice)*.

It is not surprising, then, that reviewers who overlooked the
deficiencies of what *Names* considered "the meat of the book"
were able to praise the volume as a whole with the single
qualification that it was overpriced. The *Library Journal*
"recommended [it] highly as both text and handbook for anyone
in literary studies"; the *Wilson Library Bulletin* acclaimed it as
"a carefully done and up-to-date guide"; the *Reference Book
Review* declared it to be "the best concise general guide to literary

reference books available"; the reviewer for *Names* called it "the best literary research guide I have ever seen . . . indispensable for anyone interested in literature"; *Choice* thought it "should be in the hands of all professors and serious students of literature"; *RQ* described it as "an exceptionally useful volume for those literary researchers who want to develop a greater degree of self-sufficiency in their endeavors"; and the *American Reference Books Annual* unblushingly announced that " it should stand among the top specialized reference books of the 1970s." In the presence of such misdirected acclaim, fair Reason stands aghast.

A New Edition of Chaucer

Ralph Hanna III

John H. Fisher, ed. *The Complete Poetry and Prose of Geoffrey Chaucer*. New York: Holt, Rinehart and Winston, 1977. xiii, 1040 pp.

In years to come the seventies will be remembered as one of the great epochs of Chaucerian textual criticism. During this decade two major texts have already appeared and more have been promised. Robert A. Pratt has provided a useful and attractive edition of *The Tales* and E. Talbot Donaldson, in his revision of *Chaucer's Poetry*, has expanded his selections to include nearly all the longer works. Concurrently with these publications has come the announcement of the University of Oklahoma's multivolume *Variorum Chaucer* and, more recently, of Houghton Mifflin's intention to produce a third edition of Robinson's standard text under Pratt's auspices. John H. Fisher's large volume, like Robinson's an inclusive edition of the works, has now appeared and invites judgment within this context.[1]

Physically, Fisher's is a most imposing volume, considerably larger and weightier than any other available text. This size reflects Fisher's intent, which is comprehensiveness: all the works are here, including the entire *Romaunt* and, for the first time in any collected edition, *The Equatorie of the Planets*.[2] The texts are presented in double column, clearly printed and leaded to give an attractive measure of white (although the format permits only rather narrow margins). These texts provide no surprises, having been conservatively prepared, primarily on the basis of published collations and the Chaucer Society prints. Fisher does innovate in his claim to present nonnormalized versions, texts that follow closely the spellings of selected manuscripts. All annotation of the text appears at the foot of the page "so that each page can be read without reference to other parts of the book or to other reference tools" (p. vii). These notes vary in extensiveness according to context, but quite regularly occupy one-quarter of the page; they treat such conventional matters as difficult words and phrases, obscure allusions, and relevant source material, but they also contain a generous selection of the recorded variants to the published text (e.g., from Hengwrt and related texts for *The Canterbury Tales*, from Fairfax 16 for *The Parliament of Fowls*).

Although Fisher's own statements suggest that the textual materials are separable from the remainder of the volume, he provides other forms of annotation not without their own richness. Fisher gives quite liberal introductions to the individual works, including separate essays for each of the ten fragments (here called "parts") of *The Canterbury Tales*. These are not Robinsonian *précis* of past scholarship but at least partly interpretative efforts that often direct the reader to important full-length scholarly discussions. These essays are supplemented by four brief discussions at the rear of the volume (pp. 951-72); these treat the history of Chaucer's reception, the life, language and versification (this essay and the preceding supplemented by materials inside the covers), and the methodology by which the text was established. Climaxing this plethora of materials, Fisher presents a bibliography with 1,570 entries which "lists everything published from 1964 to 1974 and many important items before and after those years" (p. viii). At the end of the volume (in most, but not all, copies) is a skeletal glossary of difficult and repeated forms (pp. 1033-40). Visually, the reader will be stimulated by five plates showing manuscript versions and black-and-white reproductions of the Ellesmere portraits (with Chaucer's detached from *Melibee* and presented with *Thopas*); his comprehension of the texts of *Astrolabe* and *Equatorie* will be significantly aided by the inclusion of twenty-five manuscript diagrams. Fisher's *Poetry and Prose* proves a quite substantial work indeed.

Describing Fisher's volume, even in these bald terms, only partially indicates the monumental labor that has gone into the production of this text. And amidst the quantity of riches here assembled, it is perhaps ungenerous to cavil. But if one reads through this volume and checks up on Fisher's claims and his presentation, one will discover numerous things that will disconcert, disappoint, and, at last, put one off. For me at least, Fisher's *Prose and Poetry* is an impressive failure because he manages to convince me, as I read, that he lacks both the critical sense and the rigor necessary for his task. In making this criticism, I do not wish to imply that this volume has not been prepared with a good deal of care or that it is not well-written and often graceful in presenting its materials. Rather, the most fundamental problem is that Fisher seems to have no sense of audience. The volume, in fact, presupposes at least a multiple audience, and in trying to meet this broad demand, Fisher adopts (perhaps inadvertently) postures and standards apt to be only marginally useful to anyone. The merits of the volume appear even less substantial if one considers it with other texts it might replace (or viably compete with).

The problem of audience is most clearly approached in terms of one portion of Fisher's efforts, his bibliography. It is discussed in the preface where Fisher gives his most explicit (and perhaps only) statement about his intended readership: "The notes and essays are intended to help readers to understand and appreciate the text. If they wish to delve further into the world of Chauceriana, the bibliography of 1570 items appended to this edition will reveal the variety and sophistication of contemporary Chaucer scholarship and criticism" (p. 8). From this statement one gathers that the intended audience is composed of undergraduate students and general readers, those who like literature and who are not research scholars. Surely this is an appropriate audience and one deserving of well-made texts. But when one scans the bibliography, supposedly prepared with the beginning student or interested private reader in mind, one has to experience a certain measure of surprise. In the first place, such an audience needs a concise, selective bibliography, one that can direct them efficiently to straightforward yet authoritative materials. To a certain extent, for the period to 1964 and for that after 1974, Fisher performs that function admirably—more than two hundred carefully selected old chestnuts and a handful of important recent books are included. Unfortunately for the would-be student, they are buried, largely by the deliberately extensive entries for 1964-1974. As a result, the bibliography becomes extremely difficult for the beginner to use, especially insofar as it shares the difficulty inherent in all unannotated enumerative listings—the tendency for all entries, be they one-page items in *Notes and Queries* or Donald R. Howard's *The Idea of The Canterbury Tales*, to appear perhaps equally relevant. This situation seems to me only partially ameliorated by Fisher's inclusion of selected bibliographical materials in the introductory essays elsewhere in the volume. In spite of the wealth of material here, an audience of students or general readers might be better served by the carefully selected few pages of suggestions in Dyson, by Rowland's *Companion*, or, for actual texts, by Burrow's anthology.[3]

These criticisms represent only an external response to the type of bibliography Fisher presents; on leafing through the assembled materials, one discovers other problems. The principles of inclusion produce serious anomalies, if the audience is visualized as beginning readers. Materials creep in which either will interest this audience only slightly or which the audience will almost certainly find useless. As one example of the first tendency, one might point to bibliography items 1-52, a survey of editions, complete through Tyrwhitt and covering selected modern texts with a range of sophistication from Manly-Rickert to paperbacks produced explicitly for students. For the first of these items, for example, a reference to Muscatine might well suffice as directing students to a single source outlining with precision the history of the text.[4] It seems unlikely that most beginners will have much interest in these matters or in such items as 206-60. A number of entries, whatever their intrinsic merit, remain thoroughly inaccessible to such a beginning audience, for Fisher includes items in such languages as Japanese and Lithuanian (see items 143, 168, 199, 395, 396, and 442). Fisher's bibliography, as it stands, will not serve well the audience for whom the author says he has intended it. If fact, Fisher has quite another audience in mind—the advanced graduate student or research scholar who is the instructor of the audience for whom the work has explicitly been prepared.

The bibliography is actually a scholarly contribution, one quite independent of other parts of the volume and directed to quite a different audience than much of the annotation. Fisher wishes to make a serious and needed scholarly contribution, to provide a bibliographic tool to succeed Crawford, with its 1963 cutoff.[5] This lacuna in scholarly knowledge, of course, accounts for Fisher's decision to provide inclusive coverage of a recent decade of scholarship. And in these terms the bibliography—especially in its clear arrangement by subject and tale headings—provides a very useful contribution. But this is a contribution that must be examined and evaluated in terms different from those applied to the remainder of the volume.

From such a scholarly perspective Fisher's bibliography is unacceptable. So far as I can tell, the work has been compiled by reordering the items listed in the *MLA International Bibliography*. (A comment on the choice of a 1974 cutoff date, p. 975, tends to confirm this suspicion.) Although the MHRA bibliography is mentioned with MLA, and although it is duly listed (item 74), it has not, so far as my researches go, been consulted. Thus, Fisher replicates every mistake and every omission in a standard, but incomplete, research tool. As an example, in an hour's search for materials written on *The Pardoner's Tale* during the period 1964-1968 I found six omissions (not all, it turns out, are *Pardoner's Tale* items, but all are unknown to Fisher). These include an edition by a major university press with a forty-nine-page critical introduction and two pamphlets approaching fifty pages each.[6] More damningly, Fisher has put the bibliography together so mechanically that, in the material surveyed, he includes three articles published outside his stated temporal limits for no other reason than the fact that MLA did not list these items until its 1964 edition. (None of the three seems to fit the criteria for inclusion of pre-1964 items.) This bibliography will not stand scholarly scrutiny, and so the effort to address a second, professional audience seems abortive.

The problems epitomized by the bibliography pervade the whole book. The author continually presents kinds of explanation or documentation inappropriate for or irrelevant to beginning readers. But if these materials are examined with the scrupulousness appropriate to the scholarly audience whom Fisher is apparently also trying to reach, both presentation and substance are invariably flawed. Fisher continually aspires to a scholarly rigor not altogether necessary for a student edition and routinely shows himself incapable of the meticulous accuracy literary scholarship demands.

Two further examples of this tendency should suffice. One unique quality of this edition is Fisher's determination to present a text in an orthographic form as close to the manuscript versions as possible. In this decision the editor implicitly rejects those systems of regularization and normalization of forms silently practiced by generations of past editors. Further, unlike any past normalizer, Fisher provides admirably clear rules for his handling of textual details (p. 966). This decision, in itself, is entirely laudable, for even professional Chaucerians may not have examined manuscript versions and may thus remain unaware of the extent to which all modern texts cosmeticize the surviving versions of the poet's works. At the same time, although Fisher's student audience will probably not experience any increased difficulty in comprehending Chaucer, for most of them this unique feature of Fisher's edition will not prove an item of great interest. Again, Fisher innovates for the benefit of a secondary, professional audience.

Unfortunately, either Fisher's principles as announced are not complete, or he has proofread carelessly,[7] or he has simply been slovenly in his handling of the manuscripts. Fisher's work is inconsistent in quality. Ellesmere, the base for *The Canterbury Tales*, is a manuscript with constantly presentable spellings, and it is reproduced with tolerable accuracy; other texts reveal a greater editorial propensity to vary from manuscript forms. Outside of *The Canterbury Tales* Fisher regularly replaces manuscript *hyr* with *hire* and ignores manuscript *hys, hyt, hym*, and *yn* in favor of forms with *i*; regularizes the vowels of unstressed syllables to *-e-* (in spite of some rhyme evidence that *-i-* pronunciations may be authorial); adds and omits *-e*'s from the manuscripts at will, including in the prose works where no metrical logic can be at issue; adjusts such spellings as *seyht* (to *seyth*, *Boece* III p 4:13 and a normal form in the base text), *theere* (to *there* and *ther*), *iwrowht* (to *iwroughte*, *Parliament of Fowls* 123, again a normal form, here and elsewhere), and *thurgh* (to *thorugh*, *Troilus and Criseyde* II:102, again a normal form). Further, so far as I can tell, *swyche*, *nat*, and *wil* are generalized, although inconsistently, throughout all texts, regardless of manuscript forms. Inconsistencies abound—for example, at *Troilus* II:160 Fisher drops *-e* of MS *trowthe* but retains it, in the same metrical context, at II:170. To be as generous as possible about this state of things, Fisher apparently discovered only belatedly the mess that nonnormalized manuscript readings could involve and, like all editors before him, resorted to normalization of the text. But he appears to have normalized subconsciously, for his discussion of the text provides not a sign of self-awareness, much less notice to the reader, that all is not as the manuscripts present it. Once again, from a scholarly perspective, the claims of the book are, to put the matter most neutrally, severely overstated.[8]

A second and specifically textual area shows similar failures of execution: "In addition to indicating all the substantive changes in the copy text, the textual notes in italics at the foot of each page give a sampling of the more interesting variants from important manuscripts. These are intended to convey a sense of the texture of the poetry, not to provide the basis for textual criticism" (p. 966).[9] Again, Fisher provides a form of annotation whose relevance to an audience of beginners may be questioned. Students frequently experience considerable frustration in grappling with Chaucer's language without having to contend with the added suggestion that the language may not be Chaucer's. Consequently, this material again probably appeals to Fisher's secondary audience of professional Chaucerians. Such information is helpful, especially insofar as it may indicate to the unwary the extent to which our knowledge of what Chaucer wrote reflects an eclectic pastiche of readings derived from a variety of manuscripts. On this score one may wish to question Fisher's selectivity of presentation, as well as his recording of significant textual suggestions (e.g., various suggestions are noted at *Canterbury Tales* A 3485, but Donaldson's magisterial treatment—bibliography item 854—is ignored at D117). And in *The Parliament of Fowls*, where the textual situation is extremely difficult, the "effort . . . to record all substantive variations between G and F" (p. 969) is very far from complete.[10] Again, the impressiveness of Fisher's claims founders on the rocks of indifferent execution.

In spite of these problems which concern the specialist, there remains the possibility of viewing the edition as a modified success. That is, insofar as Fisher fulfills his responsibilities to his primary audience of students and general readers and provides an adequate degree of reliable annotation, one might judge the work of value. As I have noted, the volume has extensive annotation, various in its scope and content; I can only scan and comment briefly on its quality.

The notes to the text, instantly available through foot of the page placement, form the most useful part of the volume. In them Fisher provides a large amount of basic information about textual details and difficulties. There are some occasional confusions: the italicized textual data clutters the page, for example. More seriously, Fisher is fond of presenting lemmata separated by ellipses; this punctuation obscures two radically different functions, for ellipses join two individual words needing separate glossing but also indicate a full phrase to be glossed. Phrasal glosses are quite frequently incomplete or provide definitions that make no sense in the context of Chaucer's lines; see those for *The General Prologue*, lines 165, 534, 550 (perhaps a comma has dropped out), and 679. Fullness of glossing remains indubitably a matter of taste, but students will miss authoritative interpretations of such lexical items as *worthy* ("honorable by virtue of military prowess," *Gen Prol*, line 43), *sheene* ("bright, shiny," *Gen Prol*, line 160), *bar the pris* ("took the prize for, was pre-eminent at," *Gen Prol*, 237), *as nowthe* ("for the present," *Gen Prol*, line 462), *meschief* ("misfortune," *Gen Prol*, line 493), *clennesse* ("virtue," *Gen Prol*, line 506), *leet* ("abandoned," *Gen Prol*, line 508), and *ylad* ("carried," *Gen Prol*, line 530). In some cases Fisher assumes that the devoted student can figure out archaic forms for himself; but some deceptively transparent items whose Middle English nuances do not correspond with modern primary connotations probably should have been defined. Omissions of this type are the only real blemishes here, for the lexical glosses given are generally apt and accurate.[11]

The annotation Fisher provides in essay form does not rival the textual materials in either informativeness or accuracy. Linguistic and metrical help is particularly sketchy, limited to something under four pages of text, the brief and laconic wordlist, and a useful phonetic summary inside the back cover. Information about these subjects frequently shows inaccuracies and misunderstandings, e.g., the unqualified statement that "the auxiliary verb [in Chaucer's Middle English] was usually a form of *be* rather than *have*" (p. 964). Brevity also marks the essay on Chaucer's critical reception, to such an extent that no reader will be able to decide whether Fisher recognizes Dryden's importance to the critical tradition. And the materials on the life, without any warning that the views stated are potentially controversial, attempts some revision of the canon and dating of individual works. (Fisher denies Chaucer any share in *The Romaunt of the Rose*, although it is printed in the text; he assigns *The Parliament of Fowls* to 1377, before *The House of Fame*, because he believes it satirizes the plans for the marriage of Richard II and Marie of France; and he tends to minimize so far as possible the amount of *The Canterbury Tales* which can be assigned to the 1390s.)

The critical essays that preface the individual works show similar unevenness so far as help for students is concerned. Although Fisher has made an effort in the volume to collect most contemporary criticism, he regularly fails to avail himself of its riches, and a great many older views of marginal interest to modern students (such matters as sources, areas of apparent revision, tale order, historical allegory) are brought forth for their instruction. The amount of sheer misstatement or incorrect information provided is also unfortunately high: e.g., the two discussions of *Boece* (pp. 8, 814-15) conflate what are two different things: the obvious intention of the work (to discuss true and false goods, proper and improper uses of this world) and Chaucer's use of the work (as a digest of quotable quotes about cosmic governance); the discussion of *The Parson's Tale* and its sources (pp. 345-46) sets forth views untenable either since the publication of bibliography items 1265-66 or after any reading of *Le Somme le Roi*; the claims that Chaucer "created a new language, half English and half French" and that "the metre [of *The Book of the Duchess*] is French" are simply untrue (see bibliography items 252 and 1440). Although some fine material gets interspersed (for example, a moving paragraph on Chaucer's medievality and modernity, p. 146), Fisher's literary annotation falls short of being generally useful.

The value of this volume, then, consists in its comprehensiveness, its making available to a broad audience the entire Chaucer canon. In this respect Fisher's work plainly outstrips all other available student texts, which deliberately ignore the prose and cover in varying degrees the breadth of the poetry. However, even this contribution proves a somewhat evanescent virtue if one visualizes the text as a classroom tool: even in a yearlong undergraduate course, one experiences some difficulty in covering adequately much more than *The Canterbury Tales*, *Troilus*, and the major dream visions. And even if one chooses to read *Boece*, the most important prose text, student comprehension is apt to be improved by use of a modern translation, rather than Chaucer's version, whatever its historical value. Again, I think, Fisher's scholarly enthusiasm has produced a work that is without an audience, for other texts will probably serve this classroom need far better.

In my view, there is only a single classroom text over which Fisher represents a substantial improvement—the current, second edition of Robinson. Fisher's relatively greater insistence on current scholarly problems, his more pointed introductory materials, his more available and fuller textual annotation should cause those who teach from Robinson to reevaluate their choice. But for those who have given up on reading the entire canon with undergraduates and have abandoned Robinson for some other text, Fisher will offer very little not otherwise available. For perspicacity on textual matters and direct annotation of Chaucer's words, Fisher and Baugh are about equivalent in value and Donaldson at least marginally superior. And the instructor who chooses Fisher's *Poetry and Prose* over either of these texts should, I think, be aware of major and irreplaceable losses of annotation. Baugh provides a lucid exposition of Chaucer's language (pp. xxii-xlii, especially valuable for its comments on syntax) and a quite extensive glossary with a wide panoply of spelling and grammatical forms (pp. 543-616; as Fisher notes, p. 1033, unparalleled since Skeat).[12] And although Fisher's essays on the poems may be somewhat more current in their outlook and of greater literary value than Baugh's introductory materials, both pale before the humanity and grace of Donaldson's extensive "Commentary" on the text (pp. 1031-1144). Donaldson also provides grammatical and metrical materials of greater sophistication than Fisher's, although without Baugh's extensiveness (pp. 1001-20); and his word list, brief but at least as full as Fisher's (pp. 1145-63), better aids the student reader in recognizing a Chaucerian pronunciation of lexical items. Given these alternatives, few careful instructors should choose this book—fewer still, I would suppose, after the appearance (perhaps a decade hence) of a revised Robinson or one-volume *Variorum*-based text.

There remain Fisher's other claims to the reader's attention— those items that seem superadded to a passible student text for the benefit of a more sophisticated audience. Such an audience will be better served elsewhere. There exists a competing bibliography for the decade Fisher covers; the manuscript spellings behind Robinson's hygienic text can be recovered in the reprinted volumes of the Chaucer Society, or, better still, from inexpensive microfilms ordered from those libraries where the original texts now repose; full collations are available in Manly-Rickert, Root, and Koch.[13] It pains me, in the face of such extensive labor as Professor Fisher has obviously performed, to say that this volume is of very limited use.

Notes

1. Pratt, *The Tales of Canterbury* (Boston: Houghton Mifflin, 1974); Donaldson, *Chaucer's Poetry: An Anthology for the Modern Reader*, 2d ed. (New York: Ronald, 1975); F. N. Robinson, *The Works of Geoffrey Chaucer*, 2d ed. (Boston: Houghton Mifflin, 1957); later I will also refer to Albert C. Baugh, *Chaucer's Major Poetry* (New York: Appleton, 1963).

2. *Equatorie* was ascribed to the poet by Derek J. Price in his edition (Cambridge: Cambridge Univ. Press, 1955), pp. 149-66.

3. J. A. Burrow, in A. E. Dyson, ed., *English Poetry: Select Bibliographical Guides* (London: Oxford Univ. Press, 1971), pp. 1-14; Beryl Rowland, ed., *Companion to Chaucer Studies* (London: Oxford Univ. Press, 1968); J.A. Burrow, ed., *Geoffrey Chaucer: A Critical Anthology* (Baltimore: Penguin, 1969).

4. Charles Muscatine, *The Book of Geoffrey Chaucer: An Account of the Publications of Chaucer's Works from the Fifteenth Century to Modern Times* (San Francisco: Book Club of Calif., 1963).

5. William R. Crawford, *Bibliography of Chaucer 1954-63* (Seattle: Univ. of Washington Press, 1967); in this discussion I have had to rely on my own findings, since Lorrayne Y. Baird's *A Bibliography of Chaucer, 1964-1973* (Boston: G. K. Hall, 1977) was not available.

6. J. C. Bright and P. M. Birch, *Four Essays on Chaucer* (Sydney: Brooks, 1967); Christopher Brookhouse, "The Confessions of Three Pilgrims," *Laurel Review*, 8 (1968), 49-56; Gilbert A. Case, *Geoffrey Chaucer's "The Pardoner's Tale"* (Adelaide: Rigby, 1968); James M. Kiehl, "Dryden's Zimri and Chaucer's Pardoner: A Comparative Study of Verse Portraiture," *Thoth*, 6 (1965), 3-12; Ian Robinson, "Chaucer's Religious Tales," *Critical Review*, 10 (1967), 18-32; A. C. Spearing, ed., *The Pardoner's Prologue and Tale* (Cambridge: Cambridge Univ. Press, 1965). Although it is difficult to extrapolate from spot checks, I would estimate Fisher's bibliography as missing at least ten percent of the published 1964-74 items.

7. This second alternative remains a distinct possibility, since typographical errors are considerably more abundant than they should be, e.g., *Alcone* for *Alcyone* (p. 565, col. 1, line 2), *Alunas* for *Alanus* (p. 565, col. 2, line 1), *Deguiville* (p. 668, line 29, but *Deguilleville recte*, p. 673), *Dalbury* for *Dahlberg* (p. 711, col. 2, line 25), *Southerland* for *Sutherland* (*recte* elsewhere, p. 711, col. 1, line 18); *Persall* for *Pearsall* (bibl. 398); *Omagery* for *Imagery* (bibl. 1105); *Fran* for *Frank* (bibl. 1295); *Kasmann* for *Käsmann* (bibl. 1381), *Cogan* for *Clogan* (bibl. 1553).

8. I base my findings on spot checks of hundred-line passages against the relevant Chaucer Society prints (which, I recognize, on past experience, not always to be accurate representations of the manuscript). I have surveyed *The Canterbury Tales* A 2421-2536, B^2 3187-3298, *The Parliament of Fowls* 85-182,

Troilus II: 78-175, and *Boece* IIIp4:1-67 (in this last case, against the base manuscript, Cambridge Ii.iii.21).

9. In passing, I wonder a good deal about the second sentence here. As I understand the responsibilities of the textual critic, "the texture of [Chaucer's] poetry" refers to matters authorial. The fact that scribes may, at points, have distorted what the poet wrote is of interest but has nothing to do with "the texture of the poetry."

10. Fisher's rather cavalier attitude toward "substantive variants" may be at issue here. For in spite of claims to reproduce them all, the editor reserves to himself (items 8 and 9, p. 996) the right to correct silently "obvious miswritings" and "filler words needed or not needed for scansion," all of which are substantive decisions that pass without a trace in the notes. A complete report on Fairfax 16 for *The Parliament of Fowls* 302-99 would require the following additions to Fisher's notes: 317 aray] F suche array; 327 And, 328 But] F *transposes;* 358 the²] F *om.;* 361 the²] F *om.;* 369 everiche] F eche; 381 noumberes] F novmbre; 383 hed] F *om.;* 386 how] F how that; 389 Youre] F With youre. The variant at 352 is mistranscribed, at least as I understand Fisher's principles (see item 6, p. 966): F reads fressh, and -e is editorial (and metrically required). In addition, Fisher's notes to 330, 349, and 370 give nonsubstantive spelling variants, and 387-90 erroneous information, at least with regard to F, which has *gouernaunce* for both rhymes.

11. The glossary, not in the first printing, helps to fill the student's need; but only three of the items cited above are there, and the student will still not discover that *leet* is past tense. Historical information of import to the text seems somewhat shakier than information on lexical items; for example, to provide an accurate account of *Gen Prol*, lines 411-34, the following changes and additions seem necessary:

411 *physik* (unglossed): physical science, the study of nature, hence theoretical medicine (as distinguished from the practical act of healing; see 413); *doctor* here is, of course, the title conferred by a university degree.

416 *houres* (misglossed, since *kepte* connotes potentially baleful influences): not simply "favorable hours," but both "those hours deemed important through the Physician's knowledge of astrology" and, probably, "the critical hours of a recurrent fever," or "those hours in which a particular humor or elementary quality dominates the patient's constitution."

417 *fortunen* (unglossed): "calculate propitious and unpropitious times (with especial reference to)."

417 *ascendant* (one of the overly inclusive ellipses leaves the word unglossed): "the position of a planet when it exercises its greatest influence," or "that planet in a position to exert maximum influence."

420 *hoot . . . drye* (misglossed, cf. the different use of *humor* in the next
line): "The four elementary qualities or *dynamoi;* from the
combination of these qualities medieval scientists believed the four
elements (earth, air, fire, and water) and the four humours, bodily
fluids determining temperament and health (blood, phlegm, bile or
choler, and melancholy), were produced. Cf. for the elementary
qualities, *The Parliament of Fowls,* lines 380-81; and for Chaucer's
reliance on the humoral theory of temperament or complexion, *The
General Prologue,* lines 333, 587, and 625.

429 *Esculapius* (misidentified): the legendary Greek god of healing.

433 *Constantyn* (misidentified): a North African (d. 1087) who
introduced Greek and Arabic medical texts to southern Italy; he may
or may not have been a physician or a Christian.

12. A full glossary to the works by Norman Davis is in preparation.

13. J. M. Manly and Edith Rickert, *The Text of the Canterbury Tales:
Studied on the Basis of All Known Manuscripts,* 8 vols. (Chicago: Univ. of
Chicago Press, 1940); Robert K. Root, *The Book of Troilus and Criseyde by
Geoffrey Chaucer* (Princeton: Princeton Univ. Press, 1926); and John Koch,
Geoffrey Chaucer: Kleinere Dichtungen (Heidelberg: Winter, 1928).

Imperial Criticism

Gerhard Joseph

A. Dwight Culler. *The Poetry of Tennyson*. New Haven: Yale University Press, 1977. 276 pp.

In each of his three books A. Dwight Culler initially ascends a magisterial height in order to survey the "Idea" of his subject. That maneuver, which he first attempted in *The Imperial Intellect: A Study of Cardinal Newman's Educational Idea* (New Haven: Yale Univ. Press, 1955), is of course a characteristically Victorian procedure, and Culler may well have learned it from the first Victorian whose imaginative country he set out to chart. For as Newman tells us in *The Idea of a University*,

if we would improve the intellect, first of all we must ascend; we cannot gain real knowledge on a level; we must generalize, we must reduce to method, we must have a grasp of principles, and group and shape our acquisitions by means of them. It matters not whether our field of operation be wide or limited; in every case, to command it, is to mount above it. Who has not felt the irritation of mind and impatience created by a deep, rich country, visited for the first time, with winding lanes, and high hedges, and green steeps, and tangled woods, and everything smiling indeed, but in a maze? The feeling comes upon us in a strange city, when we have no map of its streets. Hence you hear of practiced travellers, when they first come into a place, mounting some high hill or church tower, by way of reconnoitring its neighborhood. In like manner, you must be above your knowledge, not under it, or it will oppress you; and the more you have of it, the greater will be the load.

[Discourse VI, Section 7]

The recourse to an "imperial" altitude in Culler's second book, *Imaginative Reason: The Poetry of Matthew Arnold* (Yale Univ. Press, 1966), takes the guise of the Arnoldian dictum with which, as epigraph, that work opens: if Keats and Browning "must begin with an Idea of the world in order not to be prevailed over by the world's multitudinousness" (p. 3), the critic must likewise start with an Idea, must initially reconnoiter the maze of his poet's career from above. In that spirit Culler finds it advisable in his introduction to "mount up into a tower and gain a general view of Arnold's imaginative world" (p. 3), a perspective that reveals a three-regioned landscape, a triadic pattern of history, and a group of related symbolic protagonists, again "three or four in number" (p. 12). Although in the ensuing chapters Culler may provide careful explications of individual poems, we sense that his overriding purpose is to elicit a holistic, oeuvre impression and that he has adopted that purpose from Arnold himself and, behind him, Newman—and behind *Newman* the Coleridge of the "Preliminary Treatise on Method." Thus, in his subordination of exegetic detail to a triadic nineteenth-century thesis-antithesis-synthesis dialectic, Culler may be seen as the critical equivalent of Arnold's ideal artist whose architectonic ability to order a coherent action counts for more than the ability to throw off a variety of profound thoughts and images.

Culler's latest book, a study of Tennyson, methodologically resembles his earlier work by positing and elaborating upon an initial Idea; and *The Poetry of Tennyson* may be considered a specific sequel to the Arnold study in that this scheme is once more dialectical in articulation. Briefly, Culler argues that the Victorian geological debate between "catastrophists" and "uniformitarians" had its literary correlative: nineteenth-century writers too may be divided into catastrophists such as Carlyle who undergo and celebrate sudden, apocalyptic conversion and temperate uniformitarians like George Eliot whose works show that modulated change is the law of life, certainly of social existence. Historically, to move from the Romantic to the Victorian period is to move from literary catastrophism to uniformitarianism, and Tennyson is said to be in no way as representative of his age as in the arc he traces between the two attitudes toward life. Beginning as a catastrophist in response to Milton and the great Romantics, he drifted in the middle of his career towards uniformitarianism (*In Memoriam* with its speaker's painfully slow recovery from Hallam's death being the central "gradualist" document), but then, as his vision darkened in later years, he returned to his earlier apocalyptic mode. In place of the "two Tennysons" formulations that have moved through the criticism since Harold Nicholson in 1923 designed the notion of a linear development with an intermediate change of direction, Culler finds the figure in Tennyson's carpet to be a triadic cycle (a tripartite design that James Kincaid has also recently described, on genre principles, in *Tennyson's Major Poems: The Comic and Ironic Patterns* [Yale Univ. Press, 1975]).

But there is a price to be paid for the ascent to the critical tower for a commanding view. The Victorian mind—and its modern interpreter—may wish both to see a complicated subject "steadily" and "whole" *and* to see the individual part of that subject "as in itself it really is" (in Arnold's version of the antinomy). But however much he may have praised a Sophocles or a Goethe for their accommodation of universals and particulars, of whole and part, Arnold's own epistemological fragmentation suggests the difficulty of such bifocal vision. And Culler, committed to the Newman/Arnold ideal of conceptual coherency, is beset by the same dangers that threatened the synoptic ambitions of his Victorian masters. If one's ascent to comprehensive altitudes is a flight from unmanageable multitudinousness, one cannot help oversimplifying local effects.

Broad patterns do have the aesthetic virtue of clarity. Thus, Culler's composite method elicts a series of characters who recur in Tennyson's early poetry: in a brief, early apocalyptic phase, unmediated vision comes to the poet upon the height directly (as in, say, "Armageddon" or "Timbuctoo"). But very quickly Tennyson's artist-figures suffer an "Icarian fall," from a semidivine to a human condition, and the visionary "gleam" floats down from the heights upon a "stream of melody," which is now received by such "fallen" poet-figures as Claribel, Mariana, and the Lady of Shalott—maidens immured within a "garden of the mind." As the melody of the maiden's song or the "river" of her tears "flows out of the garden past the great city of the plain" (p. 29), the important question for Tennyson becomes how this divine flow will be received in the cities of man. In the early poetry the poet-figure is a priest or goddess, and the uninitiate are warned to stay away from the sacred grove of the imagination. In a second state the poet-figure yearns to communicate with mortals, but they are inattentive or false. And in a third, mature phase a mortal Auditor of divine music, now a relatively aggressive male quester rather than a deserted maiden, is able to communicate that music to the world. Alternatively in that third phase, the Auditor of Seer may be condemned by the gods to worldly ineffectiveness as the price of his vision, or his heroic striving may unsuit him to that political gradualism with which vision must spread through the world. Therefore, in the poems of the thirties Tennyson will sometimes introduce still another figure, an Enactor (Telemachus, Bedivere) to carry out the divine message that the Auditor (Ulysses, Arthur) has heard, a younger political mediator like Menoeceus who can translate into action the vision that Tiresias has seen.

While the rough truth of the design is evident enough, one must also note a certain flattening, a breadth rather than a nuance of response to individual poems. For one thing, Tennyson is made to sound suspiciously like Arnold: the Tennysonian stream of melody that floats down from the heights through a garden of the mind past a city of the plain has an uncanny resemblance to the equally schematized River of Life which passes through a Forest Glade and the Cities of the Darkling Plain before reaching the Wide-Glimmering Sea in Culler's Arnold book. And Arnold's repertory of protagonists who appear at different points of the symbolic topography (Madman, Slave, Strayed Reveller, Quietist, Sage) is matched by Tennyson's Apocalyptic Prophet or Revolutionary, Isolated Maiden, Civilized Englishman addressing his Civilized Peers, and Ancient Sage.

Within Culler's groupings of Tennyson's work one occasionally feels a like sacrifice of distinction for the sake of coherency in pattern. Every protagonist, for instance, that Culler considers in the early poetry—the maiden of "Anacaona," Claribel, the Kraken, Oenone, the Lady of Shalott, the Hesperidean Sisters, and the Dying Swan—is a poet-figure whose salient feature is an inability to make much of an impression upon his or her respective auditor. And these listeners are hierarchically ranked by Culler's synoptic method:

If one were to range the auditors of song on some kind of scale according to their response, the lowest would certainly be the Spaniards [of "Anacaona"]. How Claribel died and by whose hand we do not know, but the harsh and puritanical Angelo, the abandoner of Mariana, would be next, or perhaps his fellows in heaven who stoked the fires for the Kraken. Then would come the faithless Paris, the betrayer of Oenone, and after him Lancelot, who simply did not listen, did not think. Next would be the mariners who "mused/Whispering to each other half in fear," and after them Hanno [of "The Hesperides"], who listened though he could not linger. [p. 57]

Again, the general point is well worth making, and Culler's auditory ladder makes an approximate sense—even if the rungs of that ladder are hewn in part from his imagination rather than from the hard matter of the poetry. In "Claribel" there is no auditor at all; a "harsh and puritanical Angelo" may figure in *Measure for Measure*, but the brief tag from the play that introduces "Mariana" is hardly enough to give the intentionally shadowy "he" who "cometh not" so palpable an identity. And even if we grant the allegorization of the Kraken into yet another poet-figure, the "fellows in heaven who stoked the fires" for the sea monster do not exist in the poem but are sheer interpolations intended to confirm Culler's pattern. Alan Roper contends in *Arnold's Poetic Landscapes* (Baltimore: Johns Hopkins, 1969)— the plural is intended as a direct attack upon Culler's notion of a single composite landscape—that Culler too often judges the success of individual poems by the comprehensiveness with which they allude to and clarify the total symbolic topography that he has initially posited. Culler thus can read into "The Scholar-Gipsy" a landscape detail that is not present (the cities of the burning plain) in order to demonstrate that what he considers Arnold's finest poem combines for once most of his— Culler's?—composite landscape. In the above passage and some others from the Tennyson book a similar tendency seems to be at work.

It is important not to exaggerate these effects of overdetermination, however, for they are only minor flaws. Culler's larger Idea of Tennyson's imaginative world—his catastrophist/uniformitarian thesis—is never crudely constitutive or binding. Culler is generally willing to let that initial formulation shape his reading of individual poems with an admirable restraint and tact.

Furthermore, that thesis allows him to concentrate upon groups of poems that have been relatively neglected. Because the "gradualist" impulse is said to be central to Tennyson's creative life, Culler is able to look with original insight at the wise and temperate gradualism of the political poems of 1831-1834; to bring a new intellectual sympathy to the English idyls, those domestic poems "of the middle range of life and of the middle class" which he finds the most undervalued in proportion to their worth in all of Tennyson's work; and to conclude his study with high praise for the occasional poems of social converse whose Horatian stance of the civilized Englishman addressing his noble peers in his own voice strikes Culler as the most naturally Tennysonian attitude. While he certainly does not scant the mystical, apocalyptic Tennyson, one feels that this Tennyson of the middle range is the one for whom Culler has an unusually strong admiration. This is the Tennyson whom he wishes not so much to characterize—since others have defined that tonality—as to give a new primacy, weight, and intellectual respectability. Thus the English idyls are "works of subtle and delicate art"; they are "among the finest of Tennyson's poems," certainly among the "happiest" of his works. Enveloped in a "golden haze, a lucent atmosphere," they are at the same time marked by ironic juxtapositions and unresolved conflicts which give them a "dryness and classicality" rare in Tennyson. Whether "The Gardener's Daughter," "The Miller's Daughter," "Walking to the Mall," "Audley Court," "Edwin Morris," and "The Golden Year" merit such celebration each reader may decide for himself. But Culler's full and intelligent discussion of these and other "poems of the middle range" at least gives them the fair hearing they have rarely enjoyed in recent times.

Puritanism in Two Dimensions

Peter C. Carafiol

Francis J. Bremer. *The Puritan Experiment: New England Society from Bradford to Edwards.* Introduction by Alden T. Vaughan. New York: St. Martin's Press, 1976. 255 pp.

In his preface Francis Bremer describes the genesis of *The Puritan Experiment* in his inability to direct his students to a "one book" introduction to colonial New England. Bremer, and Alden T. Vaughan, who wrote the introduction, argue that this work offers a needed overview, a "synthesis," as Vaughan puts it, of the proliferating Puritan scholarship since Miller's *Orthodoxy in Massachusetts.* The book is intended for "those who want to familiarize themselves quickly with the field as well as those who wish an introduction for more extensive study" (p. vii). This is a most ambitious project, one that requires a significant act of imagination from the scholar-author, a radical intellectual displacement into the perspective of a beginning student. It is, on the other hand, a project that must inevitably seem inadequate to the community of scholars who examine (and review) it, who will first be struck with its possibly unavoidable oversimplification or neglect of issues that the experienced student of the field knows to be crucial.

The Puritan Experiment does not deal successfully with the challenges it raises for itself. In the end it is defeated by its own high aspirations. Although the book claims to address beginning students of Puritanism, it is troubled throughout by confusion about its audience. For an introductory work it throws out far too many unexplained technical terms and historical references. How is the novice to understand Bremer's discussion of the conflicts among the Marian exiles when those conflicts depended on differences between the Genevan position and the 1552 Prayer Book that Bremer neither describes nor explains. Later, when Genevan practice is finally outlined and labeled "the hallmark of Puritan ideology" (p. 9), it is far from clear why its familiar propositions are so crucial, since we have not been enlightened about the issues in the theological debate from which they arose. Similarly, the Elizabethan Settlement is mentioned, but its tenets (or even the motives behind it) are never clearly described as they should be for beginning students. Such lapses are the norm. Especially in the early chapters, when Bremer is trying to cover the whole history of Puritanism up to the settlement in the New World, the book seems dominated by a desire to squeeze in as many facts as possible even at the expense of adequate explanation. The narrative is thin cloth indeed, hung on hundreds of particulars which dominate the presentation and seem to be its real reason for being. Labels replace ideas, and while these labels might call the essential issues to mind for the expert, they could only send the novice running in frustration for his encyclopedia (not, perhaps, so unhappy a result) or more likely turn him away from Puritan studies altogether. The companion of this underexplanation is Bremer's occasional lapse into over-explanation. In some cases it is simply a matter of detail. Why, for instance, does he bother to tell us that Cotton Mather is Increase Mather's son when he fails to explain so many facts which seem more compelling? In other cases, however, the problem is more substantial and therefore still more difficult to understand. Bremer's discussion of the companies that preceded the Massachusetts Bay Company in efforts to settle New England fills three pages (the same space he devotes to the Half-Way Covenant) and includes numerous obscure details (the original capital of the New England Company, the membership of the Council of New England) that are inappropriate to an introductory work and seem to be included simply because they are at hand. Such inconsistency reflects a fundamental and distressing uncertainty about what to say and what to omit.

Such excessive allegiance to historical fact twists thought and disrupts the logic of Bremer's organization. The entire work breaks apart on a disjunction between fact and idea. He alternated chapters of historical narrative and thematic description, almost as if he were juggling the two modes of Puritan scholarship Alden Vaughan describes in the introduction: the pre-Miller external style and the more introspective treatments since then. Bremer offers precious little rationale for his inconsistent emphasis on history and cultural issues. The historical chapters are bound together by diachrony. But their otherwise orderly and businesslike, if uninspired, movement is interrupted by thematic chapters on church, state, society, art, and race that seem tangential, despite the fact that we feel the need of more such material throughout the text. Whatever justification this organization may possess in Bremer's mind is never explained and is certainly not self-evident. The effect of this scraping and jarring between chapters is to fracture our sense of chronology and alienate the spirit of Puritan culture from its historical substance.

Bremer seems simply uncomfortable, even clumsy, with ideas. He is far more at home with straight historical exposition, where he is often clear and precise, if not lively or profound. His discussions of relations between the church and the state in New England and of the breakdown of clerical authority in particular are admirably succinct without being sketchy as are, say, the opening pages on the English origins of Puritanism. Ultimately, however, Bremer's segregation of history and idea emasculates both. Divided from issues, the historical narratives are generally lifeless lists of events without motive or personality, in which we lose our way for want of relation to human and cultural interests. Occasionally they read like a simple crib sheet of "important dates" for dutiful memorization. Thematic issues on the other hand are deprived of the factual substance, the human actions, through which they were originally enacted, and as a result they are often abstract to the point of uselessness. We are told, for instance, that the fall of the English Puritan regime created "doubts" in New England, that it made New Englanders "suspicious of change," sending religious and political thought "off in new directions" (despite their suspiciousness of change), and leading ultimately to "enduring institutions of social and cultural life" (p. 171). Such large shapes lack the detail that might create a genuine understanding of Puritan culture.

The only truly lively moments occur in two anecdotes where Bremer manages to capture the humanity of Puritan life. One is about Roger Williams rowing from Providence to Newport to debate three Quakers before a hostile crowd, the other is about a minister, Hansard Knollys, whose preference for his maid's bed over his own led to a scandal and his removal. With these amusing exceptions, however, Bremer does not stray from the straight and colorless historical path. As a result, his dexterity in debunking such popular misconceptions as that of a Puritan theocracy cannot compensate for his own contribution to other and still more damaging myths, principally that of the grey-clad, severe, and unfeeling Puritan religious fanatics, embracing their inhumane faith at the expense of life's natural pleasures. In Bremer's treatment all life is drawn out of the subject, leaving only abstract historical details and still more abstract and infinitely unappealing theology. The accurate picture of Puritan vitality and creativity, though dutifully acknowledged once or twice, cannot break through the textbook tone and manner of Bremer's prose. It is just this ability to capture the life of Puritan culture that has marked the best recent work in Puritanism.[1] To fail to do so is especially dangerous in a work intended for new students in the field, who might be either encouraged or dissuaded from continuing their studies by the impressions they take away from this introductory work.

By cleaving to what can now, happily, be called an old-fashioned view of Puritan art, Bremer misses an excellent chance to portray the vitality, flexibility, and creativity of the Puritan mind, and therefore to present the Puritans in their most attractive posture to students viewing them for the first time. The tone is set in the introduction, where Alden Vaughan does not even mention art among modern scholarly concerns with Puritanism, unless we are to assume that it is included— one might say lost—in "cultural" concerns. That neglect is confirmed in the scant seven pages devoted to Puritan literature. According to Bremer, Puritan literature was rigidly utilitarian. Puritan sermons, for instance, should be valued for their "logical organization and direct, plain style" (p. 186), a view that slights the verbal wit, metaphorical richness, and literary merit that have been so convincingly displayed by David Minter, Emory Elliott, and others.[2] Puritan histories receive praise for their readability, objectivity, lack of flamboyance, simplicity, and unadorned grace of expression. Mather's *Magnalia*, on the other hand, is treated as an aberration and implicitly criticized for its massive size, its flamboyant style and eclectic subject matter, and its failure to conform to Bremer's notions of a "coherent history" (p. 189). In short, Bremer praises these (until recently) neglected Puritan art forms in proportion as they seem to suppress individuality and creativity in favor of work-a-day objectivity.

As these preconceptions carry over into Bremer's brief discussion of Puritan poetry, they are still more damaging. Bremer seems untouched by the fact (which he does not mention) that Puritan New England produced more poetry proportionately than any other period of American history.[3] Although he fudges with an "at least," Bremer can discover only "three poets who wrote extensively . . . and whose works merit inclusion in anthologies of American literature" (p. 189). A simple look into Harrison Meserole's anthology of seventeenth-century American poetry would surely broaden this shockingly narrow view. Having limited Puritan poets to three, Bremer then dispatches Wigglesworth, Bradstreet, and Taylor in a total of two and a half pages (less than he devotes to the Lords of Trade and Plantations), praising Bradstreet when she achieved a "simpler, more lyrical expression" (p. 190) in "Contemplations," expressing a certain perplexity that Wigglesworth's "swift ballad meter and internal rhymes" were "widely hailed" (p. 190) in their day, and making no comment at all on Taylor, except to say, as he did with Cotton Mather, that Taylor's rugged language was "unlike any other colonial literary productions" (p. 191). Significantly, except in his discussion of Bradstreet, which leans heavily on one article by Robert Richardson, Bremer sticks to the critical evaluations of Puritan literature by Kenneth Murdock and Samuel Eliot Morrison.[4] He bends their excellent though dated work to a vision of the Puritans as the founders of a great nation, practical inventors of American institutions and therefore far stronger, as Bremer would have it, in the practical sciences than in the arts, pragmatic rather than imaginative. This is simply not an accurate view, and it is certainly not one that should be encouraged among undergraduates and graduate students.

All of the uncertainty in *The Puritan Experiment* about audience and organization can be traced to Bremer's reluctance to make plain his own critical stance. The book simply lacks an argument to provide coherence. Strictly speaking, this is not Bremer's failing; it is his intention. He represents the book as a synthesis which, as Vaughan writes, "does not argue strongly for a single interpretive framework" (p. xi). The book seems to have been designed on the dubious premise that point of view is a troublesome but surmountable limitation, one that intrudes upon accurate historical observation and distorts the truth. Admittedly, point of view (which might also be described as having something to say) limits scope as it provides coherence, but the contrary effort to see everything (or even to see two things at once, Melville tells us) produces only a chaos of unrelated or ill-related facts and fragmentary thoughts. In the absence of the absolute authority, the supreme point of view, of a Puritan God, objectivity in scholarship or elsewhere is not productive, not even (for mere mortals) possible. Vaughan's introduction, which argues the value of Bremer's objective approach and is the strongest section of the book, happens also to be the only section with an argument. Still more significantly, it is the only part of the book that provides documentation. This unheard-of omission is its most debilitating weakness, one of which the Puritans, who documented everything, would have sternly disapproved. Not only does Bremer not cite sources, but in at least one case where he quotes a secondary source, he fails to give any hint at the identity of the author. In several other places the title of the quoted work remains a mystery. The list of readings Bremer offers in place of footnotes includes a selection from the standard works on the subjects he covers. But no list of relevant texts can replace full documentation, and there is nothing in this list that is not readily available elsewhere.[5] Such unsound scholarly practice calls all Bremer's work into question.

Without conventional documentation, a reader is lost. He cannot trace Bremer's statements to their sources or determine how his assertions relate to the scholarly consensus or begin to assess their validity. This lack of documentation seems to be a result of Bremer's attempt to achieve "objectivity," to disclaim his own presence in the text, disclaiming at the same time responsibility for its assertions.

Without a thesis, Bremer has no focus for critical judgment, adopting instead a fair-mindedness so scrupulous that it amounts to saying nothing. His brief description of the Puritans' theological sources seems to say, decisively, that they read *everything*. Though he distinguishes Puritans from Anglicans by saying that Puritans subordinated their reading to Scripture, he never says how the Anglicans differed. Similarly, his attempt to account for the Puritan migration is so even-handed as to lose all point. The one motive he does offer, the sense of corporate election, comes totally without examples or substance. He ventures only that Puritans embraced their mission somewhat more strongly than their contemporaries. So watery a treatment seems especially unenlightening after the riches recent criticism, especially that of Sacvan Bercovitch, has mined from this central Puritan motive.[6] By keeping himself out of his narrative as shaper and interpreter of his subject, Bremer necessarily clouds troublesome issues. If he actually *did* present different sides of critical debates where they exist (as Vaughan says he does), the book would be far better for it. But, in fact, Bremer has so detached himself from his subject in order to avoid imposing personal opinions that he is left with only the cold facts and neglects the issues that make those facts significant. Although he notes the critical controversy over whether the Salem congregation adopted separatist principles, he does not explain why the issue of separatism is important, and therefore he gives his reader no insight into what was at stake in Salem. Such writing lacks substance and life, the substance and life of Puritan culture, a lack Bremer occasionally tries to correct with an inflated rhetoric designed to end chapters with feeling. But the bland context he has established reveals the essential emptiness of assertions that

Puritan civilization would "serve as a model for seventeenth-century England and for later generations of New Englanders" (p. 74), or that Roger Williams and Anne Hutchinson "in learning to live with each other, advanced the cause of religious freedom in the western world" (p. 75), or that Puritan science made contributions that "would stir the emulation of later generations" (p. 197).

Not only does Bremer's portrayal of Puritanism suffer from his quest for objectivity, but the objectivity he seeks is unattainable as well as undesirable. Seeking it, he loses the advantages of a critical perspective and retains the disadvantages. Inevitably, opinions and assumptions creep in. Each choice Bremer makes, each decision, is an interpretive act that reflects his critical preconceptions. He would have been better off, then, to acknowledge his own views and express them deliberately rather than accidentally. His discussion of Anne Hutchinson's conflict with the Boston clergy, for example, is full of question-begging judgments that carry a distinct anti-Hutchinson tone. His description of her "errors" and his attempt to dissociate her views from those of Cotton and Wheelwright portray her as far more of an aberration within Puritan society than she actually was. Throughout the discussion the Boston ministers appear in the right (Cotton "bowed" to their "widsom"), and Hutchinson seems merely a political inconvenience whose banishment left only "the loose ends . . . to be tied up" (p. 72). This treatment reveals a narrowly political interest that ignores the larger spiritual and philosophical issues Hutchinson raised. A political preoccupation colors much of the book and helps to account for its neglect of more humanistic enterprises. Politics and economics intrude even where Bremer himself asserts that they do not belong. The New Haven colony, he says, was not prominent in commerce but was known for its religious zeal. Yet in the five pages devoted to New Haven only one paragraph deals with theology, while the rest dwells on boundary disputes and manufactures.

It is not my intention here to fault Professor Bremer for failing to do something he did not intend. On the contrary, I simply argue that his methods defeat his stated purposes. An introductory work to Puritanism would be a valuable contribution (though it might be hard to improve on Miller and Johnson's two-volume anthology as an introductory text). Bremer, however, seems to have misconceived the task. A book for new students of Puritanism has a still greater responsibility than a more advanced, specialized study to convey a coherent view of Puritan thought and culture. It must, of course, include the facts, but it should imbed them in the human motives and issues that give facts meaning and life. It should do full justice to the variety and creativity of Puritan expression, for it will surely have to overcome the unattractive myths of Puritan rigidity and austerity that owe more to Hawthorne and to late nineteenth-century scholarship than to the Puritans themselves. Puritan culture was lively, imaginative, even heroic in its attempt to mold human life to the divine pattern. This vital struggle between the ideal and the merely human produced the excitement of the Puritan experiment. Too much of that excitement is missing from Bremer's book.

Notes

1. Numerous works come to mind in this connection. In addition to those mentioned below, they include Larzer Ziff, *Puritanism in America* (New York: Viking, 1973), Edmund S. Morgan, *Visible Saints* (New York: New York Univ. Press, 1963), David D. Hall, *The Faithful Shepherd* (Chapel Hill: Univ. of North Carolina Press, 1972), and numerous shorter works by such scholars as Karl Keller, David Minter, Jesper Rosenmeir, Mason Lowance, and Norman Grabo.

2. See David Minter, *The Interpreted Design as a Structural Principle in American Prose* (New Haven: Yale Univ. Press, 1969), pp. 50-66, and Emory Elliott, *Power and the Pulpit in Puritan New England* (Princeton: Princeton Univ. Press, 1975). Elliott provides a selective list of works on the art of the Puritan sermon that suggests the true size and richness of the field, p. 10. n. 8.

3. Sacvan Bercovitch, ed., *The American Puritan Imagination* (New York: Cambridge Univ. Press, 1974), p. 3.

4. Robert D. Richardson, Jr., "The Puritan Poetry of Anne Bradstreet," *Texas Studies in Literature and Language*, 9 (1967), 317-31.

5. There are excellent bibliographies in Bercovitch, *The American Puritan Imagination*, Elliott, *Power and the Pulpit*, and Perry Miller and Thomas Johnson, eds., *The Puritans* (New York: Harper & Row, 1963).

6. Sacvan Bercovitch, *The Puritan Origins of the American Self* (New Haven: Yale Univ. Press, 1976).

"Illuminating Distortions" and the Dickens Critics

Richard J. Dunn

Albert J. Guérard. *The Triumph of the Novel: Dickens, Dostoevsky, Faulkner.* New York: Oxford University Press, 1976. 365 pp.

Robert Newsom. *Dickens on the Romantic Side of Familiar Things:* Bleak House *and the Novel Tradition.* New York: Columbia University Press, 1977. ix, 173 pp.

Robert B. Partlow, Jr., ed. *Dickens Studies Annual.* Vols. V, VI. Carbondale: Southern Illinois University Press, 1976, 1977. xviii, 215 pp.; xix, 210 pp.

John Romano. *Dickens and Reality.* New York: Columbia University Press, 1978. 187 pp.

Geoffrey Thurley. *The Dickens Myth: Its Genesis and Structure.* New York: St. Martin's Press, 1976. 379 pp.

Jane Vogel. *Allegory in Dickens.* University: University of Alabama Press, 1977. xvi, 347 pp.

Barry Westburg. *The Confessional Fictions of Charles Dickens.* Dekalb: Northern Illinois University Press, 1977. xxiii, 223 pp.

It is tempting to consider at length the illuminating distortions of some recent Dickens studies and to attempt correction of the distortion and dim illumination of others, but the title of this review essay points more immediately to critical theories and practices of the best recent work. Several years ago Albert J. Guérard defined fiction's "illuminating distortions" as metonymical moments that contain keys to scenes or to a book's larger meaning. More grotesque than realistic, fantastic than mimetic, the illuminating distortion reveals sources of a fiction's creative energy and of its dynamic power over readers.[1] Guérard grants a tentative quality to these moments and to

criticism that depends on locating them but thinks this is a way
to understand the dynamics of authorial creation and of a
novel's effect on us. More recently J. Hillis Miller has suggested
that when we select representative examples from works of
literature we are dealing necesarily with only suggested
contiguity or contingency; Miller thus finds much literary study
based on the extremely problematic assumption of valid
synechdoche.[2] As I understand Guérard's theory of illuminating
distortion, and as I see him, Robert Newsom, and John Romano
looking at parts of Dickens's novels that either represent or
resemble the larger issues of his writing and of novelistic art, it is
helpful to remember Miller's caveat about synechdoche. While
writing most perceptively about Dickens and fiction, these
critics, like Miller in his recent essay on the linguistic moment,
bring together "places of passage through which . . . the current
of meaning found in longer works momentarily pauses or
traverses."[3]

Guérard's *The Triumph of the Novel*, Newsom's *Dickens on
the Romantic Side of Familiar Things*, and Romano's *Dickens
and Reality* are all excellent studies of Dickens's imaginative
processes and of the ways his novels work as the idiosyncratic
artist heightens the critical reader's own idiosyncratic
imagination. Guérard declares his intention to write a rhetoric
of antirealism, and he shows the commanding part played by
unconscious creation and highly liberated fantasy in Dickens,
Dostoevsky, and Faulkner. Newsom, using *Bleak House* as his
test case, explores the tension in that novel's sustained play
between the empirical and the fictional. Romano, in similarly
short space, comes closer to Guérard's range of reference by
starting with *War and Peace* and *Our Mutual Friend* to argue
that all formal closure in fiction is by definition artificial and
that the realist writer greatly resents the unreality of artistic
convention. These books read well together; their authors
articulate essential issues of imaginative novel writing. They are
careful to avoid cumbersome terminology and scholarly para-
phernalia that would cramp their own prose, and, even as they
speculate in broad psychological and philosophical directions,
they acknowledge the futility of easy syntheses to fit Dickens, the
novel, and all Dickens and novel readers.

To hold together idiosyncratic textual examples and more general questions of formal structure, these critics must think and write clearly. All three recognize the dual impulses of chaos and control that Guérard finds basic to Dickens's temperament, but all three retain firm control over their own books. Unfortunately, some other recent treatments of Dickens lack this control; chaos prevails in Jane Vogel's *Allegory in Dickens*, and in several others there are important questions raised and fresh readings offered that really never come forward with full force. At least one of these books, Geoffrey Thurley's *The Dickens Myth*, buries its best insights in a massive critical synthesis that becomes burdensome by repetition.

Because Guérard, Newsom, and Romano produce such an impressive collective rhetoric of antirealism, it would be hoped that recurring antirealist arguments in Thurley, Vogel, Barry Westburg, and the latest volumes of the *Dickens Studies Annual* were equally strong. In lengthy rejection of what (à la Leavis) he finds to be the wrongheadedness of several critics (once more Robert Garis receives his Cambridge-style lashing), Thurley suggests that as a writer "of the expressionist type" Dickens has a characteristic tendency in the direction of hysteria. Thurley's use of the term *myth* is deliberately double; myth is the pattern of fantasies about which Dickens grew more artistically self-conscious, and it is also the conception he had of himself as a person experiencing the spiritual discontents of upward-striving modern society. Westburg, in *The Confessional Fictions of Charles Dickens*, takes a similar line but, with more limited focus on three novels, shows Dickens developing most as a writer each time he makes development itself a central theme. Although Westburg avoids the deadly novel-by-novel march through Dickens that Thurley makes, he still reasserts the obvious too often. The myth *did* reappear, confession *did* take various forms, Dickens's art *did* move toward some world view. The best of both Westburg and Thurley comes in their understanding of what happened to Dickens's childhood vision. This too is a familiar subject, but both manage to approach it freshly and therefore both talk intelligently about *Oliver Twist*, *David Copperfield*, and *Great Expectations*. Thurley believes that the gradual growth of Dickens's art must be measured against the decline of his imaginative fertility as reflected in the gradual freezing of his childhood vision. Westburg, by considering the maturing consciousness of Dickens's characters, finds that the principal task of the hero is to get free of origins while simultaneously acknowledging them. Only Pip begins to succeed in these terms, but the general struggle is hardly original for heroes (couldn't we make some of the same argument for Tom Jones?). One of Westburg's conclusions is that "a novel cannot be itself and interpret itself at the same time" (p. 182). He may be right about a number of novels, and self-interpretation as he sees it may be a different process from the kind of self-consciousness that gives formal tension to novels, but it seems to me that the critical methodology of Guérard and also of Newsom and Romano shows Dickens's best fiction simultaneously being itself and interpreting itself. Westburg and Thurley more readily grant the omnipresence of Dickens in his fictions. Self-interpretation of Dickens, if not of fictional processes, therefore comes in first-person narration and in the vocalizations of an intrusive narrator. Guérard, however, notices many Dickensian voices and gives a chapter to their rhetorical effects, which range from a grave interiorizing to self-conscious flights of rhetorical exercise and more tiresome jog-trot.

Westburg realizes the structural significance of repeated images that contribute to the complexity of a novel's vision. In *Copperfield* he traces the monstrous narcissism of mirror images repeatedly looked *at* rather than *into*: these seem perfect instances of Guérard's illuminating distortions. But Romano, in studying an even more patterned mirroring in *Our Mutual Friend*, and Newsom, in pointing out the subtle repetitions of the *Bleak House* opening number, press further with their readings. Westburg understands Copperfield's failure to look into things as prelude to the ending's "purely mythic consolations" that reaffirm "a pervasive interest in the retrograde tendencies of the psyche" (p. 109). But Romano is able to take exemplary passages even further to find in *Our Mutual Friend's* second chapter "a parable of mimesis" (p. 25), because novels, like mirrors, *are* what they reflect. In their different ways, then, both Westburg and Romano are concerned with fiction's boundaries (and implicitly both are concerned with criticism's boundaries), but Westburg is less venturesome because he so often limits discussion to the characters' consciousnesses. More freely extrapolating his examples, Romano locates a metonymy that signals "with imperfect closure . . . a certain area of experience actually located on the world's horizon" (p. 68). Guérard finds dynamic quality in fiction's illuminating distortions; the dynamics of realism for Romano arise less from the aberrant vision than from hints at what cannot be seen at all.

The "outlying, formless real world" that novels aspire to but cannot grasp, according to Romano (who looks closest at *Our Mutual Friend* and *Dombey and Son*), is precisely Newsom's concern in his impressive reading of *Bleak House*. He at once distinguishes this novel's unsettling double perspective from a more definitive alien vision by showing Dickens's simultaneous presentation of the romantic and the familiar. The novel thus challenges readers to recognize the human relationship we have with problematic objects, events, and other people. Thus, from the start of *Bleak House* much of reality seems in suspended animation. The opening number holds many causal relationships in suspension to prohibit the reader any clear discriminations among overlapping attributes and details. The most striking part of Newsom's argument is his discussion of the phenomena Freud described as "uncanny." Outlining the competing frames of reference that characterize uncanny experience, Newsom, in more detail than Romano usually presents and with psychological insights as perceptive as many of Guérard's, refines the general view of Dickens's writing as hallucinatory and dreamlike. Unlike Thurley or Westburg, who tend to turn fictional perspectives inward on Dickens, Newsom thinks the novel's divided selves are "the necessary effect of living in a world which is chiefly characterized by its repression and suppression of the past" (p. 92). Newsom does not deny the personal motive forces, and a later biographically excursive chapter studies Dickens's mourning of his father and of fathers in general as it goes on to suggest some fascinating parallels between *Bleak House* and *In Memoriam.*

But it is to Guérard that we must turn to see how well comparative reading may be handled. It is not here possible to comment separately about his treatments of Dostoevsky and Faulkner, but throughout *The Triumph of the Novel* Guérard stresses the creative process and the illuminating distortions that are interesting even in his writers' lesser works. An early chapter uses *Oliver Twist, The Double,* and "The Bear" to suggest how the antirealist impulse works within the fabric of the familiar. Although we must go to Newsom or Romano for more detailed discussion of the dynamic relationship of strange and familiar in later Dickens novels, Guérard in a few pages convinces us that *Oliver Twist* contains a prototypic pattern of mysterious connections and hidden relationships. In a second generally comparative chapter Guérard discusses the paradoxical sympathies of all three novelists, recognizing the author's attraction to such forceful characters as Quilp, Fagin, and Sairey Gamp—figures with preternatural energy and long impervious to moral restriction. Guérard here shares Donald Fanger's sense that Dickens could be possessed by his devilish villains, although Guérard on the whole expands greatly Fanger's basic argument that Dickens's contribution to fiction is a "circumstantial realism . . . tinged romantically with the sense of strangeness and wonder."[4] Psychologically tuned to evident compulsions and conflicts, Guérard keeps in the foreground the essential literary question of whether his novelists' versions of tabooed acts and relationships, strong antisocial repugnances, and threatening obsessions strengthened or weakened their fiction. The heart of his study is three chapters that examine the "forbidden games" of his writers.

With Dickens the game is one of forbidden marriage. Guérard examines again the well-known story of Mary Hogarth's special meaning to Dickens's creative life. He surveys her reappearances in the novels, all of which make clear that the novelist maintained a troubling fantasy of an ideal virginal love, lost but still in some sense alive to him. For the most part the Mary fantasy with its attendant "forbidden game" of violation did not stimulate great writing. But in *The Old Curiosity Shop*, a decidedly inferior total effort, Guérard finds tense moments when "childish purity and passivity are exposed, nearly as dangerously as in Dostoevsky, to active sensuality and other threats of violence" (p. 79). In an incisive reading of this threatened purity, Guérard sees through the perpetual nightmare of Quilp to understand that, paradoxically, it is the grandfather who represents a greater threat. It is he who robs her, though Quilp threatens to rob them both; it is he who has a dual personality—gentle, childish, easily led, but also frighteningly rejuvenated when he steps behind the screen to gamble. Although he is finally restored to sanity, the chastening eventually costs Nell her life, thereby preserving the fantasy by proving the Mary figure invulnerable to the greatest threats of male sexuality. When Guérard turns to other forbidden games in *The Insulted and the Injured* and in *Sanctuary*, he is necessarily not so attentive to biography as he continues to demonstrate the interesting effects of the writers' obsessions (Dostoevsky's pedophilia and Faulkner's generalized misogyny) on generally undervalued novels.

Three other chapters of Guérard's free-ranging book turn to subjects he believes worthy of further study—the various authorial voices in Dickens, conscious and unconscious understanding in Dostoevsky, the development of innovative forms and liberated style in Faulkner. He concludes with separate long essays on novels he thinks highly representative of the liberated imagination—*Martin Chuzzlewit* (a hard choice before *Our Mutual Friend*), *The Possessed*, and *Absalom, Absalom!*. *Chuzzlewit* indeed lacks the tidiness of structure that limits the imaginative expansiveness of so many nineteenth and early twentieth-century novels, and it surely shows Dickens at the height of his imaginative powers, creating many varieties of life that express themselves in absurd mannerism and speech. Through parallels with *Heart of Darkness*, Guérard shows the darkening vision of Dickens's grotesque American Eden, and, unsurprisingly, he recognizes a Dostoevskian power in the characterization of Jonas Chuzzlewit. Like most intelligent readers he sees the stage presence of Pecksniff as a traditional comic character, less unique than the marvelous Gamp. In her there are depths of ordinary existence that "anchor the flights of fantasy in the poignant everyday" (p. 260).

Guérard carefully describes his critical methods. He finds himself sharing Frank Kermode's view that novels resist structural analysis, but he does think that "any discoverable 'deep structure' is likely to be psychological" (p. 17). A novelist himself and best known for his studies of Hardy, Conrad, and Gide, Guérard is concerned first with creative process and with rhetorical effect. He uses a psychological but nonpsycho-analytical approach to enigmatic scenes or events; he values highly novelistic energy and tension between sympathy and judgment. He discriminates also between the effects of first and second readings. All in all, Guérard's critical method works unobtrusively (he even invites readers to skip his prefatory description of method). He brings to this impressive volume the intellectual energy that led him long ago to want to " 'record . . . the impulse toward the sombre and ironic distortions, the psychological explorations, the dislocations in form of many novelists writing in the middle of the twentieth century' " (p. 11). Beginning here with Dickens, he studies the great nineteenth-century novelist as part of an illumination of "the centrality and culminating force of the three novelists and their anti-realist love of the strange" (p. 13).

From a critic of Guérard's stature we expect an easy combination of psychological with other critical methods, but it is a pleasant surprise to find a generally skillful blending of critical approaches in first books such as Romano's and Newsom's. They at times spin toward rhetorical abstraction, but at least their work avoids such psychologically reductive statements as Thurley sometimes makes. For instance, he earnestly informs us that "the action of *The Old Curiosity Shop* really begins with the penetration of Quilp, the sexual aggressor, into the fragile womb of the Shop in search of Nell, whom he at once frightens out into the wide world" (p. 52). But even breakdowns of critical sensibility are perhaps tolerable when compared with Jane Vogel's long study committed to the principle that Dickens was everywhere a devout (and seemingly deliberate) Christian allegorist. Vogel finds allegory loosing new meaning everywhere in Dickens but centers mostly on *David Copperfield*. For all its metaphoric richness, her description of her task is actually modest: "Gazing on so vast an uncharted Pacific as Dickensian allegory for the first time, one is dazed by its visionary riches, obviously more than any one maiden-voyaging book could hope to traverse in a first crossing, much less hold" (p. xi). Her effort is Titanic, overwhelming, doomed; by contrast it gives Guérard and the others the critical purity of a Thor Heyerdahl.

Rather than follow Vogel's incredible linkings (such as *H*eep and *H*ittite), it is more reasonable to accept Guérard's point that Dickens was a great writer who presided uneasily over a rich fantasy life. With Quilp as a kind of proto-Snopes, Dickens could indeed be on the devil's side quite often. Recent volumes of the *Dickens Studies Annual* examine various manifestations of this rich fantasy life. In the 1976 edition, Leonard Manheim draws upon Karl Menninger to discuss Dickens's "HEROES, *heroes*, and heroids." As do Westburg and Thurley in their longer studies, Manheim makes much of the suffering Dickens felt from the injury and imperfection life dealt him. In the same volume James Marlow's "Dickens' Romance: The Novel as Other" works even more theoretically and (like Romano) centers on the paradoxes of fictional form. In an argument that might well be expanded, Marlow insists that to move the fancy successfully a novel must establish its irreducible otherness. He surveys Dickens's own comments about fiction and describes his self-consciousness about how best to engage his reader's fancy. More than Newsom (and certainly more than Romano) would grant, Marlow thinks it possible "to isolate not only the agency—fancy—by which Dickens hopes to make people better but also the consistent element in every aspect of his Romance" (p. 39). The moral burden upon fancy is clear, and we recall how to Leavis it was the redemptive feature of Dickens's art. Thus Marlow's reminder of the fantasy as the morally liberating agency for movement from self to other comes as a reassertion. And although it appeared before Romano's *Dickens and Reality*, Marlow's essay retains a forceful and teleologically confident counterargument to Romano's sense of novelistic limits, because Marlow insists that fiction takes us beyond limited self-consciousness. The more enigmatic "otherness" of specific characters expressive of a more general guilt and secrecy is the subject for Stanley Tick's fine "Toward Jaggers," and the 1976 *Annual* concludes with Lawrence Frank's "The Intelligibility of Madness in *Our Mutual Friend* and *The Mystery of Edwin Drood*." Frank finds Dickens's gothicism more akin to that of the underground man than to the gothic monk; it becomes a way to explore "the nature of unconscious forces and their elusive, often indefinable, manifestations [of] . . . modern consciousness itself" (p. 195).

The 1977 *Dickens Studies Annual* gives continued attention to psychological processes behind and in Dickens's novels, although both volumes contain a good balance of critical perspectives. Albert D. Hutter's "Reconstructive Autobiography: The Experience at Warren's Blacking" treats concisely much of the biographical argument that Thurley narrates more torturously in *The Dickens Myth*. Like Guérard, Hutter has a fine understanding of the complex relationships between Dickens's literary self-consciousness and his less clearly articulated psychic impulses. The essay argues positive dynamic quality for Dickens's responses to the apparent traumas of adult life. Hutter finds that previous descriptions of the Warren's experience are often distorted, and he stresses the normality of some of Dickens's reactions—Dickens continued to use his adult memory of the blacking warehouse in ways that "say as much about the idiosyncratic nature of his personality and charm as about neurosis" (p. 13).

Also interested in the fictional consequences of Dickens's confrontations with the deepest stimulants to his imagination, Robert E. Lougy believes the novelist experienced the terror of discontinuity and separation which Geoffrey Hartman finds in Wordsworth. Lougy's "Remembrances of Death Past and Future: A Reading of *David Copperfield*" is one of the finest studies ever published of this much-discussed novel. It is a thoughtful, sensitive reading with critical acuity that reminds one of J. Hillis Miller's and James Kincaid's best writing. Like

Guérard, Newsom, and Romano, Lougy works with a concern
for genre as he finds *David Copperfield* struggling with formal
tradition. As does Westburg, he notes the problem of the ending
but finds "haunting and compelling beauty" coming from the
book's effort to procrastinate as far as possible its final stasis.
There are multiple possibilities for self-deception and illusion
because *Copperfield* is a novel both of remembering and
forgetting, "encouraged by the very structures that the narrator's
memory clings to, in particular to the structures of a past
tranquilized by an inherited vocabulary and by the narrative
form of the novel itself" (p. 75). Lougy appreciates the
profundity of the novelistic imagination's borderline existence.
As he remarks when wondering where the nineteenth-century
novel, and this one in particular, may go after the "Tempest"
chapter, "There is not . . . a permanent correspondence or
identity between the center of the circle (the narrator's memory
and imagination) and its periphery, that social landscape he
traverses" (p. 92). But as Lougy notes, Dickens found comfort in
form; "Dickens gazes deeply into the inner regions of the self
and hears from within image-haunted winds, but what he sees
and hears sends him back toward the protection of definition
and form. There he must deny, or attempt to deny, those
demonic voices that sing of freedom and its terrors" (p. 100).

Dickens critics may long argue over the sources and the
precise power of these voices; some will find them neither
terrifying nor liberating, but the best contemporary work on
Dickens centers on the liberating imagination, the novelistic
vision that restlessly resisted conventional formal statement.[5] To
so respond, these critics must necessarily acknowledge the force
of the grotesque and the uncanny in Dickens's novels. Thus, for
all their critical sophistication, it is not surprising for these
commentators often to sound like (and occasionally refer to)
Chesterton on Dickens. To recognize these qualities of
Dickensian vision is to say little more than critics since Ruskin
have about Dickens, but to realize, as do Guérard, Newsom, and
Romano, how basic his antirealistic impulses are to novelistic
art is to expand Dickens criticism and contemporary thought
about the novel.

Writers on Dickens in the mid-seventies have shown once more how frequently and how variously, how personally and how collectively, the repressed past finds its way into the peculiar present of a novel. When a troubling past preempts more pedestrian rendering of present "realities," mimesis yields to strangely illuminating distortions—the madman will peek at us from the window of Blunderstone Rookery; the odd figure will leer from the drawing-room mirror. Thus with Romano we can understand the need to sacrifice conventional form for vision in great nineteenth-century works—not only in novels but in the songs of Whitman, the dazzling light of Turner paintings, and in the great ideational indulgences of Dostoevsky. But as Romano must also acknowledge, many nineteenth-century novels fall short of greatness at the point their creative burden fails to push them out of conventional shapes.

Novel criticism is not a scientific analysis; it may describe, but only up to a point. It may define, but it must do so surely with an imaginative flexibility that responds to the fiction's own flexibility. It may be that the newest, most novel novel criticism is a new New Criticism that begins with text, takes into account various pretexts and contexts, and returns to study the ways fictions stretch their self-defining boundaries. These boundaries are in large part psychic and temporal. In every fiction-making and in every imaginative reading there is a very personal time-binding task—a commitment to words, paragraphs, and larger verbal structures. With sometimes frustrating literalism, the novel form completes itself even when explicitly protesting the artificialities of closure. (For a brilliant exposition of this dilemma, see Ronald Sukenick's *Out*.) But as we look once more at the nineteenth-century "realists," those inheritors of various romantic anxieties, we find that "realism" was a paradoxically valuable restriction. The realist's awareness of limits, particularly Dickens's sensitivity to both the familiar and the romantic, permitted the fancy to roam all the more freely.

These contemporary critics certainly comprehend that the boundaries of fiction, and of much fiction criticism, are teleologic, and the confident critic does not lose confidence when artistic process seems to manifest no clear purpose or design. Thus they accept romance *and* reality, fiction *and* fact. Novel criticism at its best today accepts the nineteenth century's own distinction of various grades of imaginative life, though it may best reject oversimplified concepts of the imagination. Guérard thus spots "oddities of rhythm and diction; compression or outlandish elaboration, and all the quickenings of consciousness induced by analogy, by symbol, by myth" (p. 13). Romano can argue that individuals stand in relation to others as a work of art stands in relation to the world, and thus definitions of a work's boundaries become questions of identity. In both instances the critics share Newsom's opinion that realists are not the only highly serious practitioners of novelistic art. The course of my generalizations about these critics suggests that they have moved beyond the older New Critical practice. They bring sophisticated awareness of psychology and philosophy to their work; they are current with structuralist thought. But like the New Critics of several decades ago, they return from theory to examine the novel's specific statements; they acknowledge the psychic and philosophic importance of empty space yet remain attentive to what fills those spacious Dickens novels. They recognize the difficulties of verbalization yet attend to verbal constructions. If critics continue to be serious in their work but willingly yield to the imaginative distortions that reveal creative energy, we may continue to read Dickens with an appreciation of his idiosyncrasies as those of a genre and of a genius.

Notes

1. "The Illuminating Distortion," *Novel*, 5 (1972), 101.

2. "Nature and the Linguistic Moment," in *Nature and the Victorian Imagination*, ed. U. C. Knoepflmacher and G. B. Tennyson (Berkeley: Univ. of California Press, 1977), p. 442.

3. *Ibid.*

4. *Dostoevsky and Romantic Realism: A Study of Dostoevsky in Relation to Balzac, Dickens, Gogol* (Cambridge, Mass.: Harvard Univ. Press, 1965), p. 72.

5. It should be noted that although Guerard, Newsom, and Romano break much fresh ground, their work extends some central interests of Fanger's *Dostoevsky and Romantic Realism*, A. O. J. Cockshut's *The Imagination of Charles Dickens* (London: Collins, 1961), John Carey's *The Violent Effigy: A*

Study of Dickens' Imagination (London: Faber and Faber, 1973), Garrett Stewart's *Dickens and the Trials of Imagination* (Cambridge, Mass.: Harvard Univ. Press, 1974), and Fred Kaplan's *Dickens and Mesmerism: The Hidden Springs of Fiction* (Princeton: Princeton Univ. Press, 1975).

Critical Discrimination and Editorial Judgment

Wayne R. Kime

A Hazard of New Fortunes. Introduction by Everett Carter.
Notes to the Text and Text Established by David J. Nordloh,
Don L. Cook, James P. Elliott, David Kleinman, and Robert D.
Schildgen. Bloomington: Indiana University Press, 1976. xxix,
558 pp. An approved text of the Center for Editions of American
Authors.

The Leatherwood God. Introduction and Notes to the Text by
Eugene Pattison. Text Established by David J. Nordloh, with
James P. Elliott and Robert D. Schildgen. Bloomington:
Indiana University Press, 1976. xxix, 253 pp. An approved text
of the Center for Editions of American Authors.

These critical editions of *A Hazard of New Fortunes* (1889) and
The Leatherwood God (1916), numbered 16 and 27, respectively,
in a series eventually to include forty-one volumes, are
characteristic productions of the Howells Edition, whose texts
and textual apparatuses have earned a reputation over the past
decade for accuracy, authoritativeness, and elegant economy.[1]
Based on the formidable resources of the Howells Center at
Indiana University and on extensive collation of manuscripts
and printed texts in other repositories; edited by teams of
scholars, most of whose members have participated in earlier
Howells Edition volumes; and supervised throughout the
production process with painstaking care, the works are a credit
to the dedicated thoroughness of those who have cooperated in
their preparation. Spot collations of additional copies of *A
Hazard of New Fortunes* and *The Leatherwood God* against the
textual apparatuses of the two volumes have revealed no
discrepancies.[2] Page-line references in the apparatuses are
invariably accurate, and a resolute search for errata has turned
up only a brief list, suggesting that these works set forth with
scrupulous care Howells's intentions for his texts, insofar as the
editors have been able to determine them.[3]

As befits participants in an enterprise whose printed results promise, when complete, to occupy a five- or six-foot shelf, in their independent contributions to these volumes the editors have adhered rigorously to a principle of economy, of including no more material than what is judged necessary to insure authoritativeness. In each instance the general introduction and the explanatory notes to the text reveal this bias with special clarity. The preliminary discussions summarizing the histories of the two works' authorship, their places in Howells's career, and their contemporary receptions are enriched by a modest amount of illustrative material such as quotations from Howells's letters; but even though well chosen, these added features do not alter one's impression that the commentaries are essentially spare compilations of dates and facts. The introductions are the less successful for their compression, tending at some points to raise questions left unanswered and to point out issues left unresolved. For example, in demonstrating that *A Hazard of New Fortunes* was in its final chapters "firmly based on the actuality" of the times, Everett Carter writes that "Howells found materials for his dramatic incidents . . . in the news reports" of the New York City traction strike of January-February 1889. Carter then quotes passages from contemporary newspaper articles, observing that "from this reality Howells built the climax of his novel" (pp. xxi, xxii). But just how literally are we to take these statements? Carter suggests not merely that the author sought verisimilitude for his novel but that he actually pored over the newspapers in order to satisfy himself in that regard. If the latter was indeed the case, it is certainly worth knowing; but if the newspaper articles are not to be regarded as explicit "sources," then Carter's rationale for including quotations from them is not entirely clear. With similar inconclusiveness Eugene Pattison observes in his introduction to *The Leatherwood God* that upon its publication the work was recognized at once as a " 'radical departure from Mr. Howells' accustomed manner' " (p. xxvi), an experiment in the mode of historical romance which in earlier years the author had disdained.[4] But except to point out that Howells had long been "fascinated" by the interlude in Ohio history that took fictionalized form in *The Leatherwood God*, Pattison says next to nothing of his apparent setting aside his own creed as a fictionist.[5] A justifiable concern for economy and objective factuality may well have dictated the occasionally open-ended character of Carter's and Pattison's generally helpful introductions, but given a bit more space they could have succeeded in appearing impartial where now they seem inconsequent or unfocused. In both volumes the explanatory notes to the text are also brief but are clear and reliable.[6] Remarkably, the Howells Edition's practice of separating responsibility between personnel assigned to the historical-explanatory and to the textual sides of the two undertakings has in neither instance resulted in serious overlapping, inconsistency, or other potential embarrassment.

The most arduous and original scholarly effort expended in preparing these editions of *A Hazard of New Fortunes* and *The Leatherwood God*, both of which bear the seal of approval of the Center for Editions of American Authors, has of course been directed toward the texts themselves. In their work on the two volumes the editors have encountered textual situations which, though in some ways quite different, have posed similar problems. In both cases only scattered external evidence is available concerning Howells's authorship and revision of the multiple potentially authoritative texts of the works. At the same time, however, collation reveals numerous substantive variants which are quite possibly authorial in origin. Even hypothetically to round out the two textual histories, it is thus necessary in each case to infer the processes of revision in large part through analysis of the patterns of variation amongst the textual witnesses, and thereby to develop a rationale for identifying the author's latest intentions. Moreover, since Howells's intentions are construed to be distinct from those of his editors, it is also necessary to distinguish between readings altered by the author and those resulting from editorial or compositorial intrusion.

The discussions in the two textual commentaries of the external evidence and the patterns of variation which together suggest the hypothetical scenarios for Howells's writing and revision make fascinating if strenuous reading. Initialed by David J. Nordloh, these lean commentaries are exemplary for their lucid presentation of complex data and relationships, bringing into focus a confusion of permutations and recalcitrant details. Nevertheless, the syntheses of textual history advanced in the discussions do seem somewhat tidier than the evidence warrants. In the effort not merely to shave the textual commentaries to suitable brevity but, at an earlier and more important stage, to translate conjectural sets of relationships into practical policies for editorial choice, the hypotheses seem to have solidified into accepted facts. The result is that the claims of potentially viable textual alternatives from outside the tentatively inferred frameworks are on occasion discounted or overlooked. The sharply focused sets of supposed relationships appear at times to have precluded an open-minded assessment of all the possibilities.

As adduced by Nordloh, the textual history of *A Hazard of New Fortunes* is that proof sheets for *Harper's Weekly*, where the novel appeared serially between 23 March and 16 November 1889, were revised and forwarded in eleven installments by Howells to his British publisher, David Douglas of Edinburgh. Douglas set type from the installments and from it pulled eleven sets of proofs which, to obtain British copyright for the work, he deposited at Stationer's Hall between 1 April and 1 November of the same year. He then prepared from the standing type a set of stereotype plates which, after use for a two-volume edition which he published on 2 December, he shipped to Harper and Brothers in New York. After making some changes of their own, Harper produced a two-volume edition registered at the Library of Congress on 27 January 1890. Meanwhile, in late November 1889 Harper had also published a one-volume edition of the novel in its Franklin Square Library series. This latter typesetting derived, independently of the Douglas copyright parts and the versions which succeeded them, from some prepublication form of the *Harper's Weekly* text. One other edition appeared during Howells's lifetime, as a volume in the discontinued Library Edition of the author's work (1911).

In their effort to discover Howells's final intentions as embodied in these texts, the editors adopted as a working principle that "the crucial area of textual variation lies in the relationship of the *Harper's Weekly* text to the Douglas copyright deposit parts" (pp. 525-26). That is, for some chapters in his novel the author would have had an opportunity to revise the copy he sent abroad to Douglas after the opportunity to revise magazine proofs had already passed; for others, he conversely would have been able to revise the *Harper's Weekly* proofs after he had sent an earlier version to Douglas. By means of a table (pp. 526-27) correlating the dates of the *Harper's Weekly* publication and the deposit of Douglas copyright parts for the successive portions of the novel, Nordloh demonstrates that for deposit parts 1 through 3 and 8 through 11 Howells would at almost all times have had an opportunity further to revise proofs for the magazine after forwarding copy to Douglas; but that for parts 4 through 7 the situation is reversed: he could probably have revised copy for Douglas after the corresponding magazine chapters were beyond his control.[7] The fruit of this analysis is therefore an informed disposition to consider seriously the substantive variant readings of the surviving Douglas copyright parts 4 through 7 as possible emendations into the copy-text (specified as the *Harper's Weekly* version, "the form with which Howells took the greatest care in revision—as he did with the first printed appearance of all his work"—p. 526). And as it happens, the editors' "more subjective critical judgments" (p. 530) concerning the superiority of specific variant readings in the portions of *A Hazard of New Fortunes* which conform to Douglas parts 4 through 7 generally favor those in the Douglas texts. Thus, of the sixty-two emendations of the copy-text made for the present edition, sixty-one derive from the deposit copy, forty-three of which correspond to parts 4 through 7.

Throughout these nice calculations of dating and estimations of possible authority the one-volume Franklin Square Library text, which "shows striking agreement in a good many cases with variants appearing in what the chronology of the text would indicate is the later revised form," and which it will be recalled derived independently of the Douglas-Harper line from *Harper's Weekly* proofs, is in effect thrown out of court.

Nordloh speculates reasonably that, when preparing copy to forward to Douglas, Howells perhaps "marked duplicate sets of the magazine proofs for those sections already past his control in *Harper's Weekly* and returned one copy of these marked sets to Harper for their accumulation and eventual use" (p. 531) in setting the Franklin Square Library volume. But even though such a procedure would place the latter text at the very latest acknowledged stage of revision, the possibility that it includes unique authorial readings is not entertained; in fact, the text is explicitly dismissed as an authoritative source of emendations.[8] Without claiming for the Franklin Square Library edition an overall significance equal either to the *Harper's Weekly* text or to the Douglas copyright parts, I would like to point out a few instances in which, on the assumption that the one-volume Harper edition (abbreviated in the tables as D and cited thus hereafter) carries no independent authority, the editors have set aside its testimony in an offhand and perhaps precipitate manner.

In "one of the most difficult editorial decisions" made in the establishment of their critical text, the Howells editors replace a reading shared by the copy-text and D, "not yet" in "The *primo tenore* statue of Garibaldi had not yet taken possession of the place" (55.23-24) with "already," which occurs consistently in the Douglas-Harper line. As they observe, the choice of "already" over "not yet" turns upon the chronology of the novel. Drawing upon Howells's preface prepared for the abortive Library Edition, they cite among other details the author's reference to the New York traction strike of January-February 1889 as occurring "Opportunely" for his fictive purposes;[9] and since, as they note, "the statue of Garibaldi . . . was erected [in Washington Square] in 1888" and "Howells' choice of detail seems to place the [published] fiction at roughly the same time as the historical events upon which it draws" (pp. 537-38), they deduce that—1889 following 1888— "already" is the correct choice. But Howells's reference to the statue of Garibaldi occurs near the beginning of the novel, not near its close, where the portrayal of the strike is introduced. A survey of the work's time-scheme indicates that the action begins in the fall of 1887, proceeds at an even pace through 1888, reaches the period of its tragic complications in early 1889, and closes—conspicuously switching to the present tense—at the time the final chapters were serialized, in the fall of 1889.[10] Within this scheme, the reference to the Garibaldi statue is made during the portrayal of events in October 1887, before the erection of the statue, so that the rejected copy-text and D reading is certainly the correct one. Oddly, in their treatment of this crux the editors seem to overlook their own conclusion that Howells could have altered proofs of the issue of *Harper's Weekly* containing the debated reading *after* he had sent copy to Douglas which, presumably, included the erroneous "already" reading.[11] At any rate, it is enough to observe that the D text, copy for which Howells could in fact have reviewed and revised long after either the proofs he sent to Douglas or those he sent to *Harper's Weekly*, corroborates the accurate copy-text reading.

Two further points singled out for comment in the textual apparatus will suggest more clearly the attitude of mind in which, because they do not entertain the possibility of Howells's marking *Harper's Weekly* proofs for D after sending proofs to Douglas, or else of his purposely marking the proofs for D at the same time but marking them somewhat differently, the editors summarily dismiss readings unique to D. At 186.34-187.1 in the present text, a small cluster of variants occurs between D and all the other witnesses, as follows:

All texts but D	*D*
. . . March refused to believe this as he looked round on the abounding evidences of misery, and guiltily remembered his neglect of his old friend.	. . . March refused to believe this as he looked round on these evidences of misery, and remembered his neglect of his friend.

According to the Howells editors the D readings "are unconvincing as authorial or editorial revisions," and the "only explanation which fits the circumstances is a typographical one"; namely, that the substitution in D of "these" for copy-text "the abounding" and the omission from D of copy-text "guiltily" and "old" could have insured "an exact parallelism of lines at the chapter break" of the one-volume edition, which was printed in a double-column format (pp. 539-40). But just why are the changes, regarded in themselves, "unconvincing" as possibly by Howells? Even a reader unfamiliar with the novel would, I suspect, sense in these small omissions a toning down, a backing away from direct emotional appeal. And since Howells elsewhere brought his narrative almost but not quite to the verge of melodrama, as if to suggest the profound moral import of his fable without expressly requiring a proportionate emotional response from the reader,[12] this cautious muting of effect seems plausible as a revision, if not by the author then certainly by someone sensitive to his aims. The "typographical" suggestion by the present editors tacitly denies the muted D reading its day in court as potentially an authorial change.

The textual editors and also the author of the introduction do bring critical considerations to bear in their comments on a second variant reading unique to D. The problem, at 24.7, is again a chronological one: "I've refused it" in all the texts but D, in which the reading is "I shall refuse it." Without detailing the context of these alternative declarations by the protagonist Basil March, we may simply note that while both Everett Carter and his textual colleagues affirm the superiority of "I've refused it" over the D reading on critical grounds, in both discussions there is really no contest anyway: to Carter, the D variant "is a correction that a well-meaning typesetter or proofreader might have made" (p. xxiv); to the textual editors D is, after all, "a form of the text over which Howells did not exercise control" (p. 536). Yet once it is supposed that D could possibly represent Howells's intentions at this point, both arguments of its inferiority become less than convincing.[13] The working principle that the variants between *Harper's Weekly* and the Douglas deposit parts are alone "crucial" to Howells's intentions for *A Hazard of New Fortunes* seems to have taken so firm and exclusive a hold over the editors that the thirty-four substantive readings unique to D are never taken very seriously. Yet no conclusive evidence is presented to warrant the assumption that Howells did not participate in the preparation of D.[14] While according due recognition to an editorial

performance that overall is a *tour de force* of informed
speculation, acute and meticulous, I suggest that a less sharply
focused conception of the potentially authoritative forms of *A
Hazard of New Fortunes* would have permitted a more careful
evaluation, largely on critical grounds, of the variant readings
in D as potential emendations into the text.

Complicated and occasionally subject to debate though it may
be, the textual evidence surrounding *A Hazard of New Fortunes*
is simplicity itself in comparison with the elaborate patterns of
completion, correction, and revision that appear to interrelate
the potentially authoritative versions of *The Leatherwood God.*
As summarized by Nordloh, hypothetically the several texts of
this late work originated in the following manner. An extant
typescript of the entire novel, prepared from an author's
manuscript that also survives for the first nine chapters, was
revised by Howells, further revised by an editor of the Century
Company, and set in galleys and then page proofs for a Century
book edition. Howells revised some form of these proofs for the
serialization of the work in the *Century Magazine,* where it
appeared monthly between April and November 1916. A further
revised set of book proofs went to Herbert Jenkins Limited,
London; and a still further revised set finally formed the basis
for the Century book edition, which was deposited at the
Library of Congress on 2 November 1916. An edition by Louis
Conard of Paris appeared in 1918 and "was certainly prepared
from a copy of the Jenkins edition, either printed book or late
proof stage" (p. 174). Nordloh's neat account of the
transmission of the text is consistent with "the predominant
characteristics of textual variation among these forms"—
namely,

the greater correspondence of the magazine text than of the Century
and Jenkins editions with the substantive readings of Howells' revised
typescript, the greater relative agreement of Century and Jenkins texts
with each other than with the other forms, and the apparently
independent authoritative readings of both magazine and Century
book. More specifically, this outline comprehends three complicated
and pervasive patterns of variation: first, the ·agreement of the
magazine text with Howells' revised typescript against the Century
and Jenkins editions; second, the independent variation of both

magazine and Century edition from the agreement of typescript and
Jenkins edition; and, third, the independent variation of the book
editions on the one hand and the magazine on the other against the
typescript. [pp. 175-76]

The novel took shape along two distinct lines of transmission—one resulting in the *Century Magazine* and the other, and
later, in the Century book edition. Accordingly Nordloh
addresses the question whether there are in fact two different
literary entities bearing the title *The Leatherwood God*. His
determination, which seems defensible, is that the author's
revisions along the two lines suggest "not consciously variant
intentions but separate attentions" (p. 179). Since both sets of
independent revisions represent stages of Howells's attention to
the work conceived as a single entity, both are regarded as
possessing legitimate claims as potential emendations into the
copy-text (specified as for the first nine chapters the author's
manuscript and for subsequent chapters the typescript, as
revised by Howells but not as revised by the Century editor).
Thus in the present edition the author's "independent revisions
have been accepted as completely as possible . . . on the grounds
that though they derive from a fragmented sense of the material
they nevertheless tend to represent more of the individual
elements of Howells' total attention than the exclusive
emphasis on either line of transmission could produce" (p. 179).
At points of mutual disagreement the Century book edition
takes priority, Howells having "had apparent control over the
book text after magazine installments had already been printed"
(p. 181). But as a whole the critical text of *The Leatherwood
God* established by the editors represents, not the author's "final
intention," but a synthesis or conglomerate designated as his
"realized intention" (p. 180).[15]

In order to extract from the several authorities the
components of the author's own total attention to the novel, the
editors are thus obliged to distinguish between readings
"apparently Howells' own" (p. 181) and those which proceed
from other sources. Eschewing a concern for the "best"
intention, they are compelled nonetheless to rely largely upon
considerations of style—of which readings might be character-

istic of Howells—as a guide in making emendations. Enforced by the scarcity of external information, this repeated necessity of making editorial judgments on the basis of critical discriminations is onerous but inescapable; for as the Century editor's numerous revisions of Howells's already revised typescript attest, it is entirely possible that extra-authorial tampering played its part in each one of the printed texts under consideration.[16]

Given these circumstances, one can imagine the heartfelt relief with which the editors dismissed the Conard edition of 1918 from their attention as potentially a repository of authorial changes. They present no secondary evidence of Howells's involvement, direct or otherwise, with the Conard edition, but the assumption they have made is clear from the statement by Nordloh that "all substantive variants [in the Conard text] from the Jenkins edition are apparently compositorial lapses—dropped words and phrases or typographical errors—and not the results of authorial revision or conscious editorial clarification" (p. 174). However, a review of the thirty-nine readings unique to the Conard edition (cited on p. 174, n. 9) does not confirm this summary characterization. A few Conard readings do make no sense (for example, in the list of rejected substantives see the entries for 6.3, 127.33, 144.5), but the great majority reflect a definite streamlining (10.3-4, 36.19, 37.8), clarifying (55.32, 128.34-35, 130.13), even correcting (144.15), certainly "conscious" intention, whosoever it may be. In fact, these minor changes of from one to eight words are quite similar both in length and in kind to the variant readings in those texts which the editors entertain as potentially authoritative. No useful purpose whatever is served by this tendentious description of the Conard variants, except perhaps that it helps bring into focus the need for a fuller explanation in the volume's textual apparatus of the reasons why particular variant readings are judged to be authorial, editorial, or compositorial in origin.

The question of authorship is briefly taken up in some of the textual notes on entries in the lists of emendations and rejected substantives. For example, at 69.31 all the authorities agree on the reading "All-mighty" except for the *Century Magazine*, which reads "all-powerful." An emendation to "All-powerful" is made by the Howells editors, with this explanation: "The present edition accepts the apparently authorial substantive revision made here in the magazine text, but retains the capitalized form which is consistent with Howells' usage in other instances of such epithets" (p. 201). But just why is the unique *Century Magazine* reading "apparently authorial"? Difficult or impossible as it may be to set forth a definitive identification of "all-powerful" as authorial on critical grounds alone, some effort in that direction is worth making. "The interested reader," that not altogether mythical personage, can only be benefited by a brief account of the issues and perceptions underlying a delicate editorial judgment such as this one. Providing a short commentary equips the reader with an indispensable basis for his study of the editorial principles in operation from crux to crux.[17] Not including such a note lends an appearance of finality to the textual apparatus which diverts attention from the necessary provisionality of the critical text itself.

The adherence in the textual apparatus of *The Leatherwood God* to essentially the same spare format which with some modifications has characterized earlier volumes of the Howells Edition is regrettable in this respect, for it has tended to obscure the editors' chronic problem of identifying variant readings as authorial or otherwise.[18] At many points, it is true, the hypothetical chronology of texts functions implicitly (and in circular fashion) as a rationale for accepting variant readings from the text apparently revised last by Howells. Thus at 110.21 the locution "slowly he crept by," which is found in the copy-text and all the others but one, is emended to "he crept slowly by," the reading of the Century book edition.[19] On the other hand, at many points the hypothetical chronology has no bearing on the decision to emend. At 94.13 the unique *Century Magazine* reading "desecrated" is acceptable over "dishonored," which occurs in the copy-text and also in the texts assumed to be supervised by Howells after the *Century Magazine*; and the same pattern occurs at 98.6, where "outraged" in the magazine version is preferred over "desecrated" in all the others. At 76.5 "her," which concludes a sentence in the *Century Magazine*, is selected over "her; then he sank at her side" in the copy-text and Jenkins and Conard texts, and also over "her before he sank at her side" in the Century book edition. Since the hypothetical scenario for the genesis of *The Leatherwood God* is insufficient by itself to insure that any particular variant reading is certainly Howells's own, in each of the above instances the editors' critical acumen—their sensitivity to Howells's aims and methods—has evidently played a crucial role in their decision to emend. Granting, as we all should, that textual editorship is a fundamental act of criticism and that familiarity with an author's practice imparts to an attentive individual a heightened sensitivity to the author's mind and style, it follows that in explaining the nuances of perception that underlie their decisions the Howells editors likely have a valuable range of insights to offer. Certainly, were the textual apparatus of *The Leatherwood God* to include a quantity of the brief annotations I am suggesting, it would be a bulkier production than the present one; and, just as certainly, the critical text it included would still be ineluctably provisional. Nevertheless, the explicit acknowledgment it would contain of the extent to which critical discriminations have influenced the judgments of its editors (and we may presume also the recounted acts of judgment themselves) would warrant the additional space and expense.[20]

Thus far the Howells Edition has managed with enviable grace to reconcile the opposing claims of thoroughness and economy by laying only the essential evidence before the readers of the individual volumes, having first winnowed away what Nordloh terms "unuseable textual information" (*The Leatherwood God*, p. 172). Yet given the difficult circumstances which surround the textual histories of *A Hazard of New Fortunes* and more particularly *The Leatherwood God*, some lessening of the effort to achieve tidy conciseness seems justified. When a textual editor's critical tact has been brought into play in an unusual degree, as is preeminently the case with the latter volume, he owes us a particular accounting—tentative and subjective though it may be—of why he has done to the copy-text what he has. In thus taking his stand, the editor as critic demonstrates that while not all the problems he has encountered admit of definite solution, in dealing with them he has tested the full resources of his learning and his sensibility.

Notes

1. For a general survey of the early history and accomplishments of the Howells Edition, see Hershel Parker, "The First Nine Volumes of A Selected Edition of W. D. Howells: A Review Article," *Proof*, 2 (1972), 319-32. Two further Howells volumes have intervened between the works noticed by Parker and those under consideration here: *April Hopes* (1974) and *Years of My Youth and Three Essays* (1975).

2. The copies used for checking are *A Hazard of New Fortunes*, 2 vols. (New York: Harper and Brothers, 1889) in the collection of Wayne R. Kime; *The Leatherwood God* (New York: The Century Company, 1916) in the University of Toronto Library (PS/2025/L43/1916).

3. In *A Hazard of New Fortunes*, p. xvi, n. 25.4, "Tildon" should be "Tilden"; 299.35 "uphappy" should be "unhappy"; 528.6 "authorized" should be "unauthorized." In *The Leatherwood God*, 229.8 "he crept slowly by," should apparently not include the comma (see 248.20).

4. The quotation is cited as from Frederick Taber Cooper, "The Story of a False Prophet," *Publishers' Weekly*, 90 (1916), 1403.

5. Pattison observes only that Howells recognized the anomalousness of his writing historical fiction and that he developed "a rationale for writing fiction about regional history": namely, "that 'the parochial' in novels was preferable to the national or universal" (pp. xvi, xvii). On the other hand, Pattison does discuss Howells's motives for undertaking the historical research that lay behind *The Leatherwood God* ("to discover the meaning and significance of the past in order to instruct the present," p. xv), and he demonstrates how Howells sought "to be faithful to . . . historical data while transmuting it into fiction" (p. xix; see pp. xix-xxi).

6. The scope of the details selected for annotation seems well judged, though if anything the editors might have cast their nets a bit more widely. For example, how many readers would be able to identify without assistance the unannotated term *sweet-oil* at 82.25 in *A Hazard of New Fortunes*, or would understand the colloquialism *train* at 155.35 in the same work to mean "act sportively, romp, 'carry on' "? (Howells's use of "train" here is the earliest instance cited by the OED of the word's use in that sense.)

7. In the textual commentary to *The Rise of Silas Lapham* (1971), pp. 375-78, Nordloh sets forth a similar arrangement of dated Douglas copyright deposit parts in relation to corresponding dated sections of the novel's serial

magazine publication in order to identify those portions of either composite text which probably represent the author's latest intentions.

8. According to Nordloh, the Franklin Square Library text "bears no evidence of Howells' attention to its substantives or accidentals"; rather, "it contains a great number of non-authorial variants" (p. 531). According to Everett Carter, the differences between the Franklin Square Library text, the magazine version, and the two-volume Harper edition "all indicate the superior authority of both the two-volume text and of the *Harper's Weekly* serialization over the one-volume text which has heretofore been regarded as the first edition" (p. xxiv).

9. The preface, entitled "Bibliographical," is reprinted in the present edition, pp. 3-6; the quotation is from p. 4. Also included as an appendix to the volume, pp. 501-10, is a transcription of a typescript, entitled "Autobiographical," which apparently was an early draft of the preface.

10. The time-scheme of *A Hazard of New Fortunes* may be inferred from the following selective series of page-line references to the present edition: 29.14-15, 45.18, 55.24 ["not yet"], 57.2-3, 57.11-12, 103.15-16, 122.17-21, 152.29, 154.33, 181.34-35, 258.6, 281.1, 287.11-12, 290.35, 307.33, 314.36-315.1, 321.8, 346.13, 365.7-8, 380.21-24, 392.1, 398.11-12, 403.37, 456.9, 480.30-31, 490.30-31, 494.5-7, 494.23-25, 495.22-23.

11. The reference to the Garibaldi statue is in Book I, Chapter 8, of the novel, which appeared in *Harper's Weekly* on 20 April 1889. According to Nordloh, Howells "could have revised the 20 April, 27 April, and 4 May installments, and this after revision of the material intended for Douglas" (p. 529).

12. For example, see *A Hazard of New Fortunes*, pp. 64-65, 70-71, 250-51, 443.

13. According to Everett Carter, since at the time Basil March makes his statement he has not yet refused a job which has been offered him, "the one-volume reading is logically consistent"; but, while the "I've refused it" reading may be "logically inconsistent," it is "psychologically much more interesting." Indeed, Carter claims it is the very "brush-stroke of the master," for "it shows March reacting with all of the outrage parents feel at the selfishness of their children, and all the childlike petulance which is designed to make the child feel as guilty as possible" (p. xxiv). As to logical consistency versus inconsistency, a review of the two chapters preceding March's speech shows that in his own mind March actually has decided to decline the job offer—see 16.3, 16.8-9, and 23.24. In this sense, "I've refused it" is not at all logically inconsistent, as Carter avers. More importantly, the notion that March reacts with "outrage" and "childlike petulance" proceeds from a misreading of the tone of the scene. In lightly mocking his children's want of perspective and sense of proportion, March is ending a discussion on a note of teasing irony which he has already sounded during its course. For example, see 22.15-20, 22.27. He is not regarding his children in anywhere nearly so harsh or so serious a light as Carter suggests.

The authors of the discussion in textual notes claim that the change to "I shall refuse it" weakens "the ironic mood with which March has been playing throughout the scene" (p. 536). But so far as I can tell, the replacement of one reading with the other involves no weakening but only the exchange of one form of irony for another.

14. The only evidence adduced that bears on this matter is Everett Carter's reference to a letter from Howells to Harper and Brothers, dated 11 December 1890, in "the Harper & Row contract files." The reference is in a footnote documenting a statement about D: "Howells showed little interest in this edition, on which he was paid a ten per cent royalty, and devoted all his attention to the two-volume edition, the plates for which he would supply, and on which he was paid a royalty of twelve and one-half per cent" (p. xxiii). The letter cited in the footnote would seem to include statements of terms; but does it also reveal in some way the degrees of Howells's interest in the one-volume and two-volume editions?

15. For a recent survey of approaches to the concept of "intention" as it is variously defined in textual study, see G. Thomas Tanselle, "The Editorial Problem of Final Authorial Intention," *Studies in Bibliography*, 29 (1976), 167-211.

16. The editorial markings on the typescript are discussed on pp. 172-73 of the present edition and are further discussed and listed, subdivided according to type, on pp. 191-96.

17. And, of course, in so doing it enables the reader more readily to correct errors of editorial judgment when they occur. The textual notes to *The Leatherwood God* provide an instance of the helpfulness of this procedure. As emended on the sole authority of the present editors, a sentence in Chapter 4 of the novel (31.31-35) reads: "Often she stopped, and wondered at herself; it seemed impossible that she could be thinking it, be doing it, but she was thinking and doing it, and at sundown she knew by the eager shadow of a man in the doorway, pausing to listen if the baby were awake, all had been thought and done." Here the copy-text reading "sundown, when" is replaced by "sundown" with the explanation that the change "is the least arbitrary way to correct editorially a grammatically incomplete sentence that went unnoticed in all the early forms of the text" (p. 200). But as it appears in the copy-text the sentence is grammatically complete: "when" introduces an adverbial clause which modifies "sundown," and the construction "sundown . . . awake" is subordinate to the final independent clause "all had been thought and done." Perhaps the confusion here was caused by Howells's unnecessary comma after "doorway," which renders it ambiguous whether the person "pausing" is "a man" [Howells's intention] or "she."

18. This is not at all to suggest that the editors have been less than candid in acknowledging the difficulties they have had to face. Once for all, in the textual commentary Nordloh forthrightly defines as one variety of emendation made into the copy-text "those revisions and completions of the text which

were introduced by Howells himself (insofar as the present editors have been able to distinguish these from mere editorial sophistication and compositorial error)" (p. 180). What is missing are explicit and detailed indications, in the tables and the textual notes, of the persistence of these difficulties from beginning to end of the critical text.

As an indication of the editors' awareness that persons other than Howells may have been responsible for variant readings, notice the passive voice cautiously employed by Nordloh in discussing a point in *The Leatherwood God* where three different readings occur among the various texts: "the original typescript reading was changed . . . this reading was retained . . . the book proofs were changed later," and so on (p. 177).

19. In the tables of Emendations and Rejected Substantives in *The Leatherwood God*, readings from the seven textual authorities are listed in order according to "a somewhat synthetic chronology" which is "based primarily on the order of completion or publication" but "does not precisely indicate the true relationship of the texts in point of time." For example, in the present instance the Century book edition reading is listed as if from a text which precedes the Jenkins, whereas in an important sense the reverse is apparently true: the Jenkins had its origin in a prepublication form of the Century book edition (see pp. 229, 248). Because the list of emendations includes only readings which antedate (according to the synthetic chronology) the adopted readings, it often occurs that a variant reading which in regard to the author's intention antedates the accepted reading is listed among the Rejected Substantives, as if it reflected a later intention. A certain amount of page turning and mental gymnastics is necessary to cope with this procedure when one reviews the textual history and surveys the options available at particular points. Aware of the difficulty, the editors express hope that "the straightforwardness of the presentation of evidence will offset the inconvenience these conventions must inevitably cause" (p. 185). Unquestionably the evidence is presented in a straightforward manner; but since the chronology for arrangement is a synthetic one anyway, much would have been gained in ready comprehensibility if the Century book edition readings had been listed after those of the Jenkins and Conard, rather than before as they now appear.

20. All very well in the abstract, one may say, but who is going to underwrite the production of such an expanded textual apparatus? Given the steadily rising costs incurred by academic publishers and the distressing cutbacks in university budgets, long-term projects like the Howells Edition have had to take satisfaction in appending to their critical texts whatever textual discussions could be financed, no matter what of importance must be excluded as impracticable. As it happens, publication even of the present critical *text* of *A Hazard of New Fortunes* was delayed owing to a want of funds. In that harsh light Don L. Cook's sober comment of 1974 in his "Afterword: The CEAA Program" merits reiteration: "unless funds, federal or other, are found to meet the publishing costs of these volumes, a good deal of

the literary heritage that the NEH has done so much to preserve and restore will continue to gather dust in printers' shops and filing cabinets while students and scholars continue to employ corrupt texts of our classic American authors" (J. Albert Robbins, ed., *American Literary Scholarship: An Annual, 1972* [Durham: Duke Univ. Press, 1974], p. 417).

Notwithstanding the financial situation, the fact remains that in order fully and accurately to represent the editorial processes involved in the establishment of critical texts for most modern writings, some accounting of the specifically critical issues which have been encountered and dealt with is necessary. Now that university presses have begun seriously to experiment with alternative forms of publication, perhaps the time is ripe to consider issuing future critical editions of literary texts in tandem formats through multiple media. For example, the basic trade edition of *The Leatherwood God*, with historical introduction and spare textual apparatus, might appear more or less as it does now, as a traditional bound volume. But for research libraries and for professional students a supplementary package, including a much fuller textual discussion and perhaps additional material such as transcribed early drafts, pertinent correspondence, source material, and collation data might be made available in microform or as xerox-from-microfilm.

The *New* Milton Criticism

Joseph Wittreich

Edward Le Comte. *Milton and Sex*. New York: Columbia University Press, 1978. x, 154 pp.

Roland Mushat Frye. *Milton's Imagery and the Visual Arts: Iconographic Tradition in the Epic Poems*. Princeton: Princeton University Press, 1978. xxv, 408 pp. 261 illus.

Christopher Hill. *Milton and the English Revolution*. New York: Viking Press, 1977. xviii, 541 pp.

Mary Ann Radzinowicz. *Toward Samson Agonistes: The Growth of Milton's Mind*. Princeton: Princeton University Press, 1978. xxiii, 435 pp.

> the jury which sits in judgment upon a poet . . .
> must be impanneled by Time from the selectest of
> the wise of many generations.
> —Percy Bysshe Shelley

Only two Miltonists currently in academe can properly lay claim to the deanship of Milton studies: Arnold Stein and John Steadman. Neither, I presume, would aspire to the office. But each, with no less than three Milton books, possesses the credentials; and each, in recent years, has issued a position paper, as it were, on the current state of Milton criticism. Stein's statement appears as a preface to his recent book, Steadman's as the preludium essay to a special issue of *Milton Studies*. What form, what harmony Stein finds in this now burgeoning plant of Milton criticism "is produced by competing hothouses, forced growth and altered timetables" with the result that "promising opinions exhaust themselves and are retired to the compost in record speed."[1] Steadman advances a less gloomy prognosis, representing Milton criticism as now adding "reason to imagination, seeking a judicious compromise between the

historical approach and modern critical methods"—as now
striving "to be honest both to the poet's intent and to the
reader's response."[2] From Steadman's vantage point, the
conditions are right—the time is ripe—for a new Milton
criticism.

That was 1975. It is now 1978; and in the last year four
volumes of a projected eight-volume *Milton Encyclopedia* have
appeared (generally consolidations of knowledge are backward
looking, but the volumes that have appeared so far are
remarkable for their forward gaze). In addition four books,
which range from not so good to excellent, have been published
(those by Le Comte, Frye, Hill, and Radzinowicz); and three
others (by Edward Tayler, Joan Webber, and Joseph Wittreich)
are promised for the fall or winter. If there is a new Milton
criticism those books just off the press may reveal something of
its nature, may suggest what criticism for the next few years will
be up to. My attention here will be directed toward these four
recently published books, though it is noteworthy that none of
the items mentioned above is a dissertation or tenure book (none
belongs to the genre that John Wallace calls *publicatio*). All are
the work of seasoned Miltonists—the outgrowth of years of
research, tempered by years of teaching. The books by Hill and
Frye evidence the point in the extreme: *Milton and the English
Revolution* is the culmination of a lifetime's effort; and *Milton's
Imagery and the Visual Arts,* Frye acknowledges in his preface,
involves a subject that has been on his mind for "some
twenty-five years": "the last decade has been almost entirely
devoted to research on this subject" (p. xxiii).

Milton and Sex, with its bristling wit and flair for eloquence,
is an eminently readable book (the most readable of this lot). It
will intrigue the generalist and interest the specialist, even
where it annoys him. One only wishes that there were fewer
causes of annoyance, beginning with the epigraphs which make
one wonder why, if no one has spoken more expansively or more
resoundingly on this topic, Le Comte has chosen to do so. And
that, I suspect, is not their rhetorical function.

Le Comte's book moves through Milton's life and works "in
chronological order, deviating only when topical order is more

compelling" (p. ix). The first chapter ranges over Milton's early poetry, tracking the same ground, essentially, as John Shawcross has previously done; but Le Comte's accents differ from Shawcross's, and so too do his conclusions. Literarily, chapter two deals with the early prose and bibliography, with Milton's first marriage—"the big, traumatic event" (p. ix). However, it is the remaining portion of the book (chapters 3 through 7) which contains the most sustained literary analysis and which consequently will command the attention of most Miltonists. The discussion of Milton's attitude toward women in *The History of Britain* is masterfully conducted, and the critical excursions into Milton's last poems are threaded with useful insights; still *Milton and Sex* lacks the intellectual toughness and general brilliance of Le Comte's earlier study *Yet Once More* (1953).

Both the strengths and weakness of this book become apparent in its last chapters. Le Comte is particularly adept at sorting out fact from fiction and at relating Milton's life and ideas, especially on marriage and divorce, to the last poems. Yet in these pages one often wishes that Le Comte were in closer contact with, and therefore more directly responsive to, previous criticism—to J. B. Trapp's proposition, for instance, that the frequency with which Milton asserts "the equation Eve-Mary . . . [is] the reverse of the antifeminist trend" in historical Christianity (the index, by the way, gives a blind reference to Trapp); or to John Collier's thesis that Eve is the true "hero" of Milton's epic.[3] A keen intelligence shows through in these pages, but so too do certain prejudices, as when Le Comte speaks of that "spokesperson for Women's Liberation [who] has alluded . . . to 'Milton's diarrhetic outpourings of misogynism' " (p. 53) or as when he alludes to "a 1975 article that has nothing but length over previous speculations [and that] in this direction [read: homosexuality] furnishes no scrap of evidence" (p. 118). It is admirable, I suppose, that Le Comte does not beleaguer his generalist reader with lists of critics nor burden him with the minute particulars of scholarly debate, for his objective is *to inform*. Yet repeatedly Le Comte risks misinforming. It is as if, in our own enlightened times, only a feminist critic would think to raise the spectre of Milton's misogyny. At least the "spokesperson," Mary Daly, is named in a footnote; but the author of that 1975 article who, it is said, "perverts Latin and imagery" (p. 118) and accords Milton the label of "homosexual" remains anonymous, receives no footnote, though critical tact and good manners would seem *here* to require one. But this book is sometimes short on tact and, at times, shorter still on essential information.

Minimally, one might expect that a book on Milton and sex, which raises the issue of the poet's alleged homosexuality, would come forth with the following facts: (1) Most recently this subject has been considered by John Shawcross in "Milton and Diodati: An Essay in Psychodynamic Meaning," *Milton Studies*, 9 (1975), 127-63. (2) That essay steers clear of labeling Milton a homosexual, though it does locate a sexual crisis in his life and does speak of the poet's "latent homosexualism." (3) Lacking hard evidence, all such suggestion exists in the realm of speculation, as it still does in the case of Lord Byron; this is a critical problem, not evidence of critical dereliction. (4) Such suggestions have been set forth before, but with decidedly different motives (John Shawcross hopes to bring us closer to understanding the poet, whereas Robert Graves is driven to deprecating him). (5) By no means a subject invented by modern criticism, Milton's supposed homosexuality figures prominently in an attack on the poet by Richard Leigh (see *The Transproser Rehears'd*, 1673): here Leigh not only calls Milton a homosexual but insinuates that such a liaison exists between Milton and Marvell (the first of these allegations dates back to the early 1650s). (6) Marvell's dedicatory verses accompanying the 1674 edition of *Paradise Lost*, written as a point-by-point rejoinder to Leigh's criticisms of Milton, very tactfully raise the related issue of Milton's supposed effeminacy, suggesting that the muscular poetry of *Paradise Lost* contrasts with the effeminate (tagged and pointed) verse of his contemporaries.

With this information on the board, again minimally, one might expect some attention to be given the following questions: How often does the charge of homosexuality figure in the harsh, name-calling polemics of the seventeenth century?

What is its history in the rhetoric of abuse? Where, specifically, *and why*, does homosexuality figure, either implicity or explicitly, in Milton's writings? As to where, Le Comte cites the salient cases: "the first edition of *Comus* takes its epigraph from this [Virgil's second]—homosexual—eclogue" (p. 9). The generalist will find out a bit more if he pursues the bibliographical datum in the footnote; the specialist will probably find less here than he already knows, or has surmised. Yet what all would wish for none will get: *an explanation*. What is Milton doing—not just here but in that other instance? In *Paradise Regained*, Belial proposes that Satan tempt Jesus carnally, with beautiful women—a suggestion that Satan thereupon dismisses with scorn. But when the banquet temptation is devised, included in it are "tall stripling youths . . . of fairer hue/Than Ganymede," together with "Nymphs . . . Niades . . . And ladies of th' Hesperides" (II. 352-57). The boys are mentioned first, and previously Ganymede has been referred to by Milton as a representative of homosexual culture. This is a demonstrable fact about Milton's poem, seeming to require no substantiation from criticism. Le Comte's strategy, though, is to allow Barbara Lewalski to voice the discomfiting facts, and he thereby frees himself from the responsibility of elucidation. No reviewer would have to belabor this point if Le Comte had labored with his subject.

Oddly, Le Comte's subject, which ought to elicit from him serious and extended exposition, more often is the occasion for good (and sometimes not so good) one-liners: "Adam is a Restoration playboy with a hangover . . . . He responds like a man with an erection, 'Bone of my bone thou art' " (pp. 97, 99). As such instances accumulate, they create the impression (and I think it is a false impression) that the critic is high-handed but not high-minded. Here is yet another such instance: "One mouth, another mouth—how much difference is there, as such indulgences as fellatio and cunnilingus prove?" (p. 70). This instance is particularly revealing, for it takes us to the very heart of the problem this book evinces. The title may startle (no less so than the book's dustjacket), its author may speak of "fellatio, buggery . . . and glass dildos" (p. 10), but he is finally not at ease—is in fact very awkward—in the vicinity of his subject. In consequence, *Milton and Sex* seems to mock at its admirable appeal: "I don't think that anything in Milton is un-Miltonic. Preconceptions must be shed" (p. 10).

Uneasiness and awkwardness are compounded, moreover, with carelessness as when we are reminded that the serpent, historically, "had been given a woman's face" and then are told: "Even one of Milton's illustrators, J. H. Fuseli, was carried away—illegitimately—by this tradition" (p. 73; Fuseli's name does not appear in the index which, alas, is only an index of names). For substantiation, we are sent to figure 96 in Marcia Pointon's *Milton and English Art* to find a poor and misleading reproduction of Fuseli's painting which, as it happens, is reproduced as figure 30 by Gert Schiff.[4] There the serpent's head is unmistakably masculine, presuming, of course, that we take a moustache to be a masculine denominator and presuming, too, that the wings of Mercury (also evident in the Pointon reproduction) are an indicator of sex. When one remembers Milton's strategy of regularly representing Satan as God's ape, the brilliance of Fuseli's design comes into focus: Mercury, renowned for his eloquence and emblematized by the serpent, is often figured as the false god who drives souls into hell, contrasting with the true god who is their deliverer. And more to what should have been Le Comte's concern: as Alexander Ross, among others, explains, Mercury is hermaphroditic—half masculine, half feminine.

Contrary to its professed purpose, Le Comte's book does not help us to shed preconceptions; it only fosters them. However, correctives are forthcoming this year—in the subtle and sensitive probings of Edward Tayler's book and in the enlightened and humane considerations, especially of androgyny, that figure so richly in Joan Webber's study of the epics. In the meantime, we can await William Kerrigan's full-length study that will make Le Comte's declaration, "Freudian interpretations of Milton are rare" (p. 108), less of a truth and that will bring us closer, one hopes, to a psychoanalytic interpretation of the last poems. Such an effort will be particularly welcome in view of Christopher Hill's recent reminder: Milton was Freud's favorite poet.

One book that does effectively dispel certain preconceptions about Milton is Roland Frye's *Milton's Imagery and the Visual Arts*. In an imaginary conversation Leigh Hunt has Alexander Pope say of Milton: "With all his regard for the poets of Italy . . .

he has said not a word of their painters, nor scarcely alluded to painting throughout his works . . . . If he had loved painting, he would not have held his tongue about it . . . . I believe he had no eyes for pictures."[5] Frye thinks differently and so mounts an argument in behalf of a criticism that would study the visual component of Milton's epics. This book is the finest testimony we have to Thomas Warton's proposition that Milton's poetry is "a perpetual fund of picturesque description"; it is a noble extension and elaboration of Francis Peck's still earlier declaration: "The same kind of taste is seen in writing; & MILTON has it . . . to a degree beyond what we have ever found in any modern painter and sculptor, not excepting RAFAELLE himself . . . . His *Eden*, his chaos, hell, heaven; his human figures, his angels good & evil, his MEDIATOR, his GOD, all is superior to what is elsewhere to be found; all are . . . like what RAFAELLE'S pictures exhibit."[6] No book of this year, indeed very few books of any year, would have been so pleasurable to research and so painfully difficult to organize and write. It is inevitable, perhaps, that any such book would not make easy cover-to-cover reading; and that, in consequence, it is likely to be dipped into here and there, and used occasionally for reference. It must be said of *Milton's Imagery*, though, that Frye has been painstaking in making his materials accessible and that, with the possible exception of a few finely printed modern editions, this is undeniably the most handsome Milton book of the century.

Frye is overly modest in the claims he makes for *Milton's Imagery*: "I have merely written an introduction to reading Milton with a more adequate visual recognition. Other scholars will surely amplify what I have done here, and correct my oversights, omissions, and errors, but at least a beginning has been made" (p. 350). Actually, the "beginning" antedate's Frye's book: both J. B. Trapp and A. C. Labriola (not to mention Milton's early editors) broke the ground for iconographic study of Milton. Frye, on the other hand, blazes a trail for iconographic study of the epics—a more ample one for *Paradise Lost*, however, than for *Paradise Regained*.

Frye is too exacting a scholar to require much correction of
error, though in a book of such splendor there are perhaps too
many oversights: "Jeffry Spencer . . . he" for "Jeffry Spencer . . .
she" is one example—a jumbling of gender that is compounded
in the index by the shuffling of all references to Edmund
Spenser into the entry for "Spenser, Jeffry B." There is
inattention to the spelling of names, hence "Keightly" for
Thomas *Keightley*, "Ann" for *Anne* Davidson Ferry, and
"Taylor" for Edward *Tayler* (see pp. 49, 150, 215, 388), and
sometimes to names themselves, thus "John" for *Thomas*
Middleton Raysor (p. 116); not to mention imprecision in the
citation of bibliographical data (the date of Raysor's edition is
1960, not "1962" or "n.d."). On occasion, a word or phrase is
ill-chosen ("Adam's pudendum," p. 266, or "self-deified self," p.
111); and in at least one instance, excision would seem desirable:

For several years, I have tried the following experiment with bright
undergraduate English majors. After they have completed a close study
of the Shakespearean presentations of Hamlet and of Lear, I have
shown a number of Renaissance and later portraits of intelligent
young princes and authoritative old kings, and have asked each
student to identify the artistic version which comes closest to the
literary characterizations. The identifications have been so varied that
no pattern emerges. *This is admittedly a rather simple-minded
experiment.* [p. 86, my italics]

Milton's Imagery is too sophisticated a book for that sort of
irrelevancy; and physiognomy is a more *definite* art, both in the
Renaissance and the eighteenth century, than Frye's subsequent
remarks allow. Better: we should have learned here that Sergi
Eisenstein credits *Paradise Lost* with teaching him an array of
visual techniques and find explored in this context what Angus
Fletcher means by calling *Paradise Lost* a cosmic picture show.
    Evident throughout this book is a compulsion to simplify
which can mislead and which, more alarmingly, can cause one
to teeter on the brink of error. Here are some striking instances.
Frye wishes to discredit "any degrading identification of
Pandaemonium with the chief church of Roman Catholicism";
and though such an association derives from eighteenth-century
commentary, there is much to Frye's argument, much in it that

is compelling, Yet it is downright misleading to suggest, with regard to Roman Catholicism, that "Milton's days of sectarian controversy and bickering were over" (p. 135), were *behind* him; or to argue, in the context of *Paradise Regained*, that while the younger Milton might express "anticlerical and antipapal sentiments," the older Milton, "a more ecumenical spirit" (p. 343), would not. Milton's attack on popery in the otherwise broadly tolerant tract *Of True Religion* (1673) proves otherwise. Equally misleading, and quite confusing, is the distinction Frye draws between elders and angels: "elders are not angels," he says flatly (p. 187). What then are they? According to the Geneva Bible, "by these [the four and twenty elders] are ment all the holie copanie of the heaues"; and similarly Gustav Davidson observes, "the Elders *are* angels."[7]

Accuracy becomes an issue elsewhere. For instance, Coleridge is singled out as "the first to notice the similarities between this painting [Raphael's *Creation of the Animals*] and Milton's description" (p. 161). In fact, Thomas Newton noted this correspondence much earlier, and he drew, at the same time, yet another visual parallel to Milton's creation story: "the famous picture of the morning by Guido . . . . The picture is on a cieling at Rome; but there are copies of it in England, and an excellent print by Jac. Frey."[8] It is not immediately clear why the Salvatore Rosa painting, which, though mentioned by H. J. Todd, and actually nominated as a source for *Paradise Regained* by Charles Dunster, is regarded as "much too late to be of relevance to our inquiry" (p. 344). (Rosa's dates are 1615-1673.) Additionally, Todd mentions a further visual analogue; but this suggestion (as he acknowledges) derives from Thyer and is first printed by Newton, whose note makes clear that this reference is not to "an engraving by Vischer" (as Frye reports on p. 344) but to "a design of David Vinkboon's": "It is to be met with among Vischer's cuts to the Bible, and is ingrav'd by Landerfelt."[9] Given Frye's later interests, it would seem pertinent to note here that Salvatore Rosa painted two different temptations of St. Anthony; and given Frye's thesis, it would seem appropriate to invoke the authority of earlier criticism. As Charles Dunster

observes, "Bp. Warburton and Dr. Jortin both . . . [believe] that
this description [PR IV.421 ff.] is taken from the legend, or the
pictures, of the Temptation of St. Anthony."[10]

As one considers Frye's thesis within the context of the whole
history of Milton criticism, it becomes increasingly evident that,
historically, more attention has been given to the visual
component in Milton's art than Frye's chapter "Milton's Visual
Imagination and the Critics" allows. There are those many
annotations by eighteenth-century editors that anticipate Frye's
discoveries. Indeed, Frye's insight regarding Uriel riding a
sunbeam is advanced by Newton: the episode, says Milton's
early editor, derives from "some capital picture of some great
Italian master, where an Angel is ready to descend in like
manner. I since recollect it is from a picture of Annibal
Caracci." But more important, there are annotations, a
significant number of them, that should have encouraged Frye
to expand his discussion at certain points. Relating Michael's
sword in Book VI of *Paradise Lost* to the two-handed engine of
Lycidas, Newton explains both in terms of the visual arts: "The
two-handed engin is the two-handed Gothic sword, with which
the painters draw him [Michael and St. Peter]."[11] And in an
analogous instance, referring to the ministry of angels in
Paradise Regained, Charles Dunster reminds us of "an
Assumption of the Virgin, by Guido, in St. Ambrosio's Church
at Genoa; only the motion of the whole groupe there is
ascending.—If it is not from any famous painting, it is certainly
a subject for one."[12]

Oversights, simplifications, a few inaccuracies, and some
notable omissions are a source of confusion and confinement in
Frye's book, but no one need be confounded by his thesis or by
his ultimate achievement. Frye banishes the notion that Milton
possessed a faulty visual imagination, arguing instead that "an
awareness of the visual heritage of art will enrich our responses"
to Milton's epics and explaining that his analyses "are
undertaken to show the traditional ways of seeing things that
the arts can reveal to us, and not to identify a particular painting
or sculpture as the source for this or that line in Milton" (p. 4).
Frye's interest is in the genius a poet displays while "distilling,

transmitting, and applying" his knowledge of visual traditions, precipitating them "into new fusions of perfect aesthetic propriety" (pp. 6-7). That argument, unfolded skillfully, is everywhere buttressed by significant detail and shrewd perception. Occasionally Frye comes close to asserting a source, as in his discussions of the Beccafumi bas relief (p. 83), Michelangelo Naccherino's marble statuary group (p. 105), and Raphael's *Creation of the Animals* (pp. 161-62). When Frye relinquishes his characteristic stance, however, he has the authority of history, criticism, and freshly discovered detail to authenticate his role as source finder. But these are exceptional instances. More regularly, Frye is concerned with visual icons and their traditions as they intrude upon Milton's poem and affect our response to it.

The discussion of *Paradise Lost* encompasses a multiplicity of traditions and involves the entire field of Milton's epic—hell, heaven, Eden, the battle in heaven, the fall (before and after), the expulsion, together with Milton's whole cast of characters. The discussion of Satan is particularly successful; and if a base in earlier criticism had been provided, especially here, one would have a much stronger sense of Frye's originality. Newton had contended, for example, that "the greatest masters in painting had not such sublime ideas as Milton, and among all their Devils have drawn no portrait comparble to this; as every body must allow who hath seen the pictures or the prints of Michael and the Devil by Raphael, or of the same by Guido, or the last judgment by Michael Angelo."[13] Frye has seen them all, and more; his book reproduces most of them. But Frye thinks differently from Newton, and his argument is weighty. Frye tells the story of Satan's deformation (in Medieval art) and rehabilitation (in Renaissance art), and he explains that while Milton cannot ignore those distortions entirely he does put them "at some distance from his devils" (p. 74). Moreover, Frye demonstrates that "sixteenth- and seventeenth-century artists produced numerous devils that are quite fairly and constructively comparable with those of *Paradise Lost*" (p. 81) and, in a discussion of many-headed devils, establishes visual analogues to Milton's depictions of Moloch, Belial, and

Beelzebub. Here Frye is provocative—and no less so in his
discussions of demonic tears, Sin and Death, "darkness visible,"
and the Limbo of Vanity as "the *reductio ad absurdum* of the
apotheosis ceiling" (p. 212).

Frye's critical successes result from strict adherence to the
methodological principle so emphatically stated within his
book: "Sophisticated readers need to be aware not only of what
Milton incorporated in his epic[s] but also of what he excluded
from it [them] . . . . The variation from an established
iconographic scheme is at least as important as adherence to it"
(pp. 77, 153). But surrendering that principle, perhaps
unwittingly, in the chapter on *Paradise Regained*, Frye makes
that discussion a dim shadow of what in potentiality it might
have been. The critic's initial assumption about artistic
representations of the wilderness story may, in fact, need some
qualification: "The story of Christ in the Wilderness had been
presented in objective visual forms for centuries before Milton's
time . . . and the works of those artists provided a reservoir of
images in terms of which men and women had been accustomed
to imagining the physical components of the authoritative
accounts in the Gospels" (p. 4). There is an artistic tradition
behind this episode, to be sure, but it is not so prominent as Frye
leads us to believe; and its importance may lie in the fact that so
often it supplements—it does not merely project—the scriptural
rendering of this story. Gertrud Schiller provides the corrective:
"no Early Christian representation of the Temptation is
known . . . probably none was executed"; at no period in the
history of Christian art was Christ's temptation "a particularly
prominent pictorial theme; indeed *it was strikingly rare*, even
among New Testament cycles."[14] Here particularly, then, the
paradigm must be established and variations upon it tabulated.

Alongside Schiller's corrective, it may be useful to set forth the
following propositions:

1. The subject of Christ's temptations seems to have been
   more popular among biblical illustrators than painters.
2. When the entire tradition (biblical illustration, as well as
   painting) is assembled, it is possible to discriminate
   between different ways of handling this subject:

   a. Sometimes a single temptation is depicted, usually the first, and so allowed to represent metaphorically all the others.

   b. More often the first temptation is figured in the foreground and all the others in the background.

   c. In some instances this New Testament subject is represented within a cycle painting that relates this one episode to others in Christ's life.

   d. In other instances this episode is combined with an Old Testament subject, often one that invokes the idea of blood sacrifice.

   e. At still other times the subject of Christ's temptation is combined with that of his crucifixion.

These propositions yield two firm principles for the study of this particular artistic tradition. First, it is difficult, if not altogether impossible, to discuss this tradition without at the same time invoking the concept of typology (the concept scarcely figures in Frye's book and is given no entry in its index). Second, it is impossible to talk about this tradition without addressing its theological content—at least to talk about it in any *meaningful* way.

Frye recognizes that "some of Milton's most brilliant theology" (p. 320) is set forth in *Paradise Regained*; but without registering a consciousness of this tradition, which pairs the wilderness story and the crucifixion, Frye is in no position, as he usually is in his discussion of *Paradise Lost*, to show the individual talent encountering tradition and thereupon subjecting it to radical transformation. In his own assessment of Milton's brief epic, Frye reverses the historical estimate of the poem: it contains "some of Milton's most brilliant theology . . . though not . . . his finest poetry" (p. 320). Historically, criticism has argued just the opposite: that while *Paradise Regained* contains some of his grandest poetry, particularly in its fourth book, the poem errs wildly in its theology by humanizing Jesus, thereby tearing him from the firmament. One man's great poem may be another's lesser poem; one man's erroneous theology may be another's brilliant theology—that is clear enough. But it is worth recalling here that Milton himself valued *Paradise*

Regained enormously, putting a higher estimate on it than Frye does; and worth remembering too that the brilliance of Milton's theology in the brief epic—not at all an established fact of Milton criticism and as yet not a major subject of criticism on that poem—deserves the attention that Frye withholds from it.

Ultimately, one must ask how much Frye has withheld from his book, and asking that question leads to this assessment: *Milton's Imagery* is an important book, though not one of first importance. Its stature, finally, is diminished by procedures that eventuate in too many exclusions. More compelling supporting evidence for Frye's thesis than either Milton's Italian journey or his Italian acquaintances is provided by the visual component of Milton's early poetry. Thomas Warton alone offers convincing visual analogues for the Nativity Ode, *Comus, Arcades,* and, most notably, *Il Penseroso.* Once recognized, the presence of this visual element in *all* Milton's poetry is to be explained by reference to Renaissance critical theory, which pertains to all the arts and which proceeds from the assumption that they have been individually disfigured by the Fall. Division, separation— the terms used to describe the fallen human condition—apply equally to the arts. At one time integrated, they too have become fragmented, so that any artist who, like Milton, would restore the Golden Age must restore the arts themselves to the unity of their unfallen condition. *Milton's Imagery* has little grounding in art theory and none in critical theory pertaining to the various arts; nor does it take its bearings in the rich tradition of eighteenth-century commentary that begins discourse on Frye's subject, even as it advances ideas to which Frye remains a stranger. There is a message here for Miltonists generally: we cannot rely on critical samplings like those provided by the Critical Heritage Series to pursue problems as specialized as those with which Frye is dealing. Given the peculiarities of the new Variorum Milton, not the least of which is its post-1800 orientation, there is simply no substitute for the work of critical excavation: we must do the digging ourselves. And as we begin digging, we will discover that, while Frye's perceptions sometimes represent an advance upon earlier criticism and sometimes are preempted by it, on other occasions they are also

challenged by an earlier criticism. Alluding to that visual
tradition which portrays Satan as a Franciscan friar (i.e., a Gray
friar) or hermit, Frye argues that Milton "entirely ignores" this
disguise in *Paradise Regained* (p. 343). Charles Dunster, on the
other hand, contends that Satan, who had already appeared as
such a friar in *In Quintum Novembris*, recalls, however
elusively, this same tradition when, in *Paradise Regained*, he
bows "his gray dissimulation" (I.498), the first temptation now
completed.[15] Traditions not directly invoked may rise up
through insinuation or, as seems to be the case here as well,
through a striking and significant transference. Jesus, after all,
is led into the desert as a "glorious Eremite" (I. 8-9). And,
futhermore, traditions that manifest themselves in the visual arts
may be fed by literary and theological traditions which, in turn,
may prove to be a poet's ultimate authority. In this regard, we
must learn to distinguish again, as an earlier criticism had done,
between pictures Milton draws from nature, pictures he draws
from books, and pictures he draws from painting.

Within its own limitations, Frye's book achieves impressive
results; but those limits, finally, are too narrowly set—too much
of relevance is pushed beyond the scope of this book. Yet it is
worth cataloguing the exclusions, for they indicate the kinds of
studies that *Milton's Imagery*, certain to be an influential book,
ought to provoke. Frye has realized his objective, and realized it
mightily: to provide a dictionary of Milton's visual icons. What
we need now is a scanning of historical perception—what
paintings, what illustrations, what emblems have commentators
hitherto thought relevant to Milton's art, not just to his epics
but to his early poetry and, later, his prose works? Frye chooses
not to consider Milton's illustrators. If one regards them as
critics of the poet (and they are that certainly), their exclusion is
understandable; but one may also regard them in the way that
Frye regards George Romney, as being in direct contact with the
iconographic traditions that inform Milton's art and, indeed, as
focusing those traditions. Henry Aldrich's three contributions to
the Medina series are as good an example as any; for they derive,
respectively, from Raphael's Michael and the Devil, from
Mantegna's Descent into Limbo, and from Raphael's

Expulsion. Furthermore, not all illustrations are adaptations from Milton's poem; some, antedating *Paradise Lost*, are adapted to Milton's poem, in which case the compiler is engaged, like Frye himself, in discovering visual counterparts and so contributes in important ways to our understanding of Frye's subject.[16] Quite properly, Frye excludes from discussion the thorny subject of Milton's influence upon the arts; yet in the very act of mentioning that subject, he sets it forth for future inquiry. And there is the related subject of Milton's influence on the Bible—how, subsequent to the epics and under their sway, conventional scriptural readings become altered. *Paradise Regained* is probably more influential in this respect than *Paradise Lost*. Though he devotes most of his attention to Milton's reliance on paintings for his descriptive passages, on occasion Frye ventures into a quite different but related area—that of visual effects. There are discussions of Milton's using "incremental repetition . . . so as to provide various perspectives upon . . . and modifications of events, places, characters, and ideas" (p. 56); of Milton's giving us "not a single picture, but rather a series of pictures in motion" (p. 110); and of Milton's constructing the final books of *Paradise Lost* "according to the established principles of multiscenic design in pictorial art" (p. 301). Such discussions, however abbreviated, push us into the area of what John Bender calls "literary pictorialism" and thereby suggest the need for a study of Milton comparable to the one Bender has provided for Spenser.[17] And such a study would necessarily travel over ground that Frye leaves untouched: Renaissance theories of optics, of perspective, for example. Finally, the very best confirmation of Frye's thesis, that Milton is a profoundly pictorial artist, is to be found in Milton's largest aesthetic commitment. The poet has been called a prophet, or visionary, and is said to write prophecies. But scarcely any attention has been given to that one generic feature of prophecy: its dependence upon the verbal and the visual (pictures, hieroglyphs, emblems), its insistence upon intervolving the two so as to create a composite art form, and its consequent development, through these very strategies, of a dialectic of the senses. What one must finally attend to is the way in which aesthetic and intention harmonize as a chord: Milton's intention is to achieve an emancipation of consciousness; his strategy is to realize this goal through an emancipation of the senses. The eye altering alters all.

Frye's persistent claim, that "we should not always insist upon finding . . . [Milton's] sources in books" (p. 132), is reiterated with still greater emphasis by Christopher Hill: "It is a prevalent donnish assumption that ideas are transmitted principally by books . . . . My not very daring suggestion is that Milton got his ideas not only from books but also by talking to his contemporaries" (p. 5; cf. pp. 76-77). Reviewers of Hill's book *Milton and the English Revolution* have tended to fault it for this eminently sensible proposition; they have also convicted Hill for labeling Milton—a temptation that, in all fairness, Hill is resolute in resisting:

Milton himself was not an extreme radical, Leveller, Digger, or Ranter. He agreed with these groups on some issues, but only on some. What I suggest is that this is the milieu in which we should set Milton . . . . He remained the great eclectic, the asserter of Christian doctrine who was a member of no church. [p. 99]

Lest I be misunderstood, I repeat that I do not think Milton was a Leveller, a Ranter, a Muggletonian or a Behmenist. Rather I suggest that we should see him living in a state of permanent dialogue with radical views which he could not wholly accept, yet some of which greatly attracted him. [pp. 113-14]

Milton and the English Revolution is a daring, courageous book, its objective being to set Milton studies on a new course. Like Frye, Hill is bent upon dispelling preconceptions about Milton; but now the stakes are greater, the effort is more prodigious, and the consequences all the more important. According to Hill, we do not need yet another study of Milton and his classical or patristic sources; we need instead a proliferation of studies that will see Milton in relation to his contemporaries; that will, as Hill would have it, "put Milton back into history" (p. 119). Like David Masson's monumental effort of the nineteenth century, this book studies Milton "in connexion with the . . . History of His Times" (Masson's subtitle); yet unlike Masson's work, it does not flow with, but against, the prevailing currents of criticism. *Milton and the English Revolution* is written for the new age and to the future generations, and Hill's accomplishment here is in every way proportionate to his undertaking. This is a colossal book, fiery in its thought and consuming in its interest. Of our time, this study is for all time—a new classic in criticism. For good reason, then, it was the recipient of the 1977 James Holly Hanford Award.

Hill does not leave for inference—he sharply formulates—the kind of work which, in the aftermath of his book, remains to be done. We need, first, a new study of Milton's contemporary reputation—William Riley Parker "looked in the wrong places" and so misgauged it (pp. 2, 8, 99, 229); "Milton's relation to . . . [the] underground of thought has not yet been properly investigated" (p. 5): "A wider study of Milton and preceding ideas about the relation of the sexes is needed. There are general histories of Unitarianism and Socinianism in which Milton's name occurs; but no study of his ideas in the light of this tradition, also strong in the English underground. There is no work on Milton and contemporary millenarianism, antinomianism, materialism or Hermeticism . . . . There is a book to be written on 'Milton and Fludd' which will be far more important than any studies of Milton's classical and patristic sources" (p. 6). And further: "There is a good book to be written . . . on the subject of taverns and ale-houses as centres of political information and organization during the English Revolution" (p. 97); "A 'source' for *Paradise Regained* to which more attention might be paid is William Perkins's *The Combate between Christ and the Devill displayed*" (p. 427); "Milton concealed his views so successfully that in the eighteenth and nineteenth centuries he came to be regarded as the orthodox Puritan poet . . . . There are many ironies here to be incorporated into the history of English popular culture when it comes to be written" (p. 465). And on and on. No Miltonist, at least for some time, will have to forbear the perennial complaint from students: "But there is nothing more to be done." There is plenty to be done!—by way of augmenting Hill's study, by way of readjusting some of its accents, by way of refining and sometimes sharpening its perceptions.

Milton and the English Revolution is a giant step forward for historical criticism, but here it should be noted: Hill is a better reader of history than of texts (and he thinks better than he writes). Yet even as an historian he is not flawless, not even in those areas where he seems to be speaking with supreme authority. Indeed, to a literary historian, his methods may seem too haphazard. One might reasonably expect completeness on the subject of Milton the Revolutionary from a bibliography as exhaustive as the one accompanying Hill's book. However, Merritt Hughes's "Milton as a Revolutionary" receives no entry; nor does the admittedly troublesome, though germane, study by Hugh Richmond.[18] Others like Christopher Caudwell have written about Milton from Hill's own ideological perspective, and while Caudwell *is* mentioned in the bibliography, his signally relevant studies *Illusion and Reality* (1937; rpt. 1967) and *Romance and Realism* (1970) go unnoticed. Inasmuch as Milton's millenarianism is inextricably involved in Hill's subject, one might expect to find a citation here for Marjorie Reeves's *The Influence of Prophecy in the Later Middle Ages* (1969), which maintains a lively concern with the issues Hill brings forward for discussion, or to Michael Fixler's "The Apocalypse within *Paradise Lost*," printed in *New Essays on Paradise Lost* (1969). It seems odd, moreover, that a bibliography which contains so many items of tangential interest nowhere mentions John Steadman and that a book which spars repeatedly with William Riley Parker, quarreling with his assumptions and presumptions, does not include *Milton: A Biography* (1968) in the roll call of its bibliography.

Hill is at his best forging the history of an idea and tracing its projection through the intricacies of Milton's prose tracts. In the course of illuminating these tracts, he presents the finest essays we have on Milton's various heresies and the finest introduction to date for *De Doctrina Christiana*. The radical ideas embodied here are extended with supreme skill to *Paradise Lost* and used convincingly to illuminate it. Hill's Milton is of a piece and so, like Blake, may at times alter his opinions, but never his principles. Indeed, Hill's arguments are marshaled with such care and mounted with such force that, when he focuses the political element in *Paradise Lost*, all readers of this book should readily give their assent. Hill does this by reporting an exchange between Theodore Haak and H. L. Benthem and by then explaining that the latter gathered that "Milton's poem was really about politics in Restoration England," that " 'This very wily politician . . . concealed under . . . [a] disguise exactly the sort of lament . . . his friends had originally suspected' " and feared (p. 391). If Hill misrepresents here, it is only in minimizing the extent to which earlier criticism was similarly sensitive to the political dimensions of Milton's epic—to its thinly veiled and intermittent political allegory. One eighteenth-century critic, for example, can speak of "the passage relating to Nimrod, at the beginning of the twelfth book, which *has always been supposed* to allude to . . . [Milton's] own times"; and another, even if suspicious of historical allegorizings of the poem, can write:

Abdiel may be the Poet himself . . . . It needs not be told what nation he points at in the twelfth book.
    "Yet sometimes nations will descend so low . . . ."
Again, how plain are the civil wars imagined in the sixth book? The Michaels and Gabriels, &c. would have lengthened out the battles endless; nor would a solution have been found, had not Cromwell, putting on celestial armour (for this was Milton's opinion) like the Messiah all armed in heavenly panoply, and ascending his fiery chariot, driven over the malignant heads of those who would maintain tyrannic sway.[19]

The point is not that everyone in the eighteenth century subscribed to such an interpretation but that this kind of reading was sufficiently common, especially in the periodical press, that its aptness could be debated. On *Paradise Lost*, Hill has done his homework, and the results are dazzling.

But when we turn to his discussion of *Paradise Regained*, where the research is partial, or to *Samson Agonistes*, where the research is highly selective and ridden by ideology, we find interpretations that are themselves partial (in both senses of the word) and, in the case of *Samson*, deeply troubling. Part of the problem is that Hill restricts himself so completely to the idea that Milton's radical contemporaries are the source for the poet's ideas that he does not consider the possibility that they themselves had sources in an earlier radical literature and, occasionally, may have directed Milton to them. Joachim of Fiore is one example. He presents a perspective on the wilderness story that Milton may very well have had in mind while writing *Paradise Regained*—a perspective that conceives of this story as a summoning of all men to spiritual adventure, which, beginning in self-transformation, ends in cultural renewal:

Clear the eyes of the mind from all dusts of the earth; leave the tumults of crowds and the clamour of words; follow the angel in spirit into the desert; ascend with the same angel into the great and high mountain; there you will behold high truths hidden from the beginning of time and from all generations . . . . For we, called in these latest times to follow the spirit rather than the letter, ought to obey, going from illumination to illumination, from the first heaven to the second, and from the second to the third, from the place of darkness into the light of the moon, that at last we may come out of the moonlight into the glory of the full Sun.[20]

In his *Leviathan*, moreover, Hobbes asks what can be the meaning of this episode, "other than that [Jesus] went into the Wildernesse; and that this . . . was a vision?" The biblical account of this episode, he says, "suiteth with the nature of a Vision."[21] It is not clear that either of these readings constitutes *the* seventeenth-century reading of the wilderness story; but it is clear that by the middle of the next century this was the way in which the biblical story was regarded and that, later, when such an interpretation was advanced by H. Cates, the commentator cited Milton's brief epic as an authority.[22] By accepting too matter-of-factly the thesis that "Milton was not an original thinker" (p. 6), Hill closes us off to the possibility that, on occasion, Milton can be original, if not in supposition at least in amplification and demonstration. *Paradise Regained* is a classic instance of Milton's setting a new interpretation for the future generations.

Hill is right, certainly, to point to William Perkins's commentary even if he does not draw out from that commentary its full implications, which, as it happens, are explored by Daniel Dyke and later by Henry Archer. Their shared belief, that the temptations of Jesus comprehend and abridge all the temptations to which mankind is subject, is developed by Dyke to the point that he acknowledges: we must cultivate the "Stoical eye of our Saviour" so as "not [to] bee moved and set agogge . . . with the beauty of a young boy . . . [we] must have continent eyes, as well as hands."[23] This passage may have some bearing on the banquet temptation alluded to earlier, where stripling youths, fairer than Ganymede, appear. Indeed, from these three commentaries, one could collect most of the components of Milton's banquet temptation. It is noteworthy, too, that the very title of Dyke's treatise, *Michael and the Dragon*, sets the temptation within an apocalyptic context by way of stressing that the weapons employed here are the apocalyptic ones, weapons not physical but spiritual, and that the warfare here is an example of how all Christian warfare is to be conducted. Here we reach beyond *Paradise Regained*, begin to push into *Samson Agonistes*, in interesting ways.

There is a tendency in Dyke's treatise, evident in an earlier one by Lancelot Andrewes, to parallel the temptations of Jesus with those of Samson. (Andrewes specifically parallels the pinnacle temptation with the scene of Samson at the pillars.) However, if Andrewes presents Delilah as Antichrist and Samson as Christ, an equation characteristic of much early commentary, Dyke moves the whole Samson myth in a direction that will eventually form one way in which the seventeenth century looked upon this scriptural episode. Having already observed that the Spirit of God leads us always to the Word, never to the theater, and having submitted the view that all impulse to kill derives from Satan rather than from God, Dyke refers to the Samson story by way of arguing that faith is man's chief weapon when he is in combat with the devil: "As the Philistins got away the Israelites weapons, so doth Satan in getting away faith from us, disarme us, to make us naked . . . . And in this faith apprehending Gods strength lies our strength, as *Samsons* in his lockes, and therefore the Divell knowing this, labours to do to us, which *Dalelah* did to *Samson*, even to cut off his lockes. And indeed when he doth this, he doth that to us, which *Samson* did to the Philistins; hee pluckes downe the pillers of the house, and so overthrowes us."[24] The equations are slippery here and thus worth underscoring: first, the Philistines = Satan; then, Delilah = Satan; finally, "pluck[ing] downe the pillars," Samson = Satan. This last equation surfaces throughout the seventeenth century, especially after the failure of the Puritan Revolution (it is not mentioned by Hill, or by Jackie Di Salvo, or, for that matter, by Michael Krouse—in each instance, I suspect, for ideological reasons).[25]

It is understandable that Hill does not mention Krouse's book (nor does he cite it in his bibliography), especially when we recall Krouse's position: that in the sixteenth and seventeenth centuries "Samson was treated exactly as he had been treated during the medieval period."[26] Perhaps no Milton book of this century is a better instance of what Hill, quoting Denis Saurat, is complaining about: " 'tak[ing] up a thread at the beginning of human culture and follow[ing] it up till it reaches Milton' " which, as a critical strategy, " 'is a pure illusion, a mere abstract fabrication of the academic mind' " (p. 5). The whole thrust of Hill's book is toward bringing criticism to a higher state of consciousness: "It is, in my view, quite wrong to see Milton in relation to anything so vague and generalized as 'the Christian tradition'" (p. 3). By looking to Henry Robinson, Lucy Hutchinson, John Lilburne, Joseph Salmon, and Robert Norwood, Hill demonstrates his point; for Krouse, denying a political dimension to *Samson*, wholly ignores the fact that Samson was the hero of the Puritan revolutionaries—the one whom John Lilburne said they might have to follow, even unto his death. Hill, then, sees what Krouse refuses to see, but he sees only the Samson who is a great deliverer. There is exclusion on both sides—Krouse's and Hill's—neither critic perceiving Samson, neither representing him, in his fallen, Satanic form. But put this aside for a moment.

Hill is right, certainly, that *his* Samson, so popular in the 1640s and '50s, would be on the mind of any contemporary

reader, especially of a play coming forth from the pen of John
Milton. Hill is right, too, that we have not given proper
attention to the difficulties Milton had, writing throughout his
life under censorship—to the lengths he had to go, to the devices
he had to employ, so as to conceal the political motives of his
last poems. They were presumably completed and written while
Milton was in seclusion and fearful of assassination—at a time
when, as Milton well knew, any false step might cost him dearly.
And herein lies the problem. Hill makes no effort to square his
suppositions with his reading of Milton's tragedy:

> About *Samson Agonistes* . . . "neo-Christians" are as mealy-mouthed
> as they are about Milton's defence of polygamy. They emphasize that
> the poem is about the regeneration of Samson. They do not emphasize
> that it is also about revenge, about political deceit and murder, and
> that the two themes are inseparable. At the end Samson may be
> regenerated, but the Philistines are dead, horribly dead, in large and
> indiscriminate numbers, even though the lower classes escaped . . . .
> Milton believed that the war against Antichrist continued, and that it
> was the duty of God's people to hit back when they could . . . . *Paradise
> Regained* could be interpreted as a pacifist poem . . . . But *Samson
> Agonistes* . . . conforms to what the *De Doctrina* tells us about the
> religious duty of hating . . . . Milton's message seems clear: however
> difficult the political circumstances, be ready to smite the Philistines
> when God gives the word. [pp. 442-43]

Earlier, Hill is just as emphatic; in this tragedy, where the
message is so "clear," Samson does not stop short of "murder"
(p. 313). Given what Samson meant to Englishmen during the
Civil War years, how could Milton get away with publishing
this play, which, by the way, has meant to others what it now
means to Hill? The words of one eighteenth-century critic, not
cited by Hill, adequately summarize Hill's own reading of the
play: "Let us consider his tragedy in this allegorical view.
Samson imprisoned and blind, and the captive state of Israel,
lively represents our blind poet, with the republican party after
the Restoration, afflicted and persecuted. But these revelling
idolators will soon pull an old house on their heads; and GOD
will send his people a deliverer." This critic suggests such an
interpretation, however, only to discredit it: "These mystical

and allegorical reveries have more amusement in them, than solid truth, and savour but little of cool criticism, where the head is required to be free from fumes and vapours, and rather sceptical than dogmatical.''[27] With regard to Hill's interpretation of *Samson Agonistes,* the best posture for the historical critic to assume is still one of skepticism.

All the evidence is not yet in; and some of it, here presented by Hill, is suspect. Take, for instance, Hill's epigraph for Chapter 31: "The heroic Samson . . . thought it not impious but pious to kill those masters who were tyrants over his country." And then listen to what Hill makes of that quotation, for which *he* has provided the ellipses: "The passage . . . is decisive evidence that Milton did not disapprove of Samson . . . . There is nothing to suggest that Milton changed his views on this matter" (p. 445). Without the entire quotation, of course, we do not know what Milton's views actually are. What Milton says is this: "The heroic Samson . . . whether prompted by God or by his own valor, slew at one stroke but a host of his country's tyrants . . . . Samson therefore thought it not impious but pious to kill those masters who were tyrants over his country, even though most of her citizens did not balk at slavery."[28] The passage questions Samson's impulse: "whether prompted by God *or* his own valor" (Milton does not say which prompted Samson); it goes on to say "Samson . . . thought"—*not* Milton thought. Milton is just as equivocal in his tragedy. The messenger who reports Samson's death says that he stood as one who prayed *or* some matter in his own mind resolved (*SA,* lines 1637-38). Nor can the messenger say for certain what created this horrible spectacle—is it providence *or* instinct of nature *or* reason disturbed? If Milton himself was able to answer that question, it was because, and only after, he entered the metaphysical bramble bushes that Hill recoils from.

Neither Hill, nor twentieth-century criticism for that matter, provides us with what we need for interpreting *Samson Agonistes*: a study of the myth, of the meanings that accrue to it in the seventeenth century and that subsequently, in that same century, are stripped from it. After the failure of the Revolution, Samson ceases to be the savior whom the people are to follow—

they have followed him too well already. The moment the
revolutionary dream begins to fade, people begin to talk about
Samson as Roger Williams earlier had done—of God's people,
of Samson, fast asleep in Delilah's lap.[29] Moreover, as it becomes
increasingly clear that Antichrist could, and perhaps during the
Revolutionary years did, disguise himself as a zealous church
member so as to appear in the world as a saint, Samson himself
comes to look like Antichrist. This realization served as a check
upon the tendency to see Samson as one of the Saints against
whom Antichrist wages battle, for it was now more evident than
ever that the Lord's battle would not be fought out in history but
was to be waged within every Christian. Hence the conclusion
that the true exemplar of Christian warfare is Jesus, not Samson;
and the scene of the battle is now the wilderness, not the pillars.
The terms of this contrast had been formulated much earlier by
Richard Bernard. Jesus, a proponent of mental fight, subdues
his enemies by the sword that comes out of his mouth; Samson,
by using the carnal sword of force and violence. Bernard then
amplifies this antithesis in order to differentiate the true from
the false prophet: the one has his wife, the other only his whore;
the one rises into a new life, the other goes down to destruction;
the one lives by the waters of the Gospel, while the other is
drunk with the blood of murder and sacrifice. Such
discriminations, when set against the stories of Jesus and
Samson, also set those figures in dramatic contrast,
discouraging the sort of typological associations that previously
were so common. And Bernard advances still other contrasts,
opposing those who go forth with the everlasting gospel and
those who ignore it; those who are killed for preaching God's
word and those who put others to death, thereby exalting the
sacrifice of blood over the gospel of love. Given this context, it is
noteworthy that Bernard should later invoke the Samson story,
representing Samson as a type of the great dragon and Delilah as
a type of the great whore.[30]

A similar realization had caused John Trapp, before the
Revolution, to say: "follow the way of Christ, assume his
burden, take up the cross" rather than "run[ning] away with it
as did Sampson with the gates of *Gaza*." Christ enables men to

escape the destruction to which Samson had doomed himself and to avoid the afflictions of spiritual blindness, imprisonment, and violent death that are visited upon the Old Testament figure. According to Trapp, Samson's life is marked by "continuance in an evill course"; and thus he is punished, "one Sinne with another."[31] Similarly, though from one point of view Thomas Godwin can see in Samson a figure who begins the deliverance that Christ accomplishes, he also feels compelled to emphasize that as a strong man Samson is but a shadow of the true strong man. Unlike Christ, Samson is a backslider, slipping again and again into sin. Were it not for the fact "that we find his name in the list of the worthies, Heb. xi," says Goodwin, we probably never would have thought Samson a "godly man."[32] Such a view of Samson, gaining prominence during the 1650s and '60s, persisted into the nineteenth century, when it was conceded that Samson is often treated as a regenerate hero, but then allowed that after his death "we find people again in idolatry, accompanied by social crimes of horrible character": "Sampson . . . did not, for all his strength, deliver his countrymen from the Philistines. Strength is the only extraordinary quality which he is recorded as possessing. He was not very moral or very wise."[33] Along with these literary representations, we should probably follow Roland Frye's lead and pursue the treatment of Samson in the visual arts where so often, as in the Medici tapestries, he is surrounded by vast numbers of dead bodies. This is not exactly the kind of tapestry, E. H. Gombrich observes, that one would like in a room.

The partial historical consciousness that Hill brings to *Samson Agonistes* (and, admittedly, is the only consciousness with which modern criticism has armed us) is equally evident in Mary Ann Radzinowicz's *Toward Samson Agonistes*—a book that despite this failing is a brilliant example of, and certain to become the chief model for, future contextual study of Milton's poetry. With total mastery of Milton's canon, Radzinowicz brings all the poetry and prose to bear on Milton's last poem. As it involves *Samson Agonistes*, this book, like Hill's, is problem-raising rather than problem-solving; but if we are ever to see further than Hill and Radzinowicz into the complexities of Milton's tragedy we will do so only by standing on their shoulders.

Toward Samson Agonistes, described in its subtitle as the growth of the poet's mind, is Milton's *Prelude* written by one of his finest critics; and this book is destined to become *the* prelude book to all serious study of Milton's canon, even if its thesis, that Milton's tragedy is his crowning achievement, does not win general acceptance and even if its first and last propositions are too crudely formulated. Milton's dialectic, like Blake's, comprehends an opposite, a negative, a third essence, which must be extirpated if the struggle of contraries is to be redeemed. And Milton's aesthetic commitment to prophecy, Radzinowicz's argument notwithstanding, is a constant—surfacing in the early verse, securing itself in the prose tracts, and not subsiding from but commanding the performance of the last poems.

This book is so thorough in its analyses, so impressive in its learning, so cogent in its arguments, and so acute and authoritative in its insights that one wishes there were no Appendix E, "The Date of Composition of *Samson Agonistes*." Insofar as Radzinowicz has an argument to make, it is made *in extenso* by the book itself. The appendix, not substantive, is merely a rhetorical flourish, marred by obtuseness—and by error. Its purpose is to demonstrate that the poem Milton published last is also his last poem; its strategy is to topple all those who have supported an early dating (i.e., Parker, et al.). The problem is that Radzinowicz's own argument proceeds by misstatement. Initially we are told that William Riley Parker "was the first to show any evidence of uncertainty" about *Samson*'s date. Later, reinforcement comes from what appears to be a comprehensive survey of what Milton's early editors and biographers had to say on this subject (that survey ends with Thomas Newton). It is disconcerting to discover, with no help from Radzinowicz, that Milton's next great editor and biographer, William Hayley, has this to say: "It is to the fate of Vane, with others of that party, and to his own personal sufferings, that the great poet alludes in [*Samson Agonistes*].... The nephew of Milton [Edward Phillips] has told us, that he could not ascertain the time when this drama was written; but it probably flowed from the heart of the indignant poet soon after his spirit had been wounded by the calamitous destiny of his friends."[34] At least one person, unbeknownst to Radzinowicz, questioned, on the basis of Phillips's remark, a late date for the play. Phillips's statement is problematic in the extreme, but context helps to clear up the meaning of at least one phrase that Radzinowicz puzzles over. Phillips is quoted as saying that "doubtless" *Paradise Regained* "was begun and finisht and Printed after the other [i.e., *Paradise Lost*] was publisht, and that *in a wonderful short space*" (p. 387; my italics). Phillips has already explained what causes him to marvel at the "wonderful short space." Hypothetically, there is a three-year period alluded to here, the time from 1667 to 1670; but in actuality, given Milton's peculiar habits of composition, which Phillips has just described, there is but a year and a half: "That his Vein never happily flow'd, but from the *Autumnal Equinoctial* to the *Vernal* . . . that in all the years he was about this Poem [*Paradise Lost*—and any other poem?] he may be said to have spent but half his time therein."[35] This information, reportedly, comes from Milton himself. The implications of this statement beg for examination, but instead we are turned to Andrew Marvell.

According to Radzinowicz, "The silence of Andrew Marvell (Milton's valued friend) concerning a tragedy by Milton about Samson strongly suggests that *Samson Agonistes* had not been written by 1667, *when Marvell wrote his poem 'On Paradise Lost' "* (p. 390; my emphasis). It is hard to entrust the dating of *Samson Agonistes* to someone who fumbles so badly in the dating of Marvell's poem. No one should object to a critic's challenging commonplace, but one should know first what the commonplaces are and why this particular one has achieved the status of historical fact. "On *Paradise Lost*" is Marvell's last poem, written as a defense of Milton in the aftermath of Richard Leigh's attack upon him (written, that is, in 1673 or early 1674). Milton himself, by the way, contemplated writing his own rejoinder. All the evidence militates against Radzinowicz's unsubstantiated assertion that the poem was written in 1667. First, the last verse paragraph of "On *Paradise Lost*" is by all accounts a response to Milton's own remarks on rhyming verse, which were not published until 1668, and perhaps also to Dryden's *The State of Innocence*, which dates even later (lines 18-22 of the poem are often cited in support of this latter hypothesis). Second, Marvell's reference to that "slender book" (line 2) presumably alludes to the fact that the quarto of 1667 is now being re-presented as an octavo volume (at least this is the construction that most of Marvell's editors have put on the line). Third, the poem takes up, one by one, the charges leveled against Milton by Richard Leigh in *The Transproser Rehears'd* (1673). In light of this evidence, other of Radzinowicz's assertions become doubtful: "Marvell refers to a blindly destructive 'Sampson' quite unlike Milton's Samson . . . . That Marvell mentioned Samson suggests that, although he cannot have seen the play . . . he may have heard of the plan for a tragedy on the subject" (p. 390). Related to this comment is one made earlier in the book:

> It is . . . clear from the image Marvell gives of "Sampson . . . in spight" . . . that he could not have seen or known or ever heard of Milton's *Samson Agonistes* . . . Milton's Samson . . . is no spiteful groper. The probability is strong that had Milton already written *Samson Agonistes* by 1667 . . . Marvell would have known of it. It would then have been too great an impropriety for Marvell to willfully liken Milton to a destructive Samson when Milton had already treated a regenerative Samson. [pp. 269-70]

One measure of the range of critical speculation in the books of this year is the fact that Christopher Hill is absolutely certain that Marvell knew of, and that he probably read, Milton's tragedy. It seems to me that *he* is right.

If we discount, as I think we must, the 1667 date for Marvell's poem, we are left with the argument that if Milton had written and published his poem, Marvell, a familiar acquaintance, would surely have known of it. *Samson Agonistes* was published in 1671, Marvell's poem written in 1673. Not only would Marvell have known of Milton's tragedy, he probably would have read it by now. Thus we are left to ponder the "impropriety," or propriety, of Marvell's allusion to Samson and of the attendant comparison, or rather contrast, of Milton and Samson. Marvell's poem is self-evidently a defense of Milton against his detractors, an attempt to mediate between Milton and his audience. The point of the allusion (it plainly asserts a contrast) is to forestall further identification of Milton with Samson, an identification that had already been encouraged by Edward Sexby: "I answer with the learned *Milton* that if God commanded these things, 'tis a sign they were lawful and commendable . . . . Neither *Sampson* nor Samuel alleged any other cause or reason for what they did, but retaliation, and the apparent justice of the actions themselves."[36] There may be identity between Samson and Milton in the tragedy, but there is also distinction, and Marvell's strategy here is to underscore the latter and thereby distinguish Samson the false prophet and destroyer from Milton the true prophet and creator, the one figure losing his life and the other being providentially spared his. That Marvell says so little in this regard is itself revealing—is evidence of sorts that a new understanding of the Samson story has begun to prevail, the Samson myth now being used to provide a critique of the revolutionary effort and to support the proposition that the cause was too good to have been fought for. Such an historical context is excluded from Radzinowicz's book, as it is from Hill's. Its omission by no means nullifies the validity of their shared interpretation, but is does affect the way they read the play and construe the contexts they invoke to explain it.

Toward Samson Agonistes evinces none of the flaws of its final appendix. Its strategy is to lead us on, a little further on, step by step and context by context—through Milton's dialectical philosophy, into his conception of history, and out again into his politics, ethics, theology, and poetics. The result is a sustained, compelling reading of *Samson* in terms of the interpretation accepted by critical orthodoxy: a drama of individual regeneration that promises cultural renewal. Never has the play, from this perspective, received so thorough an analysis nor so elaborate a justification. However one wishes to read the play, this book establishes conclusively that *Samson* is "a unified, coherent, strongly ordered work of spiritual architecture" (p. 6). This is *the* book for those who espouse *its* interpretation—tactful, learned, subtle, and (given its biases) convincing. If the book falters, it does so only by departing from its own critical manifesto, which asserts that criticism is a collaborative effort and which implies that, like *Samson* itself, it involves a dialectical procedure. Radzinowicz has adopted one perspective on this play—has advanced its premises, elucidated its implications, and authenticated its conclusions. The "thesis" is here given its finest elaboration and fullest exposure. The "antithesis," however, represented by John Carey, Irene Samuel, and Donald Bouchard, though given modest representation, is not seriously encountered and so not really disposed of either.

Like Samuel, who has clearly been a guiding hand in this book, Radzinowicz surveys a gathering of passages from Milton's prose works, all of which are said (and generally agreed) to make significant reference to the Samson story. Where Samuel reads black, however, Radzinowicz reads white. The relevant passages will be well known to Miltonists: the one in *The Reason of Church-Government* where Samson is likened to a king, his locks to the law, and Delilah to the clergy who, shearing Samson's locks, would deprive the king of his strength; in *Areopagitica* where Samson, though not named, is identified with the strong man (the English nation) rousing himself from sleep; in *Eikonoklastes* where Samson now represents the degradation of the national leader; in *The First Defense* where it is said that whether by God's power or his own Samson thinks it proper to hurl down the pillars on the Philistines; and in Book IX of *Paradise Lost* where Samson is shown succumbing to Delilah. It might be argued (I think it should be argued) that these references are usually neither positive nor negative but ambivalent. It should also be noted that no poet had a greater sense than Milton of the power of allusion, that here the allusions are sometimes direct, other times implied, with real purpose, and that if one considers the latter, at least another reference from *Eikonoklastes* must be added to the list, and that if one adds another category, one of significant silence, still another passage comes under scrutiny. There is, besides, the allusion to the Samson story in Marvell's poem; and that poem, printed at the portal of *Paradise Lost*, constitutes another, albeit negative, allusion.

Of the explicit references, the one in *The First Defense* is most favorable; but like all other such references it is qualified. Samson *thought* himself pious in hurling down the pillars, but it is not clear whether he does so because he is divinely propelled or self-motivated. That has always been the chief question in interpreting the Samson story, and Milton is steadfast in his refusal to commit himself either way. Context also qualifies any positive construction placed upon this reference. Samson is a warrior, the hero here of the New Model Army, though at the same time that Milton is praising the army for its effort he is quietly exalting himself, his own effort, above the army and its effort: the greatest of all heroes, Milton will explain in *The Second Defense*, fight not with the sword but with the pen, are engaged in warfare not carnal but spiritual. Much earlier, in the allegory of *The Reason of Church-Government*, Samson is king and his locks the law, identifications which are complicated by the fact that Milton does not have much truck with kings and, here, is concerned with asserting the primacy of the new over the old dispensation. Milton also concludes this account by reporting that Samson's final act brings great affliction upon the hero.

There are two other explicit references to Samson: in *Eikonoklastes* where he is the duped leader and in *Paradise Lost*, the duped lover. As for the implicit allusions, they are even more problematic. The first, mentioned by Radzinowicz, occurs in *Areopagitica* where the English nation is likened to a strong man rousing himelf from sleep and shaking his invincible locks. Samson is not named, it is sometimes suggested, because Milton wishes to avoid the suggestion of cultural holocaust, his concern here being with cultural renewal. It should also be noted, however, that 1643 is the year that Joseph Mede's commentary on the Book of Revelation (*A Key to the Revelation*) got by the censor. Its preface, written by Dr. Twisse, contains several sentences that may have an important bearing on this passage. There Twisse speaks of "God awaking . . . out of a sleep . . . like a giant refreshed . . . : and the Lord Christ awaking, and stirring

up his strength."[37] Here Milton may very well have omitted
specific reference to the first Samson because his reference is
really to the second Samson who succeeds, unlike the first, in
delivering his people. In *Paradise Lost* Milton is a second
Moses; England, a second Chosen People. In *Areopagitica*, most
likely, England is likened not to the historical Samson but to the
true Samson who effects not devastation but deliverance. The
second oblique reference, comparable to this one but not
mentioned by Radzinowicz, occurs in *Eikonoklastes* where
Milton speaks of those governors of nations who are "overswaid
. . . under a Feminine usurpation."[38] Samson, judging from
other references (see *SA*, lines 1058-60), would clearly represent a
type of such usurpation. And it is precisely this construction
that is placed upon the Samson story in *Paradise Lost*, where we
encounter, in unexpected quarters, another "employment" of
the Samson story, this time in the form of a significant silence.
Paradise Lost concludes, as Radzinowicz observes, with an
overview of history that "includes the life of Samson," and this
overview, she allows, receives "the curtest possible treatment,"
she thinks because of "the pressure of time": in *Samson
Agonistes*, Milton "supplies . . . what was here omitted" (pp.
289, 290). Given Radzinowicz's premises, this is a logical
conclusion. Given another set of premises, however, it is equally
logical to assume that his silence is calculated. In a poem filled
with political allusion, a reference, however abbreviated, is
possible; and such a reference, surely, would not steal the
thunder from Milton's later poem. If this were a concern, Milton
would have deleted from *Paradise Lost* the extended story of
recovering paradise that sprawls over Books XI and XII.

Once we tabulate these allusions, direct and oblique, what is
perhaps most important is that we discern an overarching
pattern suggested by them: the Milton of *Areopagitica*, if the
primary reference is actually to Samson, is concerned with
relating one phase, the supposed triumphant phase, of Samson's
life to English history. The later Milton, on the other hand,
reverts to an earlier phase in the Samson story, his objective
being to relate man's tragedy and England's tragedy to the
defeated Samson. My point is not that Radzinowicz is untrue to

Milton's poem, only that she is unfailingly true to an ideological perspective on that poem which, when the evidence is in, may have to be adjusted. Her book is written in support of the thesis that *Samson Agonistes* is Milton's "last testament," his "great summation" (pp. xviii, xix), embodying his "most advanced theological position" and enacting "his most revolutionary poetics" (p. 269). *Samson Agonistes*, Radzinowicz argues, "contains a free and open-ended theology that seems fully to have satisfied Milton" (p. 271). It is these suppositions that Milton criticism has already begun to debate and that now, so sharply focused, it is certain to debate for years to come. In this sense, *Toward Samson Agonistes*, speaking of what criticism is generally, prophesies what it will be particularly: a "building site" where Miltonists must now assemble and enter into a cooperative effort, which will enable criticism, especially of Milton's tragedy, to progress in a manner that resembles the quest for truth in *Areopagitica*. *Toward Samson Agonistes* is not only the finest critical effort of this year; it is one of the several finest of this decade. But this is also a book whose real strength resides in its substructure, not in its overarching thesis; the book will be remembered for what it says on its approach to *Samson Agonistes*, not just for what is says about the play itself.

There will always be those (and perhaps they will always constitute a minority) who challenge the controlling thesis of this book; but many of its subtheses should win universal assent: "The triad of . . . poems in the last years . . . calls for an order of analysis which moves among them and within them" (pp. xiv-xv); "the fullest response to Milton's poetry . . . comes from interpreting its message in relation to its evolution within the corpus of his works" (p. xix); Milton "created in form what he perceived was latent in content" (p. 3). Or in terms of *Samson Agonistes*: "when Milton recast the biblical story of Samson . . . he did so to challenge the preconceptions of his day" (p. 6); "to secure the ends of tragedy . . . Milton did not resort to a scholarly mode but undertook to revolutionize and modernize the genre" (p. 12); "the play works closely from scriptural sources" (p. 23), especially the Psalms and the Book of Job, Milton's reading of which issues in "the double ethical insights of *Paradise*

Regained and *Samson Agonistes*" (p. 260); "the sonnets are
expressive of a sense of community which Milton never lost" (p.
118), and together with *Lycidas* they illustrate the "embedded
political force" of so much of his verse (p. xxi); and *Paradise
Regained* is the "companion piece" of *Samson Agonistes*, the
two poems revealing an elaborate system of parallels (p. 227).
These theses are not merely asserted; they are given brilliant
demonstration.

The ultimate counsel of this book is that "Milton read
Scriptures in the way one should read Milton, attentive to
progressive relevancies" (p. 279) and that, like the scriptural
books, Milton's works are mutually reflective, mutually
illuminative of one another. No longer is the individual poem—
now the canon is—the critic's field of inquiry; and his
responsibility is one of "choosing and shaping contexts" (p. xv).
T. S. Eliot thought that the function of criticism was
elucidation. Judged by this criterion, *Toward Samson Agonistes*
excels enormously; but Radzinowicz's book is more than
elucidation and interpretation: it is exemplary exposition and
thus a model for the way in which Milton criticism should
henceforth be conducted. No longer will we be inattentive to
"processive discoveries and progressive relevancies" (p. xxi). In
this sense, to appropriate this time one of Eliot's haunting and
celebratory phrases, *Toward Samson Agonistes* is a book that
"states immensely."

To speak of a "new" Milton criticism is to imply that there is
a now old Milton criticism, that what is currently emerging
from the presses is different (notably so) from what has been
issuing from them. Start with the titles. Of those under review,
Milton and Sex is the most flashy, appears to be most trendy.
But the book itself is a rather conservative, albeit interesting,
encounter with its subject—is typical, moreover, of those studies
of the seventies which, for the most part, have been carved on
cherry stones rather than in marble. Examples of the
monograph-book abound as the recent publications by the
following authors testify: William Riggs, Keith Staveley, Austin
Dobbins, Burton Jasper Weber, Thomas Wheeler, Hugh
Richmond, and E. L. Marilla. In contrast, the books by Roland

Frye, Christopher Hill, and Mary Ann Radzinowicz are remarkable for their spaciousness: each of them is an extensive, in some way definitive, exploration of its subject; each is impressive for the leisure with which it conducts its argument, and for the fact that their respective arguments have very few loose ends. Critics, like legs, apparently need space to stretch out in. One thing that is new, then, is that Milton, after nearly a decade, is again the subject of *real* books. And in this regard Princeton University Press, through two of these books, has set a standard for other presses to emulate.

In 1957, the late Rosemond Tuve took to the BBC to lament the then current state of Milton studies: the prestige of historical studies had reached a nadir, books without footnotes were the idol, the whole discipline required to write them was unpopular. In twenty years' time the situation has altered considerably: Miltonists have returned to the rigors of scholarship without withdrawing the rewards of interpretation. They have, as if in direct response to Tuve's appeal, provided us with a series of contextual studies which set, especially the last poems, against a backdrop from which they can be studied anew.

Contextual studies have, moreover, reached a new plateau of sophistication as is suggested by the felt need to discriminate between kinds of contextualism. There are, as Radzinowicz explains in her preface, the historical contextualists (represented here by Frye and Hill): they formulate their explications "in terms of the contemporary structure of feeling and thought from which . . . [a work] derives and which it expresses" (p. xiii). In tandem, there are the "author-contextual" readers (like Le Comte and Radzinowicz herself): they are interested in "contextual placement," their objective being to bridge "the gap between the intrinsic of formalistic study of literature and the extrinsic or casual study of literature"—"to offer insights into the creative process as a continuous and subtly changing activity" (p. xiii). Both Le Comte and Radzinowicz do this, but with different degrees of success. Outside Milton studies, Earl Wasserman has provided the most eloquent articulation of their purposes:

To commit oneself to literary interpretation is necessarily to enter
the unending hermeneutic circle, with its promise of progressive
revelation. Part and whole being interdependent, the full meaning of
the part is contingent upon its role in the totality, but the nature and
significance of the totality are functions of its parts . . . . The
fundamental requirement of interpretation is always the determination of context, that is, the principle by which the parts perform their
constitutive function; and our interpretative disagreements are usually
disagreements over what the relevant context is, over whether we have
the right framework for putting the work together organically.[39]

And Wasserman is equally aware, as Miltonists are becoming
aware, of the extent to which poetry and criticism are involved
in a dialectical process that, in criticism, evolves into a
collaborative enterprise. At the extremes of that dialectic are
ideological differences (they have plagued Milton studies from
the very beginning). They may never be reconciled, but they
should be recognized and mediated. At the center of the process
is the interchange between criticisms and critics: the
structuralists in dialogue with the contextualists, this critic
contending with that one. All too often, though, the interchange
has been conducted among contemporaries with the result that
critics of one age are disenfranchised by those of another. This
tendency is particularly evident in Milton studies: *A* will
converse with *B* if *B* is at the forefront of recent criticism, but
neither *A* nor *B* will converse with *C* if *C* happens to belong to
another century. The foundations of Milton studies were laid
long ago, in the eighteenth century, by Addison and Dennis and
Johnson (who are remembered) but also, and more importantly,
by Newton and Warton and Dunster (who tend to be forgotten).
Milton criticism needs to return to its origins, and a "new"
Milton criticism ought to be mounted on those secure
foundations.

There has also developed in Milton studies a conspicuous and
perhaps predictable antagonism between English and American
criticism. The two cultures have been, and to a certain extent
remain, at odds in Milton criticism. As one listens to
Christopher Hill upbraiding the neo-Christians today, he may
remember yesterday when William Empson sniped at the whole
American establishment of Miltonists through his chiding of

"the American," "the Christian," Mr. Diekhoff (he didn't dare turn his guns on C. S. Lewis!). It is true that the American Milton industry quietly complains that the plant in England is not producing to its capacity, only to find a rude voice shouting back: *you* are producing too much, too quickly, and it is of inferior quality. A passage in Christopher Hill's book immediately comes to mind, for in it we see national pride exercising itself with a vengeance:

Milton needs to be defended from his defenders almost more than from the declining band of his enemies. There is the immensely productive Milton industry, largely in the United States of America, a great part of whose vast output appears to be concerned less with what Milton wrote (still less with enjoyment of what Milton wrote) than with the views of Professor Blank on the views of what Milton may or may not have written. Milton has been described as "the poet of scholars and academic critics"—no longer either a people's poet or a poet's poet. What a fate for the arch-enemy of academic pedantry: better dead than alive, surely! [p. 3]

Therein may lie an unsettling truth. England has been notable for the quality of its criticism—and for critical squabbling. But since those important books of the sixties (by J. B. Broadbent, 1960; Christopher Ricks, 1963; and C. A. Patrides, 1966), she has been silent. In the meantime America has been grinding at the mills, not always—but sometimes—with impressive results. But even about these successes England has been notably silent. Yet silence is golden when it is finally broken by the Oxford don and by Lady Radzinowicz (who may be said to possess and so to represent the best of both worlds: a Columbia education and a Cambridge teaching post). Hill and Radzinowicz together have helped to push Milton criticism in new directions and have defined for it new destinations. They have put Milton back into history and back into context with an intelligence and sophistication that future criticism will emulate. Their books will be its handmaidens, displaying as they both do a "heroism of mind" that, as John Steadman relates the concept to criticism, "is . . . achieved . . . not through consistent caution, but through occasional risk."[40]

Notes

1. *The Art of Presence: The Poet and Paradise Lost* (Berkeley and Los Angeles: Univ. of California Press, 1977), p. 9.

2. "The Epic as Pseudomorph: Methodology in Milton Studies," *Milton Studies*, 7 (1975), 23. There will be those, of course, who would like to modify this statement in order to say that Milton criticism is now adding imagination to reason.

3. See both Trapp's "The Iconography of the Fall of Man," in *Approaches to Paradise Lost*, ed. C. A. Patrides (Toronto: Univ. of Toronto Press, 1968), p. 258, and Collier's *Milton's Paradise List: Screenplay for Cinema of the Mind* (New York: Knopf, 1973), p. xiii.

4. See both Pointon's book, published in 1970 by the University of Manchester Press, p. 111, and Schiff's *Johann Heinrich Füsslis Milton-Galerie* (Zurich: Fretz and Wasmuth, 1963), p. 67.

5. *The Romantics on Milton: Formal Essays and Critical Asides*, ed. Joseph Wittreich (Cleveland: Press of Case Western Reserve Univ., 1970), pp. 453-54.

6. See both Warton's edition of *Poems Upon Several Occasions* (London: Printed for James Dodsley, 1785), p. 154, and Peck's *New Memoirs of the Life and Poetical Works of Mr. John Milton* (London: n.p., 1740), pp. 66-67.

7. See both *The Geneva Bible: A Facsimile of the 1560 Edition*, ed. Lloyd E. Berry (Madison: Univ. of Wisconsin Press, 1969), New Testament, p. 116, and Davidson's *A Dictionary of Angels* (New York: Free Press; London: Collier-Macmillan, 1967), p. 102 (my italics).

8. *Paradise Lost*, ed. Newton, 9th ed., 2 vols. (London: Printed for Rivington et al., 1790), II, 40. For Newton's remarks on Raphael's painting, see II, 50.

9. See *Paradise Regained*, ed. Newton, new ed., 2 vols. (London: Printed for Strahan et al., 1785), I, 31.

10. For Dunster's remark, see *Milton's Paradise Regained: Two Eighteenth-Century Critiques*, ed. Joseph Wittreich (Gainesville, Fla.: Scholars' Facsimiles and Reprints, 1971), p. 245.

11. *Paradise Lost*, ed. Newton, I, 302, 449.

12. *Milton's Paradise Regained*, ed. Wittreich, p. 260.

13. *Paradise Lost*, ed. Newton, I, 65-66.

14. *Iconography of Christian Art*, trans. Janet Seligman (Greenwich, Conn.: New York Graphic Society, 1971), pp. 143-44 (my italics).

15. *Milton's Paradise Regained*, ed. Wittreich, pp. 36, 53.

16. On Aldrich's sources and their derivations, see Suzanne Boorsch, "The 1688 *Paradise Lost* and Dr. Aldrich," *Metropolitan Museum Journal*, 6 (1972), 136-49. And for examples of such illustrations, see *Il Paradiso Perduto*, 2 vols.

(Paris: Giovanni Alberto Tumermani, 1740), and by the same publisher the different edition of 1742.

17. See *Spenser and Literary Pictorialism* (Princeton: Princeton Univ. Press, 1972).

18. Hughes's only book, *Ten Perspectives on Milton* (New Haven: Yale Univ. Press, 1965), concludes with this essay (see pp. 240-75); and see, too, Richmond's *The Christian Revolutionary: John Milton* (Berkeley and Los Angeles: Univ. of California Press, 1974).

19. *Appendix to the Memoirs of Thomas Hollis*, comp. by Francis Blackburne (London: [Printed by J. Nichols], 1780), pp. 612-13, 615 (my italics).

20. The passage is quoted by Marjorie Reeves in *The Influence of Prophecy in the Later Middle Ages: A Study of Joachimism* (Oxford: Clarendon Press, 1969), p. 292.

21. *Leviathan*, ed. C. B. MacPherson (Middlesex, Eng.: Pelican, 1968), p. 662 (IV. 45).

22. See, e.g., Hugh Farmer, *An Inquiry into the Nature and Design of Christ's Temptations in the Wilderness* (London: Printed for A. Millar, 1761). Farmer published an appendix to this commentary in 1765, along with a second enlarged edition; and a third edition, with still more additions, was published in 1775. For Cates's commentary, which follows Farmer's and invokes Milton as an authority, see *Lent Sermons: or, An Inquiry into the Nature and Design of Christ's Temptations in the Wilderness* (London: Printed for C. Cradock and W. Joy, 1813).

23. See Dyke's *Michael and the Dragon, or Christ tempted and Satan foyled* (London: Printed by John Beale, 1635), p. 318. I am using the sixth impression (the first dates from ca. 1614). See also Archer's *The Personall Reign of Christ upon Earth* (London: Printed by Benjamin Allen, 1642), p. 18.

24. Dyke, *Michael and the Dragon*, p. 242; but also Andrewes, *The Wonderfull Combate (for Gods glorie and Mans Salvation) between Christ and Satan* (London: Printed for John Charlwood, 1592), pp. 69-74.

25. Neither Krouse's work nor Di Salvo's is mentioned by Hill; see Krouse's *Milton's Samson and the Christian Tradition* (Princeton: Princeton Univ. Press for Univ. of Cincinnati, 1949), and Di Salvo's " 'The Lord's Battells': *Samson Agonistes* and the Puritan Revolution,"*Milton Studies*, 4 (1972), 39-62. Di Salvo's essay, especially, has great bearing on Hill's argument.

26. *Milton's Samson*, p. 72.

27. *Appendix to the Memoirs of Thomas Hollis*, p. 624.

28. *The First Defense*, in *Complete Prose Works of John Milton*, ed. Don M. Wolfe et al. (New Haven: Yale Univ. Press, 1953—), IV, i, 402.

29. Hill knows of this tradition, for he cites Roger Williams's remarks in *Antichrist in Seventeenth-Century England* (London: Oxford Univ. Press, 1971), pp. 126-27.

30. *A Key of the Knowledge for the Opening of the Secret Mysteries of St. Johns Mysticall Revelation* (London: Felix Kyngston, 1617), pp. 34-36.

31. *God's Love-Tokens, and the Afflicated Mans Lessons* (London: Richard Badger, 1637), pp. 42, 63, 113-14, 141.

32. See Goodwin's "The Folly of Relapsing after Peace Spoken" and *Of Christ the Mediator*, in *The Works of Thomas Goodwin*, 12 vols. (Edinburgh: James Nichol, 1861-66), III, 419; V, 152-53, 158.

33. See the anonymous *Song of the Prophets* (London: Orr and Smith, 1835), pp. 91-92.

34. *The Life of Milton*, ed. Joseph Wittreich (Gainesville, Fla.: Scholars' Facsimiles and Reprints, 1970), pp. 165, 167-68. I am quoting from the second edition, published in 1796; the first, expurgated, edition was published in 1794.

35. *The Early Lives of Milton*, ed. Helen Darbishire (London: Constable, 1932), p. 73.

36. *Killing, No Murder* (1659), quoted by William Riley Parker, *Milton's Contemporary Reputation* (Columbus: Ohio State Univ. Press, 1940), p. 97.

37. Mede's commentary was translated by Richard More and introduced by Dr. Twisse (London: Printed for Phil. Stephens, 1643), unpaginated preface.

38. *Complete Prose Works*, III, 421.

39. *Shelley: A Critical Reading* (Baltimore: Johns Hopkins Press, 1971), p. vii.

40. "The Epic as Pseudomorph," p. 25.

New Approaches to the Trollope Problem

Francis Russell Hart

James R. Kincaid. *The Novels of Anthony Trollope*. Oxford: Clarendon Press, 1977. xiii, 302 pp.

John Halperin. *Trollope & Politics: A Study of the Pallisers & Others*. London: The Macmillan Press Ltd.; New York: Barnes and Noble, 1977. x, 318 pp.

If Henry James had not committed his memorial partial portrait of Anthony Trollope, modern Trollopians would have had to invent it. For most of them begin with a kick at that partially straw man. James's essay is not without genuine insight and admiration, but one hears only of two major complaints. First, Trollope persisted recklessly in intruding upon, and destroying, the illusion of reality in his fiction. Second, Trollope was a master of the commonplace and chronicled it without "strong intrinsic tone." James Kincaid sets about defending Trollope against the first with a genre study fueled by the post-Jamesian poetics of Frye and Wayne Booth. John Halperin attacks the second in an exhaustively documented reading of Trollope's conservative political attitudes, chiefly in the Palliser novels. Taken together—not easy, since two books could hardly be more different—they help to explain why Trollope seems to the modern reader at once so comfortably remote (Victorian pastoral) and so uncomfortably familiar (the complex ambiguity that C. P. Snow and Ruth apRoberts have identified as relativism or Situation Ethics). These two books also arouse slight nostalgia for the naive days before Trollope became a subject for academic criticism.

Ten years ago Gordon Ray rejoiced that Trollope had so far survived without academic resuscitation. Some of us, nodding approval, could recall delightful chance encounters with other closet Trollopians. Peter Taylor told me once that anyone who disliked Trollope simply did not comprehend the essential novel, and I understood and agreed. Some of us had our anecdotes of the sort Elizabeth Bowen dramatized in 1946 on the BBC: a young soldier, leaving for the front, stops by to bid an uncle farewell, asks for a book to take with him, specifies Trollope, and shocks his earnest uncle. It is understandable, then, why Lionel Stevenson would have to report in 1966 that "there is something of a chaos in Trollope studies" (*Victorian Fiction: A Guide to Research*). But that innocent anarchy was not to last.

Thesis directors (myself included) had already caught the bug from A. O. J. Cockshut's pioneering *Anthony Trollope: A Critical Study* (1955; reprinted in America, 1968) with its thesis that "Trollope is a gloomier, more introspective, more satirical, and more profound writer than he is usually credited with being." The sixties produced numerous dissertations, and from them came the books and articles that have made the past decade for Trollope a time of academic revival. "With the work of recent critics," notes Kincaid, "most notably A. O. J. Cockshut, Robert Polhemus, J. Hillis Miller, and Ruth apRoberts, a new image of Trollope's novels has begun to emerge, one that is certainly more strikingly modern, tougher, more ironic and complex" (pp. 10-11). While accepting the new image, Kincaid and Halperin provide a usefully historical corrective. As the field becomes crowded, critical stances become subtler and critical manners are strained. Kincaid is the inclusive critic: placing himself vis à vis his antecedents, his is a rhetoric of both/and; he finds meaning and value even as he differs. Halperin is the exclusive critic with a rhetoric of either/or, bent on "exorcising" or "laying to rest" the "utter nonsense," the "silly" errors, that persisted until he came along. Kincaid's certainly makes for better manners, but the value of the books had best be sought in spite of manners.

Both face the insoluble problem of how to deal justly but comprehensively in a single volume with such a huge corpus: the novels alone number forty-seven. Old-fashioned enthusiasts relied on vague topical groupings and stressed their favorites. Rebellious modernists claimed a growing pessimism in

Trollope and stressed the "dark" later books. Polhemus sought bravely to consider the whole relative to the portmanteau theme of a "changing world," and apRoberts argued generally for a consistency in Trollope's art, religion, and philosophy: "his distinguishing consistency, his 'one-ness,' can best be thought of as a relativism, arrived at by means of the multiple ironic perspective . . . . His stance is that of what we now call Situation Ethics, and I propose that he has a corresponding Situation Aesthetics."[1] Kincaid (who disagrees persuasively with apRoberts) and Halperin (who disagrees with almost everyone) are more prudent. They focus their attention more sharply, and they must pay the price. For Kincaid arranges all the other novels as "experiments" and "variations" ancillary to the Barset and Palliser series. And Halperin argues a general thesis about Trollope's politics chiefly through an excessively detailed thematic exegesis of the six Palliser novels.

Kincaid's study is formal, and its chief value is in its balanced presentation of Trollope's Victorian form as essentially "mixed," accommodating the "closed" form of his eighteenth-century inheritance to the demands of a new kind of moral realism for "open" form. Kincaid wisely insists that we read Trollope no more as if he were a "modern" than as if he were a late Augustan, and that the "trap" in which Victorian novelists were caught (as described by Barbara Hardy) be seen as rich in possibility. The question remains whether Kincaid's properly historical perspective is properly served by a strong application of Northrop Frye and his mythoi of comedy and irony. Moreover, in the treatments of non-Barset, non-Palliser books, one is sometimes given the impression that Trollope wrote novels "to test methods and values," to "explore the possibilities" of a mode, to "explore . . . the use of unconventional moral centers," with the effect of a "curious formal duplicity or ambiguity" (p. 144). But while such intentions are unlikely, the effect is surely what many readers have found baffling, and Kincaid's emphasis on rhetoric and mode seems to me crucial to an understanding of Trollope's attitudes. Kincaid's is the best book I have read about Trollope's novels.

Halperin's interest in form is limited to his concern with thematic coherence, and that concern is to show that the "social" and the "private"—Halperin is, I believe, mistaken to identify them—are always closely interrelated with the "political." Formal interest is largely excluded by one of Halperin's chief purposes: to prove the extent to which Trollope's is "fiction that is true"—that is, drawn from actual political life and character. He argues this even against Trollope himself, citing the *Autobiography* in one of its most interesting passages:

> The personages with whose names my pages had been familiar, and perhaps even the minds of some of my readers—the Brocks, De Terriers, Monks, Greshams, and Daubeneys—had been more or less portraits, not of living men, but of living political characters .... Now and again there comes a burst of human nature . . . but as a rule, the men submit themselves to be shaped and fashioned, and to be formed into tools .... These are the men who are publicly useful, and whom the necessities of the age supply.[2]

Palliser, Trollope recalls, was otherwise. Now the distinction between "living men" (such as Palliser) and "living characters" is so crucial to the central mystery of Trollope's characterology as to justify quotation here and further comment later. But Halperin's purpose seems to have led to misunderstanding. Trollope does not deny that the "characters" are from the life; he admits he has "had [his] mind much exercised in *watching* them" (*Autobiography*, p. 298; emphasis mine). Rather, his distinction is between two kinds of observed human reality: the "characters" who have relinquished their identities to the pebbly-smoothness of institutional behavior and the "living men" who could not or would not do so.

Halperin's other main thesis is of the nature and importance of politics in Trollope's fiction. One may not have noticed so much previous uncertainty, however, as Halperin alleges: "It has been fashionable, as we know, to say that Trollope's political novels are not 'really' political—that, despite surfaces, there is no politics in them to speak of. It has also been usual for critics to separate the political and social worlds they find in the Palliser novels and to miss or ignore the important ways in

which these worlds are connected" (p. 203). It is true that critics
once argued over which novels to call "political." But C. P.
Snow some time ago referred to Trollope's "studies of the
human political process—as opposed to his sketches of
political ideas, in which he wasn't much interested."[3] Polhemus
speaks of the interdependence in Trollope of private lives and
political conditions and concludes that "his steady interest in
the effects of history and of power relationships on everyday life
made him essentially a political novelist."[4] And apRoberts has
this excellent definition of the central significance of politics for
Trollope: "Politics is not a specialised, sharply demarcated field
of study; it is only the study of social man in his most practical
aspects, man trying to act, to achieve something, not by himself,
but in concert with other men. We can discover the ways of
society through the study of real men functioning in a specific
political structure, or government."[5] Society, in short, has
become the center of politics. As J. S. Mill long ago warned, and
as social theorists (Arendt, Sennett) have more recently argued,
Trollope's century saw the emergence of the "social" as the only
public life, and with it a growing confusion of "public" and
"private." The real pathos of Hardings and Pallisers is that, for
all their public-spiritedness, they can find no effective place in
society; they are shy private men with public moralities.

Or put it this way: The central problem in Trollope is
worldliness—in the sense of wealth and power—and it includes
the political, the social, and the ecclesiastical. The Trollope we
are accustomed to hear described as facilely accommodated to his
own worldly age is the Trollope whose spokesmen—the
Grantlys, the Madame Maxes, the Winifred Hurtles—tirelessly
urge the good to seek wealth and power lest the bad take them
all. The Trollope that puzzles us in such company is the one
whose imagination lives with the Hardings, the Pallisers, even
the Roger Carburys—and, yes, the Madame Maxes when they
resolutely decline their ducal inheritances—the people whose
devotion to moral principle is too personal to allow them to
smooth away their scruples and give all their energies to
acquisition.

Halperin and Kincaid both recognize as central in Trollope a concern for the problematic relations of public and private life. But Kincaid finds in Trollope the view that "public morality, the morality of abstractions and slogans, is no morality at all" (p. 100). Halperin, on the other hand, quotes Dr. Wortle to the effect that "no man [has] a right to regard his own moral life as isolated from the lives of others around him . . . a man cannot isolate the morals, the manners, the ways of his life from the morals of others"; and from *The Claverings* the view that "no man has a right to be peculiar." In short, as Muriel Spark would say, there is no such thing as a purely private morality. In fact, the Ciceronian-Anglican Trollope of apRoberts's interpretation clearly believed in a public morality. But he lived in a time when public morality was turning into "abstractions and slogans"—into unreality, which is to say inauthenticity, of thought and word. So his men of public morality find it growingly difficult to lead public lives. Indeed, Trollope's cardinal aim as a novelist—total intimacy between character and author, character and reader—helped to further the very confusion of public and private that caused the difficulty, for it helped to establish the belief that only intimacy could be real.

Consider the most basic problem of political attitude in Trollope. Commenting on *Phineas Finn* in 1869, the *Dublin Review* wonders: "Mr. Anthony Trollope wishes to become a member of Parliament. It is difficult to understand why he of all men should be smitten by such a sore temptation . . . . He can hardly be supposed to have retained to this time of his life any illusions as to the magic value of the letters M.P."[6] The yearning is still alive in the *Autobiography*, written (as Halperin notes) after *The Prime Minister*. Why? But is this not also the larger question of attitude and tone throughout Trollope: why does he view with such sustained interest and compassion a human world he knows to be seriously flawed, weak, unstable, corrupt—as Lady Carbury is corrupt, as Harding is weak, as Palliser is divided and pedestrian? This question comes down to the central mystery of Trollope's intimate imaginative relationship to certain of his characters.

The passage from the *Autobiography* concerning Palliser, Glencora, and Crawley is revealing in its juxtaposition of the moral and the real. It ends: "Taking him altogether, I think that Plantagenet Palliser stands more firmly on the ground than any other personage I have created" (p. 155). The end follows a sustained emphasis on his scheme of the wide canvas, the conducting of characters from book to book, the growth in reality through a combination of consistency and change. In what sense, then, is Palliser most "firmly on the ground" and thus his creator's favorite? Is it because he is "a very noble gentleman," "as near Trollope's ideal as any," and therefore of unique didactic value?[7] Is it because he served so well as Trollope's "safety-valve," his means of having a "fling at the political doings of the day which every man likes to take"?[8] Or is it because, for all his public status and public morality, he is a "living man," one whose public life has not destroyed his identity and thus one who can be the fullest embodiment of the conflict Trollope felt? The fundamental value conflict in Trollope is revealed when we focus on his complex relation to characters such as these—characters he thought of most because they were most "real," characters who fail to become effectively "public" because they cannot permit institutions to turn them to smooth pebbles, and yet characters whose defensive privacy makes them in the mind of the Trollope of public morality somehow *inferior* (Trollope's word: *Autobiography*, p. 298). "People are not dull to me," says Palliser to Glencora in *The Prime Minister* (quoted by Halperin, p. 224), "if [only] they are real"—if only they satisfy what is called in *The Way We Live Now* "the taste for flesh and blood." But what if shams and abstractions, however distasteful, appear to be of greater public use? What if deception and illusion are social necessities? To cope with such a possibility, Thackeray chose the way of the satirist, displaying the universal sham and leaving the reader with a bewildered sense of vanity. But Trollope rejected the satiric way and chose instead to seek and fashion, through intimacy with his creations, the reality he missed in society, as Rousseau did with his *Héloise*. And because he continued to insist that they be measured by a public morality he was not sure existed, the reader is left with the sense of ambiguity—in rhetoric, in political stance—which Kincaid and Halperin seek so thoroughly to explain in their very different ways.

Notes

1. Ruth apRoberts, *Trollope: Artist and Moralist* (London: Chatto and Windus, 1971), pp. 52, 125.

2. Anthony Trollope, *An Autobiography*, introd. by B. A. Booth (Berkeley and Los Angeles: Univ. of California Press, 1947), pp. 297-98.

3. C. P. Snow, *Trollope* (London: Macmillan, 1975), p. 109.

4. Robert M. Polhemus, *The Changing World of Anthony Trollope* (Berkeley and Los Angeles: Univ. of California Press, 1968), p. 10.

5. apRoberts, *Trollope: Artist and Moralist*, p. 128.

6. Quoted in Arthur Pollard, "Trollope's Political Novels," Inaugural Lecture, University of Hull (1968), p. 5.

7. Ibid., pp. 18-19.

8. Trollope, *Autobiography*, pp. 151, 155.

American Literary Bibliography—
FPAA Style

William Matheson

First Printings of American Authors: Contributions Toward Descriptive Checklists. Matthew J. Bruccoli, Series Editor. Detroit, Gale Research Company, 1977-78. Vols. I-III.

First Printings of American Authors is the most ambitious multiple-author bibliography treating the total output of a wide range of American authors published to date. At the time this review is being written three volumes of a projected four have been published, describing in turn 124, 108, and 60 authors. This total surpasses the 280 authors projected for the *Bibliography of American Literature* and the 186 authors in Jacob Blanck's fourth edition of *Merle Johnson's American First Editions.*[1] Given the diminishing totals as publication has progressed, however, there is now some question whether, with the publication of volume four, *FPAA* will achieve the more than 500 authors promised in the advance publicity.

The serious collecting of contemporary American authors is a relatively recent phenomenon. The traditionally recognized first "bibliography" devoted to modern American literature, the *Catalogue of First Editions of American Authors*, dates back to 1885; and two other works, Herbert S. Stone's *First Editions of American Authors* and P. K. Foley's *American Authors, 1795-1895*, were published in the 1890s.[2] Despite the existence of these pioneer works, David Randall recommended the collecting of modern American writers as a "new path" as recently as 1934. In an essay entitled "American First Editions, 1900-1933," Randall observed that "the rise of an important group of book collectors specializing largely in the first editions of the works of modern authors" dates back "little more than a decade."[3] In the years since Randall's statement, two multiple-author bibliographies of American writers have guided the collector—

the fourth edition of Johnson-Blanck's *American First Editions*
and Jacob Blanck's *Bibliography of American Literature*,
published in six volumes to date, with two more volumes in
preparation. *BAL* differs from *FPAA* in the fullness of its
descriptions, in covering editions beyond the first, in including
a very wide range of secondary items, and in excluding authors
who died after the end of 1930. The Johnson-Blanck
bibliography is more directly comparable, aiming also to
provide abbreviated information enabling the user to identify a
first printing. *FPAA* provides three kinds of information not in
Johnson-Blanck: the publisher's name, information on first
English printings, and reduced facsimiles of at least one title
page for every author and for a sprinkling of dust jackets,
bindings, and bibliographic points. *FPAA* has two levels of
description for English printings. For "featured" authors it
provides as much information about the first English printing
as the first American. For the writers given standard treatment,
information on first English printings is recorded without any
attempt to bracket elements not appearing on the title page and
with no indication of the status of the English printing (whether
a new edition, reprint, etc.). Thirty-four authors are featured in
Volume I and nine each in Volumes II and III. Featured authors
are indicated by an asterisk in the table of contents in each
volume. It would have been much easier to use *FPAA* if the
entries themselves had been marked. In commenting on Volume
I, reviewers have variously cited the figure 33 and 34 for featured
authors. Only 33 authors are asterisked in the table of contents,
but Djuna Barnes is a featured writer, though not so indicated,
on the basis of the treatment of her English printings. The
cumulative index for Volume III gives still another total by
failing to asterisk Robert Creeley, Thoreau, and William Carlos
Williams. That index also gives an inaccurate picture of the
total number of authors in the first three volumes by omitting
John Barth and James Purdy.

A fair assessment of a work of the complexity of *FPAA* can
only be made after extended use. In the limited time in which
this reviewer has worked with the three volumes at hand, he has
been frustrated by the lack of information about the principles

of selection. In the preface to *BAL*, Blanck describes the procedures by which a consensus was reached on the authors to be included, noting that "present popularity" was not a factor. The *BAL* authors, "in their own time at least, were known and read." In the preface to the first edition of *American First Editions*, Johnson notes that "every name represents an author whose works are to-day (1928) being collected to greater or less extent."[4] *FPAA* states as its rationale that it (1) identifies the first printings of "established authors whose work has been the subject of bibliographical scholarship," (2) "makes an initial contribution toward identifying the first printings of authors— many still writing—whose work has not previously attracted bibliographical attention," (3) reflects "the editors' sense of collecting and scholarly interest—and the ability of a contributor to provide a particular list," and (4) is the product of "a special effort . . . to include significant authors for whom no adequate bibliography or checklist is available."[5] Thirteen of the 292 authors included in the first three volumes of *FPAA* have been or will be described in *BAL*. Does their inclusion in *FPAA* indicate that new bibliographical discoveries have been made, that these authors are particularly collected today, or simply that a contributor volunteered to prepare the entry? *FPAA* includes two authors earlier than any in *BAL*—Anne Bradstreet and William Bradford—and the following authors who were potential candidates for *BAL* on the basis of birthdates but who are not included in that work: Richard Alsop, John James Audubon, Mather Byles, Harry Crosby, Theodore Dwight, William Elliott, Frederic Henry Hedge, Samuel Johnson, George Cabot Lodge, Samuel Longfellow, Frances Newman, Elizabeth Palmer Peabody, Elizabeth Waties Allston Pringle, George Ripley, Elihu Hubbard Smith, Bradford Torrey, and Mercy Otis Warren. In the first three volumes *FPAA* treats four authors dropped from the fourth edition of Johnson-Blanck: Thomas Beer, Alice Brown, Hart Crane, and Stark Young, as well as 32 writers who are included in that work.

In *FPAA* there are dozens of authors whose names are completely unfamiliar to this reviewer. The question of who (to use the introduction's terms) is "collected" or "established" is a vexed one, as any rare books librarian who has tried to outguess the future well knows. In the preparation of *FPAA*, was "the spirit of prophecy" one of the guiding principles, unlike the other two works just mentioned? In rejecting the role of prophets, Johnson and Blanck put Hart Crane in the third edition of *American First Editions* but dropped him for the fourth, included Ezra Pound in editions two and three but left him out of four, and never listed the following in any of their editions, despite the fact that they had all published a substantial body of work by 1942: Nathanael West (dead by 1942), F. Scott Fitzgerald (dead by 1942), T. S. Eliot, Marianne Moore, William Carlos Williams, Wallace Stevens, John Peale Bishop, Allen Tate, John Gould Fletcher, Robert Penn Warren, Edmund Wilson, and Gertrude Stein. Though Faulkner and Hemingway got in early (both of them are included in editions two, three, and four) and Steinbeck made it into Volume IV, most of the twentieth-century American writers whose work is most avidly collected today were ignored by Johnson-Blanck. In such a situation a reviewer hardly feels comfortable complaining about the selection in *FPAA*, however much he may regret the failure to find information on an author of particular interest to him and however much he may wonder about the collecting interest in authors he never recalls having seen listed in a dealer's catalog or other usual collector sources. Instead he feels extremely curious about the "admittedly impressionistic" selection procedures employed by the editors (I, xix). Perhaps in devoting many pages to authors whose total output, as recorded in the work at hand, is one (Humphrey Cobb), two, three, or four books, the editors want to be sure they have not omitted some future great. There is some question in these instances whether they might simply have said in the introduction that these authors offered promise for the collector but had published too little to justify their being included at this time. Certainly the inclusion of such authors, the practice of starting the description of each author on the recto of a leaf, the generous spacing within each section, and the extensive use of facsimiles have produced a work vastly larger and more expensive than the fourth edition of Johnson-Blanck, which in one of its many incarnations was available in a pocket-size format.

If, as has often been said, fashions in book collecting follow closely on the heels of published bibliographies, it will be interesting to see what affect *FPAA* will have on collecting. This reviewer would have liked the introduction to have given some guidance to collectors. By emphasizing first printings and by not providing a statement on the importance of later impressions and editions, *FPAA* moves against the drift of present-day collecting. In his brief foreword in Volume I, Fredson Bowers comments on the importance of the private collector and says *"even* [my italics] the cult of 'the first of the firstness' in contemporary novels may lead to the sorting out of evidence that ends with textual significance" (I, xv). Implicit in this remark is G. Thomas Tanselle's point that "the traditions of book collecting have stressed the importance of 'first editions' (meaning first printings), with the result that many copies of first printings have been saved (frequently for their supposed monetary value) and many copies of later printings discarded (because there was little market for them—except as 'reading' copies regarded as replaceable when worn out by other 'reading' copies of any edition)."[6] The editors of the texts of major American writers have forcefully pointed out the need for preservation of later printings and editions. They are part of the evidence and must be scrutinized as carefully as the "firsts."

In any given listing *FPAA* sets out to record in a first section all the works, including books, pamphlets, and broadsides, entirely or substantially by an author; in a second section all books edited or translated by that author, including those with introductions or other material; and in a third section biographical, critical, and bibliographical studies about the author. Since many of the writers included have published relatively little or have not yet been the subjects of close study, the full apparatus is relevant only part of the time. In a standard entry for a first American printing, *FPAA* transcribes the titles in caps. Place of publication and publisher are recorded in abbreviated form. The date is given as it appears in the work. Imprint information not on the title page is bracketed. Enough information is given to identify the first printing, quoted in the precise form used in the book. Facsimiles are a feature throughout, but in Volume III the number significantly increases, in large part accounting for the fact that the 60 authors take almost as many pages as the 124 authors in Volume I (432 pages as compared to 412). The *Guide for Contributors* instructs the compiler of a list to examine the book whenever possible. When copies are not available, "staff researchers at the Library of Congress can provide Xeroxes of title pages, copyright pages, and colophons." When an item cannot be located but is known to exist, the contributor is instructed to include it but to "indicate clearly [that] the entry has been made on the basis of secondary sources."[7] Though occasional items are indicated as "not seen," one would have been happier if all entries prepared from photocopies, without inspection of the actual item, had been marked in some way.

In the introduction the editors observe that it "is both unavoidable and desirable" that "there is considerable flexibility from list to list in FPAA" (I, xx). This surely means "flexibility" in such matters as limiting the number of secondary entries for a writer who has published extensively, not in following the rules for recording information. This question arises because *FPAA* is, even on short acquaintance, a frustratingly inconsistent and inaccurate work. In Volume I, despite clear instructions to contributors on the use of the term *wrappers* (they are defined as synonymous with printed wrappers), the following are encountered: printed paper wrappers, paper wrappers, wrappers, paperbound, pamphlet, and stiff wrappers, all apparently used interchangeably. By Volume III the descriptions are almost entirely standardized in this regard. Though "particular collector interest" is given as the justification for including information in dust jacket variants, no mention is made of the variant in the dust jacket in Sinclair Lewis's *The Innocents*. In 1978 in the auction sale of the Jonathan Goodwin collection, a copy of *The Innocents* in the "first issue" dust jacket brought a price of $500. The birthdate of Jack Kerouac is incorrectly given as 1939. In various instances the existence of advance copies is noted, but two of the most sought-after advance copies, if price can be taken as a fair guide, Thomas Pynchon's *V* and Jack Kerouac's *The Town & the City*, are not mentioned. In Johnson-Blanck there is some attempt to distinguish ephemeral items by indicating their size (as, for example, the four-page and eighteen-page indications for two secondary items in the Edwin Markham section). In *FPAA* the user rarely can visualize the size or the binding of a work being described. It is not safe to assume that a book is bound in cloth when no information to the contrary is provided. In the section on Wallace Stevens, there is no indication that such important books as *Owl's Clover*, the Alcestis Press edition of *Ideas of Order*, or *A Primitive Like an Orb* were issued in wrappers. Since the Stevens section was prepared by J. M. Edelstein, who has published a definitive bibliography of Stevens, the failure to indicate wrappers can only be the result of some confusion in editorial signals. It would be tedious to list all the instances in which Avon books are not listed as being in wrappers. Works with such marked collector interest as Djuna Barnes's first book, *The Book of Repulsive Women*, John Hawkes's first book, *Fiasco Hall*, and Marianne Moore's *Marriage*, to take three instances, are not described as being in wrappers.

Though facsimiles are widely used, the out-of-the-way item that one would most like to see reproduced is often the very one overlooked. Despite the fact that for Flannery O'Connor's small body of work (seven principal entries and one secondary entry in *FPAA*) ten facsimiles of title pages and dust jackets are provided, there is none for a work which this reviewer had not heard of before and in which he was particularly interested, *Some Aspects of the Grotesque in Southern Fiction* ("[n.p., 1960]. 20 copies"). How large is this "book"? Is it really clothbound or is this another instance of failure to indicate wrappers? Is it actually a publication or was it distributed at a lecture or used in course work? Is nothing known about the publisher, or was this information not given because it is not in the work itself? Questions of this kind keep arising when one uses *FPAA*.

The Eudora Welty entries offer a demonstration of various kinds of inaccuracies and inconsistencies. Here again there is no

indication that *Three Papers on Fiction, A Sweet Devouring,*
and *A Flock of Guinea Hens Seen from a Car* are in wrappers.
Throughout the Welty section punctuation not on the title page
is routinely supplied, consistent with grammatical sense. In
other sections of *FPAA* (James Merrill, James Purdy, Robinson
Jeffers, etc., etc.) the contributors do not supply punctuation in
transcribing the title page. The entry for *One Time, One Place*
fails to bracket the date on the title page, though it is not found
there in either the trade or limited printings. Though *A Flock of
Guinea Hens Seen from a Car* has no title page, there is no
indication that a cover title has been used. The entry for the
limited printing of *One Time, One Place* says that it is signed by
the author "on a page [sic] tipped into the book immediately
after the front endpaper." In the limited printing of *The Opti-
mist's Daughter* the tipped-in leaf is in the same place in the copy
examined, but here the *FPAA* entry says that it is "tipped into
the front of the book." Does the tipped-in leaf vary in location
from one copy to another (which should be indicated) or is this a
case of imprecision in description? Though the imprint
information is bracketed for *A Pageant of Birds,* inspection of a
first printing shows that the full imprint appears on the title
page. In the description of one of the secondary entries, the
ephemeral exhibit catalogue of John Rood, the entry transposes
the word order on the title page. There are binding variants not
noted on copies of *The Bride of the Inisfallen* reading "first
edition" on the verso of the title page.

Such a high level of inaccuracy is not typical of *FPAA.* Its
occasional presence suggests that the editors placed too great
reliance on the listings submitted by the contributors. The user,
as a result, is left with constant doubts about the accuracy of the
descriptions. In some instances, omissions rather than errors are
the problem. *FPAA* provides information on book appearances
before an author's first book in a good many cases but omits it
for such widely collected authors in volume one as James Agee,
John Berryman, Hart Crane, Richard Eberhart, and Robert
McAlmon. In the entry for Yvor Winters, a book Winters
translated in collaboration with John Meem (*Diadems and
Fagots*) is not listed, though some dealers have speculated that

this may be his first "book," preceding *The Immobile Wind.* Outright omissions of this kind, however, do not appear to be common in *FPAA.*

Though flawed by inaccuracies and inconsistencies and frustating to use because of its failure to take its users' needs fully into account, *FPAA* contains information about a large number of writers whose work is not otherwise described and makes available compact descriptions of other authors more fully described elsewhere. *FPAA*, in its careful application of the terms *edition, printing, issue,* and *state,* follows commendable standards. The transcription of printed information on the verso of the title page is carefully and accurately done in all entries examined. A distinguished group of contributors has assisted in its preparation. If all the waste space were eliminated and the bulk of this work correspondingly reduced and if the four separate (and very aggravating) alphabets were merged into one, this set could be reviewed with a great deal more enthusiasm. These are matters which could be dealt with in a second edition. If *First Printings of American Authors* reaches a fourth edition, it may well have as warm a place in our hearts as the 1942 edition of Johnson-Blanck's *American First Editions.*

Notes

1. Jacob Blanck, *Bibliography of American Literature,* 6 vols. (New Haven: Yale Univ. Press, 1955-73); *Merle Johnson's American First Editions,* rev. and enl. by Jacob Blanck. 4th ed. (New York: Bowker, 1942).

2. *Catalogue of First Editions of American Authors* (New York: Leon and Brother, 1885); Herbert S. Stone, *First Editions of American Authors* (Cambridge, Mass.: Stone & Kimball, 1893); P. K. Foley, *American Authors, 1795-1895* (Boston: Printed for Subscribers, 1897).

3. David Randall, "American First Editions, 1900-1933," in *New Paths in Book Collecting: Essays by Various Hands,* ed. John Carter (New York: Scribner's, 1934), pp. 193, 197.

4. *BAL,* I, xi; Merle Johnson, *American First Editions* (New York: Bowker, 1929), p. v.

5. *A Guide for Contributors to First Printings of American Authors* (Detroit: Gale, 1977), p. 1.

6. G. Thomas Tanselle, "Bibliographers and the Library," *Library Trends,* 25 (1977), 757.

7. *A Guide for Contributors,* p. 3.

Tromping through Fairyland: Two Books on Melville's Tales

Hershel Parker

Marvin Fisher. *Going Under: Melville's Short Fiction and the American 1850s*. Baton Rouge: Louisiana State University Press, 1977. xii, 216 pp.

William B. Dillingham. *Melville's Short Fiction, 1853-1856*. Athens: University of Georgia Press, 1977. 390 pp.

Aside from juvenilia and a fin of *The Whale* ("The Town-Ho's Story," which appeared in the October 1851 *Harper's*), all of Melville's surviving short stories were written between 1853 and 1856, the year he published *The Piazza Tales* and completed *The Confidence-Man*. There are fourteen stories (seventeen if you count each half of a diptych) and "The Piazza," a sketch written as an introduction to the five *Piazza Tales*. All the stories appeared in two American magazines, *Putnam's* and *Harper's*, with the exception of "The Two Temples," which was rejected by *Putnam's* and remained unpublished until the 1920s. During 1852 and early 1853 Melville had worked on "the story of Agatha" and seems to have submitted it in some form to the Harpers in 1853, but the manuscript apparently does not survive and no published story has been discovered. During 1853 and 1854 Melville worked on a book for the Harpers to be called *The Tortoise-Hunters*, completing substantial portions which are not known to be extant, although some short passages may have been cannibalized for the first two sketches in "The Encantadas." And during 1854 and 1855 Melville serialized *Israel Potter* in *Putnam's* before its publication as a book (1855). Determining the sequence in which Melville composed, submitted, and published the writings of 1853-1856 (which also include a little sketch called "The 'Gees") constitutes a fascinating problem for a literary detective, one of absolutely crucial importance for understanding Melville's life and his artistry. Neither book being reviewed here shows any awareness that such a problem exists.

The Confidence-Man, published in 1857, was the tenth book of Melville's eleven-year career. After it he lived thirty-four years, publishing only four books of poetry, two of them in editions of twenty-five copies each. The year 1857 marked the end of his struggle to meet two contradictory compulsions—to be as popular as he needed to be if he were to support his family and to be as profound as he thought he could be if he gave rein to his imagination and intellect. *Typee* (1846) and *Omoo* (1847) were highly embroidered autobiographical accounts, one of captivity among South Sea cannibals, the other of Polynesian beachcombing. They created few tensions within him, for each was as good as he could write at the time and each was a popular success. To be sure, John Wiley tardily censored *Typee*, but Melville was free to work his resentments into the manuscript of *Omoo* and peddle it to the Harpers. The conflict began in *Mardi* (1849), Melville's massive Rabelaisian and Burtonian grab bag of realistic South Sea adventure, satirical island-hopping in an imaginary archipelago, and allegorical travelog through European and American politics. It was his declaration of the literary independence he was to achieve in *Moby-Dick*, but most reviewers wanted another racy tale from the hearty sailor-writer, not a litterateur's portable symposium on art, religion, philosophy, and politics. To compensate for *Mardi*, Melville wrote the realistic *Redburn* (1849) and *White-Jacket* (1850), both in a four-month stretch in the heat of the New York summer of 1849. He regarded them as "two *jobs*" which he had "done for money—being forced to it, as other men are to sawing wood." While finishing *Moby-Dick* (1851), he wrote to Nathaniel Hawthorne: "What I feel most moved to write, that is banned—it will not pay. Yet, altogether, write the *other* way I cannot. So the product is a final hash, and all my books are botches." In *Pierre* (1852) he undertook his most strenuous challenge: to write a great book that the feminine book-buying audience would accept as "a regular romance, with a mysterious plot to it, & stirring passions at work." Simultaneously, it was to pursue a psychological analysis more profound than any he had grappled with in *Moby-Dick*: "Leviathan is not the biggest fish;—I have heard of Krakens."[1] In early January of 1852, when he was halfway or more through the manuscript, the Harpers assessed its prospects and offered Melville a punitive contract, twenty cents on the dollar after costs instead of the old terms of fifty cents on the dollar. Shattered by the implications of the contract (it meant his career might well be over) and stung simultaneously by belated January reviews of *Moby-Dick*, Melville lost his disciplined concentration and wrote his current turmoil into the manuscript, thereby losing any chance that *Pierre* would be "regular" enough to delude any romance-reader. Even before *Pierre* was published, the New York literary clique gossiped that it showed Melville had written himself out. More than one reviewer called the book insane, and a New York paper printed a sober news item: "Herman Melville Crazy."

In the months after the publication of *Pierre*, Melville's artistic purpose wavered, and his robust young sailor's body deteriorated. Ridden by demons (the palpable debt-demon among them), Melville settled down in his new isolation in the Berkshires to less Titanic literary efforts, the writing of short stories and serials for *Putnam's* and *Harper's*—all anonymous, according to magazine policy, but frequently attributed to Melville by newspaper and magazine editors to whom anonymous authorship was an open secret. Several of the stories between *Pierre* and *The Confidence-Man* are of almost pathological secrecy, innocuous enough to be palmed off on his genteel publishers but concealing outrageous religious, sexual, and mock-autobiographical allegories. At times his literary works became for Melville the means of expressing his true attitudes by elaborately convoluted aesthetic dodges. *Israel Potter* and *The Confidence-Man* are tightly linked to these tales by recurrent subjects, ideas, and character types, by geographical settings, and by recurrent allusions and imagery. Parts of *The Confidence-Man*—some of the stories told by various characters—may actually have been salvaged from magazine pieces that had never quite been put into publishable shape. Like some of the stories, it reveals a love of allegory as inveterate as Hawthorne's own and is written in a shifty, deceptive style appropriate to a once-popular author who had perforce become a literary sleight-of-hand man. None of the intricate relationships between the longer and the shorter works of 1853-1856 is explored in the two books reviewed here. Both books restrict themselves to the stories, except that Marvin Fisher also discusses Melville's last published review, "Hawthorne and His Mosses."

A confession may be useful: after mailing off my Melville chapter for *American Literary Scholarship, 1977*, I caught myself poised on a stepstool in the act of putting both these volumes up with books I keep but don't consult—Vincent Kenny's *Herman Melville's "Clarel,"* R. Bruce Bickley, Jr.'s *The Method of Melville's Short Fiction*, Edward S. Grejda's *The Common Continent of Men*, Charles E. Knolim's *Melville's "Benito Cereno,"* the Penguin *Moby-Dick, The Strange Story of the Great Whale Also Known as Big Mac*, and a poor man's association item, *Pierre of the Big Top. Going Under* and *Melville's Short Fiction, 1853-1856* had to descend for this review, but they will yet make it up to those rarefied realms. For without being at all cynical, opportunistic, or perverse, without being even irresponsible by prevailing academic standards, these are books that we do not need. They are too late for what they are—fair-to-middling critical explications all but indistinguishable from dozens or even hundreds of fair-to-middling critical explications published over the last four decades. As such, they make it futile for a reviewer to attempt to engage in any discussion of the comments on particular stories.

Marvin Fisher and William B. Dillingham seem to have gotten themselves into the business of bookmaking without having bookly things to say. Fisher, who published a dozen or so parts of this short study over the course of a dozen years (it is hard to be sure, since he does not identify which parts had been previously printed), begins with a cagy attempt to "justify and explain the work that follows," since "any informed readers would naturally ask whether we really need another study of Herman Melville's short fiction, whether this work, like much of the literary criticism emanating from university faculties, might be another laborious effort to mine a nearly exhausted vein of medium-yield ore" (p. ix). The real danger was that Fisher might not rise to the challenge of writing memorably about a Golconda of a subject, and his comments reverberate like leftover pleas that a publisher accept his manuscript. There is an oddly makeshift quality about the book, beginning with the spine, where the inexplicable title GOING UNDER goes down.

Dillingham's book is no makeshift affair, and he is correspondingly less defensive. Presumably he had a publisher lined up from the time of his *An Artist in the Rigging* (1972) and could luxuriate in writing a very long book-book without having to publish piecemeal as he composed. But Dillingham has built the whole study (almost twice as long as Fisher's) upon a false premise. "What has not been generally recognized," he says, is that Melville in his short fiction "carried the technique of concealment even further" that in earlier works like *Moby-Dick* and *Pierre*. Melville

> wrote as he did in these stories for two basic reasons: concealment and artistic experimentation. He camouflaged meanings because concealment had already become a characteristic of his nature as a writer, because the articulation of a private vision in coded language, as it were, served the ends of both therapy and art, and because the magazines he was writing for demanded palatable art for queasy minds. One motive furthered the other: greater concealment led to greater experimentation. What appear to be inoffensive and somewhat amateurish sketches composed for the masses are in reality highly sophisticated and poetically compacted works often of unsurpassed originality. [pp. 7-8]

What Dillingham says "has not been generally recognized" has in fact been the cornerstone of modern criticism, from as early as Jay Leyda's 1949 introduction to his edition of Melville's stories:

> The detection of the symbolism in Melville's stories will go on forever with no more help from him than he gives in the stories themselves. Even at first glance they look far from innocent, but the idea that they contain specific, personal undercurrents is generally unrecognized without the aid of such recent pointers as handled by E. H. Eby and Merton M. Sealts . . . . Buried in each story is at least one hint for the hunter; sometimes it is a named book spread open before the searching reader—as Jonathan Edwards' *Inquiry into the Freedom of the Will* is

opened in "Bartleby," or *The Rise and Progress of Religion in the Soul*, by Philip Doddridge, lies conspicuously on the Coulters' chimney-shelf in "Poor Man's Pudding," or John Locke's image (of the newborn baby as a blank sheet of paper) that transforms the "nine minutes" of "The Tartarus of Maids" to nine weary months. Or the search may have to go deeper, into Melville's sources, to throw more light on his intentions.[2]

Leyda says much more in this vein, and so does Elizabeth S. Foster in her introduction to *The Confidence-Man* (1954), an edition which is not mentioned by either Fisher or Dillingham, and the same idea recurs as a critical commonplace in my foreword to the Norton edition of *The Confidence-Man* (1971). Leyda told the simple truth in 1949 when he said Melville's technique was "generally unrecognized," but Dillingham is quite misleading when he says in 1977 that it "has not been generally recognized."

Writing in 1972, Leyda acknowledged that there "are brilliant analysts who have won the right to interpretation," yet insisted that "their imitators are too often motivated by their schools' and their ambitions' demand to show 'more in print'—and if this can be done without leaving your study, all the better." Leyda appealed for professors to turn away from benumbing, piddling criticism and pursue biographical research: "With so much left to be known, how can we allow the present state of our knowledge to freeze and become permanently acceptable? Perhaps we have become too content with the biographical materials already at our disposal. And this contentment leads away from simple logic and towards such habitual self-deceit!"[3] Leyda's indictment applies to Fisher and Dillingham equally. Fisher can write a sentence like this: "Melville may have used a pseudonym [in 'The Encantadas'] because he had accepted an advance from Harper Brothers for a proposed work on the Galapagos tortoise after having submitted 'The Encantadas' to Putman's" (p. 29). (I assume "Putman's" must be a compositorial error for "*Putnam's*.") The sentence would take half a page to straighten out, so I will merely indicate the most obvious fault: the chronology is backwards, for the advance from Harpers came first. This kind of error makes a difference.

Dillingham, likewise, can confidently assert that Melville wrote "Hawthorne and His Mosses" before he met Hawthorne and that Melville transcribed "Monody" on "the title page of his copy of Hawthorne's *Our Old Home*" (pp. 92, 99). Scholarship simply does not speak audibly from the pages of either book.

Consider the order in which Fisher and Dillingham treat the pieces (or "articles," as Melville and his contemporaries often said). Fisher proceeds this way: "Hawthorne and His Mosses"; "The Piazza"; "The Encantadas"; "The Two Temples"; "Poor Man's Pudding and Rich Man's Crumbs"; "The Paradise of Bachelors and the Tartarus of Maids"; "The Bell-Tower"; "Benito Cereno"; "The Lightning-Rod Man"; "The Apple-Tree Table"; "Jimmy Rose"; "The Fiddler"; "The Happy Failure"; "Cock-A-Doodle-Doo!"; "Bartleby"; "I and My Chimney." Fisher's arrangement has so little to do with the sequence of composition or publication that you wonder why he bothers to call *The Piazza Tales* "a short story cycle, with ascertainable lines of connection and integration" (p. xi). He aims openly to disarm the reader: "My approach to these stories [all of them, not just *The Piazza Tales*] is not strictly chronological but rather thematic, though I have kept chronological development in mind and discussed it when it seemed relevant" (p. xi). I don't believe a word of that, for you can't keep chronological development in mind unless you know the chronology, and Fisher plainly does not. He probably means the sequence of publication, which is only a rough guide to the sequence of composition; but even so you cannot plausibly subtitle a book *"Melville's Short Fiction and the American 1850s"* unless you keep in the foreground Melville's chronologically changing responses to the American 1850s, something Fisher fails to do.

Dillingham's order is much nearer the order of publication (or that of submission, in the case of "The Two Temples"): "Bartleby"; "Cock-A-Doodle-Doo!"; "The Encantadas"; "The Two Temples"; "Poor Man's Pudding and Rich Man's Crumbs"; "The Happy Failure"; "The Fiddler"; "The Lightning-Rod Man"; "The Paradise of Bachelors and the Tartarus of Maids"; "The Bell-Tower"; "Benito Cereno"; "I and My Chimney"; "Jimmy Rose"; "The Piazza"; and "The Apple-Tree Table." Much more than Fisher does, Dillingham keeps an eye on "the American 1850s," the contemporary events and journalistic commonplaces which might have affected the tales. With Dillingham you at least know roughly why you are where you are, but neither writer has thought of the possibility that he might clarify the sequence in which Melville composed and submitted the stories. As I said earlier, it strikes me that establishing the order of these pieces is important—that it might even be the first thing a responsible scholar would do if he were planning to write a book about them.

As far as I know, Merton M. Sealts, Jr., is not writing a book about the stories, but he is editing them for the Northwestern-Newberry Edition, due out in 1979. Merely by using documents which have been available to everyone, mainly in *The Melville Log* and *The Letters of Herman Melville*, Sealts has performed an extraordinary act of scholarship in redating the composition and submission of the stories. Without giving interpretive readings himself, Sealts provides evidence for a thorough scholarly-critical rethinking of them all. The next good book to appear on the stories—the *first* really good book to appear on the stories—will study them in the order of their composition, relate them to Melville's experiences in the 1850s, and read them against the background of contemporary events. Also, of course, the writer of such a good book would read the stories along with the longer works written concurrently, *Israel Potter* and *The Confidence-Man*, and study them in relation to all of Melville's writings and his lifelong philosophical, religious, social, and aesthetic preoccupations.

There was no excuse for Fisher's and Dillingham's not working out the chronology of composition and submission as Sealts did, since the evidence was available, but they also had the simple bad luck to go to press just too late to take any account, assuming they wanted to, of some very significant new biographical information, particularly two letters published in *American Literature* (November 1977). Both written in May 1856 to Lemuel Shaw, Melville's father-in-law, they deal with Melville's need to transfer the title of his farm so as to keep it out of the hands of a creditor. Here is new, anguishing proof of Melville's desperate financial plight. The appearance of several such documents has already stamped both books *Out-of-Date*.

Something else must be said: criticism of literary masterpieces should be written in prose that aspires toward the quality of the works being discussed, but neither Fisher nor Dillingham rises even to the level of resourceful competence. Here is Fisher twice tripping over his abstractions and his "as's": "In fact, the concept of point of view is technique as well as theme in these stories and constitutes a good part of Melville's modernity . . . . This concept of point of view as theme as well as technique not only connects Melville's separately published stories, but also joins him and his work with the twentieth century and constitutes a good part of his modernity" (pp. x, 16). Printer's gremlins in this sort of prose are merely accomplices. Within the bodies of Fisher's sentences single words and phrases keep poking out like bones through skin. And the prose in Dillingham's book is relentlessly pedestrian. His device of the reassuringly recapitulative "then" at the outset of his paragraphs is so overworked as to instill suspicion rather than trust. From the chapter on "Bartleby" come these examples: "'Bartleby,' then, is concerned chiefly . . . . This, then, Melville is saying . . . . The lawyer, then presents Bartleby with . . . . Bartleby's portrait, then, is . . . . " Or sample these from the chapter on "The Encantadas": "The shadow of the tortoise, then, is cast . . . . The narrator, then, has seen both sides of the tortoise . . . . These, then, were the subjects that occupied Melville's mind . . . . In Melville's relationship with Hawthorne, then, the green world . . . . " Here is an aesthetic judgment Rex Reed might have formulated: "This passage crackles with irony" (p. 45). Dillingham can unblushingly refer to "the biblical Old Testament," in apparent distinction from other Old Testaments, or else in redundant capitulation to the ignorance of a fallen generation, and he can proceed undizzied by the Ferris wheel effect of this: "Without exception it is impossible to understand these stories without coming to an understanding of the narrative voice" (p. 11). That's dangerous prose to read on a full stomach.

Such writing not only stultifies or startles, it also debases and defiles. While reading Fisher and Dillingham, I found myself stopping again and again to read one of the tales or a part of a tale to reassure myself that the grandeur I remembered was still there. Invariably the power in Melville's stories made these two books look all the drearier by contrast. In this spirit of getting back to the stories, I want to draw this review to a close with the passage from "The Piazza" that Dillingham quotes as conveying the narrator's "exaggerated sense of the length of the journey and the weariness with which he proceeds" (p. 323):

By the side of pebbly waters—waters the cheerier for their solitude; beneath swaying fir-boughs, petted by no season, but still green in all, on I journeyed—my horse and I; on, by an old saw-mill, bound down and hushed with vines, that his grating voice no more was heard; on, by a deep flume clove through snowy marble, vernal-tinted, where freshet eddies had, on each side, spun out empty chapels in the living rock; on, where Jacks-in-the-Pulpit, like their Baptist namesake, preached but to the wilderness; on, where a huge, cross-grain block, fern-bedded, showed where, in forgotten times, man after man had tried to split it, but lost his wedges for his pains—which wedges yet rusted in their holes; on, where, ages past, in step-like ledges of a cascade, skull-hollow pots had been churned out by ceaseless whirling of a flint-stone, ever wearing, but itself unworn; on, by wild rapids pouring into a secret pool, but soothed by circling there awhile, issued forth serenely; on, to less broken ground, and by a little ring, where, truly, fairies must have danced, or else some wheel-tire been heated— for all was bare; still on, and up, and out into a hanging orchard, where maidenly looked down upon me a crescent moon, from morning.

I would have thought that these sequential glimpses into the narrator's mind during his aesthetic adventuring might convey something rather finer than weariness. No matter about such commentaries: the stories do remain, after all, undamaged by the criticism. And when Sealts's edition appears, we can all read them—and *Israel Potter* and *The Confidence-Man*—in the order of their composition and begin all over again our attempts to measure the majesty that infuses so much of the writings of 1853-1856. More profoundly than ever we will feel pleasure and awe in perceiving the complex coherency of Melville's mordant vision of himself and his times, and rejoice in watching the functioning of his new styles forged in private agonies but used at last to communicate, not to conceal.

Notes

1. *The Letters of Herman Melville*, ed. Merrell R. Davis and William H. Gilman (New Haven: Yale Univ. Press, 1960), pp. 91, 128, 150, 143.

2. *The Complete Stories of Herman Melville*, ed. Jay Leyda (New York: Random House, 1949), pp. xxiii-xxiv.

3. "Herman Melville, 1972," in *"The Chief Glory of Every People": Essays on Classic American Writers*, ed. Matthew J. Bruccoli (Carbondale: Southern Illinois Univ. Press, 1973), p. 164.

Bowers's Collected Essays

G. Thomas Tanselle

Fredson Bowers. *Essays in Bibliography, Text, and Editing.*
Charlottesville: Published for the Bibliographical Society of the
University of Virginia by the University Press of Virginia, 1975. viii, 550
pp.

The Bibliographical Society of the University of Virginia has
fittingly honored Fredson Bowers on the occasion of his
retirement as Linden Kent Memorial Professor of English
Literature at the University of Virginia by publishing a volume
of his uncollected essays. The book, carefully and handsomely
produced, contains a generous selection—made by Professor
Bowers himself—from among his most celebrated articles. It is
surely one of the most important books published by this society,
which has made many notable contributions to modern
bibliography, including, of course, its sponsorship of *Studies in
Bibliography*, edited from the beginning by Professor Bowers.
Because the essays have become so familiar, the volume cannot
have quite the same impact which the essays had when they were
first published; but the book nevertheless takes its place as one of
the landmarks in the history of bibliography, for it brings
together a number of essays which have helped change the course
of bibliographical studies, written by the man who has
dominated the field for the last quarter-century. Those who
already know these essays will be glad to have them available in
more convenient form (previously one had to search them out in
various journals and several pamphlets); and some who have not
read them before may now be exposed to them. This volume goes
on the shelf next to W. W. Greg's *Collected Papers* (1966), another
cumulation of seminal pieces, by the scholar who held the field
for several decades before Professor Bowers. And one would need
only add to these two R. B. McKerrow's *An Introduction to
Bibliography* (1927), and perhaps a few other titles by the same

three men, to have a shelf containing the basic documents which created modern analytical, descriptive, and textual bibliography.

The new volume, however, is not to be regarded simply as a collection of documents of historic value: the essays read as well now as when they were written, and many of the points they make are unlikely ever to be stated more forcefully or effectively. Certain minor details, naturally, have been superseded or modified by subsequent research—and in these instances Professor Bowers has generally provided new footnotes citing more recent scholarship. But one turns to this volume less for the facts about particular cases than for the more general statements of rationale, and the essays have clearly been chosen on the basis of the breadth of their significance. They abound in trenchant passages which will remain useful for reference and quotation, and the volume will be a continuing force in bibliographical study. Professor Bowers was therefore right not to undertake any large-scale revision of the essays: in the first place, they do not really require revision; in the second, they have been so widely consulted and quoted in their present forms that the publication of different versions of these classic pieces would create a somewhat awkward situation. What Professor Bowers has done, according to Irby B. Cauthen's foreword, is to make only a few insertions and "some minor deletions." Any "substantial new material" is placed in square brackets, and inserted footnotes are keyed by asterisks (not numbers, as the original footnotes are). Aside from the added citations of scholarship (see pp. 12, 20, 25, 32, 53, 74, 131, 199, 206, 317, 336, 449, 527), the new material consists principally of brief comments which extend the discussion of specific points (see pp. 42, 57, 201, 207, 208, 279, 339, 344, 400, 418, 499). Some of these qualify his conclusions, as when he recognizes that later compositor studies which take evidence only from short lines have marked an advance over the method he used (p. 346); others indicate his evaluations of recent bibliographers, as when he criticizes D. F. McKenzie's "Printers of the Mind" (p. 250) or refers to Philip Gaskell's "general distrust of analytical evidence" (p. 207). Among the most interesting additions are those of biographical anecdote: he describes how G. B. Harrison's eloquence once persuaded him to accept an argument on literary grounds which was later proved wrong on bibliographical grounds (p. 7), and he comments on his "first fumbling approaches to the text of Thomas Dekker" and the two "salutary" shocks, administered by W. W. Greg and J. G. McManaway, which, he says, "assisted me to become a bibliographer" (pp. 8, 205).

The twenty-six essays, which are thus basically unchanged, represent the various aspects of bibliography to which Professor Bowers has made important contributions and in the process reflect his principal interests at different stages of his career. They are sensibly grouped into four sections, the first of which—on bibliography in general—is called "The Bibliographical Way," taking its title from a 1958 lecture at the University of Kansas. This section contains six pieces, ranging from 1949 to 1971. As might be expected of such general statements, all were originally delivered as papers at meetings: "Bibliography and the University" at the University of Pennsylvania in 1949, "Some Relations of Bibliography to Editorial Problems" before the English Institute in the same year, "Bibliography, Pure Bibliography, and Literary Studies" before the Bibliographical Society of America in 1952, "The Bibliographical Way" at Kansas six years later, "Bibliography and Modern Librarianship" in California as the 1966 Zeitlin-VerBrugge and Howell Lecture, and "Four Faces of Bibliography" before a Bibliographical Society of Canada Colloquium in 1971. When placed side by side these essays are not unduly repetitive and constitute a remarkably well-rounded apologia for the whole field of bibliographical work. The fourth and fifth have previously been available only as pamphlets, and the first and last were published in journals which are not everywhere readily available; now it is a simple matter to read them all consecutively, and they should become required reading for all students in the humanities (for that matter, the points they make should be understood by scholars in all fields, since all scholars have occasion to consult printed texts). Because they attempt to convey a way of thinking (as the title "The Bibliographical Way" suggests), each reinforces the others from a slightly different angle, and the final effect is cumulative. Anyone who has read through these 106 pages will have a better understanding of the bibliographical approach than if he had read only one or two of the essays. This part of the book will probably be the least used by practicing bibliographers, for they (or at least some of them) are already well acquainted with the point of view expressed here; but for others—for anyone who wishes to learn what modern bibliography is about and why it is important—this may be the most often consulted section of the book. Certainly it represents one of the best-known aspects of Professor Bowers's career—his role as an ardent advocate of bibliographical study.

The second division of the book takes up descriptive bibliography, the field in which Professor Bowers made his first major book-length contribution to bibliography. His *Principles of Bibliographical Description* was published in 1949, and it remains the work of his which has probably had the widest influence. It codified and further refined the tradition of description which had been developing in the hands of Pollard, McKerrow, and Greg, and it has now been the standard work for nearly three decades. Scarcely any bibliographical description— even an incidental one in an article—has been written in that time which has not been influenced in some way by the *Principles.* Although Professor Bowers published two important articles on description before 1949, what he has chosen for inclusion in the present volume are three essays written after that date, essays which can therefore be said to reflect his thinking on description as it has developed after the time of the *Principles.* The first and third of these are addresses delivered on two occasions, fifteen years apart, before the Bibliographical Society in London (and subsequently published in *The Library*): "Purposes of Descriptive Bibliography with Some Remarks on Methods" (1952) and "Bibliography Revisited" (1967). The former is an excellent basic statement, which strongly affirms the position that bibliography is "an independent discipline of scholarship and not merely an ancillary technique to literary investigation" (p. 134); the latter is a brilliant reflection on the present state of descriptive bibliography, confronting in particular the difficult problem of the relation between the "degressive principle" and the role of a descriptive bibliography as a history of the publication of an author's works (not just of first or important editions). The essay in between, "Bibliography and Restoration Drama," read at a Clark Library seminar in 1966 and published in pamphlet form, is more restricted in scope; but it does record some of the techniques employed in Professor Bowers's long-term project for describing Restoration drama and contains useful statements regarding the importance of the examination of multiple copies and the role of analytical bibliography in description.

The next part of the book turns directly to analytical bibliography and presents six essays, dating from 1941 to 1954. The 1941 paper, "The Headline in Early Books," read before the English Institute in September of that year, is the earliest essay in the volume and the only one from before America's entrance into World War II. Professor Bowers served with the United States Navy during the war, and before that time he had just got started on his investigation of analytical techniques for examining Renaissance books. The first approach on which he published major work was the use of the evidence offered by running titles and headlines—in an article in *The Library* in 1938 and then in the 1941 paper. The study of headlines and the resulting identification of skeleton formes have proved to be powerful tools for establishing in detail the history of the progress of a book through the press, and Professor Bowers's two articles, along with one of Charlton Hinman's in the same volume of the *English Institute Annual*, are the pioneer statements of this technique. Following the war, Professor Bowers continued to explore the implications of running-title evidence, especially what conclusions it would lead to regarding Elizabethan proofreading procedures; and the next two essays, taking Greg's 1940 monograph on *King Lear* as their point of departure, move in this direction: "An Examination of the Method of Proof Correction in *King Lear* Q1" (1947) and "Elizabethan Proofing" (1948). These essays, which have been central in the development of thinking on this subject, are examples of analytical bibliography at its best and should be counted among the principal classics in this field. Two shorter pieces from the 1940s follow: "Running-Title Evidence for Determining Half-Sheet Imposition" (1948), showing another important use of headline study; and "Bibliographical Evidence from the Printer's Measure" (1949), the first formal description of another useful technique. The concluding essay in this section, "Motteux's *Love's a Jest* (1696): A Running-Title and Presswork Problem," from the next decade (1954), is the least important of the six, but it does show Professor Bowers still finding new significance in running titles at a time when his principal interest had turned in another direction. His achievements in the field of analytical bibliography are fairly represented by this selection of essays, though none of them lays the general foundations of the study in quite the same way as two of the essays on descriptive bibliography do for that field. He has, however, performed that service elsewhere: his Lyell Lectures (*Bibliography and Textual Criticism*, 1964)—which in my opinion have not received the attention they deserve—confront the question of the logical validity of the conclusions reached in analytical bibliography and provide a rationale for analytical study. It may be that Hinman's *The Printing and Proof-Reading of the First Folio of Shakespeare* (1963)—in its massive assemblage and expert deployment of all the analytical techniques which had been developed over several decades—more nearly occupies the position in analytical bibliography which Bowers's *Principles* does in descriptive bibliography. But Professor Bowers's contributions to analytical bibliography—essays like those included in this volume, his Lyell Lectures, and his hospitality to analytical articles in the pages of *Studies in Bibliography*, where much of the important postwar work appeared—remain basic.

The final section of the volume, "Textual Criticism and Editing," is the largest, containing eleven essays and occupying about half the total number of pages in the book. The first essay dates symbolically from 1950, reflecting the fact that as of the 1950s Professor Bowers's attention has been chiefly directed to editorial matters, with his first major edition, the Dekker, beginning publication in 1953; and the last essay, from 1973, is the most recent in the volume, reflecting the fact that his editing activities have continued to the present, with editions of Hawthorne and Stephen Crane beginning in the 1960s and of Marlowe and William James in the 1970s (not to mention the editions of Beaumont and Fletcher, Dryden, Fielding, and others with which he has been associated). This extensive and varied editorial experience, ranging over works from three and a half centuries and encompassing drama, fiction, poetry, and nonfiction in both manuscript and printed form, provides an unmatched fund of illustrative detail to support theoretical discussions; indeed, one can observe, reading these essays chronologically, that the examples keep pace with the editions concurrently in progress. Professor Bowers's editorial accomplishments have been both in theory and in practice, and these essays show the intimate relationship between the two.

Roughly the first half of this section involves examples from pre-nineteenth-century literature, and in the later part the illustrations are more likely to come from nineteenth-century literature. The first essay, "Current Theories of Copy-Text, with an Illustration from Dryden" (1950), was Professor Bowers's first major article on textual theory, and it contains his first exposition of Greg's rationale of copy-text—the approach which, as a result of his championship, has now been generally accepted as standard for scholarly editions, at least in the English-speaking world. It is followed by a basic statement of the rationale for "Old-Spelling Editions of Dramatic Texts" (from the T. W. Baldwin festschrift, 1958). The next two essays are the only ones in the volume which come from other books by Professor Bowers: "Textual Criticism and the Literary Critic," from his Sandars Lectures (1958), published as *Textual and Literary Criticism* (1959), is one of his best-known essays and has played an important role as a classic gathering of examples (from all periods) illustrating the impact of bibliography and textual work on literary interpretation; "The Folio *Othello:* Compositor E,"from his Lyell Lectures (1959), is a more detailed and specialized piece, but one which effectively shows the relationship between analytical bibliography and editing. Just what is involved in the new kind of scholarly edition of which the Dekker was the prototype is clearly set forth in the next essay, "Established Texts and Definitive Editions" (1962). Its illustrations come from Dryden and Shakespeare, and it can be paired with a later essay included here, "Practical Texts and

Definitive Editions" (1968), where the examples are drawn from Hawthorne. This later essay is noteworthy for the distinction it sets up between classroom, or "practical," editions and full-scale scholarly editions. With the exception of a detailed review (1964) of the second volume of the Yale Johnson, the rest of the essays concentrate on the nineteenth century. "Old Wine in New Bottles: Problems of Machine Printing" (1966) is an exploratory survey, citing examples from Hawthorne; and "The Facsimile of Whitman's Blue Book" (1969) is a review dealing with problems in recording alterations in nineteenth-century manuscript material. The final two essays are important general articles which take many of their illustrations from Stephen Crane. The first of them, "Multiple Authority: New Problems and Concepts of Copy-Text" (1972), is destined to be regarded, it seems to me, as one of Professor Bowers's greatest contributions—indeed, I should group it and Greg's "The Rationale of Copy-Text" together as the two central documents for modern editorial theory. Greg deals with textual situations in which there is straightforward linear descent from text to text; Bowers, after a searching analysis of Greg's theory, moves on to work out an approach to radiating texts—that is, texts which are equidistant from a lost authoritative document (as in the newspaper syndication of Stephen Crane's war reports, the problem which stimulated Professor Bowers's thinking on this subject). The other essay, "Remarks on Eclectic Texts" (1973), is more wide-ranging in choice of examples and more summarizing in nature—and therefore especially appropriate as a concluding essay. In taking up "eclecticism," it goes to the heart of the problem which has prevented some people from accepting a critical approach to editing, and it presents another powerful statement of the value of providing, in each case, "as authoritative a reconstruction of the full text as the documents allow, not editions of the separate documents, except when the distance is so great as to make eclectic reconstruction impossible" (p. 528).

These twenty-six essays, then, are well chosen to represent much of Professor Bowers's best and most significant work. But anyone acquainted with that work will also think of other worthy candidates for inclusion. For instance, there is "Some Principles for Scholarly Editions of American Authors" (1964), which is important historically for its application of Greg's rationale to nineteenth-century American literature and which therefore underlies the whole CEAA program. There is also the introduction to "Textual Criticism" in the MLA pamphlet *The Aims and Methods of Scholarship in the Modern Languages and Literatures* (1963)—certainly one of the best distillations of his approach to editing and, because of its publication in this pamphlet, one of his most widely read pieces. Other possibilities are the 1958 article on "Textual Criticism" in the *Encyclopaedia Britannica;* two articles on the editing of Shakespeare, "A Definitive Text of Shakespeare: Problems and Methods" (1953) and "Shakespeare's Text and the Bibliographical Method" (1954); an important one on the development of editorial theory, "McKerrow's Editorial Principles for Shakespeare Reconsidered" (1955); and "The New Look in Editing" (1970). Another general essay which might have gone into the opening section is the 1959 *Library Trends* article, "The Function of Bibliography." And, since reviews are (rightly) included in the volume, two other well-known ones of general interest which might have been admitted are the 1955 review of the Yale reproduction of the First Folio (along with the related 1952 article on "The Problem of the Variant Forme in a Facsimile Edition") and the 1968 review of the Clarendon *Oliver Twist.* Obviously, there is far too much appropriate material to be encompassed in a single volume, as an examination of "A Checklist of Publications to 1976"— appended to this volume—shows. Recorded there are about 150 articles and notes, in addition to two dozen reviews, several books and pamphlets, and the amazing total of forty-one volumes of scholarly editions. It is no criticism of the present volume, however, to wish that more could have been included in it. (Indeed, the only real quarrel I have with it is that no index has been provided. Because these essays—and frequently the footnotes to them—provide a running commentary on much of the bibliographical scholarship of the time and because the interrelationships among descriptive, analytical, and textual bibliography result in comments on one field turning up in essays largely on another, an index would have been particularly valuable.)

A book of this kind is necessarily retrospective (as the list of publications and the biographical chronology at the end confirm); all too often the discussion of such volumes must be a valedictory exercise as well. Happily the case is quite different here, for Professor Bowers is not likely to allow the number of volumes he has edited to remain at forty-one for very long. His list of publications is only an interim list, and in fact it is already out of date. Since the appearance of this volume, he has published five substantial essays: "Transcription of Manuscripts: The Record of Variants" (in *Studies in Bibliography*, 1976), which is included at the end of the list as forthcoming and is mentioned in an addendum to the Whitman Blue Book review (p. 446); "Scholarship and Editing" (*PBSA*, Second Quarter 1976), delivered before the Bibliographical Society of America in January 1976; "Recovering the Author's Intentions"(*Pages*, 1976); a penetrating review of the first volume of Peter H. Nidditch's edition of Locke (*Library*, December 1976); and "Greg's 'Rationale of Copy-Text' Revisited" (*Studies in Bibliography*, 1978), which draws impressively on a wide range of material. At this rate a second volume of collected essays will be needed shortly (and will provide an opportunity for including some of those earlier essays I have alluded to). In the meantime, it is good to have this single volume, which is not only a record of one man's mastery of and dominance over his field but also a work of enduring usefulness. In 1949 (in the opening essay of this volume) Professor Bowers remarked that "a new trend in scholarship is developing," based on analytical bibliography and its results. The fact that this trend did actually develop—and develop extensively—in the years that followed is an indication of his own influence. These essays mirror the development of bibliographical thinking because their author has been largely responsible for that development, and bibliographers will look forward with interest to the continuation of this process.

Middle English Alliterative Revivals

N. F. Blake

T. Turville-Petre. *The Alliterative Revival.* Cambridge: D. S.
Brewer; Totowa, N.J.: Rowman and Littlefield, 1977. 152 pp.

It is a pleasure to welcome this new book about the alliterative
revival not only because it is well written but also because it
encourages a reconsideration of the many problems associated
with that concept. Turville-Petre surveys first the origins of the
revival and then its nature: what poems were written and where
and what their audience was. The next two chapters are more
technical, dealing respectively with meter and poetic diction.
The fifth chapter is devoted to the art of narrative; and the book
concludes with an epilogue, "After the Revival," which looks
cursorily at some Scottish and later English alliterative poems.
An important omission is a discussion on the desirability of
writing a book on this topic. In Middle English studies it is
characteristic to discuss works of one genre (e.g., romance, lyric)
or of one author together because such works may reasonably be
felt to share common aims and ideals. To write on the
alliterative revival implies that a metrical form is so important
as to override all other features of poetry, as if the poems that are
alliterative have sufficient in common to differentiate them from
other Middle English poems. This, as Turville-Petre is aware, is
not true, for alliterative poems that are romances have more in
common with other romances than with alliterative poems.
Hence, in a book on the revival either there will be no center,
because too many disparate works are discussed, or else poems
that stand apart will be misunderstood or undervalued; in this
book *Piers Plowman* is hardly given the attention it deserves.
When one finishes the book, one is left with the impression that
the author thinks the poems written in the Northwest Midlands
in the second half of the fourteenth century constitute the true

alliterative revival and the others are precursors or unfortunate aberrations. Alliteration is too arbitrary an organizing principle to impose on some Middle English poems, and in a sensitive critic like Turville-Petre it results in a book that is often trying to break out of the restrictions of such an unwelcome restraint. There seems no reason to deny that the writing of alliterative poems was as much the result of the urge to create vernacular poetry in the fourteenth century as those poems written in "foreign" meters. Which metrical form was chosen may owe more to geography than to content. Hence, it might not be too much of a paradox to say that the best book on the alliterative revival is likely to be the one which takes as its theme that such a book is unnecessary because it organizes Middle English poetry in the wrong way. Such a theme would at least allow the author to dwell fairly on the differences as well as the similarities among alliterative poems.

Taking his cue from some recent suggestions, Turville-Petre shows that the theory of the survival of alliterative poetry through oral transmission at a "popular" level is untenable.[1] He states the case against this view with lucidity and then goes on to show that alliteration as a structural technique survived in prose throughout the Middle English period. Since there is little formal distinction between alliterative prose and poetry, he is able to prove that the alliterative revival was a recreation from the traditions of alliterative prose. Though he argues this case ably, his book otherwise completely disregards prose. This seems almost willful, for if the two are so close that one form generates the other, it is difficult to see how one can be treated independently of the other. Like so many others, he holds the view that prose is a lower type of creative activity which may have played a role in generating alliterative poetry but is otherwise of no importance. This neglect of prose leads to several infelicities in the book. The first concerns the genesis of fourteenth-century alliterative poetry. Turville-Petre thinks that there is only one alliterative revival, and he is at pains to outline the development toward the classical alliterative poems of the Northwest Midlands in the late fourteenth century, after which there was a decline. At the same time he often pinpoints how the alliterative poetry of the Southwest Midlands differs from that of the Northwest Midlands: metrical techniques, diction, and subject matter are particularly noted. He is consequently forced to regard the poetry of the Southwest Midlands as a "departure from the practices of the alliterative tradition" (p. 31). The implications of this statement are not faced squarely, for if *Piers Plowman* (a Southwest Midlands work) represents a departure, it may be that the tradition portrayed is incorrect. If prose could generate alliterative poetry, there is no reason to suppose that this happened only once or in one area. If alliterative prose and poetry are so closely linked that the former could easily lead to the latter, this may well have happened in many places at different times. There is, in fact, not one alliterative revival but several. It is simpler and less confusing to imagine that at least the Southwest Midlands, the Northwest Midlands, and Scotland staged their own revivals. While we do not have to suppose that these developed in total isolation from one another, the influences upon each would be different. The audience, for example, may have differed: the further north, the more socially elevated the audience was. One of these influences was the prose written in the area in question. It need not surprise us that the ornate alliterative prose of the North, such as we find in Rolle, generated the more ornate alliterative poetry of the Northwest Midlands, whereas the more restrained alliterative prose of southern sermons, for example, engendered the alliterative poetry of *Piers Plowman*.

Furthermore, the interaction between poetry and prose is likely to have been a continuing process; it is wrong to think of it as something that merely generated the poetry once. The two would exist in close kinship, prose being the less regular alliteratively of the two forms. Prose continued to nourish the poetry and supply it with vocabulary, subject matter, and an audience. This fact may be important in trying to realize why alliterative poetry decayed so quickly, something Turville-Petre finds inexplicable (p. 122). It is often thought that it could not compete with the rhyming meters popularized by Chaucer in the London area. However, this may not be the whole story, for what happened in the fifteenth century was a turning away from alliterative prose in favor of a less studied prose (influenced by Wyclif) or of a prose with a French style (influenced by Chaucer). The growth in translations from French expedited this process. As soon as that happened, alliterative poetry was no longer nourished from underneath, as it were; it became a superstructure resting on no foundations. It is hardly surprising that this superstructure should collapse. That there was no alliterative prose by the end of the fifteenth century is shown by Malory, whose prose reveals the influence of alliterative poetry, not of prose alliterative writings. He did not inherit an alliterative prose tradition. That he was to that extent an anomaly is shown by the speed with which his prose was converted by Caxton into the more usual French-based prose. In the Middle Ages prose remained a highly literary form, a fact neglected by too many scholars to their own loss. The story of Middle English alliterative poetry cannot be understood without taking prose into account.

The position of prose may have some bearing on the relationship between alliterative poets and those of the Chaucerian school, of which Turville-Petre writes: "It is only a slight oversimplification to say that the two schools of poetry co-existed without contact" (p. 36). He does not tell us what he would regard as proof of mutual influence. The alliterative poets, for their part, used rhymes, stanzas, French loanwords, and themes, such as the Arthurian setting, found also in poems of the Chaucerian school. The two schools share techniques of rhetorical description, common attitudes, narrative structures, and many items of vocabulary. That Burrow can describe both alliterative and Chaucerian poems as "Ricardian" indicates they have much in common.[2] It is true that the poems of the Chaucerian school do not have the characteristic alliterative words. But the standard language had not developed by the fourteenth century, and it is hardly surprising that poets writing outside London should use their own regional vocabulary just as the London poets used theirs. It is also true that many of the shared features may have been drawn independently by each school from common French sources. But as I have explained elsewhere, though it is easier to point to foreign than to native borrowings, we do not need to exclude the latter.[3] Some foreign borrowings may have come to some poets through English intermediaries. Alliteration and Chaucerian meters are metrical systems which are chosen deliberately by the poets, in part because of geographical considerations. These metrical systems may encourage certain restraints in vocabulary, but we do not need to make vocabulary so important that we discount other influences. While it is possible that Chaucer knew none of the better alliterative poems from the Northwest Midlands, he was certainly familiar with alliteration, and he used it decoratively. He may have learned of this from prose rather than from poetry, but it is not helpful to divide the two into watertight compartments. The neglect of prose encourages us to separate alliterative poetry from Chaucerian poetry; but it is more likely that the situation was more fluid than this book allows, with frequent interchange between poetry and prose and across geographical areas. It may be difficult to prove such interchange definitively, though Turville-Petre might have gone some way to showing evidence of it had he examined the contents of some manuscripts in depth.

An example of the interaction between the alliterative and Chaucerian traditions which might have been investigated by the author is found in Hoccleve's *La Male Regle*. There we find the following lines:

> But what / me longed aftir nouelrie,
> As yeeres yonge yernen day by day;
> And now my smert accusith my folie.[4]

The expression "As yeeres yonge yernen" echoes the words that are the leitmotiv of the first stanza of the second fitt in *Sir Gawain and the Green Knight*. In Hoccleve the formula is used to emphasize the inexorable passage of time, for as a youth he was intent only on wasting time in the search for new experiences—a search dismissed as foolish because one is not devoting oneself to worthwhile ends. It need hardly be stated that this situation echoes that in *Gawain* in which members of the court are "in her first age" (line 54) and Arthur is "childgered" (line 86). Arthur and the court are equally interested in witnessing marvels and new wonders (lines 90-99).

The passage of the seasons underlines the deceptive nature of that attitude, and in the poem we see how Gawain learns to see the world in a more mature light. The green girdle will remind him of man's folly. While I would not wish to claim that Hoccleve knew *Sir Gawain and the Green Knight*, the similarity in vocabulary and theme indicates that the two poetic traditions were able to draw on the same sources for ideas and language. What these sources were needs fuller investigation.

It follows from what I have written that I cannot accept the author's contention that there is a basic or classical form of Middle English alliterative poetry. Turville-Petre assumes that alliterative prose generated a kind of crude alliterative poetry which was then refined by later poets until it reached the basic alliterative meter of aa/ax. Writers who fail to observe this pattern are said to distort the basic alliterative rhythm, as the author claims is true of *Piers Plowman* (p. 60). It is strange that a scholar who recognizes so clearly that alliterative poems have such different styles and alliterative patterns should nevertheless wish to force all such poems into the rigid framework of a straightforward rise and fall theory. The fact that some poets are more regular than others in their use of the aa/ax pattern does not mean that all poets recognized this as the norm and were trying, unsuccessfully, to achieve it. This approach to Middle English alliterative poetry arises in part from a comparison of it with classical Old English alliteration and in part from evaluating Middle English poetry in isolation from prose. For to insist on a basic aa/ax pattern imposes on alliteration a regularity characteristic of a poetic meter and sets the works written in that meter apart from prose. But poets whose poetic ancestry lay in alliterative prose would surely have no objection to using aaa/ax or xaa/ax rhythms. Indeed, poets accustomed to alliterative prose would almost certainly expect a variety of patterns. Furthermore, that sense units are often confined to a single line rather than spilling over to the next as in classical Old English poetry may also have resulted from the influence of alliterative prose, where the alliterative scheme was confined within a sense unit. To explain this development as a feature arising from changes in the language is insufficient.

Forcing alliterative poetry into the straightjacket of a single development from shaky start to maturity to a decline results in an undervaluing of those poems that are not in the classical style. Indeed the author's attitude to the style in *Piers Plowman* is ambiguous. He recognizes that its meter is a distortion of the basic rhythm (e.g., pp. 59-60), but it is unclear whether he regards that as a sign of inventiveness or of a decline. To accept the former undermines his theory of a basic rhythm; to accept the latter undervalues *Piers Plowman*. The alliterative tradition was never still: it was a tradition of constant experiment. Poets tried a variety of different alliterative patterns and combined alliteration with an amazing range of different stanzas and rhyming forms. The striking thing about alliterative poetry is its sheer inventiveness, vitality, and exuberance—all features this book tends to underplay. The glory of this poetry is its variety, and in this it compares very favorably with Chaucerian poetry, which is often largely derivative and stereotyped.

The chapter on diction contains much good sense, though the author is forced to make unwarranted deductions about style because of his assumption of a unified alliterative tradition. Thus the absence of the traditional alliterative vocabulary in *Piers Plowman* is said to be "a stylistic decision" because Langland was "looking for a readership that was not localised and not necessarily accustomed to alliterative verse" (p. 71). But, as we have seen already, Langland's poem differs in so many respects from the poetry of the Northwest Midlands that to consider it a deviation from a norm is not helpful. Indeed, in Turville-Petre's terms the major problem is to decide why Langland used alliterative meter at all since he shares so few of what are here accepted as the basic features of alliterative style. But he never considers this difficulty. Langland used a different basic alliterative rhythm from the poets of the Northwest Midlands. He used the vocabulary characteristic of the alliterative style found in the Southwest Midlands, and we need not assume that there was much conscious decision-making about style on Langland's part in that process. Little point is served by comparing *Piers Plowman* with all other alliterative poems; it can profitably be compared only with those in its own tradition.

In his analysis of the vocabulary Turville-Petre tries to draw a distinction between words of French origin, which are "technical," and those of Scandinavian origin, which are "colloquial." He does not explain what he means by these terms. Are we to assume that the French words were not colloquial and that they were borrowed from written documents, whether technical or literary? If so, what does that tell us about the intellectual level of the audience? In fact, this division created by the author is a false one. Why is a description of hunting more technical than a description of rocks and natural scenery? Are there not technical terms for describing the latter? Naturally cultural innovations and customs introduced during the Middle English period are likely to be expressed in a vocabulary of French derivation since most of them had been imported from France. But there seems no reason to doubt that these French words were current at the same colloquial level as those of Scandinavian origin: men talked about hunting as much as, if not more than, about scenery. It is not of much importance if the vocabulary was of French origin in one case and of Scandinavian in the other. Turville-Petre evidently feels that the Scandinavian words were chosen by the poets for their expressive power. But this idea surely conflicts with his claim that they were colloquial words. If *torres* and *gill* (p. 77), for example, are words found in a dialect area, their use in a poem written in that area does not imply that the poet felt them to be particularly significant. Quite the contrary: he was merely choosing words he heard every day. People living outside that area might well regard the words as expressive, but it is not normally thought that alliterative poems were composed outside the dialect area where such words were frequent. In general the vocabulary, whether of French or Scandinavian origin, is likely to have been drawn partly from the colloquial level and partly from the literary tradition, particularly prose. Here alliterative poetry is no different from the poetry of most ages. To emphasize the colloquial nature of some elements in the vocabulary as though they represent something particularly significant will lead only to a distortion in the criticism of alliterative poems.

The chapter "The Art of Narrative" is the least successful, not so much for its content as its assumptions. The author deliberately avoids drawing examples from *Sir Gawain and the Green Knight, Pearl,* and *Piers Plowman* because they "have received, and will continue to receive, an undue share of critical attention" (p. 93). This statement implies that this chapter is not so much an account of narrative techniques as a critical evaluation of the poems that are included. For if this chapter were really devoted to elucidating the mechanisms of narrative presentation to show how alliterative poetry differs from other poetry, it is difficult to see how these three poems could be avoided. After all, the chapters on style and diction draw freely upon them—and rightly so. But this chapter never analyzes narrative in the same way as diction and style are analyzed; indeed, the author seems uncertain what narrative techniques are and how they might be presented in a more formal manner. Furthermore, it is not certain that "alliterative poetry is above all else the poetry of narrative" (p. 94). The strength of *Piers Plowman* might well be thought to reside in its presentation of theological ideas, and many might feel that *Sir Gawain and the Green Knight* is as much a descriptive as a narrative poem. In my opinion, emphasizing narrative at the expense of other features prevents a balanced approach to the merits of alliterative poetry. It also suggests that alliterative poems are as different from Chaucerian poetry in this feature as in style and diction—a proposition unlikely to command widespread support.

The epilogue deals very briefly and inadequately with Scottish and later English alliterative poetry. Once again the author's theory that there is a classical Middle English alliteration leads him to adopt an uncomfortable stance. He recognizes the literary worth of some of the poems discussed, but he is unable to give them the attention or credit they deserve because to him they represent a falling away from the standards of the poetry of the late fourteenth century.

The book contains a bibliography only of the poems of the Alliterative Revival of the late fourteenth and fifteenth centuries. Earlier poems like Layamon's *Brut* are not listed, and

there is no bibliography of secondary material. There are
generally few misprints in the text. In the quotations the author
has seen fit to expand and punctuate his chosen editions in his
own way. This can lead to infelicities, as when on p. 14 he
expands the ampersand to *and* instead of *ant* in *Seinte Maherete*.
The Middle English passages are provided with glosses and
sometimes complete translations. How much ought to be
glossed is a different matter, but in general the author has done
his job well. All in all, then, this is a careful and well-written
work which makes its points clearly and moderately. But
Turville-Petre does not fully follow through some of his ideas,
and he therefore fails to do full justice to alliterative poetry.

Notes

1. L. D. Benson, "The Literary Character of Anglo-Saxon Formulaic
Poetry," *PMLA*, 81 (1966), 334-41; R. F. Lawrence, "The Formulaic Theory
and its Application to English Alliterative Poetry," in *Essays on Style and
Language*, ed. R. Fowler (London: Routledge & Kegan Paul, 1966), pp. 166-83;
and N. F. Blake, "Rhythmical Alliteration," *Modern Philology*, 67 (1969-70),
118-24.

2. Cf. J. A. Burrow, *Ricardian Poetry* (London: Routledge & Kegan Paul,
1971).

3. N. F. Blake, *The English Language in Medieval Literature* (London:
Dent, 1977), pp. 27-33.

4. F. J. Furnivall and I. Gollancz, *Hoccleve's Works: The Minor Poems*, rev.
ed. by J. Mitchell and A. I. Doyle, EETS E. S. 61, 73 (London: Oxford Univ.
Press, 1970), p. 26.

Old Wessex, New Wessex

Samuel Hynes

The New Wessex Edition of Thomas Hardy. New York: St. Martin's Press, 1977-78.

The best place to begin a review of the *New* Wessex Edition is with the *old* one—The Wessex Edition of the Works of Thomas Hardy in Prose and Verse with Prefaces and Notes, published by Macmillan, London, in 1912-13, with supplementary volumes in 1914, 1919, 1926, and 1931. The Old Wessex had a complicated history. It began, in Hardy's mind, as an "Edition de luxe," something that he wanted badly. Tennyson had one, Kipling had one, and if Hardy also had one he would have before him material proof, on expensive paper and between elegant boards, that his literary status was permanently high: it would be a sort of public honor, like his Order of Merit.

Hardy first mentioned this dream, in a casual, off-hand way, in a letter to Macmillan in 1902, while he was still negotiating his change of publisher from Harper to Macmillan.[1] A couple of years later he mentioned it again in a wistful way, but Macmillan didn't take the hint until 1910, when a limited edition was finally proposed, to be published jointly with Harper in New York. Hardy set to work revising the texts of his novels and writing a General Preface for this new edition, but at the end of the year the deal with Harper collapsed, and Macmillan offered instead a more modest scheme, a "definitive edition," but a less grand one, to be published solely by themselves. Hardy agreed, and his revisions and Preface went into the new project, which became the Wessex Edition. (He didn't give up on the Edition de luxe, though, and it finally appeared in 1919-20 as the Mellstock Edition.)

Hardy took the Wessex Edition very seriously: he revised the texts of novels and poems, wrote new prefaces and revised old ones, and read proofs of the entire edition (in a letter quoted in

The Later Years he mentions working for ten hours one day over the proofs of *The Return of the Native,* which suggests how much importance he attached to the edition—and also the stamina that he had at the age of nearly seventy-two).[2] Once the edition had been published Hardy regarded it (not altogether accurately) as definitive, and when editors and anthologists wrote to him for permissions he usually referred them to the Wessex Edition as having the most correct texts. Richard Purdy overstates the case a bit when he writes in his bibliography of Hardy that "the Wessex Edition is in every sense the definitive edition of Hardy's work and the last authority in questions of text."[3] This is not at all true of the verse, and there are also some minor exceptions to be made about the novels, but he is certainly expressing Hardy's own view of the matter.

The Old Wessex was what a gentleman's Library Edition used to be—a uniform set of handsome, well-bound volumes, printed in a large and readable type on good-quality paper, and decorated with suitable illustrations. But it was more than that: it was a serious attempt at definitiveness. The carefully corrected texts had the author's approval, each volume contained a preface by the author (most of them new or enlarged for the occasion), and the long General Preface in Volume I set forth the author's own sense of his achievement. The only other item included was a two-page map of Wessex at the back of each volume—the familiar one, adapted by Emery Walker from Hardy's own drawing. There was no other apparatus beyond a few footnotes by Hardy: presumably the gentleman in his library needed nothing more.

The New Wessex Edition is very different. It is, in fact, two editions: one in hard covers, which we might call the new Library Edition, and another in paperback, which is obviously meant primarily for the classroom. In most cases the contents of these two editions are the same; nevertheless they are best dealt with separately, especially since only one—the paperback— seems likely to appear in the United States complete.

Let us begin, briefly, with Macmillan London's hardcover Library Edition, since it at least *looks* like the parent edition. The texts and prefaces used in it are essentially those of the Old

Wessex (plus some corrections that Hardy wanted made), but the volumes are a good deal less handsome than their predecessors: the evocative frontispiece photographs are gone; the two-page map has been replaced by a less detailed, less readable one-page version; and the old plum-colored binding has given way to a drab institutional green. Still, the page is a clear and readable one, and the books have sewn signatures, so that presumably the pages won't fall out onto the gentleman's library floor. As far as appearance is concerned, Macmillan has done just about as well as the economics of book publishing today will allow; we can all lament the passing of the New York Edition of Henry James and such treasures, but we must accept the fact that they are gone for good: the handsome uniform edition is as dead as the Flora-Dora Girls. And for even this present utilitarian set you'll have to order from England.

Though the most attractive physical features of the Old Wessex are gone, there are also some additions to the new editions. Each volume of the novels contains the following: a biographical chronology of Hardy's life; a list of his major works; acknowledgments; an introduction by a Hardy scholar; explanatory notes; a note on the text; Hardy's General Preface (in every volume!); a glossary of place-names. Some individual volumes also have special appendixes (see below for details). All of these additions are essentially what the textbook publishers call "aids to study," and no doubt students will find them useful, but they cluster a little oddly around the text of the Library Edition, which no student is likely to own. Will the general reader find it convenient to have the same brief biography in every volume of his edition? And the same General Preface? And will he require introductions? These aids may have their place in the paperbacks, but since the two editions are not printed from the same plates, uniformity between the two is not an economic matter, and I can think of no other reason for shoving the material into an edition evidently intended for a general reading public. And I can't help thinking that if all this unnecessary stuff had been left out, the savings in fees and typesetting cost might have paid to put those fine frontispieces back in.

In addition to the novels, the New Wessex Library Edition includes five other volumes: F. B. Pinion's three volumes of Hardy's stories (blue binding), James Gibson's *Complete Poems* (red binding), and Harold Orel's *Dynasts* (plum binding). These volumes do not contain the uniform apparatus of the novels, but are edited and introduced in ways appropriate to their particular needs. They are not my concern in this review, and I mention them only in passing because they do not seem quite to belong to the edition, though Macmillan has labeled them all "New Wessex Edition." None of the five appears in the paperback version.

The paperback, classroom edition can be dealt with collectively and more briefly, since as far as the novels are concerned it is identical in content with the Library Edition. There are, of course, the obvious and inevitable differences: the smaller page and smaller type, the narrow inner margins, the coarse paper, the glued binding. And there are the covers—posed color photographs of characters in quaint period costumes: Tess and Angel (or is that Alec d'Urberville with his head in her lap?), Marty and Giles, Swithin and Lady Constantine—all looking like stills from some terrible television serial. Wrap the books in plain brown wrappers and they will do as excellent classroom textbooks—carefully edited, with the best texts available, informative notes, and some good, solid scholarship in evidence (for example in the notes on the texts, where the problems of manuscript, periodical version, first edition, and later printings are set forth in sufficient detail to give an intelligent undergraduate some notion of just what a textual problem *is*).

I have said nothing about the introductions to the novels, which Macmillan may well regard as the most attractive feature of their new edition. All are new, and all are by writers who are either established Hardy scholars or known literary critics. Still, I question the value of such essays to either the Library or the classroom edition. It is, I know, a long-established convention that textbooks should have such introductions. But though the custom keeps many scholars in work, the utility of their efforts is not at all evident. Most of the readers of this review will probably be teachers. Let me ask them, then: How often do you actually *use* an introduction in teaching a novel? How often do you even encourage your students to read it? How often is information provided there that is essential to an accurate reading of the book? How often do the critic's ideas simply get in your way? Barbara Hardy, in a sensible footnote to her introduction to *The Trumpet Major*, urges her readers to read the novel *before* reading the introduction; but the best way to achieve that end, I would suggest, would be to detach the introduction from the novel altogether and print it somewhere else. This is not to say that these introductions—at least the best of them—are not excellent critical essays; I do not question the value of criticism as such, but only the value of criticism-as-instruction and the assumption that classic English novels *need* introducing in this way.

I realize that I should say something about the individual volumes in the edition; but to write a lengthy commentary on each seems a tedious and unnecessary exercise. What follows is therefore as concise an account of what is special in each volume as I could contrive. In addition I have adopted the method perfected by the late Herr Baedeker (and by Stella Gibbons in *Cold Comfort Farm*), and have assigned to each volume one, two, or three stars, according to my sense of the merit of introductions and apparatus. Three of the novels—*A Pair of Blue Eyes, A Laodicean,* and *The Return of the Native*—were not available in the American edition at the time of writing, and I have used the English paperback edition in these cases. The order of the assessments is alphabetical.

Desperate Remedies, introduction by C. J. P. Beatty.*

A maundering, sometimes far-fetched essay—though I recognize the difficulty of writing about such a weak novel. Appendixes include a list of "Poems by Hardy Associated with *Desperate Remedies*" (some of the associations are extremely tenuous) and the text of the song "The Seven Trades," one verse of which is sung in the novel.

Far from the Madding Crowd, introduction by John Bayley.***
Incongruity and separateness in the novel, as signs of Hardy's divided consciousness. Style a bit inflated, but a suggestive and intelligent essay.

The Hand of Ethelberta, introduction by Robert Gittings.*
Gittings takes the treatment of class, the most interesting thing in the novel, to be "a simplistic and wholesale blackening of the upper classes." Some pointless hovering over biographical issues (inevitable, perhaps, from Hardy's most recent biographer). Not much critical interest.

Jude the Obscure, introduction by Terry Eagleton.**
A Marxist reading, which is strong on the social content, but weak on the other aspects of the novel—the sexual psychology, the ideas of human evolution, religion.

A Laodicean, introduction by Barbara Hardy.***
A model of how to deal with a bad novel; Mrs. Hardy discusses the feminism and the autobiographical elements in the book, and analyzes Hardy's revisions, but she also gives her attention to why it is unsuccessful. The notes are by Ernest Hardy.

The Mayor of Casterbridge, introduction by Ian Gregor.***
A first-rate essay, full of critical insights, often only briefly sketched—one wishes Gregor had had more space. Focuses on the central issues of the book, so that it really *is* an introduction. Useful appendix on the time-scheme of the novel.

A Pair of Blue Eyes, introduction by Ronald Blythe.**
A running commentary more than an essay, never demonstrably wrong, but never very acutely right. The text incorporates Hardy's revisions of 1919-20.

The Return of the Native, introduction by Derwent May.*
A rather old-fashioned critical essay, concerned almost entirely with the motives and behavior of the principal characters and quarreling unnecessarily with minor critics.

Tess of the d'Urbervilles, introduction by P. N. Furbank.***
Notes more than essay, but the notes are by an original and acute critic, and they are rich in ideas—Wessex as a parable, *Tess* as an allegory, Hardy's place outside the moral tradition of English fiction.

The Trumpet Major, introduction by Barbara Hardy.***
On Hardy's historical consciousness: a critical essay of depth and grace. The notes are by Laurel Brake and Ernest Hardy; there is also a useful note on the sources of the novel.

Two on a Tower, introduction by F. B. Pinion.**
A real effort to introduce, covering many points briefly, though with a consequent loss of unity. The full note on the text compares manuscript, serial, and first edition readings.

Under the Greenwood Tree, introduction by Geoffrey Grigson.*
A rather superficial, patronizing view of the novel, which seriously undervalues it; Grigson is hard on Hardy for his treatment of the rustics, and on the whole matter of Wessex, which he argues "diluted, sentimentalized and popularized" Hardy's impact. A "Note on Country-dances" quotes two interesting letters by Hardy.

The Well-Beloved, introduction by Hillis Miller.**
A phenomenological essay that finds ingenious reasons for thinking the novel is better than it is, but nevertheless intelligent and suggestive—especially on the relations between this late novel and the themes of the poetry that followed. A long appendix quotes passages from the 1892 serial version that were changed in the final text. Notes are by Edward Mendelson.

The Woodlanders, introduction by David Lodge.***
One of the best essays I've read on this somewhat neglected novel; especially good on the ritualistic and anthropological content. Appendixes on Hardy's revisions and on the time-scheme of the novel.

Such conclusions as I have to offer about the New Wessex Edition I have already expressed: the paperbacks are the best classroom texts that I have seen (in spite of the extraordinary vulgarity of the covers); the hardbound volumes are ill-conceived as a library edition, and are sadly inferior, not only to the original Wessex Edition, but also to the more modest Library Edition that Macmillan published in the late forties. Neither is, strictly speaking, a *scholarly* edition—and neither pretends to be; though the editors recognize and sometimes comment on textual variants, they don't deal with them systematically. So the chore of a full scholarly edition remains to be done. Hardy, more than most Victorian novelists, would repay that kind of attention; for his variants record not only the development of a very odd imagination, but also the restraints and distortions imposed on him by the taste and literary morals of his time, against which his imagination worked for expression.

Notes

1. The Hardy-Macmillan correspondence is in the British Library, Additional Manuscript numbers 54923-54925.

2. Florence Emily Hardy, *The Later Years of Thomas Hardy* (New York: Macmillan, 1930), p. 151.

3. Richard Little Purdy, *Thomas Hardy: A Bibliographical Study* (Oxford: Clarendon, 1954), p. 286.

Books before Printing: A Codicological Catalogue

Jean F. Preston

N. R. Ker. *Medieval Manuscripts in British Libraries.* Vol. II, Abbotsford—Keele. Oxford: Clarendon Press, 1977. xliii, 999 pp.

This book is a tour de force by one man, N. R. Ker, who this year celebrates his seventieth birthday. With fifty years' experience of manuscripts behind him and a remarkable memory, there is no man alive better fitted to catalogue the uncatalogued medieval manuscripts in British libraries. For this is the project initiated by the Manuscripts Sub-Committee of the Standing Conference on National and University Libraries (SCONUL); it asked Mr. Ker to describe the manuscripts in the many small collections in Britain (usually less than fifty manuscripts, often a mere handful) and to provide information about the published catalogues of medieval manuscripts in the fifty or so large collections (with well over fifty manuscripts apiece). All the collections are institutional; no personal or private libraries are included. The first volume was published in 1969 and covered collections in and around London, with the promise of two companion volumes to cover Aberdeen to Liverpool and Maidstone to York, respectively. The present volume is the first of these.

In fact the present volume is more than double the size of the London one (999 pages compared with 437) and gets only as far as Keele on its alphabetical way to Liverpool. Ker tells us in his preface (pp. v-vi) what he covers: for the twenty-two large collections in this volume he gives full references to existing catalogues, and he provides descriptions of the uncatalogued manuscripts in a dozen of them and of all the manuscripts in one of them (Eton College); he gives "abbreviated descriptions" to enable users to locate the medieval items in the general catalogues of the National Libraries of Scotland and of Wales. He also catalogues all the medieval books in the small collections on his list; most of these belong to nine cathedrals, four Benedictine abbeys, three universities, eight Cambridge colleges, six theological colleges, fifteen public libraries, art galleries and museums, and to the odd school or parish church with one or two books. He makes very little general comment about the manuscripts he found, apart from there being alchemy at Glasgow university, astronomy and astrology at the Edinburgh Royal Observatory, and Books of Hours and Bibles everywhere. There is much Latin theology and devotional literature, very little vernacular; the Middle English can be counted on one hand, one of the more interesting volumes being the Coventry Hoccleve manuscript (and Ker tells us, on p. 412, the story of its disappearance and reemergence to be purchased by the enlightened Corporation in 1962). Among the less well known collections, Newnham College, Cambridge, has some choice gifts from Yates Thompson; and Cardiff Public Library is a surprisingly rich collection, apparently assembled by an enterprising librarian in the 1920s.

The variation of treatment according to what is available leads to some inconsistencies and a subjective choice of what collections or what manuscripts Ker feels like describing more fully. For example, Eton College is one of the large collections where one would expect a reference to M. R. James's *Descriptive Catalogue of the Manuscripts in the Library at Eton College*, (Cambridge Univ. Press, 1895), with Ker's descriptions of later acquisitions. But Ker generously decided to describe afresh all of the 144 Eton manuscripts; clearly he loves the collection and cannot resist describing the manuscripts of his old school, on many aspects of which he has already appeared in print.[1] He has so much new information to add that he could not contain it all within the confines of mere additions and corrections; it would make a volume on its own, longer than James's *Catalogue*. Ker also decided to include binding fragments, although in Volume I he specifically excluded them. Here again his own interests dictated his decision, for he is known for both his *Medieval Libraries of Great Britain* and his *Pastedowns in Oxford Bindings*, and he is uniquely knowledgeable on both subjects.[2] He has therefore included binding fragments found in six capitular and diocesan records, and he is particularly full on Canterbury, reconstructing the activities of the sixteenth-century binders. Probably he alone can identify and localize these materials, some of which he shows have never left the institution where they were originally written.

The size of the entry bears no relationship to the importance or the interest of the manuscript; compilations of anonymous sermons tend to receive the longest treatment as Ker meticulously tracks them all down, identifying even incomplete pieces. Exeter Cathedral's two best known manuscripts must be the Exon Domesday and the Exeter Book, both of the eleventh century. Both have had much written about them, been described in print, and reproduced. Here we find no descriptions, but seven pages (pp. 800-7) concerned solely with the physical description of Exon Domesday, with very careful tabulation of the leaves and observations on the sections, culminating in comments on the number of scribes employed and how the book was put together. These comments show how the minute observations of a palaeographer can add up to new historical findings the historian cannot ignore. Similarly, there is no description of the Exeter Book (p. 807), as Ker gives references to the 1937 description and facsimile and to his own 1957 *Catalogue of Manuscripts containing Anglo-Saxon*; he takes the opportunity to correct what he calls "defective collation in Ker," and provides a new one. The small size of this entry and the lack of the usual italic title makes the Exeter Book very easy to miss, surrounded, as it is, by long descriptions of the other Exeter manuscripts. Wherever possible, Ker refers to descriptions elsewhere and omits further particulars here. This habit can be tiresome, especially if the other publication is obscure or simply not handy. In the entry for Eton College MS 44, for example, there is nothing about the contents but a reference to his own essay in *Litterae Textuales*.[3] As a result of this practice some of the entries are distinctly lopsided, because Ker mentions only what he has to add and the real description of the manuscript has to be sought elsewhere. The mere scholar looking for manuscripts of his text can have a frustrating time.

For method, Ker in the London volume (pp. vii-xiii) set himself sixteen points to cover in his description of each manuscript: date, contents, number of leaves, foliation, material, dimensions of leaf and of written space, pricking, ruling, quiring, quire signatures and leaf signatures, catchwords, script, punctuation, decoration, binding, and *secundo folio*; in fact, he finished by noting provenance and history as a seventeenth point. This second volume uses the same method with only very slight modifications, and in his preface Ker merely refers the reader to his discussion in the previous volume. To make sense, both prefaces should be read together, as many of his comments in Volume II are meaningless without a knowledge of the preface to Volume I. These seventeen points were seminal and have now become standard practice for cataloguers of medieval manuscripts, either as the direct model or in a modified way.[4] This is the codicological method par excellence, and if the textual scholar should complain that contents are hard to find among seventeen points, he will see that the sixteen others are set apart in much smaller type.

A comparison of M. R. James's *Manuscripts in the Library of Eton College* (1895) with N. R. Ker's new descriptions of the same manuscripts can reveal both the progress of manuscript studies in the last eighty years and also the contrast between the first published work of a brilliant amateur and the mature judgment of a professional palaeographer. Ker is at his best identifying anonymous sermons and binding fragments, giving precise palaeographical and codicological details, and working out former owners (including medieval libraries) and relationships between manuscripts. James by comparison seems skimpier here than he becomes later, but he is always readable: his subjective comments give shape to the descriptions, and he has fuller coverage of illuminations, listing miniatures and often commenting on the style. In places Ker corrects him, sometimes with information not then available (such as that provided by the ultraviolet lamp,[5] or by scholarly reference books published since James's day), more often in the light of his own deductions from the manuscript and his far wider experience than James had in 1895. On matters of illustration or illumination, however, Ker simply leaves his readers to "see James's *Catalogue*." James includes Greek manuscripts and some sixteenth- and seventeenth-century volumes not covered by Ker, while Ker describes seventeen books not seen by James, including a number of fragments "happily still *in situ*." Sometimes their different approaches make the same manuscript almost unrecognizable, as with Eton College MS 26, a Bible James views as "by far the finest Vulgate in the collection. The writing and ornaments are very fine, and the contents and aspect of the book remarkable." Ker's description is far longer, and he barely notices what the book looks like, but he has nearly three pages of detailed analysis of prefaces, arguments, and other preliminary matter, making full use of Stegmüller and *Biblia Sacra*,[6] both of which are post-Jamesian scholarly tools. On the other hand James is fuller on Eton College MS 3, Bible historiale, listing the subjects of all twenty-eight miniatures and discussing their form and style; he also gives the general information that the French text is a translation of Peter Comestor's *Historia scholastica* made by Guiart des Moulins in 1291-95. Ker does not mention either Peter Comestor or Guiart des Moulins, but he refers the reader to S. Berger, *La Bible francaise au Moyen Age*, 1884, pp. 187-99 (a book available to James), where Berger discusses Pierre Comestor and Guyart Desmoulins. This is typical Ker: he assumes his reader knows his sources as well as he does. Although he refers readers to James for the miniatures, Ker gives their exact measurements (in millemeters where James uses inches), and he also describes the decoration, which James ignores—the two kinds of initials, their colors and patterns, and the "nearly continuous frame on f. 1: dogs chase hares along the lower horizontal border." On MS 5 Ker completes the identification begun by James's attempt to read the scribe's name (lacking the "t") as Elys; Ker identifies Robert Elyot, scribe, book collector, and vice-provost of Eton (d. 1499) as the man whose hand appears in twenty-two manuscripts. James describes "Binding, boards and stamped leather with medallion of crowned heads, lettered HERCULES and VENA (?). This binding, which must be of cent. XVI, occurs on many of the manuscripts." Ker, by contrast, not only identifies "Binding by Williamson" but goes on to tell us that Williamson bound twenty specified books[7] 1600-1601, fifteen of them being surviving manuscripts, most of them bearing the Hercules and Vena roll, Oldham H. M. b.2.[8] And Ker goes even further. Where James comments that "the flyleaves are from a MS. concordance to the Vulgate (cent. XV.) which is often used in connection with the HV binding," Ker identifies the leaves as from "letter E of the *Concordantiae Maiores*, (Stegmüller 3605), written in England, s. XIV[2], and used by Williamson in 1600-1601 and other years in binding nine manuscripts and two printed books." In a footnote he points out the use of leaves from a similar concordance (also Stegmüller 3605) as binding fragments in Durham Cathedral, a concordance he tells us is discussed by Richard and Mary Rouse in *Archivum Fratrum Praedicatorum*, 44 (1974), 1-30. He goes on to enumerate twenty-four more surviving leaves removed from Williamson bindings, which together form what may be the remains of the "concordance of ii partes" listed in Eton inventory of 1465.[9]

Ker is most punctilious in measuring the sizes and giving the locations of any miniatures or initials. Occasionally he gives the subjects of miniatures, but normally not with a Book of Hours unless it is what he considers worth mentioning, and his subjective judgment here too can be inconsistent.[10] He never gives any suggestion of style, nor does he attempt to attribute any miniatures. Art historians are the losers here, for a comprehensive catalogue could have catered to their interests at the same time. One misses the Eton references to James's *Catalogue*, for with the other collections there is no existing catalogue or an art-historian collaborator.[11] Perhaps it is as a result of Ker's lack of interest that of the fifty manuscripts marked "s" in the contents list, to show that scribe or illuminator is known, only one is an illuminator, one a decorator, and all the rest are scribes. Ker makes no attempt to use the miniatures to help localize or date the book as a whole, in the way he of course uses the handwriting and the *mis en page*. He is fuller on the decoration, but I have found only one small comment localizing any decoration, and that is for a French Book of Hours in Hodnet Parish Church, written for English use, with the miniatures unfortunately removed; a footnote adds that "Dr. J. J. G. Alexander tells me that such decoration as remains is English." In describing the decoration, Ker uses the number of lines as a standard of comparison to show the proportion (e.g., a five-line initial or a two-line initial), a very clear and systematic method which enables him to show the hierarchy of initials and to describe each class as a group.

In palaeographical terminology Ker shows the advance since James. It was Ker in his 1969 volume who first introduced the term *anglicana* to describe the distinctively English script often found instead of textura in English books of the fourteenth and fifteenth centuries, and who extended the Elizabethan handwriting term *secretary* backward to include the current hand commonly used for books below the textura class from the late fourteenth century onwards. These brief definitions (with plates) in Volume I were developed by his former student Malcolm B. Parkes in his important *English Cursive Book Hands*.[12] Ker is usually careful in his use of such palaeographical terms, getting just the right mixture of "current anglicana with secretary influence" and so on; but here too he is inconsistent and lapses into "written in a very good hand" or a "poor hand," both unspecified, or omits the script altogether; sometimes he only points to relationships without further description.[13]

Tucked away in the descriptions are numerous nuggets of information about medieval books and bookmaking. For example, the description of Birmingham Public Library's MS 091/MED/3 has a distinctive way of marking the quire number;[14] this turns out to be the method used by the Franciscans of Assisi and is a way of locating books from the Convent of S. Francesco there (in this case confirmed by the book's presence in the 1381 Assisi catalogue).[15] Glasgow University Library's Ferguson 104 (p. 889), dated 1364, has a German limp vellum binding minutely described and measured down to its plaited strings and central button, a beautiful

example of the new light type of binding replacing the heavy
oak boards for practical books that can be held in the hand; but
who would think of finding this information under Glasgow?
Sometimes even when one has the right entry it is hard to locate
the information: Edinburgh's Royal Observatory MS Cr. 3.2. is
marked "s" as having a named scribe, but the entry merely says
"Written at Salzburg by a named scribe" whose name is
embedded in the ten lines of Middle Low German at the
beginning of the entry. These nuggets of information need to be
made accessible, and we certainly hope that at the end of the
journey, after York, we will have full lists and indexes to retrieve
this information. Author and title indexes are essential to the
use of the *Catalogue*. Indexes of initia, of scribes and of former
owners as well as of subjects; lists of dated manuscripts and of
contemporary bindings—all these would enable us to use the
numerous codicological points at present found only by chance
when looking for something else. Computers are good at this
sort of thing, and presumably Oxford knows how to make the
results more attractive-looking than some recent computer
products. The Clarendon Press is certainly to be congratulated
on the production of the present volume; the variations of type
make such solid material look inviting, and the very thin yet
completely opaque paper makes the book a real companion
piece to the first volume, although more than double the length.

Wherever one opens this book there is some interesting tidbit
of minute observation and an impressive use of knowledge and
experience marshaled to throw light on the varying ways books
were written, produced, collected, and kept in the Middle Ages.
It is overwhelming that one man can achieve all this. For the
codicologist, fascinated like Ker by the history of the codex, this
is one of the great manuscript catalogues, by a master in the line
of Humfrey Wanley and M. R. James. We must forgive his
inconsistencies, his sometimes staccato language, his omission
of art historical comment, and his love of referring the user
elsewhere, because he gives us so much fresh information no one
else could provide. On codicological and palaeographical
points, on identification of texts, on provenance and history of
books, he is superb. We eagerly await at least two more volumes
of catalogue and the essential indexes to make this work the
indispensable scholarly tool for medievalists.

Notes

1. Perhaps the most recent publication is N. R. Ker, "Robert Elyot's Books and Annotations," *The Library*, 5th ser., 30 (1975), 233-37.

2. Royal Historical Society, Guides and Handbooks, No. 3, 2nd edition, 1964; and Oxford Bibliographical Society, new series, v. Oxford, 1954.

3. Ker, "Eton College 44 and Its Exemplar," *Litterae Textuales, Essays Presented to G. I. Lieftinck*, 1 (1972), 48-60.

4. A direct mode is the new and yet unpublished "Medieval and Renaissance Manuscripts at the University of California, Los Angeles" by Mirella Ferrari; a modified model is the *Catalogue of the Lyell Manuscripts in the Bodleian Library Oxford*, comp. Albinia de la Mare (Oxford: Clarendon Press, 1971).

5. Ultra-violet light for bringing up faded or disappeared writing, particularly ownership inscriptions, was introduced in the 1930s.

6. Stegmüller, *Repertorium Biblicum Medii Aevi*, 7 vols. (Madrid, 1950-); *Biblia Sacra iuxta Latinam vulgatum versionem . . . iussu Piu PP XI . . . edita* (Rome, 1926-).

7. Eton Accounts 1591-1602, p. 640.

8. J. B. Oldham, *English Blind-Stamped Bindings* (Cambridge: Cambridge Univ. Press, 1952).

9. *Etoniana*, ser. I, No. 28 (1921), 443.

10. This can be tantalizing, as in Edinburgh University Library MS 312 Book of Hours, which we are told has "full-page pictures of good quality on the versos . . . [including] one before article 3 (an unusual composition)." Article 3 is Horae de Sancto Spiritu, but we are given no indication as to the subject matter or style of this unusual composition.

11. This collaboration between a palaeographer and an art historian is one of the factors that makes so good J. J. G. Alexander and A. C. de la Mare, *The Italian Manuscripts in the Library of Major J. R. Abbey* (London: Faber and Faber, 1969).

12. Published by the Clarendon Press later in 1969.

13. Such as Edinburgh. Royal College of Physicians. MS written in three hands, not described, the second "not unlike Cotton Vespasian A. iii" (p. 540).

14. Page 62: "On the first recto and last verso of each quire, in center lower margin," and page 74: "each number has a short vertical stroke above and below it and a short horizontal stroke on each side of it and there are three dots, respectively red, black, and red between each horizontal and vertical stroke." Such exact descriptions enable one to recognize the distinctive marking in other manuscripts.

15. See G. Mercati, "Codici de Convento di S. Francesco in Assisi nelle bibliotece vaticane," *Studi e teste*, 41 (1924), 83-127, with facsimile. The Assisi Catlogue of 1381 was published by L. Alessandri, 1906.

W. B. Yeats: Some Recent Bibliographical and Editorial Work

Richard J. Finneran

K. P. S. Jochum. *W. B. Yeats: A Classified Bibliography of Criticism Including Additions to Allan Wade's* Bibliography of the Writings of W. B. Yeats *and a Section on the Irish Literary and Dramatic Revival.* Urbana: University of Illinois Press, 1978. xiv, 802 pp.

E. H. Mikhail, ed. *W. B. Yeats: Interviews and Recollections.* Foreword by A. Norman Jeffares. 2 vols. London: The Macmillan Press Ltd, 1977. xii, 426 pp.

A. Norman Jeffares, ed. *W. B. Yeats: The Critical Heritage.* London: Routledge & Kegan Paul, 1977. xvi, 483 pp.

Curtis Baker Bradford, ed. *W. B. Yeats: The Writing of* The Player Queen. DeKalb: Northern Illinois University Press, 1977. xxvi, 483 pp.

At the conclusion of the Yeats chapter in *Anglo-Irish Literature: A Review of Research,* I made what I knew at the time to be a doomed prophecy: that the late 1970s would come to be known as the Great Interregnum in Yeats studies, scholars and critics postponing their projects until such seminal works as the *Collected Letters* (ed. Eric Domville and John Kelly) and the authorized biography (by F. S. L. Lyons) were published.[1] In fact, as the Yeats industry labors towards the next decade, the flood of critical studies and close readings has hardly diminished; the slogan of many workers seems to be "Full speed ahead—damn accuracy and what's already been said." However, in recent years a substantial amount of energy has been directed toward bibliographical and editorial work, and the four volumes under review are a representative sampling of this activity.[2]

The most important of these books is K. P. S. Jochum's *W. B. Yeats: A Classified Bibliography of Criticism.* Many years in the making and almost as many in the printing, this volume has long been a bibliographical ghost in listings of Yeats studies: even so careful a scholar as Maurice Harmon was deceived into citing a 1976 publication date in his useful *Select Bibliography for the Study of Anglo-Irish Literature and Its Backgrounds*.[3] But it has now been published, and for once that over-used word *monumental* seems appropriate. Certainly no other single volume can do as much to raise the general level of Yeats scholarship. Jochum has listed well over six thousand items of Yeats criticism, the only deliberate exclusion of note being the Japanese material cited in Shotaro Oshima's *W. B. Yeats and Japan*.[4] Jochum has divided the entries into ten broad categories and no fewer than forty-three subsections, also providing a multitude of cross-references and eight indexes. Perhaps about half of the entries are annotated. He usually gives only a brief summary of the book or article, but some evaluations are included: thus Harold Bloom's *Yeats* "succeeds on its own terms but hardly on any others" (p. 98), or Louis MacNeice's *The Poetry of W. B. Yeats* "is still one of the sanest books written about Yeats" (p. 114). Jochum has also listed over fifteen hundred items on the Irish Literary Renaissance and its major figures, divided into three main categories and eleven subsections.

It is impossible in a brief compass even to suggest the full usefulness of this compilation. Most readers will doubtless turn first to the sections on single poems or single plays, where the major explications of each lyric or drama in the canon are either listed or cross-referenced; or to the index of selected subjects, which begins with "Mount Abiegnos" (one entry), runs through "Imagism" and the "Pennsylvania Railroad Station" (two each), and concludes with "Zen Buddhism" (six entries and a cross-reference to Buddhism). But there are riches here for even the most jaded student of Yeats criticism. Who knew, for instance, that a satire on Yeats by Edward Martyn, "Romulus and Remus," is "dull, but contains one really good line: 'As for living Miss Hollihan at least can do that for me' " (p. 537)? Or that the *Catholic Bulletin*, in the course of its diatribes against the Irish Academy of Letters, published an article entitled "The

Pollexfen Peacock Parade: Dismal Drip from Westmoreland Street," describing the Academicians as a "parade of putridity" (p. 682)? Or that "the most malignant statement ever made about Yeats" is found in a review of Arland Ussher's *Three Great Irishmen* by Thomas Bodkin: "Yeats almost deserved the dishonouring tribute of condolence which Hitler's foreign office offered to his family on his death" (p. 176)? Or that "the strangest thing that has ever happened to Yeats's poetry" is an article in *Glamour* which uses quotations from the poems as captions for a collection of fashion photographs, Jochum wryly noting that "also honored are Joyce and MacNeice" (p. 289). Or even that Thomas Wentworth Higginson of Emily Dickinson fame described *The Countess Kathleen and Various Legends and Lyrics* as "one of the most original and powerful of recent poetic volumes" (p. 449)?

One could easily go on and on, but it should be clear that the book is indeed comprehensive and is a major contribution to Yeats scholarship. It is thus unfortunate that the compilation is complete only through 1972. Although numerous works from 1973 and 1974 have been added, not all of them have been cross-referenced, and readers must find this out for themselves: Daniel Harris's important *Yeats: Coole Park and Ballylee* (1974), for instance, is not listed in the section on individual poems. I should also stress that Jochum's book takes getting used to before one feels confident in referring to it. Some works are listed two or even three times. *The Concordance to the Plays*, for example, appears in sections AB ("Additions to Allan's Wade's *Bibliography*"); AI ("Concordances"), where two reviews are cited; and G ("Books by Yeats Containing Critical and Introductory Material"), where the preface is cited. The first two occurrences are not cross-referenced; the third is, but it is omitted from the index, where the first two appear (ND, "Index of Yeats's Works"). Likewise, it is often hard to predict where a certain study will appear—in this sense the lack of a full index to titles is unfortunate. I doubt that one would expect Kimon Friar and John Malcolm Brinnin's anthology *Modern Poetry: American and British* to be in the section on "*A Vision* and Mystical, Occult and Philosophical Writings and Activities"

(FC), for instance, even though a few of its notes are on *A Vision*. Likewise, Eric Sellin's "The Oriental Influence in Modern Western Drama" is found not in section ED, "Yeats and the Nō," but in FG, "Theory of Drama and Tragedy." The inclusion of works in section G, cited above, is sometimes quite arbitrary: If the *Concordance to the Plays*, why not the *Concordance to the Poems*? The segments on the other figures of the Revival are understandably incomplete and must be considered only as good starting points. Finally, as one would have to expect, there are a few (but a very few) errors and omissions in Jochum's *Classified Bibliography*, including four items in *The Ethical Record* (New York) recently discovered by George Monteiro.⁵ It is good to know that Jochum plans to continue this project; one hopes that all users of the volume will heed his request for corrections and additions. A short list toward that end is found at the conclusion of this essay.

To turn from the work of K. P. S. Jochum to that of E. H. Mikhail is to move from the very highest standards of scholarship to perhaps the low ebb of haphazard bookmaking. *W. B. Yeats: Interviews and Recollections* is an altogether disappointing collection, a lost opportunity in Yeats studies. First of all, Mikhail clearly has no principle of selection at work. Many of the familiar anecdotes are retold, often by the same writer (compare, for instance, Lennox Robinson on pp. 256 and 287 or Frank O'Connor on pp. 267 and 340). On the other hand, many other sections are awkwardly excerpted—although with the selection from St. John Ervine, Mikhail has simply forgotten to include the section numbers for III and IV (pp. 105, 106), giving the impression that the piece is excerpted when in fact it is not. If Mikhail was attempting to represent the most important people in Yeats's life, then why nothing from Maud Gonne's *A Servant of the Queen* and only three paragraphs from her essay in *Scattering Branches*? If he was trying to make accessible obscure material, then why include thirty-four pages on *The Playboy* controversy, almost all of the readily available paperback *The Yeats We Knew*, and the interview with D. N. Dunlop included in Volume I of *Uncollected Prose* (with the same incorrect date)?⁶

But if the selections in this volume are questionable, the editing is altogether deficient. Although potted biographies and bibliographies are supplied for figures likely to be familiar to any reader, perhaps two hundred or more names, quotations, and allusions are simply passed over in silence. Even the simplest research was sometimes not done: the author of a selection entitled "Meeting Yeats," for example, is identified only as "F. H." (p. 131) when a few minutes in a research library would have disclosed his identity as Francis Hackett, the article being reprinted in his *The Invisible Censor* (1921). Many of the notes that are supplied have errors of one kind or another. One of the worst occurs when Mikhail annotates Clifford Bax's reference (p. 43) to "the lyric that begins 'Impetuous heart, be still, be still' " by stating that "Yeats did not write a lyric beginning with this line" (p. 44)—with a stroke of his pen thereby eliminating *The Countess Cathleen* from the canon. (When Louise Morgan quotes *Yeats* referring to "another poem, quite a good one, called *The Impetuous Heart*," Mikhail's response is a "sic" [p. 201].) But what may well be the low point in the editing of this collection comes when Hugh Kingsmill recalls Yeats's telling him that an earlier interview with Kingsmill had been "the best interview he had had" (p. 295). Since Mikhail is silent on this point, one can only assume he is unaware that the very piece in question is found in *Interviews and Recollections* (pp. 88-91), where it appears under the name Hugh Lunn. Even the proofreading of this collection is inferior: along the margin of a quotation in W. J. Turner's selection mysteriously appear the numbers "7 1 5 1" (p. 253).

A. Norman Jeffares's *W. B. Yeats: The Critical Heritage* is regrettably all too similar—another opportunity to make an important contribution to Yeats studies botched through careless editing. Jeffares tries to organize the 155 selections around reviews of individual volumes, beginning with Gerard Manley Hopkins and Katharine Tynan on *Mosada*, but this scheme quickly disintegrates. The section supposedly covering the 1908 *Collected Works*, for instance, concludes with an anonymous review of *Per Amica Silentia Lunae* ten years later. Many important volumes in the canon are not covered at all, including *John Sherman and Dhoya, The Shadowy Waters, Reveries over Childhood and Youth, Collected Plays, Dramatis Personae*, the 1938 *Autobiography*, and, most strangely of all, *Last Poems and Plays*. For the volumes that are included, many major voices are absent, including William Ernest Henley on *The Wanderings of Oisin*, Arthur Symons and Max Beerbohm on *The Countess Kathleen and Various Legends and Lyrics*, and Walter De La Mare and Edward Garnett on the *Collected Works*. The list of reviewers of *The Winding Stair and Other Poems* not represented reads like a Who's Who of English Poetry and Criticism in the 1930s: Richard Church, Horace Gregory, F. R. Leavis, F. O. Matthiessen, Marianne Moore, Edwin Muir, and Stephen Spender. For the major volume in the Yeats canon, the 1933 *Collected Poems*, only two notices are printed; missing are, among others, R. P. Blackmur, Babette Deutsch, Horace Gregory, Matthiessen, Spender, and Morton Dauwen Zabel. With such gaps, as well as with a general under-representation of American criticism, it seems clear that if Joyce was granted two volumes in the Critical Heritage series, his compatriot required nothing less.

But as with *Interviews and Recollections*, the major problem with *W. B. Yeats: The Critical Heritage* is the handling of what is included. Although almost all of the selections cry out for annotation, Jeffares has supplied notes to but eighteen of them. Most of these are carried over from the original sources without indication—even when a biographical sketch of John Butler Yeats on p. 61 is followed by a note on p. 65 reading "John Butler Yeats, R.H.A. (1839-1922)." Sometimes a reviewer's quotation of a Yeats poem will be replaced by a reference to a page number in the English *Collected Poems*; these are of little help to a reader with the American edition and in any event overlook the question of Yeats's later revisions to the poem quoted. The headnotes to each selection first identify the source of the material and then give a brief handbook biography and bibliography of its author. A few of these must have been the work of two different people, as that which begins "These comments are from Forrest Reid, *W. B. Yeats: A Critical Study* (1915), the first book length study of Yeats's work. Forrest Reid

(1876-1947), novelist and essayist, born in Belfast and educated in Cambridge, wrote W. B. Yeats: A Critical Study (1915)."[7] Some of the unsigned reviews are identified, but Jeffares does not consistently state that the review was first published anonymously or when the identity of the author became known—facts which can be of some interest in evaluating Yeats's opinions of his contemporaries. In two instances one must recall a passing reference in the introduction to discover the identity of an anonymous reviewer (Francis Thompson, p. 95) or "A.M." (Annie Macdonell, p. 89), neither the headnotes, the table of contents, nor the index being of any assistance. Other reviews by Thompson (p. 138) and Edward Thomas (p. 160) are not attributed; and one piece ascribed to Edward Dowden is in fact the work of Ellen M. Duncan (p. 169). Some of the articles are presented in the wrong order, those on The Winding Stair and Other Poems inexplicably following rather than preceding those on the Collected Poems. A number of the selections are misdated: that from I. A. Richards's Science and Poetry is given as 1927 (p. 280), for instance, which is twice wrong—the book was first published in 1926, but the Yeats material was not included until the second edition of 1935.

Furthermore, in the headnote to a selection entitled "Archibald MacLeish on Public Reality and Yeats's Poetry,"[8] Jeffares explains that "it appeared in an article on Public Speech and Private Speech in Poetry, 'The Yale Review', Spring 1938. The excerpt which is included here is from a later version, The Public World: Poems of Yeats, from MacLeish's book 'Poetry and Experience' (1961)" (p. 403). This is simply not true. MacLeish did publish an article in the March 1938 Yale Review, which Yeats read and approved of and which was the inspiration for his poem "Politics"; this essay was reprinted (with some slight revisions, overlooked by Jochum) in MacLeish's A Time to Speak (1941).[9] The article in Poetry and Experience is an entirely new piece, sharing with the earlier essay only the basic thesis that Yeats's involvement in the public world was essential to the greatness of his poetry.[10] Finally, although the fifty-eight page introduction by Jeffares is an adequate sketch of the response to Yeats and usefully includes some passages from reviews not reprinted, what can one make of the statement that "Yeats's drama has interested many critics, notably B. L. Reid in *William Butler Yeats: The Lyric of Tragedy*" (p. 50)? Reid's book, of course, treats the poetry exclusively.

Curtis Baker Bradford's edition of *The Player Queen* manuscripts is, like Jochum's *Classified Bibliography*, a work which has crept into several bibliographies of Yeats studies for some years before its appearance. Indeed, even in the list of Bradford's publications at the end of the volume itself, the date is incorrectly given as 1976. The edition had been essentially completed before Bradford's untimely death in October 1969. At that time it was scheduled for publication by the University of Massachusetts Press, as part of a series under the general editorship of David R. Clark (the first and only other edition in this series is *Druid Craft*).[11] When that press was unable to find the funds to publish Bradford's work, the volume was transferred to the Northern Illinois University Press, where it languished for about half a decade. All Yeatsians are familiar with the annual appearance of an announcement of imminent publication, the price increasing a few dollars each year. (I know of one scholar who, when writing to cancel her order, informed the press that since responding to their advertisement she had met, become engaged to, and married her husband, who was also waiting for a copy; the press was not amused.)

This curious publication history is of some importance in terms of the form in which the edition has at last materialized. In an open letter to potential reviewers of the book, Clark—who saw the work through the press—has disclaimed any responsibility for errors, explaining that he was denied the opportunity to read page proof, even after he had offered to travel to DeKalb at his own expense to do so. Clark also informs me that the press ignored many of the corrections which he, with Russell K. Alspach's assistance, made on the galley proofs. This situation would be deplorable for any book, but it is especially so for an edition of manuscripts. Short of laboriously checking the original manuscripts, readers will have no way of discerning errors in the text and can never be certain that what appears on the page is in fact what Yeats wrote.

With this disclaimer, one must then evaluate *The Writing of The Player Queen* in the form we have. From the mass of manuscript materials, Bradford has isolated and reconstructed some thirty-two separate drafts. The first seventeen were written from 1907 to 1910, Yeats ending up with what Bradford describes as "a full-length play, largely in verse, which is serious in tone though it has a comic ending—a 'drama' as Chekhov used the term" (pp. 5-6). Yeats then abandoned the play until 1915, when at Ezra Pound's urging he returned to the manuscript and reworked it into essentially the form we know today. This process is covered in Drafts 18-31, with Draft 32 consisting of some changes Yeats made for the 1934 *Collected Plays*. In addition to presenting the manuscript material accompanied by a running commentary, Bradford also provides an introductory essay, a chapter on the 1919 and 1922 printings which includes a lengthy discussion of the Unicorn symbol, and a concluding essay which traces the criticism of the play and offers a final assessment, calling *The Player Queen* "a triumphant success" (p. 466).

If Bradford had lived to see his work published, he would certainly have made a few minor corrections. For example, he writes that the earliest reference to *The Player Queen* is found in a letter to John Butler Yeats on 17 July 1908; however, in a letter to Mabel Dickinson on 11 June 1908, quoted a few years ago in a critical study, Yeats writes that "I spent Monday evening with Mrs. Campbell and told her the story of *The Player Queen*. She seemed delighted and [asked] to buy it . . . . I would not agree . . . . I knew that if I had to think of pleasing anybody I could not write at all."[12] Likewise, in dating Draft 5, Bradford leans heavily on the fact that the manuscript includes a tentative table of contents for the eight-volume *Collected Works*, published late in 1908; since the draft refers to only a seven-volume scheme, Bradford concludes that "a terminal date for the plan of spring 1908 should not be too far off" (p. 40). However, a letter from A. H. Bullen to Yeats, recently published in *Letters to W. B. Yeats*, establishes that the collected edition was planned for eight volumes as early as 14 March 1907.[13] Thus Draft 5, and presumably Drafts 1-4, might best be dated "early 1907," thereby verifying Yeats's claim (made in 1922) that he began the play in 1907. Also, Bradford might well have taken into account Jochum's citation of a 1910 interview in which Yeats described *The Player Queen* as "a comedy of mediaeval or Renaissance life," adding that it "will not be distinctly Irish in character, nor, indeed, will it reflect the thought of any particular nationality, though, as is but natural, it will probably bear upon it the impress which much pondering upon Ireland must give to the work of any Irishman."[14] Finally, Bradford would have expanded his list of criticism of the play to include such items as Michael Hinden's 1972 essay stressing the essential farcical nature of the work.[15]

Leaving aside such small matters, this edition raises interesting and complex questions about the proper method of editing manuscripts and the intended audience for such endeavors. Unlike the editors of *Druid Craft*, Bradford has not attempted to provide complete transcriptions of all the extant manuscripts. Although it is unfortunate that he was unaware of some relevant materials—a few scattered pages in Michael B. Yeats's collection and, more importantly, the proofs of the Coole Edition text of the play and of the *Collected Plays* in the Macmillan Archive of the British Library[16]—Bradford's intention from the start was to provide transcriptions of only some of the drafts; the remainder are either quoted from or simply paraphrased. Moreover, even in the transcriptions included there has been no attempt to "produce a diplomatic copy of the text, even in the case of passages of verse" (p. xxv). Many canceled words and passages have been silently omitted, and the final result is something approaching a fair copy of Yeats's manuscript.

The edition produced by these procedures is ultimately unsatisfactory. *The Writing of* The Player Queen should have been one of two things: either a complete and full transcription of all the extant manuscript material, a work perhaps financially impossible to produce without a subsidy but one that would have made accessible and legible for future scholars the complete record of the composition of the play; or a much smaller book, describing the process and stages of composition while quoting from the manuscripts, perhaps offering complete transcripts to interested readers in a form other than letter-press. What we have is far too long and repetitive for all but a few specialized scholars (no one can sit down and "read" this edition) and too short and simplified for that small remnant.

The next several years are likely to witness the publication of a substantial number of Yeats editions.[17] If these are to be successful, they will have to be based on logical editorial policies that have been carefully thought out—in terms of both the nature of the material being edited and the needs of the projected audience. They will also have to be undertaken with a scholarly rigor not evident in all of the volumes discussed in this essay. Perhaps we need to remind ourselves that Yeats is indeed the greatest poet in English of this century (some would claim far more) and that the opportunity to do something that will enlarge our understanding of his life and work is a high responsibility. One would hope that those who choose to publish on Yeats would bring to their work the same dedication which he brought to his.

Some Corrections & Additions for K. P. S. Jochum, *W. B. Yeats: A Classified Bibliography of Criticism*

Cited by Jochum's entry numbers. Those in brackets are suggested new entries. Those asterisked are included on the authority of either the Jeffares or Mikhail volumes under review, and thus their accuracy is not guaranteed. I have not gone beyond Jochum's terminal date of 1972.

J.5	This is a reprint of J.4 except that the text of "I saw a shepherd youth" is not included.
J.63	There are textual variants between this and J.64.
J.96	There is a third letter: (3) 18 Woburn Bldgs., [1902?], p. 193 [1969 ed.].
J.97	The date of item (5) is 1917. All the letters in J.96 and J.97 are included in J.8413.
J.499	Compiled by Andrew W. Myers.

J.504   Reissued in 1966.

J.655   First published in New York: Putnam, 1968.

[J.739a]*   Nichols, Beverley. *Twenty-Five: Being a Young Man's Candid Recollections of His Elders and Betters.* London: Jonathan Cape, 1926.

                Yeats at Oxford, pp. 36-44.

[J.762a]*   Pyper, Nancy. "Four O'clock Tea with W. B. Yeats," *Musical Life and Arts* (Winnipeg, Manitoba), 1 Dec. 1924, pp. 161-65.

[J.788a]   "Two Unpublished Letters from AE," *PLL*, 3:3 (Summer 1967), 220-28.

                Yeats and Blake, pp. 227-28.

[J.807a]   "Three Unpublished Letters from James Stephens," *PLL*, 6:1 (Winter 1970), 77-88.

                References to Yeats.

J.837   Reprinted in Wade, *Letters*.

[J.944a]*   "Plymouth Theatre," *Boston Evening Record*, 26 Sept. 1911, p. 6.

                Interview with Yeats.

[J.944b]*   "Yeats Replies to his Critics; Defends Irish Plays Being Produced Here," *Boston Post*, 5 Oct. 1911, p. 8.

                Interview with Yeats.

[J.944c]*   "A Lively Discussion over the 'Irish Plays,' " *Sunday Post* (Boston), 8 Oct. 1911, p. 37.

                Interview with Yeats.

[J.944d]*   "Yeats Defends 'The Playboy,' " *Boston Herald*, 12 Oct. 1911, p. 8.

                Interview with Yeats.

[J.944e]*   "Mr. Yeats Explains," *Boston Evening Transcript*, 13 Oct. 1911, p. 14.

                Interview with Yeats.

[J.945]*   "Abbey Theatre: Pupils' Performance; Address
               by Mr. W. B. Yeats," *Evening Telegraph*
               (Dublin), 17 Nov. 1911, p. 5.

               [This entry to go between J.945 and J.945a.]

[J.945aa]*   *"The Playboy*: Another American Surprise.
               Players Arrested; Interview with Mr. W. B. Yeats,
               Evening Telegraph (Dublin), 19 Jan. 1912, p. 3.

[J.983a]   "Irish Literary Theatre: Dinner at the Shelbourne
               Hotel," *Daily Express* (Dublin), 12 May 1899,
               pp. 5-6.

               Speech by Yeats.

[J.991a]   "Irish National Theatre," *Freeman's Journal*,
               16 March 1903, p. 6.

               Lecture by Yeats.

[J.992a]   "Irish National Theatre," *Freeman's Journal*,
               28 Dec. 1904, p. 5.

               Speech by Yeats.

[J.1024a]   Pound, Ezra. "Homage to Wilfrid Blunt," *Poetry*
               (Chicago), 3:4 (March 1914), 220-23.

               Cf. J.1023.

J.1091   The 1965 edition is substantially revised.

J.1115   Item 12 reprinted in *Dickens, Dali and Others:*
               Studies in Popular Culture (New York: Reynal
               and Hitchcock, 1946); *Critical Essays* (London:
               Secker and Warburg, 1946).

J.1156   The American edition (New York: Macmillan,
               1958) has an added "Note" in the preface.

J.1160   The third issue is dated Spring 1970 and includes
               an article on the Yeats monument in Sandy-
               mount.

[J.1180a]   Anon., "Seeker for Truth," *MD: Medical Maga-*
               zine (New York), 9:8 (August 1965), 180-87.

J.1358   Includes some remarks by Einar Lönnberg,
               pp. 199-200.

J.1528   First published Boston: Little, Brown, 1964, without the subtitle.

J.1802   Correct to *Fountains*.

J.2439   See J.175 and J.2803 for revised versions of the essays on "The Second Coming" and "The Black Tower."

J.2647   There were revised editions in 1961 and 1964.

J.2835   Reprinted as a pamphlet: London: Oxford University Press, [1965?].

J.3173   A revised version is found in J.1150.

J.3350   There was an enlarged edition, Bombay: Orient Longman, 1972.

[J.3360a]   Berryman, John. "The Ritual of W. B. Yeats," *Columbia Review*, 17 (May-June 1936), 26-32.

[J.3656a]*   *Irish Times*, 9 May 1899.
                Commentary on *The Countess Cathleen*.

J.3991a   The index applies to all editions from 1937 on.

[J.4289a]*   Watson, Sir William. *Illustrated London News*, 10 Sept. 1892.

[J.4297a]*   Lang, Andrew. *Illustrated London News*, 23 Dec. 1893.

[J.4394a]*   Anon., *Manchester Guardian*, 12 June 1903.

[J.5849a]   Le Galliene, Richard. *Young Lives* (Bristol: Arrowsmith, 1898).
                Yeats appears on pp. 308-10.

J.5911   There was a revised edition in 1922.

J.6321   Item 9: one of the letters previously published in J.166.

J.6358   The essay is an excerpt from Arthur Walkley's article. Cf. J.3767.

[J.6608a]*   "De Valera as Play Censor," *Manchester Guardian Weekly*, 30:15, 13 April 1934, p. 296.
                Yeats is quoted.

Notes

1. *Anglo-Irish Literature: A Review of Research*, ed. Richard J. Finneran (New York: Modern Language Assoc., 1976), pp. 216-314. This present essay incorporates some remarks made in a paper on current Yeats research presented at the 1978 meeting of the American Committee for Irish Studies.

2. Recent editions not treated here are *The Correspondence of Robert Bridges and W. B. Yeats*, ed. Richard J. Finneran (London: Macmillan, 1977); *Letters to W. B. Yeats*, ed. Finneran, George Mills Harper, and William M. Murphy (London: Macmillan, 1977); *Literatim Transcription of the Manuscripts of William Butler Yeats's* The Speckled Bird, ed. William H. O'Donnell (Delmar, N.Y.: Scholars' Facsimiles & Reprints, 1976); and *The Speckled Bird*, ed. O'Donnell (Toronto: McClelland and Stewart, 1977).

3. Maurice Harmon, *Select Bibliography for the Study of Anglo-Irish Literature and Its Backgrounds: An Irish Studies Handbook* (Port Credit, Ontario: P. D. Meany, 1977), p. 132.

4. Shotaro Oshima, *W. B. Yeats and Japan* (Tokyo: Hokuseido Press, 1965), pp. 149-89.

5. George Monteiro, "Addenda to Cross and Dunlop's *Yeats Criticism 1887-1965*," *PBSA*, 70 (1976), 278.

6. D. N. D[unlop], "Interview with Mr. W. B. Yeats," *Irish Theosophist*, 2 (15 Nov. 1893), 147-49. Mikhail (p. 19) follows John P. Frayne in *Uncollected Prose by W. B. Yeats*, I (New York: Columbia Univ. Press, 1970), 298, in misdating this interview 15 Oct. 1893.

7. The statement that Reid's work was "the first book length study" is untrue. The first was Horatio Sheafe Krans, *William Butler Yeats and the Irish Literary Revival* (New York: McClure, Phillips & Co., 1904). Jeffares refers to this book in the introduction (p. 14), but both there and in the index gives the name as "Horatio F. Krans."

8. Most of the titles are Jeffares's, although this is not always clearly evident (the same problem exists with the titles in *Interviews and Recollections*). At least one—"Yeats and the 'Scrutiny' Tradition" (p. 385)—is quite misleading: the review at hand, H. A. Mason's "Yeats and the English Tradition," has nothing to do with *Scrutiny* other than being published there.

9. Archibald MacLeish, "Public Speech and Private Speech in Poetry," *Yale Review*, 27 (March 1938), 536-47; *A Time to Speak: The Selected Prose* (Boston: Houghton Mifflin, 1941). In a letter to Dorothy Wellesley on 24 May 1938, Yeats wrote, "There has been an article upon my work in the *Yale Review*, which is the only article on the subject which has not bored me for years. It commends me above other modern poets because my language is 'public.' That word, which I had not thought of myself, is a word I want" (*Letters of W. B. Yeats*, ed. Allan Wade [London: Rupert Hart-Davis, 1954], pp. 908-9). The letter concludes with a draft of "Politics." Yeats found the Thomas Mann

epigraph to the poem in MacLeish's article: "Thomas Mann, who has reason to know, says of the nature of our time, that in our time the destiny of man presents its meanings in political terms" (pp. 545-46).

10. Exactly the same passage used by Jeffares appeared earlier in Raymond Cowell's *Critics on Yeats* (London: George Allen and Unwin, 1971), pp. 13-14, the editor noting that "an earlier form of this viewpoint appeared in the Spring 1938 issue of the *Yale Review* and was welcomed by Yeats" (p. 14). Jeffares gives the same imprecise date and also states that the essay "was welcomed by Yeats" (p. 403). One can only wonder if Jeffares has not relied on Cowell for his text and misread his ambiguous statement on the provenance of the essay.

11. *Druid Craft: The Writing of* The Shadowy Waters, ed. Michael J. Sidnell, George P. Mayhew, and David R. Clark (Amherst: Univ. of Massachusetts Press, 1971).

12. Quoted in Brenda S. Webster, *Yeats: A Psychoanalytic Study* (Stanford, Calif.: Stanford Univ. Press, 1973), p. 116.

13. *Letters to W. B. Yeats*, p. 180.

14. "Mr. Yeats and His New Play," *Irish Nation* (Dublin), 2 (16 July 1910), 8. In citing this item, Jochum incorrectly describes it as an "interview about the play, revealing that it was originally conceived as a puppet play" (J.3838). In the beginning of the interview "Mr. Yeats pointed out a minature model of the Abbey Theatre on which, by the help of puppets, the scenes of his new play might be arranged, and the various figures grouped and moved as in actual drama," referring to the model stage which Gordon Craig had constructed for him in January 1910. But Yeats does not suggest that *The Player Queen* had been intended as a puppet play.

15. Michael Hinden, "Yeats's Symbolic Farce: *The Player Queen*," *Modern Drama*, 14 (Feb. 1972), 441-48. Webster's study also includes an extended analysis of the play.

16. For a discussion of the British Library material and its importance in the establishment of Yeats's texts, see my "On Editing Yeats: The Text of *A Vision* (1937)," *Texas Studies in Literature and Language*, 19 (Spring 1977), 119-34; and the appendix in the forthcoming edition of *The Secret Rose*, ed. Warwick Gould, Phillip L. Marcus, and Michael J. Sidnell.

17. A critical edition of the 1925 text of *A Vision*, ed. George Mills Harper and Walter Kelly Hood, should be in print before this essay is published. I am preparing a new and comprehensive edition of *The Complete Poems*. Other editions of published materials are in progress or projected.

The Revised *STC*

William P. Williams

W. A. Jackson, F. S. Ferguson, Katharine F. Pantzer, eds. *A Short-Title Catalogue of Books Printed in England, Scotland, and Ireland and of English Books Printed Abroad 1475-1640.* Second edition, Vol. II, I-Z. London: The Bibliographical Society, 1976. xii, 494 pp.

Writing a review of the *Short-Title Catalogue,* second edition, Volume II, is very much like writing a review of the Bibliographical Society, the Modern Language Association, or the profession of letters worldwide. Scholars who work in the *STC* period have come to think of the *STC* not as a single volume (in the near future four volumes) but as a literary-historical period, an amalgam of research tools centered on the *STC* itself, and even as a microfilm series.

In 1884 George Bullen probably thought he was doing no more than producing yet another of the admirable catalogues of the holdings of the British Museum when he published a *Catalogue of Books in the Library of the British Museum . . . to the year 1640.* However, Bullen's work and other cataloguing enterprises in the first two decades of this century eventually led to the Bibliographical Society's decision in 1918 to undertake a complete retrospective bibliography of English printed books to 1640. The chief proponent of this work, and subsequently the chief editor, was A. W. Pollard of the British Museum, along with the then vice-president of the Society, G. R. Redgrave. The result, in 1926, was the *STC.* Now, after exactly a half century of intensive and extensive use by scholars, many of whom have carried their interleaved copies of the STC around the world with them, the second volume (I-Z) of the second edition has appeared. One must add that it has appeared after many years of anxious anticipation by all of us who knew how close it was to completion but kept watching professional societies struggle and founder in the economy of the late twentieth century as printing, postage, and other costs rocketed, and wondered if it would ever really be possible for the scholarly world and the Bibliographical Society to be able to afford the publication of the revised *STC* (*RSTC*). It was therefore with both pleasure and relief that we opened the pages of the *RSTC*, and we have little doubt that the remaining volumes will appear, and approximately on schedule.

The publication of the *STC* in 1926 was followed twelve years later by the commencement of the University Microfilm series "Early English Books 1475-1640" (a project which has filmed nearly all *STC* titles during the past forty years). Then in 1944 William Warner Bishop's checklist of American copies of *STC* books appeared, and six years later a second revised edition was published. Paul G. Morrison's *Index of Printers, Publishers and Booksellers* was also issued in 1950, and in 1958 David Ramage's finding-list of English copies of *STC* books appeared. Hence, thirty-two years after its publication it would be fair to say that an *STC* industry had emerged, and by that time W. A. Jackson had already begun work on a revised *STC*.

It was Pollard's intention in 1918 to produce a catalogue which contained the bare essentials for each book recorded so that the *STC* could be put in the hands of scholars at the earliest possible date. And although it took Pollard and Redgrave considerably longer than expected to do the catalogue, the entries did provide only that information necessary to produce a "handlist," as the editors called it in their preface. They went on to say that because of their desire to produce the *STC* quickly and at a reasonable cost, they had not elaborated on some entries for which they had information because they did not have available similar information for others: "The trouble is that when scrupulous care is evident in some entries, it is expected in all, and one object of this preface is to warn all users of this book that from the mixed character of its sources it is a dangerous work for any one to handle lazily, that is, without verification" (p. ix). Pollard and Redgrave thought that a proper catalogue would be produced in the future "when we know enough to make it a good one" (p. vii).

By the time Jackson was at work on the revised *STC* we apparently knew almost enough to make a good catalogue. However, when the first half of the catalogue had been revised, so much more was known about the preparation of the revision that the last half of the *RSTC* could be issued at a higher standard of accuracy and "perfection" than could the first half— and it could be issued sooner. Miss Pantzer and the Bibliographical Society therefore followed Pollard's lead by getting the book into the hands of users as soon as possible, even if that meant publishing the first two volumes in reverse order.

It is also well that the revision does not merely correct errors and add titles, but rather that it transforms the *STC* of 1926 into a catalogue which is that "good one" envisioned in 1918. Surely a crucial decision was not to renumber the entries but either to cancel, transfer (e.g., "21427 Roy, William. Rede me and be nott wrothe. [1528.] Now=1462.7."), or add by the use of a point and sequential numbers to the right of that point (two of the most impressive instances of this are "Indulgences," 14077c.1-154, and "Newsbooks," 18507.1-361). Thus a scholar need not keep both *STC* and *RSTC* on hand (as is the case with the first and second editions of volume one of Wing) in order to make use of the microfilm series or any other part of the *STC* industry.

This decision was a matter of common sense and forethought. When one compares *STC* and *RSTC* entries, one immediately becomes aware of substantial differences between the two catalogues. First, the *RSTC* makes much greater use of annotations because the editors knew more, and scholars will be forever grateful to Jackson and Pantzer for this fact. One can easily imagine the number of delays, photocopy orders, letters, and plane trips that will be avoided by annotations such as these added to 18603: "Same plates as in 18601. The L copy has the title in a border of type orns. while O, C, F have it in the engr. compartment of 18601." And one is nearly awestruck by such annotation as that found for 18533, for where *STC* had only said "(2 issues), HH," *RSTC* tells us: "Tp in two settings; above the imprint the spacing of the colon in 'God: Honor' is 'd: H' (HN) or 'd : H' (G², YK, HD). Quartersheet N² set in duplicate; Nl^r line 3 from bottom ends: 'from' (G², HN, HD) or 'frō' (YK). First

8 lines of Ll^r in 3 settings: line 1 begins: 'tichrist' (O, C); 'ry' (O, HN, HD); or 'gory' (O^5, G^2). The last is the only one that properly fits the text of K8^V." Even on a more modest level the wealth of detail, fullness of description, and care can be observed. *STC* said of 18535; "The oration and sermon made at Rome the xxvij daie of Maie, 1578. 8°. *I. Charlewood*, [1581.] Ent. 22 ap. 1581. HH." The *RSTC* entry expands, adds, and corrects in the following manner: "The oration and sermon made at Rome . . . the xxvij. daie of Maie. 1578. 8°. *I. Charlewood, seruant to the earle of Arundell*, [1581.] Ent. 22 ap. 1581. L^2 (imp.). O^4. D(imp.).; F. Answered in 19402."

Of course the revision has been expensive in terms of time, money, and space; *STC* was made up of 627 pages measuring about 250 x 185 mm., whereas just half of *RSTC* takes up 506 pages of 310 x 235 mm. This fact alone tells us that this will be the definitive retrospective bibliography of early English books, for it would seem unlikely that we will be able to afford to revise a catalogue on such lavish proportions in the forseeable future. However, it may never be necessary to reedit this work in its entirety. Certainly new titles and new variants will continue to be discovered, but it is doubtful that they will appear in such numbers that they cannot be dealt with by the issuing of fascicles prepared along the lines of the addenda and corrigenda on pages 489-94 of *RSTC*, and published perhaps every quarter of a century. Furthermore, its high standard of accuracy will make the *RSTC* definitive, though I hesitate to use such an absolute term. I know of only about a dozen errors in this work, only one or two of them more important than faulty punctuation, and almost every one known to the editor long before reviewers pointed them out. I will list below a few errors that matter, not as any kind of implied criticism of *RSTC* but so that readers may correct their copies appropriately.

14077c.14	The point is missing.
14077c.11B	The point is missing in some copies, though not in mine.
23969.5c	The *c* is unnecessary.
25471	Appears as 05471.

16633.3   Should read 16333.3 in the table of added entries
                 on page 489.

The editors must be commended for the many cross-references in
RSTC, but the Oxford University Press is not to be commended
for the odd things that happen to headings and running heads
from time to time. Someone seems to have changed his mind
between "Indulgences" (pp. 2-9) and "Newsbooks" (pp. 178-85),
for in the first instance the main entry number (14077c) is not
carried on from column to column while in the latter instance
(18507) it is. On p. 256 the author heading which begins the
second column has one more comma than the author entry at
the foot of the first column (20487.5), and on p. 146 a similar slip
between columns occurs with a digraph. Finally one
has to note the heading of the second column on p. 340,
which describes "Smith, Henry" not as a "Minister," as he had
been designated in the first column, but as a "Monster." I
assume that Miss Pantzer is not responsible for any of these
problems, nor should she be, I believe, but if this is the worst of
RSTC's errors and infelicities, then only the greatest
nonpublishing pedant would suggest that *RSTC* should not
have been rushed into print with these blemishes!

Personally, I find some unease in having Volume II without
the full front matter, which is promised to us in Volume I, but I
suppose anyone who has used Greg's *Bibliography of the
English Printed Drama* should not boggle too much at the front
matter appearing in the front, though later in time, rather than
having it appear at the back. Furthermore, all such minor points
are doubtless compensated for by knowing that eventually the
RSTC will give us a printers and booksellers index and Dr.
Philip Rider's chronological index (this last component of
RSTC had not been decided on when Volume II went to press
and consequently it is not mentioned in the preface) in a
uniform format, it is to be hoped, and all from the same source.

Now that the galleys for Volume I are making the rounds of
the libraries for final checking and we are less than two years
from having Volume I of the *RSTC*, it is perhaps an appropriate
time for the scholarly community to offer thanks to Katharine

Pantzer, not just for editing the *RSTC* but also for finding time
to answer the many questions of scholars who needed *RSTC*
information before there was an *RSTC*. Fifty years ago, at the
conclusion of the preface to the *STC*, Pollard and Redgrave
offered this hopeful prophesy: "When the Bibliographical
Society has produced this second volume [the *RSTC* in its four
volumes], it will, we believe, have put England a long way
ahead of any other country in Europe in its record of its early
printed literature" (p. xi). The labors of W. A. Jackson, F. S.
Ferguson, and Katharine F. Pantzer have surely fulfilled that
prophecy, and the scholarly community is grateful.

Gawain Douglas Re-catalogued[1]

Florence Ridley

Priscilla Bawcutt. *Gavin Douglas, A Critical Study.* Edinburgh: Edinburgh University Press, 1976. xii, 245 pp.

Mrs. Bawcutt's stated purpose here is "to present a balanced picture of Douglas, and to show the complex content in which he wrote" (preface). Her method is to list the writers, works, and experiences which could have influenced the poet, then to list details of his poetry which might reflect such influence. After reading this book, while many will agree with the author that "such an approach by no means diminishes," few will conclude that it "often illuminates" Douglas' work (p. vi).

In Chapter I she repeats the facts of Douglas' life which have been amassed from public records, comtemporary letters and early commentaries by his editors, John Small and David Coldwell;[2] but she never makes clear how these disparate details form a significant whole, specifically how what we know of the poet's life actually shaped his writing. She suggests only that in the "Palice of Honour" and in the Prologues, each of which introduces a book of his translation of the *Aeneid*, Douglas may present something of a self-portrait having "much in common with the litigious churchman" who disputed with ecclesiastical rivals in real life and is depicted by John Major and Polydore Vergil (p. 2).

Chapter II, "The Cultural Background," attempts to place Douglas in an "international, Latin speaking world" (p. 24), and to demonstrate his character as a "vernacular humanist" (p. 36). The evidence for every scrap of possibly relevant influence is cited: Scotsmen who visited Europe and Europeans who visited Scotland; means for publishing books at home and abroad; the curriculum of St. Andrews where Douglas studied; hints that he may also have studied in Paris; the imaginary dialogue between Douglas and David Cranston written by John Major, who portrays Douglas as a critic of scholastic philosophy and theology; opportunities for literary discussion which friendship with Robert Cockburn and Polydore Vergil could have provided; classical and vernacular writings owned by Douglas' contemporaries and/or mentioned in his poetry.

But John Major's portrayal of Douglas is a fiction; we are not told for how long or how well he knew Cockburn, who spent much of his time in France; and Polydore Vergil knew Douglas only during the last year of the poet's life, when the time for influential literary discussion was long past. As Mrs. Bawcutt says, the university curriculum "left few obvious traces in Douglas' poetry" (p. 26) and the presence of a writer's name "may not necessarily mean that Douglas had read him" (p. 35). Thus much of the evidence presented for an understanding of Douglas' intellect, and therefore of his poetry, remains tentative. There are some interesting observations in this chapter, such as that the Scots poet "humorously re-applies" Chaucer's line about the Prioress, "And al was conscience and tendre herte," to himself in Prologue XIII (p. 41). But mainly what we are given here are catalogues of details about Douglas and his contemporaries and of writings reflected in his poetry. These same tendencies to list traits rather than analyze trends and to reach ambiguous conclusions similarly mar the chapters that follow.

In Chapter III, "The Palice of Honour," Mrs. Bawcutt repeats the views which are generally accepted about Douglas' canon, the genre, sources, and literary relations of his dream vision, the poem's main theme (the pursuit of honour) and its basic structure (a poet's learning process). She then gives a detailed retelling of the story and finds the central conception to be ambiguous. For Douglas "honour" is equated with God, or with valor, or with virtue, and while it embodies a "rejection of all forms of earthly glory," (p. 61) yet is "more secular and this-worldly than perhaps he would admit" (p. 63).

Mrs. Bawcutt mentions Douglas' portrayal of himself, as "Both timorous and obtuse" (p. 67), but apparently without perceiving the implications of that portrayal. She merely cites aspects of "The Palice of Honour," its conscious ornateness, complex stanzaic pattern, allusions, archaisms, verbal patternings, rhetorical colours, learned polysyllables, lavish catalogues, without explaining how the persona makes these separate aspects meaningful, providing unity and significance. This persona, apparently suggested to Douglas by a similar device in "The House of Fame,"[3] is the key to the poem's endless catalogues, unevenness, self-conscious metrical fireworks, and abrupt ending. In "The Palice of Honour," a would-be poet, exploiting ad nauseam all the techniques of the dream vision, tries desperately if futilely to write his own. But in Mrs. Bawcutt's study the central importance of this figure is passed over.

Chapter IV, "Douglas's Virgil," deals with standpoints from which Douglas saw Virgil. As a Christian who defends the pagan poet by allegory. As a vernacular writer anxious to assert the superiority of his own version of the Trojan story on the grounds of its faithfulness to the original. And as a poet who admired and imitated Virgil's poetic artistry. But she is trying "to illustrate the variety of Douglas' response to Virgil, and the way in which his ideas were often shaped by tradition" (p. 90). Standpoints from which one poet views another are not necessarily responses. While she does indeed demonstrate that Douglas in his notes and Prologues stated certain attitudes toward Virgil which he shared with earlier writers, and that he occasionally quoted from Virgil, she fails to show how one poet affected the other. In what color, texture, abbreviation, amplification did Douglas' attitudes result? The next chapters, on "The *Eneados* 'Text' and 'Sentence' " and "The Eneados: 'Eloquence,' " should have made this clear, but they do not.

Chapter V answers few questions, although it addresses several: the audience to whom the *Eneados* is directed; the difficult—really unsolvable—problem of which text of Virgil Douglas used; the influence of medieval commentators, particularly Badius Ascensius, upon contents, division, and wording of the translation. It is not too difficult to make a plausible surmise, as Mrs. Bawcutt does, about why Douglas chose to translate the *Aeneid*, or to learn from his text that he depended upon Virgilian commentaries. But how did he use them? We are told only that sometimes he followed one, sometimes another, sometimes both (pp. 122-23). Did he politicize or Christianize Virgil? Although she acknowledges that Douglas "must have been aware that what Virgil said of 'onkyndly wer' and 'souerane liberte' was relevant to the Scotland of his own time" (p. 125), the critic finds in his work no political implications such as those detected by Coldwell and Bruce Dearing (p. 125).[4] He emphasizes, makes more explicit, stresses, and expands "those ideas he could reconcile with his own religion" (pp. 126-27); yet at the same time he "does not give specific Christian colouring to the underworld" (p. 125). We are left again with an uneasy sense of Mrs. Bawcutt's wavering back and forth between possibilities. When she concludes that Douglas "preserves a balance between the different elements in Virgil's poem, and much, if not all, of its complexity" (p. 127), we have been shown neither those elements nor that complexity nor Douglas' degree of success in preserving either.

What is the overall impact of the translation? What is its nature as an independent poem? How specifically does it resemble or differ from the original? Chapter VI contains an abundance of raw data which should have made it easy to answer such central critical questions, but its answers are ambiguous: Did Douglas understand Virgil's versification? "It is not easy to determine" (p. 137). Were his errors the result of carelessness or ignorance? "It is difficult to say" (p. 137). Was his use of conventional diction an asset or a drawback? In this respect, "he is not so clumsy as Lydgate, nor so subtle as Chaucer" (p. 143). Moreover, the author's presentation of seemingly endless examples, leaving the reader with a sense of having confronted stack after stack of neatly catalogued slips of paper, tends to obscure any view of the poem as a whole.

Details of Douglas' style are listed one after another under general headings: Efforts to translate Virgil's world into contemporary experience (individual words—*Merum* is "ypocras"; Dido wears a "wimple," Amata a "quafe," Ascanius a "tawbart"; ships have "forcastells" and "eftcastells"; *aes* is translated "steill," "stelyt," "irene graith," "plait of steill,"

"steill weid"). Parenthetical explanations which lend a sense of remoteness (examples). Anachronisms which lend a sense of contemporaneity (examples). Comments which underscore religious difference (many examples).

The catalogue effect of such presentation is particularly noticeable in the section dealing with Chaucer's influence, an influence Mrs. Bawcutt finds apparent in: Anglicisms (o for a, ai, or ay). Isolated words ("sche" for "scho," "morrow" for "morn," "mych" for "meikill/meikill"). Syntax ("of hym Achillys," "of hym Julius"). Archaic verb forms ("bene" for "be"; past participles with y- prefix; infinitives ending in -in, -en, -yn, -ing). Intensive prefixes (for-, to-, alto-). Variant forms or pronunciations ("drive/drevyn," "drynt/drond," "daw/day"). Chivalric attitude to love reflected in phrasing and imagery (examples); in an idealistic approach to women (more examples); in the treatment of Dido (which manages both to depart from that of Chaucer and yet to recall it).

Similar treatment is given the matter of the alliterative school's influence upon Douglas; but it seems pointless to repeat more details. None of them is incorrect. But the multitude of aspects, good and bad, which are indubitably part of Douglas' style remain unassembled fragments, so that it is ultimately impossible, at least on the basis of the evidence as presented, to accept or reject Mrs. Bawcutt's tentative opinion that Douglas remains "reasonably faithful to his original, yet has recreated Virgil's images in terms of his own language, poetic traditions, and experience of the world around him" (p. 163). The difficulty is that while the author cites abundant independent details of Douglas' language, experience, and sources, she fails to show how he used them to recreate Virgil.

She begins Chapter VII by asserting that in contrast to early anthologizers of Scots poetry, such as George Bannatyne as well as two of the best modern critics, Coldwell and Denton Fox, she reads the Prologues of the *Eneados* "not only as self-contained pieces of writing . . . but in the context within which Douglas himself placed them . . . within the Virgilian ambience" (p. 165). Although this promises fresh critical insights into each of the Prologues and its relation to Virgil, what we get in the main is a listing of sources—classical poets, medieval poets, Virgil, Horace, Ovid, Martial, Statius, Dante, Chaucer, Boccaccio, Lydgate—all of whom could have influenced Douglas, coupled with summaries of contents, descriptions of the manner in which certain Prologues are linked to (though not necessarily of how they reflect) the book they precede, and an occasional original comment, such as the suggestion that Prologue VIII "forms a grotesque parody of the opening lines of book 8" (p. 173). This is a quite plausible interpretation of the concluding portion of the Prologue, though it is somewhat too sweeping a generalization when applied to the whole. Number VIII, an attack on the evils of Douglas' own day, seems not to be "a joke, a piece of comic relief" (p. 173) throughout; but rather, as Coldwell has pointed out, a foil to the idealized state of Evander depicted by Virgil.[5]

Mrs. Bawcutt indicates that she will treat all of the Prologues as independent units within "the Virgilian ambience," yet she discusses in detail only three of the thirteen. She demonstrates fully that Prologue XII is ornate, derivative, and a hymn to the sun, but offers no explanation of its reltaion to book 12.[6] She notes the linking of Prologue to Book 7 (like other men the poet wakes and must resume his daily labor), but does not comment on the symbolic relation between the two units made clear by Coldwell: "Seven, as Douglas himself points out, on dark and gloomy winter, is a coda to the Underworld."[7]

On another suggestion of Coldwell, however, that in Prologue XIII Douglas has "a chance to explain and defend his inclusion of the extra book" (added by Maphaeus Vegius),[8] Mrs. Bawcutt expands and in so doing makes her most original contribution to an understanding of Douglas' poetry. Prologue XIII traces a Scottish evening from twilight to dawn, and here she points out how such temporal patterning reflects the poet's changing mood as he moves from rest to a resumption of labor at dawn. His dream during the night, with its reference to the dream of St. Jerome, lends Douglas' work authority, indicates his awareness of the proper Christian attitude toward pagan literature, provides him with an opportunity to express his own views and an excuse for adding something which he realized was an improper appendage to Virgil. It is a perceptive interpretation, one which takes into consideration this entire Prologue and does what the author had indicated she would do with each of them. Here she shows clearly how Prologue XIII is "a successful piece of writing in itself, yet closely linked with the book that it precedes" (p. 190).

In her concluding chapter Mrs. Bawcutt traces Douglas' subsequent reputation and effect by citing his admirers, imitators, and critics. "The *Eneados*," she says, "must . . . be related to an anonymous 'body' of English as well as Scots poets, to Chaucer, to Ascensius and other Latin commentators, and, not least, to Virgil" (p. 160). Add to the *Eneados* "The Palice of Honour" and Mrs. Bawcutt has described her consistent purpose throughout: to relate Douglas to his cultural and political context and to other authors. But to "relate" is not merely to list aspects of experience, sources, style, and the like. When on the last page, where one might hope for a final comprehensive appraisal, she sums up the poet's qualitites—not profoundly original, eccentric, pedantic, obscure, idiosyncratic, lively, humorous, honest, zestful, possessed of verbal energy, strong, comprehensive—we receive no overall impression. We cannot see the forest of Douglas' poetic achievement for the trees of Bawcutt's minutiae.

She has brought together a great deal of accurate information. Yet what we could have asked for from her book is somewhat less: less raw data suggesting that Douglas' work might have been influenced in a certain way; less repetition of material already published; and much more: more acknowledgment of studies which could assist students of Douglas and of Middle Scots poetry generally;[9] more critical insights into Douglas' own work; and most important of all, an unambiguous, comprehensive statement as to his real worth. Is he valuable only as a repository of words and images mined from other poets? Or only historically as the first British translator of the *Aeneid*? Or has he not an unique character as a poet in his own right? If so, what?

For some years there has been increasing interest in the neglected treasures of early Scots poetry, as the success of recent sessions on that topic at meetings of the Modern Language Association would indicate. But despite excellent analyses by John MacQueen, Denton Fox, Louis Brewer Hall, and A. C. Spearing of individual poems of Henryson, Douglas, and Dunbar,[10] we still badly need balanced, book-length critical appraisals of the entire corpus of each. After the publication of *Gavin Douglas: A Critical Study*, the need still remains.

Notes

1. The poet indicates the spelling of his name in "To knaw the naym of the translatour" at the end of his translation of the 12th book of the *Aeneid*: "The GAW onbrokkyn mydlyt wyth the WYNE," see Gawain Douglas, *Virgil's 'Aeneid,' Translated into Scottish Verse*, ed. David F. C. Coldwell, The Scottish Text Society, 3rd ser., 4 (Edinburgh: William Blackwood & Sons Ltd., 1960), p. 139.

2. John Small, ed., *The Poetical Works of Gavin Douglas* (Edinburgh: William Paterson, 1874), I, i-cxxvii. Coldwell, ed., *Virgil's* Aeneid, *Translated into Scottish Verse*, The Scottish Text Society, 3rd ser., 1 (Edinburgh: William Blackwood & Sons Ltd., 1964), pp. 1-38.

3. For a perceptive analysis of Chaucer's poem see Alfred David, "Literary Satire in the *House of Fame*," *PMLA*, 75 (1960), 333-39.

4. Coldwell makes such a finding in *Virgil's* Aeneid, I, 88: Bruce Dearing in "Gavin Douglas' *Eneados*: A Reinterpretation," *PMLA*, 67 (1952), 856-59.

5. Coldwell, *Virgil's* Aeneid, I, 88.

6. For a plausible explanation of the relation between Virgil's Book 12 and the prologue supplied by Douglas, see Coldwell, *Virgil's* Aeneid, I, 88.

7. Ibid.

8. Ibid; Bawcutt, pp. 186-90.

9. See, for example, J. W. Baxter, *William Dunbar, A Biographical Study* (Edinburgh: Oliver and Boyd, 1952); MacQueen, "Some Aspects of the Early Renaissance in Scotland," *Forum for Modern Language Studies*, 3 (July 1967), 204; Scott, *Dunbar*; F. H. Ridley, "Middle Scots Writers," in *A Manual of the Writings in Middle English*, ed. Albert E. Hartung, Vol. 4 (Hamden, Conn.: Shoe String Press, 1973), 961-1060, 1103-1313. These and a number of other editions, books, and articles which, although not mentioned by Mrs. Bawcutt, are of considerable value for the study of Douglas' work are identified in my article, "A Check List, 1956-1968, for Study of 'The Kingis Quair,' the Poetry of Robert Henryson, Gawin Douglas, and William Dunbar," *Studies in Scottish Literature*, 8 (July 1970), 30-51.

10. MacQueen, *Robert Henryson, A Study of the Major Narrative Poems* (Oxford: Clarendon Press, 1967), pp. 24-44; Fox, "Dunbar's 'The Golden Targe,' " *ELH*, 26 (September 1959), 324-29; Fox, "Henryson's Fables," *ELH*, 29 (December 1962), 337-56; Hall, "An Aspect of the Renaissance in Gavin Douglas' *Eneados*," *Renaissance Studies*, 7 (1960), 184-92; Spearing, " 'The Testament of Cresseid' and the High Concise Style," *Speculum*, 37 (April 1962), 208-25. Tom Scott's *Dunbar, a Critical Exposition of the Poems* (Edinburgh: Oliver and Boyd, 1966) is, of course, a book-length study, but a psychosociological rather than a literary or critical one.

Greene's Revised *Carols*

Rossell Hope Robbins

Richard Leighton Greene, ed. *The Early English Carols.* Second edition, revised and enlarged. Oxford: Clarendon Press, 1977. clxxiii, 517 pp.

In recent decades, criticism of Middle English has moved from the distinguished and talented amateurs of the nineteenth century—and what more were F. J. Furnivall, R. Morris, J. R. Lumby, who established the Early English Text Society over a hundred years ago in 1864, than inspired dilettantes?—to the footnoting professionals of today.[1] During this period some few names have become identified with a particular achievement, greater or less, so that the conditioned reflex to "pastourelle" is W. P. Jones; to "lost literature," R. M. Wilson; to "aureate terms," J. C. Mendenhall; to "political prophecy," R. Taylor; to "literary patronage," K. Holzknecht; or to "macaronic hymn," W. O. Wehrle. Though respected, these names do not reflect the breadth and scope that is evoked by Bishop Thomas Percy with his *Reliques*; Francis James Child with his *Ballads*; the Reverend Walter W. Skeat with his *Oxford Chaucer*; or Manly and Rickert with their *Texts of the Canterbury Tales*. These were giants in their day. When a study of comparable magnitude to any of these works is finally announced, knowledge of its appearance has been breeding for some time: tension mounts; the day of publication is awaited; the windows of Blackwells bulge with pristine copies, their jackets as clean as Eton choristers'. The most impecunious graduate denies himself more meals than usual to buy his own, his very own copy.

How in 1979 can anyone convey to young scholars of today the excited anticipation that greeted the appearance of Richard Leighton Greene's *Early English Carols* in 1935, at a time when who knew what a carol was? Forty years later, who does not know what a carol is, and so to most of the community of scholars, young and old, "Carols Mark II" (the phrase is Douglas Gray's) is déjà vu. Greene's classic definition of carols is automatically accepted: "poems intended [on their metrical form], or at least suitable, for singing, made up of uniform stanzas and provided with a burden which begins the piece and is to be repeated after each stanza" (p. xi). We forget that in 1935 this was new, controversial, shocking. Carleton Brown, for example, questioned this strict adherence to form: "Logical consistency may have demanded the inclusion of this piece [No. 402] in his collection, but one feels that Dr. Greene has saved his definition only by sacrificing the essential spirit of the carol . . . . But it is questionable whether one can establish these boundaries by wholly ignoring general usage and considering only metrical form."[2] Mary Sergeantson in *YWES* snubbed this landmark with a short sentence: "Greene's work on the carol deserves note" (16 [1935], 120). However, Gordon Hall Gerould, writing in the authoritative *Speculum*, appreciated the book's preeminence: "Very rarely is a scholar so fortunate, and at the same time so acute of mind and industrious, as to establish firmly for the first time the value of a literary *genre* and to present his conclusions buttressed by the whole extant body of evidence, edited with scrupulous care. This is what Professor Greene has succeeded in doing—a great task worthily accomplished."[3] Gerould's critique could be reprinted with minor revisions as a review of the 1977 version, completely reedited, all the manuscripts reexamined, the notes updated and showing an encyclopedic intimacy with the literature, and beautifully reset by the Clarendon Press in a somewhat smaller 10-point type (though the original 461 pages now number 517). This "Second Edition, Revised and Enlarged" is a magnificent monument to a giant of our days: a gentleman and a scholar. Greene is the carol; the carol is Greene.

In the half century since he presented his dissertation to Princeton University in 1929, Greene's position on the origin of the carol has not changed. Consistently he has stressed its secular (as opposed to ecclesiastical) basis. In the *Selection of English Carols* (Oxford: Clarendon Press, 1962), he wrote: "The *carole* is both an indoor and an outdoor recreation in the Middle

Ages, but its original site is out-of-doors and socially unrestricted, a 'common', a market-place, or a field by a sinister-sacred tree or perhaps one where the fairies have left the lush green circle of their own *carole*, a *platea*, as the old documents call it" (p. 51). And Greene summed up in a much-quoted sentence: "Both carol and *cantilena* owe their form to the immemorial structure of the unlettered people's dance-song: burden, stanza, burden, often linked by rhyme" (p. 43). This, of course, had been his view in 1935, and it remains his view in 1977—the second edition in fact reprints the words of the first: "The ultimate origins of the carol are non-Christian. The direct progenitors of the ring-dances of nominally Christian France and England were the dances of the pagan spring and winter festivals . . . . Yet in the fourteenth and fifteenth centuries in England, the lyric form which grew out of the round dance, the carol, is particularly associated with the service of the Christian religion."[4]

On the other hand, what Greene seems to have done over the years is to make more precise his conception of the use to which these carols were put. He still allows, as in 1935, a dual function of the carol as a song "in a company gathered for conviviality or for religious praise."[5] But in 1977 he stresses far more the use of carols for "a social gathering in a hall." He was tending toward this position with his choice of poems for his *Selection of English Carols*; the secular carols (which are indeed more attractive to a general reader) were heavily represented, and the religious underrepresented (who after all could stomach all Ryman's 119 pieces), so that "the kind of carol which predominates *in this collection* was at celebrations involving feasting or social dining" (p. 27; my italics). Greene applies this conclusion to the entire corpus of the 502 carols in his 1977 work (p. xxxviii). Indeed, he has organized this new material (pp. xxxviii-xliii) into a section called "The Carol at Feasts and Banquets." The urgent question, Which, if any, of the carol-texts here collected were actually sung in the round dance? was broached in the first edition: "The Carol surviving the Dance" (pp. lvi-lix), but in the second edition it has been subsumed in "The Carol and the Ballad" (p. lxxvi).

While Greene was at the same time both limiting the function of carols to social occasions and extending this secular function to specifically religious carols—he notes that a carol ending with a prayer "is not a sign that the piece is designed for use in church rather than for a social gathering in hall" (p. xxvii)—he still forbids any suggestion that the carols were used for nonliturgical purposes in church or churchyard (pp. cvi-cix).[6] Function is something quite distinct from the "ultimate origins of the carol" (antedating "even recorded history"—see *Selection*, p. 51), and while I am willing to concede that the English carol may not have originated in the processional hymn, nevertheless I still find it easier to believe some carols were used for religious purposes. Greene himself notes the close relationship existing "between the English carol and the non-ritual extra-liturgical carols or cantilena, which is often identical in metrical form with the vernacular carols," which he describes as due to their "common ancestors."[7] If the majority of carols had long ceased to be songs for dancing, and if none was ever used in nonliturgical ceremonies (like introducing a sermon), then it is hard to explain the survival of the carol in the late fourteenth and fifteenth centuries as a musical cum literary form (burden and stanza) designed to structure some kind of ambulatory movements. And if the carol did survive to the early Tudor period, then its practical disappearance after 1550 is inexplicable. Greene devotes a new major section to the problem of survivals (pp. lxxii-lxxix); but I believe a simpler explanation is to see the separation of movement and its attendant literary/musical expression the result of the Anglican prohibition of processions about 1550. Divorced from its function, the carol was becoming an anachronism; its place in a social gathering in a hall was usurped by the madrigal, with stanza and refrain, but freed from the dance-compelling (or procession-compelling) burden. Greene naturally recognizes the winds of change: "The carol-form appears in songs which are still sung communally in dances of various lands as well as in pieces which are for performance at the tavern table or in other situations not involving dancing" (p. lxxvi).

I do not think this is the occasion to elaborate my objections to the exclusion of church-related opportunitites for the singing of carols, for I discussed them at some length in my review of Greene's *Selections* (*Speculum*, 38 [1963], 484-87). Readers might also be directed to the double review by Douglas Gray of Greene's *Selections* and my *Early English Christmas Carols* (1961) in *Notes and Queries*, 208 (Nov. 1963), 431-32.

In addition to the new material on the pages I have already cited, further new discussion occurs in the introduction on pp. xlvi-xlviii (Kölbigk dancers; cf. *Selection*, p. 5); pp. lxxii-lxxix (Christmas carols and Scotland); pp. cxxxii-cxxxiii (survivals); pp. cxxxv-cxxxviii (minstrels; cf. *Selection*, p. 18); pp. cxli-cxliii (dancing; cf. *Selection*, p. 17). As for the notes, the majority are reproduced from the first edition, with whatever updating is necessary (new editions, new texts, corrections and additions to the commentary). To his previous headcount of 474, Greene has added some 30 carols, making a total (since he deleted old Nos. 165 and 437) of 502. Many of the new carols are secular and many are early sixteenth century. Especially useful are the notes for 115.1, 121.1, 121.2, 139.1, 311.1, 393.1, 402.1, 418.1, 418.2, 418.3, 431.1, and 468.1. For some of the original carols Greene has expanded the documentation: 10, 79, 80, 107, 114, 121, 136, 152, 266, 270, 323, 419, 423, 440, 453, 459, and 463. I would single out as especially valuable the notes to 322 ("Corpus Christi Carol"), 414.1 ("The Briar and the Periwinkle"), and 467 ("If it were not"), for these exhibit Greene's genius in melding literary and historical texts to elucidate a poem. Since Greene has previously published articles on 322 and 467, scholars are already familiar with his interpretations.[8] In the Wyatt carol (467) Greene identifies the first line of the burden and the fourth line of the second stanza as actual mottoes used by Anne Boleyn: "Ainsi sera groigne qui groigne," discontinued (on the advice of the Imperial Ambassador) because of its resemblance to the Burgundian "Groigne qui groigne et vive Bourgoigne," and "La plus heureuse," worn on the liveries of Anne's retainers after her marriage to Henry VIII. "The carol, thus viewed, becomes a striking example of the Tudor lyric which is not a general or fictitious and conventional love song, but which is connected with a real social (and here political) situation" (p. 500).   How much better would we comprehend the Middle English lyric if more critics adopted Greene's historical methodology. In deploring "a growing tendency to read into medieval lyrics more than is there," Greene notes a commentary on "Jolly Jankin" (457), with its concluding lament of a betrayed maiden:

> Benedicamus Domino: Cryst fro schame me schylde;
> Deo gracias therto: alas, I go with chylde!
> Kyrieleyson.

One critic had written: "The poet ironically juxtaposes two births: the one bringing rejoicing and hope for all sinners, the other shame. That shame, in turn, proves the necessity for Christ's birth and its celebration. Although the mass is parodied, it promises the true love which will bring the girl peace of mind." I think Greene's gentle rebuke is well given: "There is little peace of mind for the girl, nor in the use of the commonplace simile of 'wortes to the pot' does she voice 'both her admiration and her domestic hopes' " (p. 493).

Yet Greene is always courteous when he is slapping wrists, and as a "collateral descendant" he need not fear what befell "Dr. Alexander Leighton, who had his ears cut off for exercising his right of free speech too freely" (broadside, Wesleyan University, 22 October 1970). The roster of those whose writing Greene faults reads like a Who's Who of the critics of the lyric, for example: Francis Berry (p. 426), Sir Edmund Chambers (p. 426), Maurice Evans (p. 495), Stanley Eugene Fish (p. 495), David C. Fowler (p. 426), Gordon Hall Gerould (p. 426), Douglas Gray (p. 425), Neil Ker (p. 499), Stephen Manning (p. 388), Margit Sahlin (p. 493), Theodore Silverstein (p. 411), Leo Spitzer (p. xxxii), Francis Lee Utley (p. 456), Sarah Appleton Webber (p. 387), and Rosemary Woolf (p. 318). Since I myself have written extensively about the carols, my own name appears very frequently, and I suppose to appear in this register is a mark of distinction. Yet Greene is most generous in acknowledging even minor assistance from his colleagues.

If there is one aspect of Greene's scholarship I would especially emphasize, it is his reliance on the manuscripts. I fail to see how any person can write intelligently about Middle English literature until he has spent at least six months or a year in the British Library or in the Bodleian studying manuscripts. Thus I think the most useful part of Greene's revision, which will help all who start from the text in the manuscript (rather than an extrapolated poem copied from a prior edition in some Golden Treasury type of anthology), is the "Bibliography of Original Sources" (pp. 297-341). Greene's notations, for example, on the three portable manuscripts (Eng. poet. e 1, Sloane 2593, and St. John's Camb. 259) are excellent specimens of what close inspection and analysis can do: Sloane 2593, "almost certainly" written at the Benedictine monastery of Bury St. Edmunds (p. 306). Greene has placed one of its owners (a monk, John Bardell), but has left it for others to find out more about the other monk whose name appears in the manuscript, "John Wulfspett." MS Eng. poet. e 1 "comes from Beverley Minster, Yorkshire," "a place of great importance, high in the favor of Henry V, on a main route to the north, and eleventh in size among all English cities" (p. 318). Even Greene can do little more with the pocket book, MS St. John's Camb. 259, beyond saying that it is "certainly from East Anglia . . . . It has obvious similarities and correspondences" (p. 320) with the two foregoing. Greene's descriptions of the ninety-seven manuscripts with carols are models of brief informed cataloguing.

Custom requires a reviewer to find at least one typographical error and a couple of slips. I verily believe Dr. Greene and the Clarendon Press let a few intrude, just to make the readers work harder! On p. 490 a quotation mark is omitted at the beginning of line 11. On p. xxxvii, footnote 14, the reference to *Anal. Hymn.* is 114 (as given in 1935); on p. 390 (No. 155), Heuser is Vol. 14 (not 16) of the *Bonner Beiträge*; and on p. 333, Brotanek's edition, cited in full on p. 477 (No. 431), should be added to the descriptions of the manuscript. On only one issue do I dissociate myself from Greene, namely, his linking carols to witches (pp. cxlii-cxliii); his primary source (Margaret Murray) is so dishonest, tendentious, and discredited as to be useless for serious studies; and Montague Summers's erudite works are best viewed as casebooks in abnormal psychology.[9]

What is truly amazing is the absence of errors in this huge volume, and one can appreciate Greene's efforts: "The revision and insertion of material is more laborious and trying," he wrote to me on 30 April 1977, "than doing the basic copy in the first place." Coming on the heels of this volume will be Greene's second labor of love, his section on the carols for the MLA *Bibliographical Manual of the Writings in Middle English 1100-1500*, Vol. 6, in press, which will cement all Greene's knowledge into official bibliographies.

Notes

1. Furnivall considered his prefaces as personal letters to his friends—the Early English Text Society had but 400 subscribers, as he explained in *EETS*, O.S. 18 (1867), viii. Here are some examples of his delightful informality: (1) "The odd account of the origin of this Treatise—in its first lines—caught my eye as I was turning over the leaves of the Sloane Manuscript which contains it. I resolved to print it as a specimen of the curious fancies our forefathers believed in . . . . The loss of my sweet, bright, only child, Eena, and other distress, have prevented my getting up any cram on the subject of Quintessence to form a regular Preface" (*EETS*, O.S. 16 [1866]). (2) "As Adam Davy has always been down in our lists for printing, I askt Mr. George Parker to copy the old Marshal's *Dreams*, so that we might get done with him. The 'Life of Alexius,' Solomon's 'Book of Wisdom,' the well-known 'Fiftene Tokenes' in a fresh version, and the 'Lamentation of Souls', are added, just to make the Text thick enough to stand alone" (*EETS*, O.S. 69 [1878]). (3) "Of the pieces now issued some have been printed elsewhere, and of most, perhaps better texts exist; but the time that it takes to ascertain whether a poem has been printed or not, which is the best MS. of it, in what points the versions differ, &c., &c., is so great, that after some experience I find the shortest way for a man much engaged in other work, but wishing to give some time to the Society, is to make himself a foolometer and book-possessor-ometer for the majority of his fellow-members, and print whatever he either does not know, or cannot get at easily, leaving others with more leisure to print the best texts" (*EETS*, O.S. 15 [1866]).

2. *Modern Language Notes*, 52 (1937), 128.

3. Gerould, *Speculum*, 11 (1936), 298-99.

4. *Carols*, p. cxxxix; 1935, p. cxi.

5. *Carols*, 1977, p. lxxix; 1935, p. lix.

6. In my article "Middle English Carols as Processional Hymns," *Studies in Philology*, 56 (1959), 559-82, I had (I thought) presented the English carols as extraliturgical accretions: "Processions were the logical place for the introduction of the vernacular, perhaps because they were conducted outside the chancel, in the nave. Their inherent variability placed them outside the stricter liturgical formulae of the mass and offices, and exposed them more easily to accretion and change" (p. 568). Greene, who generally puts "liturgical" before processions, answers my point directly (1977, p. cvii), but it seems to me that dismissing the implied processional use of the polyphonic carols in BL MS Addit, 5665 because three of them are clearly secular (6, 133, and 348) is more of a problem than maintaining that thirty-seven carols which can have a religious function override the three "social." In editing the texts and music of my *Early English Christmas Carols* (New York: Columbia Univ. Press, 1961), a work designedly popular as the Press's "Christmas" book for that year, I worked very closely with the late Catherine Keyes Miller, who had done the first study of this Addit. MS 5665 at Yale in 1948, antedating Professor John Stevens by over a dozen years. I am the literary executor for Dr. Miller and would be glad to have musicologists go through her manuscripts.

As this review goes to press, my good friend Professor Alan H. Nelson gives me permission to print the following snippet he has found in the Mundum Book of King's College Cambridge for June 1501: "Item [?] die Junij solutis Johanni Parkar pro cantilenis viz. pro xxiiijor carols ad iiijd le carol; viijs. Et pro xij balettes ad iijd le balet: iijs. Et pro viijto ballettes ad ijd le balet: xvjd." Nelson comments: "A. B. Emden has an entry for Parker: 'Parker John. Grace that study in music at Cambridge for 3н years suffice for complete 'form' for entry in Music, granted 1502-3.' I suppose Parker copied out the carols and ballads rather than composed them. It's interesting to see such compostitions being treated so matter-of-factly, and reimbursed on a piece-work basis. Probably Parker did the work for the use of the chapel choir."

7. *Selection*, pp. 39; *Carols*, 1977, pp. cxiv-cxvii.

8. "The Meaning of the Corpus Christi Carol," *Medium Aevum*, 29 (1960), 10-21; "A Carol of Anne Boleyn by Wyatt," *Review of English Studies*, 25 (1974), 437-39.

9. See my article "The Imposture of Witchcraft," *Folklore*, 74 (1963), 545-62, based on a paper delivered to Section H, British Association for the Advancement of Science, Aberdeen, Scotland, 3 September 1963.

Trelawny and the Decay of Lying

Donald H. Reiman

Edward John Trelawny. *Adventures of a Younger Son*, ed. William St. Clair. London: Oxford University Press, 1974. xxiv, 479 pp.

William St. Clair. *Trelawny: The Incurable Romancer*. New York: The Vanguard Press, Inc., 1977. xii, 235 pp.

Noel B. Gerson. *Trelawny's World: A Biography of Edward John Trelawny*. Garden City, N.Y.: Doubleday & Company, 1977. xviii, 289 pp.

"My life," wrote Edward John Trelawny to Mary Shelley on 19 January 1831, "though I have sent it to you, as the dearest friend I have, is not written for the amusement of women; it is not a novel. If you begin clipping the wings of my true story, if you begin erasing words, you must then omit sentences, then chapters; it will be pruning an Indian jungle down to a clipped French garden." But, like the realistic author he was, seeking "£200 per volume" or not "under any circumstances . . . less than £500 [for] the three volumes," Trelawny in the same letter said that if in the "general opinion" of Shelley's friends Thomas Jefferson Hogg and Horace Smith and of "the booksellers, Colburn or others" that "there are *words* which are better omitted, why I must submit to their being omitted."[1]

As William St. Clair points out in his valuable edition of *Adventures of a Younger Son*, the original press-copy manuscript (now in the Houghton Library, Harvard University) in the hand of Charles Armitage Brown—first Keats's and then Trelawny's housemate, friend, and amanuensis—shows that numerous "excisions were made after the text left Trelawny's hands." St. Clair errs, however, in thinking that for all differences between the expurgated manuscript and the first edition, "the printer" was "simply printing his own version" [p.

xiv]; many such stylistic revisions were during this period made on proof sheets,[2] and, doubtless, if the proofs of *Adventures of a Younger Son* ever come to light, most of these changes will be found in Horace Smith's hand.[3] All these changes and deletions, whether in the manuscripts or in proofs, are equally without Trelawny's explicit authorization and St. Clair rightly restores every verbal reading that he has been able to decipher from the manuscript. He retains, however, the title given the book by Mary Shelley, rather than Trelawny's choice—*A Man's Life*—and also ignores Trelawny's explicit instructions to Mary (in his letter of 19 July 1831) to spell the name of the heroine "Zellâ" rather than "Zela."[4] St. Clair also (reluctantly) retains "the heavy punctuation of the first edition" on the grounds that "the punctuation of the manuscript is minimal and Trelawny himself cared nothing for such matters." And, without justification, he retains the "division into chapters made by the first editors . . . although it differs from the original division of the manuscript" ("Note on the Text," p. xix). These decisions leave us with an eclectic text, closer to what Trelawny wrote or approved than any other published to date, but with someone else's title, chapter divisions, and punctuation. Perhaps the next editor will have the courage to publish the work as Trelawny wished it, supplementing the punctuation only where necessary and recording all such deviations, as well as collating the first edition (1831), the 1835 Bentley's Standard Novels edition, and all other authorities.

Besides an improved text, St. Clair provides the reader of this Oxford English Novels edition with a brief introduction that is at once informative and provocative, a useful "Glossary of Strange Words, Mostly Anglo-Indian," and an excellent map that plots the voyages of the unnamed "younger son" in the East, with flags identifying the locations of key events in the narrative. Finally, there are just over six pages of "Explanatory Notes"—a mélange that includes definitions of "merry-andrew" and "blues" (defined as "bluestockings," little help, perhaps, to a modern student), historical notes, sources of quotations and allusions, and comments on manuscript changes. These notes are really too sketchy for a critical edition, often omitting the salient information necessary to make sense of the passage annotated. The note to p. 3, for example, should include the known birthdates of the six Trelawny children to show how close in age they were: Harry and John (both born in 1792), Catherine, Mira (b. 1796), Charlotte (b. 1797), and Caroline comprised the family, until Caroline died at Weymouth in 1814 or 1815.[5]

William St. Clair's interest in Edward John Trelawny seems to have developed out of Trelawny's appearance as a minor character in *That Greece Might Still Be Free*, St. Clair's interesting and important historical reassessment of the role of Western "philhellenes" in the Greek War of Independence. In that study, St. Clair concluded that most Westerners who became involved in that conflict were either dupes or rogues (Lord Byron and Samuel Gridley Howe and a handful of his American colleagues being the most notable exceptions), but he could not quite decide to which category Trelawny belonged. Even then, however, St. Clair knew that Trelawny was a liar and a poseur: "To the historian or biographer, Trelawny is an intensely irritating figure because of his uncomfortable habit of telling lies about everything he did. . . . Trelawny's aim was mainly to swagger about Greece in exotic dress and to enjoy the sensation of being a Byronic hero, a Lara or a Conrad."[6] As a minor figure in that long war that managed ultimately to involve military men, humanitarians, and statesmen from four continents, Trelawny merely afforded St. Clair a colorful interlude of two pages at the denouement of the struggle between Odysseus, Trelawny's chosen chief and brother-in-law, and the Westernized Greeks led by Alexander Mavrocordatos (to whom Shelley dedicated *Hellas*). But when St. Clair, himself a classicist and a historian by training, turned to study Trelawny's life, first in his introduction to *Adventures of a Younger Son* (or *A Man's Life*, to let the author have his way) and later in his full-scale biography, he succumbed to the intense irritation he had predicted for Trelawny's biographer.

Not all biographers, of course, have been irritated with Trelawny. Some do not even know that he was an incorrigible liar. Noel B. Gerson is one. A professional writer with forty-three

works of fiction and twenty-four previous "nonfiction" titles to
his credit (including lives of Harriet Beecher Stowe, Kit Carson,
Pocahontas, and—alas!—Mary Shelley), Gerson apparently uses
whatever materials he finds at hand in local libraries in the area
of Clinton, Connecticut, where he "lives with his family." In
that locale, almost equidistant from New Haven and New
London, he often turns up bibliographical rarities, as Alice
Green Fredman discovered. In her review of books on Mary
Shelley in the 1974 *Keats-Shelley Journal,* she notes that, while
Gerson seemed to know nothing about recent editions or
scholarship on his subject, his bibliography lists an 1894 edition
of Mary Shelley's *Works* in twenty volumes! In his "Select
Bibliography" for *Trelawny's World* he has no title later than
R. Glynn Grylls's *Trelawny* (1950), but he has discovered a
previously unknown edition of *Adventures of a Younger Son,*
also London, 1831, but in *four* volumes instead of three.

   Gerson, no stickler himself for historical (or any other kind
of) accuracy, is perfectly content to accept Trelawny's story just
about as he tells it. He even swallows the "doses of opium and
ether," followed by quinine "dissolved in wine," with which
Trelawny is supposed to have cured most of his crew when they
were stricken with cholera. As Gerson observes with
unintentional irony: "he lost only four sailors—a remarkable
record" (p. 118). Rather than feeling humiliation at being
ravaged by Trelawny's lies, Gerson simply relaxes and enjoys
them:

. . . the cynics and skeptics who came after him found it difficult to
believe that any one man could have had so many remarkable
adventures.
   These critics are similar to some gentlemen of Trelawny's own
acquaintance, who scoffed when they heard he was irresistible to
women. But his record speaks for itself. He had four wives and
mistresses without number . . . .
   He was as strong as Paul Bunyan, as gallant and courageous as
D'Artagnan, a great sailor and an even greater fighting man. As a lover
he had no peer. He consorted with the leading intellectuals of his age
as an equal and, although almost without formal education, wrote
three spectacularly successful books, two of which are still regarded as
classics. [p. xii]

Really? The story is not so simple or so grand, as William St. Clair reminds us in his introduction to Trelawny's masterpiece: "the *Adventures* is a curious mixture of fact and fiction. The first dozen or so chapters which describe his boyhood and service in the Navy contain numerous points that can be corroborated from other sources, such as family letters and Admiralty records. But the rest of the book is largely fantasy. Trelawny never deserted from the Navy and certainly did not become a privateer in the French service . . . . For some incidents in which he claimed to be personally involved, it can be shown that he drew on the experiences of friends or took over stories from books" (p. vii).

William St. Clair, a diligent historian who has devoted evenings and holidays from his civil service post in London to examining MSS in the British Library, the Public Record Office, and overseas libraries, as well as to visiting the sites of Trelawny's life in Britain, Italy, Greece, and the United States, has one goal in mind: the true facts of the case; Noel B. Gerson, the professional writer, turning out two or more books each year in Clinton, Connecticut, has another aim: to tell an interesting story. Each succeeds, but neither really asks what Trelawny's goal was and how well *he* succeeded, though each examines that aspect of Trelawny's psyche that conforms to his own purposes as a biographer.

Challenges to Trelawny's veracity had been present from the first, as St. Clair shows in *Trelawny: The Incurable Romancer*. But it was the research of Lady Anne Hill (both in Trelawny and Hawkins family letters and in the logs and muster books of the ships Trelawny served on), the results of which appeared in the 1956 *Keats-Shelley Journal*, that put modern research on Trelawny onto a solid footing. She provided a number of firm dates and facts about his life before he entered the navy and showed that he was in service on a series of Royal Navy ships throughout the period that, he tells in *A Man's Life*, he was serving with De Ruyter as a privateer under the French flag.[7] The next advance in Trelawny scholarship appeared in volumes V and VI of *Shelley and his Circle* (1973), for which I had general editorial responsibility and wrote detailed commentaries on thirteen letters from Trelawny to Augusta White (later Draper), giving a picture of his life and character in 1817-19. To these same volumes R. Glynn Grylls (Lady Rosalie Mander) contributed two important essays. The first retells Trelawny's life (of which Grylls had been the most recent biographer in 1950), incorporating Lady Anne Hill's researches, as well as new information garnered by Grylls and the staff of The Carl H. Pforzheimer Library, especially Dorothy David and Doucet Devin Fischer, from (among other sources) the records of Trelawny's three trials for divorce from the former Caroline Julia Addison, who had eloped from the irresistible Trelawny with a Captain Thomas Coleman, an infantry officer who lived in the same rooming house in Bath. An ephemeral contemporary pamphlet entitled *The Trial between Lieut. Trelawny, Plaintiff, and Capt. Coleman, Defendant, for Criminal Conversation with the Plaintiff's Wife, including the Amorous Love Letters* . . . (London, 1817)[8] shows that Trelawny had been publicly as well as privately humiliated by the defection of the young wife he had married in defiance of his family, on whom he was (as St. Clair demonstrates) still dependent for support. Grylls's second essay traces the friendship and correspondence between Trelawny and Augusta White (later the wife of William Henry Draper, who became chief justice of Upper Canada) from 1817 through 1876.

Interestingly, though Hill, Grylls, and I were fully aware that Trelawny fabricated or rearranged the facts in his writing, none of us became especially irritated at Trelawny for his creative deceptions in the account of his early life. Grylls writes: "I for one would entirely agree with Lady Anne Hill in the verdict she pronounces on this admixture of fantasy with fact: 'The proportion of truth to fiction in the *Adventures* turns out to be small, no more than one tenth. But the demarcation line between fact and fantasy is so definite—it can be dated and placed to within a week and a chapter—and the early, truly autobiographical, portion of the book is so astonishingly accurate, that Trelawny's reliability as a witness of the last days of Shelley and Byron is perhaps scarcely impaired.' "[9]

At this point William St. Clair entered Trelawny studies and continued the investigations that had proven so fruitful since 1950. For his edition of *Adventures of a Younger Son,* he discovered the probable prototype for De Ruyter in the French privateer Robert Surcouf (1773-1827), whose depredations of British and allied shipping in the Indian Ocean created panic while Trelawny served there in the Royal Navy. Unfortunately, St. Clair did not complete the investigation of Trelawny's fictional method by identifying the origin or significance of the names "De Witt" and "De Ruyter," both of which Trelawny gives his hero's mentor in *Adventures of a Younger Son.* In the first volume of Thomas Moore's *Letters and Journals of Lord Byron: with Notices of His Life,* Moore quotes from Byron's Journal for 22 November 1813 on the Dutch rebellion against Napoleon: " 'Orange Boven!' So the bees have expelled the bear that broke open their hive. Well,—if we are to have new De Witts and De Ruyters, God speed the little republic! I should like to see the Hague and the village of Brock, where they have such primitive habits [i.e., where they fight for freedom]. Yet, I don't know,—their canals would cut a poor figure by the memory of the Bosphorus . . . . No matter,—the bluff burghers, puffing freedom out of their short tobacco-pipes, might be worth seeing; though I prefer a cigar, or a hooka, with the rose-leaf mixed with the milder herb of the Levant."[10] The significance of Trelawny's choice of names is obvious: De Witt and De Ruyter (who, as Leslie A. Marchand points out in his note to the same passage in *Byron's Letters and Journals,* were Byron's variants of the names of actual Dutch defenders of liberty in the seventeenth century) represent in Byron's journal entry the struggle for liberty that is the keynote of Trelawny's book; and thoughts of that struggle carry Byron by free association to the East, where he had enjoyed personal freedom from the restraints of English society. Trelawny, who had seen—and actually fought—Dutch imperialism in the East Indies, preferred to represent his idealized privateer as an American. And as an American, De Ruyter (a.k.a. De Witt) would have spelled those names as they are found in Trelawny's manuscript—not "de Ruyter" ("de Witt"), as St. Clair "corrects" them.

In *Trelawny: The Incurable Romancer* St. Clair has added other facts and conjectures, illustrating how Trelawny did—or could have—transmuted his own experience, adventures of his close friends (Edward Ellerker Williams, for example), and facts and experiences from his reading into the stories of adventure that gave much substance both to his first book and to his later repertoire of dinner-party anecdotes. All this research and even the accompanying speculations are of great value to serious students, present and future. But William St. Clair brought to his study of Trelawny another perspective first crystallized in the third paragraph to his introduction to *Adventures of a Younger Son*:

The curious thing to most readers is that Trelawny should have wished to be identified with the hero of the book, for even by the standards of the age he is a repulsive character. He claims to be a liberal always on the side of the poor oppressed peoples of the East against the imperialist Europeans, yet he himself was surely one of the worst. . . . Violence is the essence of his character and he glories in it, whether he is killing tigers or Arabs. His first instinct on encountering any animal is to kill it, and his numerous hunting expeditions usually entail the incidental deaths of a few anonymous servants or followers. [pp. vii-viii]

Now anyone who rereads Trelawny's book will see that these statements stretch the truth. To take only one example from many, we have the encounter with the orangutan in Volume III, Chapter 2. At the end of the previous chapter, Zellâ had warned the hero that a tiger was approaching, announced by a "faoo bird" that "always gives notice of his approach." "I put a ball, over the large shot, in my carbine, and making a rest on the rocks for my gun, I determined not to fire till he attacked us; then, if I missed killing him, we were to swim out to the boat . . . ." When, to his astonishment, he "saw, not a tiger, but a gray, hairy old man," the hero is filled with curiosity, rather than violence, even though "there was a wild and sullen malignity of expression" in the eyes of the strange creature, "more like those of a demon than of a man." The hero insists on following the strange creature, though Zellâ warns him that the *"jungle admee"* is "more dangerous, cunning, and cruel than any wild beast." They cautiously follow him to his hut: "I looked round with admiration, marvelling at the good taste with which the recluse had selected a place for his hermitage." And the hero proceeds to describe in detail the beauty of the setting. Just then a cobra threatens Zellâ and, when he shouts a warning to her, the old man attacks him with a club, aiming at his head a vicious blow that he barely manages to avoid while discharging his carbine, killing his attacker with the aid of Zellâ, who "was forcing a boar-spear into his side." This reluctant killing in self-defense (though, perhaps, provoked by the hero's curiosity— and by the needs of the author for the marvelous) enables the hero and Zellâ to examine the interior of the old man's hut. Trelawny's anger and gratuitous, perjudicial hatred emerge— but not against the creature who had just tried to kill him: "We then went into his house. It differed little . . . from those of other natives of the island, only it had a greater degree of neatness and appearance of comfort. At one end of it was a partition, very ingeniously fastened, as a security. . . . There was good store of roots and fruits, carefully spread out to prevent their rotting. It might have been mistaken for the abode of a mangy mongrel Scotch philosopher." Van Scolpvelt, the ship's surgeon (whose name St. Clair spells "van Scopveld" and whose portrayal he describes as being a mere caricature, elaborated with "malicious humor" [p. x]), becomes Trelawny's spokesman in identifying the dead creature as "an orang-outang . . . really very like the genus *homo*." Addressing the hero, he continues: "Buffon says they have no sentiment of religion, and what have you? they are as brave and fierce as you are; and are very ingenious, which you are not. Besides, they are a reflective and considerate set of beings; and have the best government in the world: they divide a country into districts; are never guilty of invasion; and never infringe on the rights of others. All this is because they have no meddling priests, kings, or aristocrats. This one has been refractory—a heavy sinner . . . and doubtless banished from the community of his fellow creatures."

This killing, then, is not only motivated by the need for dangerous and adventurous incident in the genre of its narration but also justified by the situation and the nature of the being whose life the hero reluctantly takes to defend his own. The incident, like others in the book, also provides an occasion both to introduce a brief Utopian exemplum and to broaden the characterization of Van Scolpvelt from such merely malicious caricatures of his profession as the metaphor beginning Volume I, Chapter 32 ("The doctor, who had as keen a scent for blood as the carrion-kite . . . "). The doctor shows himself to be (as he had been introduced in Volume I, Chapter 30) the consistent man of science, in his positive as well as his negative qualities. Though he lacks the power of sympathizing with others' sufferings, he possesses the virtues of scientific curiosity and rational appraisal that are lacking in the emotional reactions of Zellâ and, often, in the hero himself.

Nor is St. Clair correct in saying that Louis, the "steward and purser" (a "mongrel Frenchman"), is portrayed with "malicious humor." Though he is certainly a "humours" character worthy of Ben Jonson, his ruling passion for good food makes him—as the narrator avers in his first extended description of him—an excellent steward: "We all laughed at Louis, though there was no one on board that did not feel indebted to him for his good services. He was indefatigably industrious, and having a stomach himself, like a chronometer,[11] he never missed the hour of serving out the rations; besides, he was scrupulously honest in weight and measure. Under the abundant and well-organized system of this conscientious purser we rarely had cause to complain; and he used to pride himself on the crew's increase of power and weight since his appointment" (p. 132). The question arises as to whose portrayals are more "untrue"— Trelawny's of his characters, or St. Clair's of Trelawny's motives, attitudes, and characterizations?

Returning to Trelawny's apparently gratuitous insult about the orangutan's hut resembling "the abode of a mangy mongrel Scotch philosopher," we should observe that Trelawny is speaking of Robert Owen (his Welsh name calling forth the epithet "mongrel"), who advocated such rationally neat but primitive huts for his workers and whose ideas Trelawny had attacked directly earlier in the novel:

The philanthropist Owen of Lanark, or the sage and saintly Hannah
More, and her tribe, scrawl and jabber about education, and of that
alone constituting the difference between man and man, and of nature
having sent us into the world equally disposed for good or evil.
Shakspeare and Bacon thought otherwise; and they were deep and
wise, and the others are shallow and foolish. Bacon says, "Deformed
persons are commonly even with nature; for as nature hath done ill by
them, so do they by nature . . . . "

I have been led to this digression by the memory of Aston and De
Ruyter, whose . . . lofty spirits, and gentle and loving hearts, first
awakened in my nature feelings, which had been trampled on but not
annihilated, of friendship and benevolence. [II, iv, p. 159]

Trelawny's narrative has several dimensions. At the deepest
psychological level it is a fairy tale, such as "The Firebird" or
"Cinderella," in which a child doomed (often by its parents) to a
life of poverty, obscurity, and suffering, determines to rise and—
aided by outside powers—succeeds in becoming a bright and
shining example to his own siblings and other oppressed
children. This is the myth that adds depth to several of Dickens's
novels (as J. Hillis Miller once demonstrated so movingly[12]),
"*Oliver Twist* and *Great Expectations* being archetypical
examples. The theme is obviously epecially relevant to Western
societies following the Industrial Revolution, during which the
old aristocracies of title and landed wealth gave place in turn to
commercial magnates, then to industrial barons, next to
technocrats and specialists (the "new mandarins"), and finally
in our day to mass communicators, from actors, sports heroes,
and rock music stars to local TV weathermen. But whereas most
of Dickens's heroes are filled with the guilt attendant on such a
rise in fortunes, Trelawny's narrative projects his guilt, instead,
upon his parents and the other hostile adults who haunted his
childhood. Lady Anne Hill's and St. Clair's revelations of the
character of the Rev. Samuel Seyer, schoolmaster—or, rather,
turnkey—in the school the Trelawny brothers attended at
Bristol, added to the universal portrayals of Trelawny's cruel,
parsimonious father and foolish, heartless mother, vindicate the
basic truth of his early narrative, whether the boy's acts of
defiance and revenge were wishful or actual. St. Clair's vivid
description (in Chapters 2 and 3 of *Trelawny*) of the hard

conditions in the Royal Navy and his shrewd speculations about Trelawny's individual means of coping with his pain and anger present a clear (and, I should say, true) picture of the young man attempting to compensate for the persecutions heaped upon him, partly because he had always been rebellious (and, therefore, persecuted) and did not know how to live otherwise.

Thus, above the deep psychological level of myth and fairy tale, we find a more superficial level of consciously motivated needs and responses—the level of realistic fiction. It is at the level of Bildungsroman that Noel Gerson (insofar as he does so at all) infuses a critical element into his retelling of young Trelawny's story. When De Ruyter entrusts the hero ("Trelawny") with command of the "Arab grab brig" soon after his desertion from the navy, "Trelawny" would drink only tea because, Gerson writes, "his sense of responsibility was so acute he wanted nothing to interfere with his judgment." Gerson continues: "It is of great significance that, for the first time in *Younger Son*, Trelawny mentions his awareness of personal responsibility; it had been born the moment De Ruyter gave him command of the grab. . . . this former midshipman who had detested any form of discipline suddenly saw the matter in a new light. Reasonable discipline was necessary at sea, he realized, and it was essential that a captain's orders be obeyed without delay or question" (p. 53). At this level, Gerson's sporadic and far-from-profound attempts to analyze motivations (in what he accepts almost without question as a basically true account) succeed better than St. Clair's similar efforts. For Gerson is not burdened with the additional task, which St. Clair accepts as primary, of sorting out true incident from fabrication, and thus Gerson can analyze consistently Trelawny's book, which—in whatever degree it is externally factual—remains totally true to Trelawny's inner psychological history.

St. Clair, so good at unraveling the truth of the evils Trelawny suffered in these early years, attributes almost all the good influences that appear in the story either to Trelawny's imagination (e.g., De Ruyter/Surcouf) or to Trelawny's later experience (e.g. the Zellâ of *Adventures* was actually Tarsitsa, Odysseus's sister, whom Trelawny married during his Greek sojourn). St. Clair may be factually right—though we cannot be sure that characters like De Ruyter and Aston are not drawn from people who befriended Trelawny during his naval career— but his criticisms of Trelawny's veracity are not well taken. Every Bildungsroman told retrospectively from the first-person perspective assumes the maturity of the narrator to be at least that which his experience had enabled him to achieve by the end of his narrative. Trelawny intended from the first to continue his story in a second three-decker at least through the deaths of Shelley and Byron and his own return from Greece.[13] Thus the maturity at which "Trelawny," the protagonist, had arrived by the time he began to record his experience was that of Trelawny's actual development till 1825 or 1830. It included all those maturing experiences that lay beyond Trelawny's naval career—his marriage to Caroline Addison, her elopement, and his friendship with Augusta White and her family; his life in London attending plays and socializing with actors, his divorce trials and the accompanying scandal; his travels on the Continent, including friendships with Daniel Roberts, Thomas Medwin, Edward and Jane Williams, and Sir John St. Aubyn's menage at Geneva; his brief but crystallizing friendship with the Shelley circle at Pisa, the building of vessels for Byron and Shelley, and Shelley's drowning and cremation; the Greek adventure; his visit to England in 1828-29; and, finally, his return to Italy and his new friendships with Walter Savage Landor, Charles Armitage Brown, Seymour Kirkup, and other English expatriates.

Whatever order he chose for the events, perhaps to protect some of the innocent (including his three daughters then living) by disguising names, dates, and identities, by this date Trelawny had both lived more than most men and had developed into a remarkable personality, with both forcefulness and forthright-ness (not to be confused with matter-of-factness) that impressed, angered, or frightened those who met him, depending on their own personalities, but seldom bored and was never forgotten by them. Women generally liked him better than men did; with them he was gentle and generous, as in his treatment of Augusta White and her mother and of Mary Shelley in their respective hours of need. With men he was aggressive and rivalrous, as befitted a man of his upbringing who had fought for every advantage and bit of recognition he had obtained. Yet he was, according to *all* the witnesses—even those like Joseph Severn and Robert Browning who disliked him—a remarkable character. Landor admired him. To W. M. Rossetti, Millais, and Swinburne he was a survivor of an otherwise lost race of Titans. When Richard Garnett wanted to describe Captain Edward W. Silsbee, a later forceful but eccentric admirer of Shelley, he wrote: "Mr. Silsbee was a most remarkable man; much such an one as Trelawny might have been if . . . Trelawny could have been made amiable and gracious without parting with any of his native force."[14] Beginning as an ignorant, gauche, and rebellious sailor boy, Trelawny had observed Diotima's definition of love as a sense of need or want—a desire for the good, the true, and the beautiful beyond himself, and he had set out to acquire them. To the energy and animal courage forced on him by his life at home, his school, and the navy, he added a love of learning and humane values, reading great authors from Shakespeare and Bacon to Shelley and Byron and creating a beau ideal of himself that led him from the brutality of his early hunting days to strict vegetarianism during his later years. True, he remained abrasive and easily offended, but he now picked the targets of existential wrath (bequeathed by his harsh childhood) on the basis of values that are, I think, not only defensible but admirable, even on terms and tests as stringent as William St. Clair sets for him. Trelawny's anger at class distinctions, religious cant and hypocrisy, the oppression of the darker races by imperialism and of women by unjust laws may reflect only his own memory of the oppressions from which he himself had suffered. But though he had been a beaten child, he did not become a childbeater, thus breaking the most insidiously vicious cycle of oppression known to humanity. Whether or not he defended a weaker shipmate like "Walter" from petty oppressions on board a British man-o'-war, his later knowledge that this was the proper way to act established an ideal in *A Man's Life* that was true to Trelawny's mature sense of justice— and to ours.

Henry James, in his story "The Liar," raises the question as to which person is more culpable—Colonel Capadose, who continually tells tall stories but is otherwise a decent man, or Oliver Lyon, a painter (in love with Mrs. Capadose) who sets out to expose the Colonel's "monstrous foible" to his wife in the hope of driving them apart.[15] James's tale is merely one subtle, unnoticed shot in the battle that raged throughout the Victorian Age between men of fact (Dickens's Gradgrind and Peacock's Mr. Fax) and men of imagination, between the minions of utility and the apostles of beauty. In many respects the final salvo in that stage of the war was fired by Oscar Wilde—with characteristic paradox and hyperbole—in his defense of his volume of fairy tales entitled *The Happy Prince and Other Tales*, which had been harshly handled in the *Saturday Review* on 20 October 1888. In "The Decay of Lying,"[16] Wilde attacked the matter-of-fact critic who had praised "The Nightingale and the Rose" as "the only place in the book where his artistic sense stumbled a little along with his natural history." Wilde asserted that "no doubt there will always be critics who . . . will gravely censure the teller of fairy-tales for his defective knowledge of natural history, who will measure imaginative work by their own lack of any imaginative faculty, and will hold up their ink-stained hands in horror if some honest gentleman, who has never been farther than the yew-trees of his own garden, pens a fascinating book of travels like Sir John Mandeville, or, like the great Raleigh, writes a whole history of the world, without knowing anything whatsoever about the past."[17]

Without impugning St. Clair's motives (he is certainly *not* trying to win the affection of Trelawny's audience away from him) or questioning his imaginative faculties, I must observe that Trelawny—a military-trained scion of faded gentility who (as a rebellious graduate of the school of hard knocks) despised universities, bureaucratic regulations, Scots, and mere external facts—provides an almost too tempting target for either an ivory-towered, Presbyterian, American academic like myself, or for a British civil servant out of Edinburgh by way of Oxford's "greats" like St. Clair. William St. Clair, whose scholarship and writing I admire so much that I was truly honored to persuade

him to become a Contributing Editor to volumes VIII-IX of
Shelley and his Circle, has not successfully resisted the
temptation to criticize Trelawny for exhibiting the natural
differences between creator and scholar. For Noel Gerson, a
denizen of the modern exurban Grub Street, indentured to
deliver to an uncritical publisher a brace of books each year from
the shaded shoreline of Clinton, Connecticut, Trelawny—a
remarkably gifted storyteller whom merely to paraphrase is to
write an exceptionally readable book—becomes a convenient
tool. Between them, Gerson and St. Clair come near to treating
Trelawny as Square and Thwackum tutored Tom Jones—one
inculcating a naive (but fundamentally insincere) belief in
Trelawny's native virtue and the other threatening to cane him
every time he appears to have lied or exaggerated. Their
biographies, both of which draw their raison d'etre and interest
from the original power of Trelawny as a narrative writer,
become in quite different ways patronizing distortions of a good
book, "the precious lifeblood of a master spirit, embalmed and
treasured up on purpose to a life beyond life."

Gerson is not the first—and certainly neither the most
intelligent nor the best informed—to write a biography of
Trelawny that accepts his subject's basic veracity. Besides H. J.
Massingham's *The Friend of Shelley* (1930), which Gerson cites
with approval, and R. Glynn Grylls's *Trelawny* (1950), there is
Margaret Armstrong's *Trelawny: A Man's Life* (1940), which I
picked up in a second-hand bookstore while I was in high
school and read with an avidity that presaged my later
dedication to the English Romantics. Nor—*pace* the recent
spate of press releases and popular reviews—is St. Clair the first
editor or biographer of Trelawny to view skeptically Trelawny's
claims, though he, building on the work previously cited, is the
most tenacious in documenting his demurrals. Both Edward
Garnett and H. N. Brailsford expressed their skepticism in
introductions to earlier editions of *Adventures of a Younger
Son.* Garnett, examining the question, "how far the book is
'history,' and how far romance" in his biographical
introduction for the Unwin edition (1890), concluded rightly
(without the benefit of the supporting external evidence since
adduced):

It is most likely from the internal evidence, that Trelawny began with the intention of writing his life, that as he progressed he found that a little fiction set off the facts to great advantage, and that, towards the end, the book becomes less and less of the life, and more and more of the romance. The Younger Son is an excellent stage hero by the finish . . . . But the account of his boyhood has a very real air, and if it is accepted, we see him as a self-willed, passionate boy, whose bad bringing-up developed his faults and hardened his character. . . . his experiences after 1820 seem to have suggested incidents for the years 1809 and 1810: he would probably not have shown himself burning Zela's body, had he not burned Shelley's in 1822 . . . .

It is, however, only fair to him to allow . . . that it was a work of rare brilliancy, if not of genius. . . . Its peculiar merits were perhaps not pleasing to critics of the greatest delicacy and refinement, as it is both unconventional and original. It is real, and yet a romance. How real may be seen by comparing a book of fictitious adventures with it. Let any be chosen, "Treasure Island," for example, and admirable as is Mr. Stevenson's piece of work, its characters, its encounters seem pale and shadowy beside the characters and adventures in the "Younger Son." . . .

To those who know their Dumas it will appear only natural that a translation of the "Younger Son," with an introduction by the great man, should be found in the list of his writings under the title of "Un Cadet de Famille." [pp. 8-9, 13]

Garnett concludes his penetrating analysis of Trelawny's life and writings with these words: "In the long run individuals come to be judged by their acts, and not by what they have said of themselves. Thus should it be with Trelawny. His favourite maxim, 'Believe nothing you hear, and only half of what you see,' may be applied with advantage to himself. If, to quote Mrs. Shelley again, he was 'one who wished to be thought eccentric,' he was 'noble and generous at bottom.' And with all his affectation he was thoroughly fearless" (p. 25).

Similarly, Brailsford in his introduction to the Bohn's Library Edition of *Adventures of a Younger Son* (1914), writes:

Trelawny's fact is as brilliant as the most daring fiction, and it was with no idea of conferring a left-handed compliment that Dumas held it worthy to rank with the creations of his own fancy. Fact or fiction, or an adroit mixture of both, it has all the qualities of a great novel of adventure. . . .

A novel of adventure and a chapter of adventurous autobiography must in the end stand or fall by the same merits or defects . . . . Is the tale enthralling? Are the descriptions vivid? Are the characters of the story interesting human beings skilfully portrayed? If the book can satisfy these tests it will live. Who believes that Benvenuto Cellini really achieved all the exploits and adventures of his Memoirs, and who reads them the less greedily because he was the most shameless boaster and the most unconscionable liar of the Renaissance? . . . Trelawny's book is a story of adventure told in the first person. In form it differs in no respect from such novels as Defoe's. It lives as they do, by its strong, simple English, its power to hold us by an enthralling narrative, its lively and unmannered descriptions and characterisations. [I, v-vii]

St. Clair, now engaged with an American scholar on a complete edition of Trelawny's letters, is a fine historical researcher. With other students of Trelawny, I certainly hope that this projected edition of the letters, which are not likely to be reedited as often as *A Man's Life*, will not only conform to the standards of the Center for Scholarly Editions, but will also exhibit both imaginative sympathy for the subject and patience and tenacity in discharging editorial responsibilities similar to those employed in the foregoing efforts to expose Trelawny's "lies." Such tenacity in the editing of *A Man's Life* would have produced a text that followed the author's intention (primarily evidenced in the manuscript he sent to press and in his subsequent correspondence) and would as well have identified for the reader several dozen significant quotations and allusions (such as those to Robert Owen in Volume III, Chapter 2, and to Byron's journal, via Moore's life, in the use of the names De Witt and De Ruyter). To take only two further examples (both from the two-page "Conclusion"), in the first paragraph Trelawny's oath "to *war, even to the knife,* against the triple alliance of hoary-headed imposters" (p. 464) echoes the famous reply of the Spanish patriot Palafox to the French when they demanded the surrender of Saragoza during the Peninsular War; it came to Trelawny from Byron's *Childe Harold,* Canto I, where the phrase in the eighty-sixth stanza is explained by Byron in a note.[18] And both the prose quotation on the final page and the following poetic quotation from Shelley come from *Laon and*

Cythna (*The Revolt of Islam*), the first from the preface and the latter from VIII, xxviii. Such identifications would have reinforced St. Clair's portrait of Trelawny creating himself out of the books he read. And if the critic grants the possibility that a better man might emerge from within an unloved child who followed the creative dreams of Shakespeare, Shelley, and Byron, rather than taking his inspiration from the factual world either of the Royal Navy or of Regency society, then the whole truth about Trelawny begins to emerge.

All students of the Romantic period ought to read—and scholars in the field will want to own—*Trelawny: The Incurable Romancer*. But they should also read, both before and after, Trelawny's own *Adventures of a Younger Son*. Teachers would, moreover, do both themselves and their students a favor by reviving Trelawny's classic, and placing it in the curriculum beside such other autobiographical fictions of the age as *The Prelude*, *Childe Harold's Pilgrimage*, *Sartor Resartus*, *The Red and the Black*, and *Wilhelm Meister's Apprenticeship*, if only to see how much philosophy of life an artist can embody in action instead of talk. For that purpose, the text to use, for the present, is William St. Clair's Oxford English Novels edition. And if a high school student growing up in Erie, Pennsylvania, or Clinton, Connecticut, should happen to pick up at his local bookstore or public library *Trelawny's World* by Noel B. Gerson, let us hope that it may whet his appetite to read the man's own *Adventures* (or *Life*) with an open, imaginative mind.

Notes

1. *Letters of Edward John Trelawny*, ed. H. Buxton Forman (London: Henry Frowde/Oxford Univ. Press, 1910), pp. 140-42. He ultimately received a total of £400 for the first two editions of the book.

2. Shelley, for example, wrote to Lackington that he was correcting "instances of baldness of style" in the proofs of *Frankenstein* (Shelley, *Letters*, ed. F. L. Jones [Oxford: Clarendon Press, 1964], I, 565.)

3. "Your work is in progress at last, and is being printed with great rapidity. Horace Smith undertook the revision [i.e., the proofreading]" (Mary Shelley to Trelawny, 14 June 1831; Mary Shelley, *Letters*, ed. F. L. Jones [Norman: Univ. of Oklahoma Press, 1944], II, 45).

4. See Trelawny, *Letters*, pp. 161, 164-65, 170.

5. These facts derive from *Burke's Peerage* and Anne Hill, *Trelawny's Strange Relations* (Stanford Dingley, England: Mill House Press, 1956).

6. *That Greece Might Still Be Free: The Philhellenes in the War of Independence* (London: Oxford Univ. Press, 1972), pp. 239-40.

7. "Trelawny's Family Background and Naval Career," *Keats-Shelley Journal*, V (1956), 11-32. The family letters cited in this article are quoted at greater length in Anne Hill's *Trelawny's Strange Relations*.

8. This pamphlet has rested undisturbed in the New York Public Library until Dorothy David went there seeking books to check footnotes in R. Glynn Grylls's essay.

9. Grylls, "Edward John Trelawny," *Shelley and his Circle*, V (Cambridge: Harvard Univ. Press, 1973), 41-42.

10. Moore, 1st, quarto ed. (London, 1830), I, 444. Trelawny had finished reading Moore's first volume (published on 15 January 1830) by *at least* 16 August 1830 and would thus have had plenty of time to alter the name of the privateer to De Witt (his alias) and De Ruyter before 25 October 1830, when he sent the manuscript to London in the care of George Baring (see Trelawny, *Letters*, pp. 134, 135).

11. Here is a case where overpunctuation, presumably added by the printer, has distorted or weakened Trelawny's meaning.

12. *Charles Dickens: The World of His Novels* (Cambridge: Harvard Univ. Press, 1959).

13. See Trelawny, *Letters*, p. 135.

14. *Journal of Edward Ellerker Williams, Companion of Shelley and Byron in 1821 and 1822*, introduction by Richard Garnett (London: Elkin Mathews, 1902), p. 11n.

15. "The Liar," in *The Short Stories of Henry James*, ed. Clifton Fadiman (New York: Modern Library, 1945), pp. 126-83. See also Wayne C. Booth, *The Rhetoric of Fiction* (Chicago: Univ. of Chicago Press, pp. 347-54. I answered Booth's indictment of the ambiguity of James's method both in my brief review of *The Rhetoric of Fiction* (*South Atlantic Quarterly*, 61 [1962], 427) and in an unpublished lecture entitled "Rhetorical Techniques in the Shorter Fiction of Henry James," in which I show how in "The Liar" James carefully establishes Sir David Ashmore as a trustworthy character to speak for him and for the truth of the situation.

16. First published in the *Nineteenth Century* for January 1889; revised and reprinted in *Intentions* (1891).

17. Quoted in *The Letters of Oscar Wilde*, ed. Rupert Hart-Davis (New York: Harcourt, Brace & World, 1962), p. 236n.

18. See Byron, *Poetical Works*, ed. E. H. Coleridge (London: John Murray, 1904), II, 78, 94.

Finding (and Counting) American Literary Manuscripts

John C. Broderick

J. Albert Robbins, ed. *American Literary Manuscripts: A Checklist of Holdings in Academic, Historical, and Public Libraries, Museums, and Authors' Homes in the United States.* Second edition. Athens: The University of Georgia Press, 1977. liii, 387 pp.

Not all basic reference tools are vouchsafed a second edition. Those that are should make the most of the opportunity to correct mistakes in policy and execution that may have flawed the original publication, to clarify or extend its range, and to offer new and, possibly, new *kinds* of information. The second edition of *American Literary Manuscripts (ALM 2)* improves upon its predecessor in many of these ways, though not so completely as, ideally, one might have wished.

The first edition of *American Literary Manuscripts* (1960) was prepared by the five-man committee on manuscript holdings of the MLA's American Literature Group. The preface, signed by the committee, acknowledges the assistance of one traveling field representative, Fred Hanes. Its governing assumption was that the committee would merely compile reports submitted by myriad manuscript librarians, perhaps after receiving the spur of a visit from the field representative.

ALM 2, on the other hand, boasts an editor, J. Albert Robbins, the only member of the 1960 committee still associated with the enterprise, eight regional chairmen, sixty-three regional associates, plus four assistants to the editor (chiefly computer consultants). Thus more than seventy-five people were directly involved in the preparation of *ALM 2*, to say nothing of the "hundreds of librarians who assisted" and a number of others who participated in "research and data gathering" (p. xii). Truly, a massive effort in cooperative scholarship.

The change in approach was necessitated by the facts of life. As the 1960 *ALM* recognized, the governing assumption that curators would do the committee's work for it was impracticable, especially for large research libraries. (The holdings of Harvard, Princeton, the University of Chicago, the New York Public Library, and the Library of Congress, among others, were represented in *ALM* chiefly by the imprecise plus-sign for most authors.) Reliance instead upon a large, well-organized network of associates could be expected to result in better coverage. And it does. Nevertheless, the helpful "Notes on Coverage" identifies many repositories, including some of the most important, for which *ALM 2* offers far from a complete record.

The 1960 *ALM* reported its findings in a double-column format, alphabetically by author, with a tabular report of manuscripts listed below, one line per repository, each of which was identified by the customary library symbolism. Thus the sixteenth line under Lowell, James Russell, reads:

MB MS4 L17 Cl3 Dl.

This means that four manuscripts of Lowell, seventeen of his letters, thirteen items of correspondence (i.e., letters to Lowell), and one document are in the Boston Public Library. The tabular format, even double-column, resulted in considerable white space. The listings required 421 pages.

The listings in *ALM 2* require only 362 pages, though some five hundred names have been added, the number of libraries covered has more than doubled, and almost every individual entry has been enlarged. This compression has been achieved by abandoning the tabular format in favor of a run-on paragraph entry, in which bold-face dots (bullets) separate the repository listings. The system of abbreviations is retained and refined. Although the new format undoubtedly achieved necessary economies, it produces a page difficult to scan. Scholars using *ALM 2* will probably have to convert its information into their own tabular lists for use. Bold-face printing of the entry names would have improved legibility and scanning.

Some of the difficulties the project experienced in the 1950s in securing reports from curators undoubtedly derived from the extensive listing of (sometimes unfamiliar) names for which information was requested, 2,350 in all. That number has been increased to approximately 2,800, especially to achieve better representation of black authors and "younger" twentieth-century authors. Many users of *ALM 2*, however, will believe that decisions about inclusion have been inconsistent.

For example: Janet Flanner is included but not A. J. Liebling, E. J. Kahn, Brendan Gill, or John McPhee; Larry McMurtry is included but not Larry King or Willie Morris; Tad Mosel is included (one letter at the University of Tennessee) but not Garson Kanin or Thomas Heggen; Grace Isabel Colbron (one letter at the University of Southern California), but not Kathryn Hulme, Elizabeth Janeway, Anne Morrow Lindbergh, or Marcia Davenport; Donald Justice but not John Ashbery; John Pauker but not A. R. Ammons; Mona Van Duyn but not Katherine Garrison Chapin, Josephine Jacobsen, Carolyn Kizer, or Ann Stanford; Walter Kerr but not Brooks Atkinson or even Jean Kerr; Thomas Pynchon but not Donald Barthelme; Ernie Pyle but not Lowell Thomas or Bill Mauldin; Meredith Willson but not Oscar Hammerstein II or Stephen Sondheim; Harold Robbins but not Leon Uris or Irving Wallace (Mickey Spillane is among those authors whose manuscripts were sought but not found); Herbert Cahoon but not Donald Gallup; Maxwell Perkins but not Albert Erskine, Saxe Commins, Hiram Haydn, or Irita Van Doren.

To this reviewer, the names above illustrate the difficulties in planning a comprehensive work such as *ALM 2* and the less than satisfactory way in which the compilers met some of the difficulties.

A reference tool, however, usually stands or falls not on what it omits, but on what it includes. In this respect, *ALM 2* deserves fairly high marks. A comparison of coverage for John W. DeForest, as a random example, reveals the following. *ALM* located DeForest manuscripts in eleven repositories, with the bulk of known material at Yale. Three of the eleven (Harvard, NYPL, and South Carolina), however, were represented only by plus signs ("to show significant holdings without specific count"). *ALM 2* locates DeForest manuscripts at fourteen repositories, adding the Huntington Library, Princeton, Brigham Young, the American Antiquarian Society, and the University of Rochester. The plus sign for Harvard is replaced by a specific count, twenty-six letters and one item of correspondence. The New York Public Library and University of South Carolina, on the other hand, disappear. Only three listings from the original edition remain unchanged. Random sampling of several other entries discloses much the same pattern, with the most numerous changes occurring for recent authors (Katherine Anne Porter, Ezra Pound, E. B. White), as one would expect; but many entries for earlier authors (George Whitefield, for example) are substantially improved and enlarged.

One of the most useful innovations in *ALM 2* is the inclusion of more than one hundred references to published descriptions of particular collections and a bibliographical listing of more general guides. Although inclusion of such lists is a step forward, *ALM 2*'s failure to coordinate the various information sources leads to inconsistency and omissions. Example: The entry for Robinson Jeffers includes a listing for the University of Virginia (MS7, L11, C1), with a citation to a 1960 checklist of Jeffers material at Charlottesville. That checklist, however, includes numerous letters of Una (Call) Jeffers. *ALM 2* does have an entry for Una Jeffers, but it fails to list any of her manuscripts at the University of Virginia. Similarly, a nine-page checklist of University of Virginia holdings of Charles T. Brooks is included among the references, though the holdings at Charlottesville amount to only four manuscripts and five letters. Brooks's fellow Transcendentalist Theodore Parker, on the other hand, is represented by more than one hundred fifty items in the Library of Congress, which were described in a 1966 article in the Library's *Quarterly Journal*. The article on Parker, however, is not among the references appended to *ALM 2*.

The omissions and inconsistencies cited above are matters of detail. In an undertaking of this scope, inconsistencies were inevitable, especially when the execution of policy depended upon so large a number of individuals. The blemishes cannot negate the overall usefulness of such a guide, but they serve to underscore the editor's remark: "*American Literary Manuscripts is a general guide and one should adjust his expectations accordingly*" (p. xx). Intelligent use of *ALM 2* will shorten the drudgery of some research. Nevertheless, it is an aid to research, not a substitute for it, especially research with an emphasis on *search*.

Whether the evident usefulness of *ALM 2* justifies the massive effort it took to produce it is another question, and one about which reasonable men and women will differ. The competing reference tools are the *National Union Catalog of Manuscript Collections* (*NUCMC*) and the *Guide to Archives and Manuscripts in the United States*, sponsored by the National Historical Publications (and Records) Commission and originally edited by Philip M. Hamer. The *NUCMC* is a continuing publication, the *Guide* a one-time publication, for which plans exist to keep its information current. Neither *NUCMC* nor the *Guide* attempts to supply the kind of detailed information on individual items offered in *ALM 2*. Each publication has its uses, to be sure, but whereas *NUCMC* and the *Guide*, by providing information about manuscript *collections*, not individual items, are in forms that emerge naturally, almost routinely, from standard curatorial practices, the entries in *ALM 2* must be specially created and recreated. Although some repositories maintain records of individual items, the Yale Collection of American Literature being the outstanding example, that is a luxury most curators must relinquish. Certainly for 2,800 names!

The entries in *ALM* also give an illusion of precision in a world that is comfortably imprecise. *ALM 2*, for example, credits the Library of Congress with *exactly* five letters of John Dos Passos. An annotated worksheet which the compilers obligingly left in the Library of Congress for its reference use indicates that four of the five letters reported are in the Woodrow Wilson papers, for which the Library has issued a three-volume index. Unfortunately, the four letters in the Wilson papers are from John R. Dos Passos (1844-1917), not (1896-1970). An added risk is that the seeming precision of an entry (especially when the count is low) will forestall investigation into the true holdings of a repository. Numbers and symbols look so exact.

Finally, the kind of scholarship chiefly facilitated, if not encouraged, by *ALM* is hit-and-run. A scholar interested in John Dos Passos, for example, and searching for material about him at the Library of Congress otherwise than through *ALM 2* might be encouraged by the fact that the Library holds the papers of Dos Passos's friend Archibald MacLeish and the editorial records of *Harper's Magazine*, which published his work. Approached this way, the holdings of the Library of Congress would be found to yield close to one hundred known items of correspondence rather than five, four of them ghosts. Personal papers are remarkable resources, embodying as they do the life and relationships of the person around whom they developed. A systematic exploration of such materials will usually produce results of a kind not to be compared with a mail-order request for photocopies of items from a second-hand list. Such hit-and-run scholarship is not the best use to be made of information in *ALM 2*, but it is a characteristic use.

ALM 3, if it should ever come to pass, ought to mark as significant an advance over *ALM 2* as the publication under review surpasses its predecessor. One improvement would be to abandon the specific count of items, almost always unreliable and always subject to change, in favor of a simpler system designed to alert researchers to the presence of material in particular libraries (and perhaps in particular collections). Until *ALM 3* comes along, however, students of American literature will be glad to have *ALM 2* at their elbows.

Three Views of the Nineties

Stanley Weintraub

Karl Beckson, ed. *The Memoirs of Arthur Symons: Life and Art in the 1890s*. University Park: The Pennsylvania State University Press, 1977. 284 pp.

David Crackanthorpe. *Hubert Crackanthorpe and English Realism in the 1890s*. Columbia: University of Missouri Press, 1978. xi, 183 pp.

William H. O'Donnell, ed. The Speckled Bird, *by William Butler Yeats, with Variant Versions*. Toronto: McClelland and Stewart, 1977. lix, 275 pp. (Yeats Studies Series).

Although Max Beerbohm claimed to have belonged to the "Beardsley Period," fin de siécle seems more legitimately to belong to the underrated Arthur Symons. The author of the first major study of French Symbolism, which would have a profound impact in England; the editor of one of the quintessential magazines of the nineties, *The Savoy*, with Beardsley as art editor; a poet, fictionist, critic, and memoirist whose work reflected the prevailing moods of the decade; the companion and confidant of the major poet to survive the nineties, Yeats, even to sharing rooms with him; the friend of such nineties figures as Dowson and Moore and Wilde—Symons was the ubiquitous figure of the so-called Decadence. Yet he faded out as a name to conjure with early in the new century, and readers discover with surprise that he lived to be eighty, surviving the old century by forty-five years.

Yeats called the writers among whom he lived and worked in the nineties "the tragic generation" because so many—among them Dowson, Johnson, Beardsley, and Crackanthorpe—died young. Some others might just as well have been interred with them, given the silence into which they fell and the death of their reputations—John Gray, Victor Plarr, Theodore

Wratislaw and perhaps half a dozen more, including Arthur Symons. Even before his mental breakdown in 1908 his work showed declining vigor; and afterwards, although he wrote when he was able, it was often with an incoherence that he seemed to cut through only when he could write with nostalgia about the lovingly remembered past. His unpublished *Memoirs* became a large manuscript, filled out by material pillaged from his own colorful essays, sketches, and obituary pieces; but in his lifetime it remained a hopeless tangle in which logic and grammar and chronology sometimes disintegrated. Some of the pages were numbered as if part of a larger manuscript, but even the original table of contents, if the *Memoirs* had gone that far, has disappeared. When his estate was dispersed, the pages, defying any easy editorial solution, found a resting place at Princeton.

What remained was not physically sufficient for a book, nor did the surviving pages cover Symon's life adequately enough in all its color and range. But as Karl Beckson explains in a brief but illuminating preface, he has pruned the incoherence and augmented the pieces Symons had intended to publish by adding other reminiscences—of Pater, Verlaine, J. A. Symons, Dowson, and Beardsley, all of whom were of major importance in his life—and prefaced them with Symons's "A Prelude to Life," which is more fact than fiction about the artist as a young man. As late as 1933, in a letter to his literary agent, Symons noted his intention of adding it to the still incomplete *Memoirs*. And from *Confessions*, a pitiably confused short book, Beckson has taken segments that describe Symons's mental collapse. "The result," writes Beckson, "is, I hope, a reasonably coherent, albeit episodic, account, an authentic record, in Symons's own words, of his 'loves, passions, and adventures, all of which are personal, and of the people I knew and admired during those years' " (p. 5).

As an account of the nineties it is necessarily incomplete. Symons never finished it, nor did he write about those things which did not interest him. (Symons's own omissions are indicated by ellipses, Beckson's editorial cuts by asterisks, but these are not intrusive.) But otherwise it is one of the richest contemporary records which we have of that colorful era. To a biographer the richness of the vein is measured by how often one encounters a crisp characterization or a revealing anecdote one wishes had been in hand at the writing of one's own books, and I particularly regret I could not have read Symons on Whistler before I wrote my biography of the Master. It was not so much a new turn of phrase that Symons had remembered, but a mannerism—the way in which Whistler would devastate a person in conversation. "I remember the dinner party at which I first met him," Symons wrote, "and my first impression of his fierce and impertinent chivalry on behalf of art. Some person officially connected with art was there, an urbane sentimentalist, and after every official platitude there was a sharp crackle from Whistler's corner, and it was as if a rattlesnake had leapt suddenly out. The person did not know when he was dead, and Whistler transfixed him mortally, I know not how many times; and still he smiled and talked" (p. 211).

The most memorable pages are Symons's evocation of the music halls, the ballet girls, even of the Yiddish theatre, but the book will be turned to again and again for its memories of the terrible Alfred Jarry, the youthful André Gide, the fading Algernon Swinburne, the swaggering Jimmy Whistler, the dying Aubrey Beardsley, the sordid Ernest Dowson (who lives more in Symons's nearly mythic portrait than in any real-life account). One must get used to Symons's mannered style, but even that has the flavor of his period. Beerbohm was wrong, despite Beardsley's quicksilver genius. He had flowered in the Symons Period.

There are only two references by Symons to another young editor and writer of the decade, one whose life was more brief— Hubert Crackanthrope. Yet Symons had traveled with him in Italy and summered with him in the vaguely bohemian watering place of Dieppe, across the Channel, that artists' colony which often then sheltered more of the writers associated with the nineties than London itself. The reason may be inferred from Beckson's note, which now can be updated: that Crackanthorpe, at twenty-six, "was found dead in the Seine. Whether the result [was] suicide or foul play has never been established" (p. 262). That we have no further words from Symons on Crackanthorpe—although Beckson might have incorporated an 1898 essay on his work from the *Saturday Review*—suggests deliberate reticence. For the brief biography by his grandnephew—and the first ever, although Crackanthorpe died in 1896—now makes clear that he was a suicide, and that the affair might have embarrassed other nineties figures in Symons's circle.

In some ways the Crackanthorpe biography is akin to making bricks without straw, which seems the reason for the *"and English Realism in the 1890s"* tail to the title. Despite an active and productive life, however curtailed, he left few life records— or at least few life records were permitted by his family to survive—and few of his letters to friends and colleagues are extant. Yet we do know that he came from a wealthy family and that its material success as well as its interest in the arts enabled him to evade the formal Oxbridge route for an apprenticeship with writers and an opportunity to dabble at editing his own magazine. And as David Crackanthorpe, who (indirectly) inherited Hubert's library and a few vital drafts of letters, notes, another avenue of self-education (as it had been for Symons) was an immersion in nineteenth-century French literature. Crackanthorpe was a marker of passages, and one can assume that he marked what interested him. Thus we can trace his interest in French-style realism in the books he owned which have survived him. His family seems also to have paid George Gissing (who was always short of cash) to conduct a sort of tutorial program for Crackanthorpe. This tutoring was then followed by a year of editing his family-financed literary magazine, the *Albemarle Review* (1893), a respectable journal that could afford to solicit contributions from such rising Liberal politicians as R. B. Haldane, David Lloyd George, and Herbert Gladstone, and from such writers as John Gray, Richard Le Gallienne, Herbert Horne, and Bernard Shaw. The first number even used as frontispiece Whistler's lithograph *A Song on Stone*, which created such a demand that used copies of the sixpence publication were being hawked at ten shillings a few weeks later.

No literary scholar by training or background, David Crackanthorpe has nevertheless done his homework well, filling out the documents of the foreshortened life with a thorough search of the newspaper and periodical files of the day and the published memoirs of Hubert Crackanthorpe's English and French contemporaries. Even the bibliography and index will prove helpful to scholars of the period, and one may be surprised that the author has found as much as appears in his slim book, for young Crackanthorpe, until the day of his death, was less an accomplished writer than one from whom much was beginning to be expected.

Crackanthorpe's world of promise began collapsing on his wedding day, although his first book of stories, *Wreckage*, was a success and he was to become one of the early contributors to *The Yellow Book*. Leila Macdonald, whom he married in February 1893, was never a favorite of her husband's family. Although she emerges only faintly from the shadows even now, she appears to have been a statuesque and strong-willed woman who suffered, soon after their marriage, an eye injury from an exploding lamp that left her with emotional and physical problems for which Crackanthorpe seems to have had only imperfect sympathy. Whatever the reasons, the two drifted farther and farther apart, and eventually Leila would take a lover and her husband a mistress. On the fatal last trip to Paris in November 1896, Crackanthorpe was writing at the height of his powers and was even toying with the idea of taking over the failing *Savoy* (which was expiring with the dying Beardsley) and replacing Arthur Symons as editor. But Crackanthorpe then disappeared. He had crossed the Channel with Sissie Welch, the pretty married sister of Richard Le Gallienne, and joined Leila and her lover in a ménage à quatre in a Paris apartment. It appears from this distance as an exercise in communal masochism, and the inevitable quarrels occurred. Sissie returned to London while Leila announced her intention to initiate divorce proceedings on grounds of adultery (a gentleman would not press a countercharge) and "legal cruelty." The biographer (a lawyer) interprets these in terms of the 1890s as suggesting that she had charged that she had contracted a venereal disease from her husband.

Into Paris swooped Hubert's formidable mother, to talk with her son and with his wife's solicitor. Two months later Crackanthorpe's body was dragged from the Seine so decomposed that it was only by his ring and cuff links that he could be identified. The family, led by younger brother Dayrell Crackanthorpe, damped down all rumors. His grandson now suggests that the veil was drawn to protect Dayrell's chances for a diplomatic post in Madrid. But what he preserved has now made possible more informed speculation. Very clearly Hubert Crackanthorpe was neither pushed into the flood-swollen river nor did he fall in by accident. He had performed the final service for his socially prominent family by preventing a public scandal, and he left literary London to speculate on his unfulfilled promise. Nineties realism often involved a descent into easeful death. Crackanthorpe was living out one of the themes of his own fiction.

Rather than live out *his* fiction, Symons's closest friend in the nineties, W. B. Yeats, seems to have turned to fiction in order to explore the contradictions in his own life. His never-completed *The Speckled Bird*, now published with its three draft alternative sections, is more memoir than novel, especially in the brilliant edition William O'Donnell has produced, which relates every character and every event, wherever possible, to Yeats's life and work in his twenties and early thirties. Written between 1896 and 1902, when Yeats was deeply involved with Celtic mysticism, and just after he had completed his *Secret Rose* stories, the novel ostensibly is concerned with the spiritual quest of Michael Hearne, but it is clearly spiritual autobiography.

Although Yeats was unable to put sufficient distance between his own dilemmas and those of his hero to sustain the narrative, even the fragmentary portions are sensitively written, and the episodes gain enormously in interest from their associations with Yeats's own life, work, and friends. We see the young artist trying to find a professional direction, a satisfactory religious accommodation (through occultism), and an end to his frustrations in love. Early in the novel Yeats thinly fictionalizes his boyhood fascination with literature and art, his relations with his father (also a *John* here), and the awakening of his aesthetic sensibility. I have left in the text O'Donnell's editorial machinery:

John Hearne had never read the book, but when Michael told him of it he bought him a *Morte d'Arthur*, which he had read, and talked to him one night by the sea of the coming of these tales into the Middle Ages and of the poets and painters who had made them almost as important in our time. [CANCELLED: He said, "They are a part of the holy church of romance, which should be to you and me all that the holy church of theology is to our servants." And he spoke of the gradual fading of theology and belief in the supernatural, and a gradual awakening of joy and liberty as men talked when the poems of Swinburne and the discoveries of Darwin were in the air. Michael, in whose nerves the emotions of a very different generation were already beginning to stir, listened a little indignantly, and thought not indeed of devil or angel, God or saint, but(?) of Merlin under the stone.] His imagination, which had even more than a child's prepossession with woods and waters and imaginative circumstances, found all it desired in these books, with their delight in amour and in raiment and in household things learned by the story-tellers in the courts of princes, and in giants and wizards and grotesque persons learned 'by the storytellers from a broken race that still remembered the reveries of ancient herdsmen among woods and waters. It was long before the later book, with its more passionate tales, became more important to him than the older book and when it did, its world took the ancient form and colour he read in that older book. What delighted him most in the newer book was the story of the Grail and the stories of Merlin and of Morgan le Fay and the wizard. [p. 9]

Later—one cannot list all the points at which life and art intersect—we see the Yeats figure involved in the Celtic Mysteries, and we see him unhappy over the marriage of the woman he loved to someone else, and his consolation by an older married woman. In the process we meet people who are clearly McCormick Mathers, Maud Gonne, and Olivia Shakespear (the "Diana Vernon" of the *Memoirs*), and we meet in disguise many of the writers and artists Yeats and Symons knew when they shared a flat in Fountain Court in the first days of Symons's editing of *The Savoy*. The curious Count Eric

Stenbock, in a deliciously satirical section, is Count Sobrinski, for example, and an episode in the parlor of an inn, O'Donnell tells us, referring to a Symons memoir Beckson does not use, is based upon a little Irish hotel in which Yeats, Symons, Edward Martyn, and George Moore stopped for tea on their way back from the Aran Islands in 1896.

O'Donnell's editing of the manuscripts is a model of informativeness: he provides his cross-references between manuscripts and gives explanations of allusions which parallel the *Memoirs* and the *Autobiographies*, or which are referred to in published and unpublished letters. O'Donnell makes it clear that *The Speckled Bird*, even if seldom read for its clean narrative prose and its ear for dialogue, will be read for its picture of Yeats and his circle at a turning point in his professional life. In its way it is Yeats's third memoir, and the narrative, notes, introduction, and very thorough index will be regularly consulted. Scholars who wonder whether a fragmentary or unfinished work is worth publication can take *The Speckled Bird* as text.

Imprint on History

James Wells

Lucien Febvre and Henri-Jean Martin. *The Coming of the Book: The Impact of Printing 1450-1800*. Trans. David Gerard, ed. Geoffrey Nowell-Smith and David Wootton. London: NLB; Atlantic Highlands, N.J.: Humanities Press, 1976. 378 pp.

When Lucien Febvre and Henri-Jean Martin's *L'Apparition du Livre* was published in 1958, it received little attention outside France. I closed my review in the July 1959 *Library Quarterly* with the hope that "some enterprising publisher will commission an English translation so that it may become widely known." That hope has been realized, almost twenty years later, in a translation made by David Gerard. One reason for this long delay may have been the difficulty of the task, since the style is complex and the technical vocabulary highly specialized. Gerard has provided a decent, somewhat pedestrian translation, which occasionally slips when he is faced with printers' terms. He calls a papermaker's mould a form; uses the French term *cran* for the nick, the notch used by the compositor to determine the top or bottom of a piece of type; speaks of borders as formes; calls the protective brass studs on the bindings of early books nails; and confuses the matrices used for casting types with dies. But these are minor imperfections. What is important is that a truly original and highly influential book is at least available to those who do not read French.

Theodore K. Rabb, in an excellent review in the *Times Literary Supplement* for 14 October 1977, discusses at some length the influence of *The Coming of the Book*, as it is called in English, since its original publication. He cites Robert Mandrou, Geneviève Bollème, and Marc Soriano among the French who have followed Martin's lead; in this country the book has considerably influenced the work of Elizabeth

Eisenstein, Robert Darnton, and Natalie Davis, among others, in their studies of particular aspects of French printing and publishing. It has had less impact on historians dealing with non-French subjects, although its method and point of view are certainly applicable to the study of printing and the book trade in any country, at any time.

The publishers of the English edition have omitted the foreword by Paul Chalus, which outlined the scope of *L'Evolution de l'Humanité*, the massive collection in which *L'Apparition du Livre* appeared, and which placed the book within its framework. By 1958 the first section, dealing with prehistory and antiquity, had been completed in twenty-six volumes. *L'Apparition du Livre* was the last of forty-nine volumes projected for Section 2, "The Origins of Christianity and the Middle Ages"; Sections 3 and 4 were to cover "The Modern World" and "Toward the Present," respectively. The whole was to comprise over one hundred volumes, a collective synthesis of man's thought, politics, art, science, and life. This is truly history on the grand scale; the first volume appeared in 1920, and publication continues; perhaps half the announced titles have appeared, not in order and not always by the announced authors. *L'Apparition du Livre* was assigned by Henri Berr, founder of the series, to Lucien Febvre, about 1930; it was considered a crucial volume, linking two epochs and marking a revolutionaiy step in the means of transmitting thought. Febvre planned the book but was never able to write it. In 1953 he asked his friend and disciple Henri-Jean Martin to take over the book and gave Martin his preface and plan. Febvre was able to read and approve most of the book, but the major part of the execution and the actual writing are Martin's. Martin, in his own prefatory note, takes responsibility for the book, while stating that he had put Febvre's name ahead of his own on the title page out of affection and gratitude.

Febvre's brief preface stresses that the book was not intended to be still another history of printing, since there was no need for one. Rather, its aim was to trace the book as an instrument for change during a period of great changes. The emphasis is not, as in most histories of the book, on the discovery of printing nor on the aesthetic of book design, although both these subjects are well treated. Rather, it is on the social, intellectual, and economic background of the book trade from 1450 to 1800. A number of specialists were recruited to deal with their particular areas of competence. Marcel Thomas deals with the background of the manuscript book trade; Mme. M. R. Guignard with the Chinese precedents for printing; Mme. A. Bazanoff with printing in the Slavic countries; and Father H. Bernard-Maitre with the Far East. But the emphasis is on the book in Europe, and particularly in France. This is a strength, since Martin inevitably knows the history and culture of his own country best and can introduce much new material; when writing about England, especially, he is apt to rely more upon previously published material. It is also a weakness, since the book is somewhat parochial.

The complexity of the subject matter has dictated a complex organization, thematic rather than chronological, which results in some repetition; but considering the scope of the work there is remarkably little. Marcel Thomas's introduction provides a succinct survey of the manuscript trade from the late Middle Ages to the invention of printing. He discusses the increasing audience for books which resulted from the founding of universities and the growth of a literate laity; the organization and regulation of secular and monastic scriptoria; the way in which manuscripts were produced, priced, and distributed; and the size of editions—for some manuscripts, notably Books of Hours and vernacular romances, were produced in multiple copies. The scribes, illuminators, and stationers who produced books for the manuscript market paved the way for the printers who replaced them in the fifteenth century.

Printing could not have progressed as rapidly as it did had there not been an adequate supply of paper. Vellum was not as expensive as we have thought, but it was not an easy material to print on and there would not have been enough for large editions. Paper, introduced into Italy from China via the Arabs in the twelfth century, was initially distrusted for its fragility and impermanence. But its virtues—low cost and light weight—soon won it acceptance. Paper manufacture requires two ingredients: an adequate supply of clean rags and a large supply of pure water. The first proved a bottleneck until the introduction of wood pulp and straw fibers in the nineteenth century; water was easier to find and dictated the location of the paper mills. The major mills were located on the upper reaches of rivers, which provided not only the water required for manufacture but also power and cheap transport. This was extremely important since paper is a heavy and bulky commodity; overland freight was more expensive and less dependable than water. The mills were usually near large trade centers, for ease of distribution; printers tended to set up nearby, for the same reasons: to be near the source of their primary raw material, to save on freight, and to be near their customers.

An abundant supply of paper is a prerequisite for printing, but there are others: type, ink, and presses. All these were available, in rudimentary form, before the fifteenth century. Goldsmiths knew how to cut dies, to strike moulds from them, and to cast coins and medals; the necessary metals, tin, lead, and antimony, were in use. Presses were commonly used in the manufacture of wine, cheese, oil, and other commodities. What was needed was a mould which could be adjusted for varying widths of letters; a method of assembling the cast types into lines, words, and pages. Martin does not belabor the question of who invented printing, where, or when—the subject of a vast existing literature. He gives Gutenberg his share of the credit but points out that many others were working on the problem at the same time in many places besides Mainz. The methods of producing type, composing it, and printing from it changed little from the fifteenth century until the Industrial Revolution. There were antecedents; the Chinese and Koreans used carved wooden type and cast ideographs long before, but there is no evidence that their methods were known in Europe. Images and patterns were printed from wooden blocks earlier, but this was a slow, expensive, and unsatisfactory method of printing texts. The breakthrough occurred with the invention of the type mould, which held matrices struck from engraved punches.

It took considerable time for the printed book to develop its own conventions; incunabula looked much like manuscripts in their layout and typography, with incipits, binders' signatures, initials, types, and borders copied from manuscript models. This is not surprising; incunabula were not intended to deceive buyers. Readers are conservative and would not have accepted a completely unfamiliar book. The first types were based on existing books and cursive hands; but gradually these were simplified and reduced in number for economy, with roman, italic, and black letter the only survivors. During the seventeenth century, copper engraving superseded wood blocks and considerably augmented the use of illustration for information: current events, works of art, maps, and scientific illustrations.

Binding also changed as the printed book became more common. There were no sudden changes; incunabula, like manuscripts, were bound in leather over heavy wooden boards. There were no edition bindings at first; books were sold in sets of sheets for which the purchaser commissioned a binding according to his taste and purse. Gradually cardboard superseded wood because it was cheaper and lighter and could be made from waste paper. Decoration was simplified, with panels and rolls replacing individual tools. Gold tooling, introduced into Italy from the Near East, was reserved for luxury bindings; ordinary books carried only spine titles and slight decoration. Eventually, leather was replaced by paper or cloth covers.

Martin has used archives and records extensively to document the component costs of the book: raw materials (paper, ink, type, and presses) and labor (composition and presswork). He has found much new material and has interpreted it with great skill, extrapolating from legal documents and archives a picture of the various kinds of printing shops and their working conditions. He describes the equipment of the workshop for large, medium, and small firms, and the quantity owned by each, using inventories and wills. Type, which wore out quickly, was more burdensome than presses, which did not. The purchase of type and paper required tying up considerable capital for lengthy periods; printers and publishers tried not to print more copies than could be sold quickly. Paper represented the largest fixed cost of the book well into the eighteenth century; the author received a small fee for his work, relying mainly on patronage, and printers were not well paid. Larger printer-publishers produced most of their own work, farming out some of it; smaller shops depended heavily on such outside commissions. Gradually a network of large firms was established, which traded titles and which could afford agents and travelers; they met often at the fairs in Paris, Lyons, Leipzig, Frankfurt, and other large commercial centers. A system of bills of exchange was developed to supersede barter.

When the book industry began to change and modernize, it did so quickly. Division of labor and specialization cut costs; type founders, who were by the nature of their work highly skilled, were among the first to become independent entrepreneurs. The printing industry was highly regulated; master printers preferred such control, when competition became fierce, and civil and ecclesiastical authorities demanded it in order to monitor what was printed. The craft required considerable education and a long apprenticeship; journeymen were not always sure of a job and frequently had to travel in search of one. Many of them were poorly paid and, when they tried to organize, as they did quite early, ran into fierce opposition from their masters and the state. Most of them were never able to find the capital to set up their own shops and could hope for little more than a foremanship in a large establishment. The big firms were often family held, through many generations.

One of Martin's most successful chapters treats the geography of the book, tracing the spread of printing and the emergence of such centers as Paris, Lyons, and Venice, which not only provided a large domestic market but were also export centers, shipping books throughout Europe and to the New World. The earliest customers were mainly clerics, but they were soon outnumbered by laymen, especially lawyers, who bought books for their work and for entertainment. Martin's analysis of the changing book market is new and extremely stimulating.

The Reformation brought about great changes in the book trade. It impeded or stopped the trade between Catholic and

Protestant countries; nationalism encouraged the growth of vernacular printing at the expense of Latin. Traditional centers like Leipzig and Frankfurt slipped in importance; Holland, which had high tolerance and comparatively little regulation, printed many books which were banned but popular in France. The Counter-Reformation also had its effect. In Catholic countries printing revived in the South and Cologne; Antwerp again became a great printing center, producing service books for Europe and the Americas. The Jesuits became great patrons of the printer in France and Belguim, while Protestant presses flourished along the French border in Switzerland and in Protestant areas of France.

During the seventeenth-century economic decline, many small printers failed. The rise of the vernaculars narrowed the international book trade, and increasing censorship and regulation made business more difficult. The new colonies and the provinces began to print for themselves, to save time and money.

The chapter on the changing book trade focuses on the size of editions and distribution methods. There has always been a temptation to print large editions, but unsold books tie up a great deal of capital and cost money to warehouse. The successful publisher has always been the one who is adept at gauging the size of his market. During the fifteenth century, editions of 100-150 copies were not uncommon, especially for classical texts; 1,000 copies was a large edition. By the end of the century, with better distribution, editions grew much larger, especially as prices were lowered. Successful printers like the Kobergers printed 1,500 copies. English editions were limited, by a Star Chamber decree of 1587, to 1,200-1,250 copies. This was the norm during most of the seventeenth century, although occasionally religious books or textbooks with a sure sale were issued in larger numbers. Even in the eighteenth century runs of over 2,000 copies were exceptional.

Since no single market could absorb large copies of a single title, small consignments were the rule. Transport was a major problem; books are heavy, bulky, and vulnerable to weather damage. Booksellers did not always pay promptly; printers often shipped incomplete sets of sheets. The book fair, at which volumes could be examined and appraised, played an important role in distribution; book fair catalogues, especially in Frankfurt and Leipzig, were important sales tools which became bibliographical aids. Popular literature—pamphlets, ABC's, chapbooks and the like—were generally sold by peddlars, who took an active part in the distribution of clandestine and politically dangerous works.

As editions grew larger, and contemporary writers began to expect reward for their work, publishers felt the need for protection of their investment. Counterfeiting and piracy began as early as the sixteenth century, especially in Lyons. The Italians were the first to seek legal protection, which was only local; foreign printers could pirate their work freely. Royal and ecclesiastical privileges gradually developed in France and Germany, but infractions were frequent and hard to prove, since fictitious imprints were often used. The monopolies of successful works were highly profitable and very tempting.

During the Reformation and Counter-Reformation there was increasing effort to control printing and distribution. As today, banned books were sought after. Neither the church nor the state could effectively stop their production, no matter how stringent the penalties. Booksellers and printers, motivated by conscience or greed, issued them under false imprints, smuggled them across the borders, and gambled on not getting caught.

The final chapter, "The Book as a Force for Change," is the longest, the most original, and the most important in the scheme of the work. It explores the way in which the book was used, especially in the Reformation and the Counter-Reformation, to change men's minds and lives, and the way in which the book itself changed in the process.

The first books were frank imitations of manuscripts, produced correctly, cheaply, and rapidly; they won quick acceptance and made books available to many who could not afford them before. It is estimated that some twenty million were printed before 1500 for a comparatively thinly populated world, most of whose inhabitants were illiterate. Printers rarely print to change the world. Rather, they print for profit and choose books they hope to sell. Most incunabula, about 77 percent, were in Latin. Religious works made up about 45 percent of the total; literature about 30 percent; law about 10 percent; and science about 10 percent. The Bible and liturgical books commanded a sure market, as they still do. Clergy and pious laymen bought devotional works and popular theology in vast quantities.

The early printers played an important part in increasing literacy through the provision of teaching tools; grammars and texts were among their staples. The rise of humanism increased the sale of classics, philosophy, and history. Vernacular works, few at first, were generally translations from Latin, although there were successful editions of Dante, Boccaccio, chivalric romances, and courtly poetry. While fifteenth-century scientific books included many medieval encyclopedic works and classical authors, about 57 percent of scientific incunabula were by contemporary writers, without much lasting interest. Astronomy and travel were highly popular, and there were many technical works on fortification, weaponry, and the like.

While there were few sudden spectacular changes in reading habits after the invention of printing, a sort of cultural Darwinism soon began; only the fittest of past writings survived. The press greatly assisted the humanist movement, making available favorable texts, well printed in clear roman types, to all Europe. The desire for accuracy led to a search for new, better manuscripts and to the formulation of new editorial standards based on philological principles.

By 1550 printed books had largely replaced manuscripts in libraries; by the seventeenth century, as a result of the vast output of the press, books were easily available, at comparatively low prices, to anyone who could read. Large private libraries had become fairly common. The laity soon replaced the clergy as the major buyers of books. Lawyers, who needed books as tools, and civil servants were heavy purchasers. They often built sizable collections; private libraries of 500 volumes were not uncommon in the sixteenth century. This market is reflected in the choice of books printed. The vast majority of early incunabula were religious books, which were gradually supplanted by secular works, many of them classical texts. Martin demonstrates these changes with a mass of detail from library catalogues, wills, and other sources. Using such data, he traces the rise of humanism, of Hebrew and Jewish printing, of translations and vernacular works. The demand for translations did much to fix the vernaculars by standardizing spelling, grammar, and vocabulary.

With the Reformation came a renewed demand for religious books: for the Bible, mainly in translation; for polemical works; and for devotional books. The printing press did not bring about the Reformation, but it played a central role in its development. New ideas could be spread far and wide at a great speed; Luther's works were printed in vast quantities; a new genre of informational printing, which had begun in the fifteenth century, grew enormously. Posters, placards, and pamphlets informed the populace not only of the activities of the Reformers but of the measures being taken against them; many were illustrated, for those who could not read. Printers who worked for Luther became rich. His books and pamphlets were distributed not only through the bookshops but by colporteurs, who took them into the smallest towns. Luther's translations of the Bible were printed in numerous, often large, editions; 430 editions, of the whole or parts, are recorded between 1522 and 1546; a single printer issued 37 editions of the Old Testament between 1546 and 1580. There were probably a million copies printed during the first half of the sixteenth century and even more in the second. Lefevre's translation into French was also highly successful, as were translations into other languages. Martin's figures on the number of copies printed are highly revealing.

Luther's works quickly reached other countries, probably through the Frankfurt Fairs. Many of the polemical tracts were printed abroad for the French market; there was an almost immediate attempt to suppress them. Strasbourg became an important center for the entrance of Protestant propaganda printed in Switzerland and Germany. Underground organizations in Basel and Geneva, often manned by French emigrés, worked with booksellers in France, supplying Lyons and Paris. Censorship was sporadic and ineffectual until 1534, when the

King and Parliament began to get tougher. The trade continued to flourish, however; an occasional colporteur or printer might be tried and burned, but the big well-connected establishments were rarely bothered.

The Coming of the Book is an ambitious work which attempts at the same time too much—a survey of the book trade and the society in which it was carried on from the late Middle Ages to 1500—and too little, since it stops at a period even more innovative and rapidly changing than that it covers. It would be difficult to write that second volume covering the nineteenth and twentieth centuries, but it is needed. *The Coming of the Book* has its faults: the eighteenth century is treated somewhat cursorily, and the seventeenth only slightly less so. There is too much emphasis on France. But these are minor flaws in a major work which is original, stimulating, and remarkably learned. The English publishers have not, unfortunately, served it as well as they might have. While the illustrations in the French edition were not very well printed, nor always well chosen, many of them gave new insights into the place of book illustration in the life of the times and its relationship with the other decorative arts. The plates have been omitted from the translation; fortunately the excellent maps, tracing the spread of printing, are included. The apparatus in the French edition was somewhat confusing; books cited in the excellent notes were sometimes omitted from the bibliography, which also included books not mentioned in the notes. It would have been difficult to update the bibliography and to fill some of the inexplicable gaps, especially the work of such American scholars as Ivins, Bühler, and Wroth, but to drop it is inexcusable. Nevertheless, it is good to have available at last in English one of the most important twentieth-century works dealing with the history of one of man's most durable and influential inventions.

Transcriptions with Writers

Ronald Christ

Conversations with Writers. Vol. I. Ed. Matthew J. Bruccoli, et al. Detroit: Gale Research Co., 1977, 302 pp.

Most collections of interviews are like most thrift shops: they tempt you with a chance for discovering real value with almost no work. You wander among them, looking and hoping for a "find"—something discarded that you value that will take on value in the eyes of others through your discovery. Simultaneous with this hope of discovery, however, is a certain ruthless contempt for the bulk of what's offered along with the ironic pleasure of browsing thoughtfully in the midst of trash. You're outsmarting the system, in a way.

Which is another way of saying that collections of interviews as well as thrift shops are popular museums, and like all such institutions they tend (I say *tend*) toward the vulgar and the merely curious as they conceal the few valuables they contain— if, indeed, they contain any at all. Of course some settings can mask the nature of the enterprise; the sign may read "Antiques" or the cover *Writers at Work* and we know that we are being asked to take seriously—as "art"—what is, in the very best sense of the words, popular, ephemeral, informal, dilettantish.

With interviews it is precisely the tension between lofty aspirations on the one hand and technical or autobiographical gossip on the other (both balanced against commercial interests) that gives to the form its liveliness, its power and its possibilities. (The same is true with many a Hollywood movie.) Especially if within the form we narrow down our consideration to exclude propaganda—such as presidential news conferences— or explication—like my interview with Borges in *The Paris Review*. More often than not, what remains are called "conversations" in order to convey the intentionally chatty, random quality that inspires some of the best examples in the form. Still, even in such "conversations," it is the tension between the form and the effect, between the medium and the use to which it will be put, between the attitude with which the work is undertaken and the attitude with which it is subsequently viewed that gives such efforts their distinctive nature.

Such is the case with *Conversations with Writers*, issued under the general editorial direction of Matthew J. Bruccoli, and it is precisely in the sloppy or nonexistent observance of this tension that the volume sinks into categories of pseudocriticism, pseudoliterary history and scholarship with almost no redeeming characteristics. The high aspiration of the volume is testified to in the introduction, where we are told that this first volume in a projected series has been planned (1) "to provide a forum for the leading American writers by preserving their comments on their work and careers," (2) "to provide readers with insights into the profession of authorship in our time," and (3) "to present an accurate image of the authors as individuals." But when we look at the book itself, we see how these intentions are everywhere contradicted by the choice of authors, the dull questioning, the witless editing—the failure to come to grips with what the interview offers other than a mindless recording of spoken utterance subsequently distorted through translation into another mode, the written word.

For example, here are three consecutive questions from the "conversation" with James Dickey: "Why did you decide to write a novel?" "How long did it take you to write *Deliverance?*" "I thought the novel was dead" (pp. 34-35). There is no dramatic sense here, no attempt at continuity, no imagination, and certainly no attempt at *conversation*, a word whose roots indicate a *turning with*. Just as there is none in this excerpt from the "conversation" with William Price Fox (a "leading" American writer?) which shows how "fidelity" to the spoken word evidences no loyalty at all to the speaker, the writer, *or* to the reader:

Conversations: What were the rewards of teaching for you—certainly not the money? You're still in it, obviously it means something to you.

Fox: Yeah, I'm still in it. I don't know, I think it means something because, you know, you can . . . . I've had a lot of success with students that had some talent, an awful lot. I mean like, oh, about twenty or twenty-five books, and several screen plays. I'm able to recognize talent most of the time. Whey they're too abstract I can't follow it. [p. 54]

I mean if this interview, like, you know, had been constructed or like developed or something, like, to evoke a sense of Mr. Fox's character and personal style as an author, you know, then his stumblings and repetitions and inarticulate sounds (even his lack of logical expression) might have served a real purpose, you know? Here, they merely convey an unfair awkwardness and opaqueness resulting from our triple remove from his voice— first, through the tape recording; second, through the transcription (he didn't speak with that punctuation, for example); and, third, through our reading his oral comments on the written page (listening to him we never would have had to wonder what that final "it" refers to or whether that "awful lot" signifies the quantity of his success or the number of his successful students).

The editing of these "conversations" is often faulty along other lines as well. For instance, the interviewer's second statement in the following excerpt from a conversation with Edward Gorey serves no purpose other than to guarantee that we have a record of every pointless word. Had the interviewer's interjection—try calling him a "conversationalist" or the interjection a "statement" and you'll realize the aesthetic potential that this book squanders—had this interjection been deleted, Gorey's words would make more logical sense, although it is true that some of the book's country-porch flavor might have been lost:

Conversations: Do your books get attention?

Gorey: In a word, no, very seldom. Occasionally somebody will write a brief review. *Amphigorey* got notices.

Conversations: Right.

Gorey: *The New Yorker* once reviewed, I think, *The Vinegar Works,*

and made some nasty remark on the strength of the title. That was all I
needed from them. They've never mentioned me since. [p. 150]

Such editorial presentation—such *lack* of editorial presentation—characterizes this book on almost every page. Such
presentation smacks of thoughtlessness, a will to publish no
matter what the quality (that is, a will to sell), and perhaps even
a scorn for the genuine artifices of written and spoken speech.

Similarly, the tiny, uninformative and unevocative
introductions preceding the conversations are pointless when
they are not merely embarrassing, as is this final sentence from
the paragraph heading the talk with Thomas Tryon (another
"leading" American author?): "The interview was interrupted
at one point so that the principals could make use of the
well-stocked bar in the room" (p. 253). I suppose that such Rona
Barrett coyness is intended to lend something to the "accurate
image" of Tryon as man and as author, but, on the contrary, it
only confirms the commercialism of the interview, matching
perfectly although not so flossily the commercialism of its
subject, who tailors his production to what his agent, Bob,
thinks best for his career: "But there is this book that I want to
do called 'Final Cut.' It's about Hollywood, and Bob doesn't
want two Hollywood books in a row. Ergo, my pain. And, you
know, I think anything would do—*McGuffey's Reader* by
Thomas Tryon—just anything, just to get the book out of the
way. Then I can go on and do this other thing, which is pretty
big, but it's good. So I don't know" (p. 175). Now with some
attention to subject, persona, and literary market such an
interview could be enormously entertaining and instructive;
here, it merely testifies to Tryon's being read and recorded in the
same manner, say, as John Gardner. So the conceptual and
editing problems in the book run as wide as they run deep, with
the fault showing up, as always, in the language: the blunt
jargon of the interviewer who asks Mary Hemingway (yet
another "leading" author?) "What was the actual writing span
on that?" (p. 183) reveals an insensitivity to language that is no
worse, unfortunately, than what is divulged by the other
interviewers and editors, who are equally insensitive to the very
material in which they work:

*Conversations: How do you do it? What you have been describing here
are all kinds of oral patterns that you can't get on a printed page. And
yet you are a printed-page man.*

Fox: Well, I try to do it and I just hope that people who know my work
. . . . What I detest is that speed-reading because they miss all of the
stuff; and I do a lot of that ricky-ticky stuff. [p. 76]

Speed-editing and speed-printing are just as bad, if not worse,
because they are virtually irremediable. If only the makers of this
volume had heeded Fox's words, heeded the medium in which
they are working, they might have seen that his aesthetic
problem is theirs too, or is at least analogous to it.

But no inattention to words has been spared in this anthology
which only occasionally recognizes its own nature, as in the
following exchange between the poet Robert Hayden and
Richard Layman where Layman asks: "When you were first
describing the move from Detroit to Nashville you kept referring
to 'it,' the pressures of 'it'. What did you mean by 'it'? More than
simple prejudice, I assume." And Hayden gracefully rhymes his
answer to the *it* of the question: "Oh, well, yes. It was certainly
the racial situation which in Nashville wasn't as bad as it was in
some other places in the South, but it was bad enough," and
then goes on to construct a beautiful period on the basis of
anadiplosis and anaphora: "But the racial question in the South
was of paramount importance to us because it did pretty much
limit us: limit the kind of experiences we could have, limit the
kind of things that we could do, limit opportunities in every
single way" (p. 170). These fragments are as characteristic of the
way Hayden speaks as are those I quoted from Fox, I suppose;
but what sets them off, what gives them relief is Layman's (and
Hayden's) attention to language itself, whatever its nature.

But such attention is rare in this collection, and mostly we
must rely on the principle that if an articulate, sensitive man
talks long enough he's bound to say something worthwhile once
in a while. The informing principle of the treasure hunt where
the reader does the real work after the interviewer has done the
hiding; the raison d'être of serendipity, where the reader, again,
does the discovering. Allowing for these norms we do hit upon a

few finds in *Conversations with Writers*, though not nearly enough to justify the enterprise or the reader's time.

One such find is the conversation with John Gardner, whose opening response demonstrates exactly the kind of near nonsequitur that justifies a reader's and an interviewer's time:

Conversations: You've had the best of two careers: scholar and writer. Which came first?

Gardner: I guess writing. I don't think they're very different. Insofar as scholarship is really different from sensitive reading, I think it's bad scholarship. [p. 83]

Besides the authoritative injunction in that last sentence (where Gardner is moving away from an answer to the question) we also hear the man's character, we realize again a purpose in his works that further behooves our clutching his utterance in our minds. We know, too, that there's merit in our going on with the reading. If we do, then we encounter some ideal statements from Gardner like the following: "We've got to remember we live in a democracy, and if we really believe in that principle, and I really do, we're going to have to accept some funny values. We're going to have to finally end up admitting that the best artist we ever produced, the most impressive all over the world, the most influential on all the arts, is Walt Disney, of all people" (p. 90). Vance Bourjaily (still another "leading" author?) also provides a serendipitous aperçu: "In the country they don't make any distinction between teaching and learning; they use the same verb, 'to learn,' for both functions. They say, 'He learned me.' And 'learn' is a better word than 'teach'. When I learn somebody something, I learn it myself too" (p. 21). Indirectly, Mr. Bourjaily instructs us that if we have learned anything from this book it is because we have learned it for ourselves, not because the book offers any teaching, for as Mr. Bourjaily laments in another paragraph: "They just don't edit much anymore" (p. 19).

Every book establishes its own norms, by which it must be judged and compared and known. This one establishes norms of the worst order—those of the lowest common denominator. Which is not to say that it is entirely lacking in information, for as John Gardner said, if we really believe in democracy—and I really do—we have to accept some funny values. One of these values is that the interview is a democratic form in respect to its history, its practioners, and its audiences. Consequently, among the siftings and blunderings, good things do come out in *Conversations with Writers*. My objection, however, is that such a book is not an appropriate theater for such values, since it willfully confuses high statement of purpose with shoddy practice, confuses meretricious candidates with authentic ones, and, finally, confuses the pleasure of discovering insight with that sickening taste most thrift shops and such collections deposit in our mouths: yes, there may be baguettes here; but, if we must range through all this trash to get them, is it worth it?

The Diversions of an Ardent Bibliophile

William B. Todd

Alan Noel Latimer Munby. *Essays and Papers*. Edited, with an introduction, by Nicolas Barker. London: The Scolar Press, 1978. xiii, 241 pp.

It is a curious circumstance and, lamentably, will always remain so, that many who profess some competence in interpreting the printed word are little concerned about the original edition of the works so exquisitely expounded, the original testimony of the authors themselves. Nay, the modern reprint from the local dispensary is quite adequate for their high purpose, a reprint appearing usually without any warranty, yet eagerly accepted as if it were bestowed directly from Mount Sinai. Such is their simple faith, their implicit trust in what some latter-day purveyor has thrust upon them.

Even those readers who acknowledge some authorized edition, and may occasionally consult it, are rarely impelled to possess this artifact or to trace the history of the work in question, from early inception through several vicissitudes to final repose in some dusty library. All that business involving printers, publishers, editors, collectors, sales and resales, even thievery and arson perhaps, they might reasonably argue, is quite irrelevant to explication de texte. No school of criticism has ever countenanced, much less approved, any such vagary.

Against all critical dictates, however, one may defiantly quote the late William A. Jackson, perhaps the greatest research librarian of our time. "I enjoy books," he often remarked, "but even more I enjoy books about books and, best of all, books about books about books." The same interest, more ebulliently expressed, is found in Larry Powell's *A Passion for Books* and in countless other declarations, all betraying a certain affection which the strict litterateur must regard as very peculiar indeed. And now this strange proclivity is discovered again in the

especially endearing testament of these *Essays and Papers*, a
selection from the many bibliophilic excursions of the late
librarian of King's College, Cambridge.

To account for what others would consider a wholly
inexplicable activity, Dr. Munby, or "Tim" as he was known to
all his friends, was prevailed upon late in life to reminisce about
"Book Collecting in the 1930s," one of the three pieces which
his editor, Nicolas Barker, happily added to the list previously
drawn up by the author himself. In this essay particularly we
observe, almost in set order, all the signs leading to the final,
unswerving commitment of a bibliophile. First is the early
compulsion to acquire, preserve, but not necessarily to read,
books on any subject whatever. As a schoolboy in Clifton,
Somersetshire, Munby first purchased, for two pence, the tenth
edition of a 1744 volume of sermons—a book still on his shelves
in 1973, the date of his writing. Next as he says elsewhere, is the
"will-power necessary to get rid of books" (p. 39), a rational
reaction quite ineffective in the case of the sermons, but still
operative when young Munby sold for five pounds some early
tracts on vaccination he had earlier acquired for nine pence.

Given the persistent compulsion, along with some little
discrimination, at least after the event, there should follow
certain other inducements: the encouragement of relatives
(Munby had an indulgent father and aunt), an antiquarian
bookstore near one's college (Gustave David's is remembered in
several of these essays), and in the college itself a strong
book-collecting tradition (at King's the example of Stephen
Gaselee, Maynard Keynes, Arthur Cole) continuing in the
student's own time (John Carter, John Hayward, Desmond
Flower). Thereafter one should avoid an academic routine,
which as already intimated usually serves only to deaden a real
appreciation of books, and engage instead in the lively
commerce of these original artifacts. Here Munby's experiences
could hardly be surpassed: extensive training under two of the
leading booksellers' firms in London (Quaritch and Robinson),
research in the British Museum Library, and finally the most
exciting experience of all, an education "second to none" with

the great auctioneering establishment of Sotheby's. Yet at the last as at the beginning, Munby still confesses, in 1973, "a foolish weakness for odd books," including the very recent acquisitions of a Corfu-printed modern Greek phrase book and, alongside it on his shelves, a Bombay-printed prospectus of a Persian epic poem on the exploits of British armies in India.

This final survey of experiences past and pleasures present serves to inform even the doubting reader of the real validity of Munby's many exploits in the bibliophilic world. Perhaps he will be remembered best and consulted most often for those extensive researches which, in these *Essays and Papers*, can receive only passing reference. First among these, certainly, is his five-volume account of Sir Thomas Phillipps, the very exemplar of a bibliomaniac gone completely berserk. Not unrelated was his lifetime interest in the sale catalogues of important libraries, of which he had accumulated some fifteen hundred at the time he wrote "Floreat Bibliomania" (1952) and as many as seven thousand when he came to prepare a "Postscript" (1974). Munby's encyclopedic knowledge of book sales, based upon his own remarkable collection, prompted him to edit, in a facsimile series continuing since 1964, *Sale Catalogues and Libraries of Eminent Persons*. This series will always remain an essential reference to the "literary stock" that furnished the minds of later writers. Further, in a list of Munby's own writings appended to these *Essays*, it is divulged that he was the anonymous commentator in the *Times Literary Supplement* 1950-1960 on practically all aspects of the bibliographical research reported in the leading journals of the time. Thus he had the unusual privilege, exercised in a firm yet genial way, of imposing some restraints upon the more egregious displays of bookish nonsense. (I write as one among many so admonished.) By precept then, as well as by example, Munby's influence was all-pervasive and always to good effect.

From the list of writings it is also apparent that Munby's enthusiasms had a ready audience since, except for a wartime interval, he was constantly in print every year from 1933 to 1976, sometimes producing an article, a review, or a book every month, and once (in 1952) achieving a record of fifteen contributions. Hence these eighteen essays and papers constitute a mere sampling of Munby's less extensive but no less stimulating performances. The 1952 "Floreat Bibliomania," already mentioned, is the only one, apart from the longer 1973 apologia, which defends book collecting, "an incomparably exciting sport," here against the mockery of Harold Nicolson, E. M. Forster, and other philistines. The remaining essays deal with an array of bookmen (some of them outright scoundrels), with certain notable books (Newton's *Principia*, the "Caxton" manuscript of Ovid), with questions of institutional policy on the acquisition of older books and manuscripts, and with ancient foundations worthy of commemoration (among them, of course, the author's own King's College). Throughout in this memorial collection, and elsewhere in all his work, Munby constantly celebrates the joys of a true bibliophile and never once, I believe, descends to the level of what is called literary criticism.

Waugh as Diarist

Jerome Meckier

Michael Davie, ed. *The Diaries of Evelyn Waugh*. Boston: Little, Brown and Company, 1976. 818 pp.

Now that the often unangelic Waugh is sojourning, hopefully, among the celestials, his autobiography, *A Little Learning* (1964), which stops at 1928, must remain incomplete. Christopher Sykes's official biography seems semihagiographic and a failure at best.[1] So one falls back on the novels: *Brideshead Revisited* for Oxford days, *Decline and Fall* for schoolmastering, *Vile Bodies* for the life-style of the Bright Young Things, *Black Mischief* for Ethiopian escapades, *Sword of Honour* for misadventures in World War II, and *The Ordeal of Gilbert Pinfold* for Waugh's sharpest insights into his own cantankerous temperament.

Given this unsatisfactory but tolerable situation, it is tempting to deplore *The Diaries of Evelyn Waugh*, a matter of 789 pages (340,000 words), as an insufferably long read. Pepys confined his classic diary to nine eventful years following the Restoration of Charles II; the uneconomic Waugh makes seven distinct attempts at a daily record, never persisting more than ten years or less than two. Fortunately for the persevering, these occasionally unguarded documents have a cumulative impact: they contain material that is new or corrective and much that is highly corroborative, attributes sufficient to establish them as an adequate but hardly splendid replacement for the full-length autobiography Waugh would have gracefully carved out of them.

Waugh's diaries do not excel throughout. This is not a book to be swallowed whole. If unfamiliar with *A Little Learning*, the general reader can rejoice: the first three hundred pages of the diaries, from which the only completed portion of the autobiography comes, are the best; but, alas, even they are seldom as good as the autobiography, which means that those who are more familiar with Waugh will be disappointed. Comparison of the diaries and the finished volume of autobiography suggests that the former contains raw materials for the latter, which is invariably more polished if at times, like the diaries themselves, heavily self-centered. At a fairly early stage in his career, perhaps after the success of his first two novels, Waugh began to transform what had been a boyhood exercise into a conscientious storing up of facts for future use. In the late twenties and early thirties the diaries change noticeably, remaining a confidante but becoming more of a ledger or potentially public record. Unlike Adam Fenwick-Symes and the deservedly inconspicuous Johnny Hoop, who plan in *Vile Bodies* to issue callow autobiographies while still in their twenties, Waugh would not publish beforehand, but he would carefully anticipate the future, only to be thwarted, along with his expectant readers, by his own mortality.

Conceivably, Waugh planned to destroy the diaries once he finished the autobiography. It seems certain that he did not view his private record as an independent literary production, although his immensely readable prose style is in evidence as early as 1920. Diarists are obliged to pretend to have no thought of the printer. In Waugh's case, even if he periodically reread his diaries and on one occasion edited them, it is difficult to believe he contemplated or desired their publication. The decision to print was made after his death by his second wife and eldest son.

By Pepysian standards Waugh has scant right to be called a diarist at all. Several of the most important events in his life go deliberately unrecorded. Breaks between attempts at a daily record come at first without discernible cause. There are no entries for his career at Oxford. More regrettably, none exist for the period Davie rightly designates "a watershed" (p. 305): the time between winter 1928 and spring 1930, during which, having married and divorced Evelyn Gardner, Waugh gravitates, perhaps as a consequence, toward Roman Catholicism. More precisely, the twenties diary ends with an entry for 23 November 1928, and the diary for the thirties commences on 19 May 1930. But again in August of that year there is a two-month interruption, during which, in September, Father Martin D'Arcy, S. J., receives Waugh into the Catholic Church. Subsequent accounts of a trip to Addis Ababa for the Emperor's coronation selfishly save the critical religious epiphany Waugh experienced at Debra Lebanos for *Remote People*.[2]

A reason for pauses in Waugh's diaries gradually presents itself. Unless one posits some sort of psychological obstruction, whereby the novelist desires to keep a diary but is compelled to suppress his most private moments, especially such embarrassments as his lunacy in 1954 (the hallucinations described in *The Ordeal of Gilbert Pinfold*), Waugh must have used his notebooks to record mainly ordinary, otherwise forgettable events in his life, a way of binding each to each of days mostly unexceptionable. A suicide attempt, watersheds, conversions and epiphanies—Waugh seems to have no doubt that he can recall these at length and at will, without assistance from a diary. Moreover, he prefers to recall them for oblique, indirect treatment in novels and travel books, never confronting them head-on in the diaries. In the midst of crises, then, the diaries are always suspended until life returns to normal. For whatever reason interruptions occur, they severely limit the autobiographical value of Waugh's diaries and turn one back again toward the novels.

The conclusion that Waugh reserves his diaries for the unexceptionable receives support from the only personal opinion Waugh expressed about the function of private journals: "Nobody wants to read other people's reflections on life and religion and politics," he maintained, "but the routine of their day, properly recorded, is always interesting, and will become more so as conditions change with the years."[3] Waugh's religious and political reflections are liberally sprinkled throughout his travel books. Interspersed with events of the day, such meditations would have enhanced the appeal of his diaries. Without them, Waugh's routine, in early life and later on, seldom rivals the sense of being close to power and greatness readers vicariously experience on a day in the life of Pepys. One regrets that Waugh, as diarist, should have been temperamentally indisposed to the confessional mode or else guilty of serious misjudgment about the kind of diary posterity wanted him to write.

In "The Twenties Diary" several glaring deficiencies, besides the reluctance to record crises, begin to appear in the diarist. One soon detests Waugh's penchant for listing all social engagements, replete with guest list; here, certainly, is an incessant, repetitive round of vile parties. Hangovers are duly noted; vomitings, whether by Waugh himself or his companions, meticulously tabulated. None of it seems to have been in the least pleasurable, a sense that comes across in the early novels that reuse some of this material. Extensive record-keeping—names, dates, places—is de rigueur for all serious diarists; some of the people with whom the diarist celebrates may later achieve fame, as happens, for example, with Waugh's acquaintance Henry Yorke (the novelist Henry Green). But most of the luminaries Waugh mentions have suffered a just eclipse. Scandalous elements in the diaries have lost their power to shock. When Waugh, unlike Pepys, becomes more famous than most of his friends, he often appears to posterity to be name-dropping the names of obscurities. Davie abets this weakness by annotating fully at the bottom of every page and in a thirteen-page Appendix of Names that seems needlessly modeled on the DNB.

And yet, despite the avalanche of parties, persons, and pubs, Waugh's diaries offer few coherent portraits of other people, a disappointing performance for a novelist with so good an eye, and another indication that the diaries, from the 1920s onward, were intended chiefly as a compendium of facts to stir the memory of the eventual autobiographer. One gets a rewarding glimpse of Arthur Waugh, pompously referred to as "Chapman and Hall," finding with pleasure an obscenity in the Bayeux Tapestry, but the full-dress portrait in A Little Learning is much better. Satiric cameos of Alec Waugh, whom his brother called "Baldhead," show him mired in a bohemian world of third-raters but cannot compensate for Evelyn's customary reticence about his mother and both of his wives.

Ultimately, Waugh seems most secretive about himself. His diaries are only intermittently given to self-assessment, although a considerable amount of distaste for self is ubiquitous, never quite overshadowed by his distaste for others. Perhaps a diarist should appreciate himself and other people more than Waugh did, which is to say that satirists make unlikely diarists. Even Waugh's reading during the formative years between Oxford and *Decline and Fall* must be gleaned from scattered asides, such as his praise for T. S. Eliot's "marvellously good" poems that have "a most impressive flavour of the major prophets about them" (p. 242).

Taken by sections in accord with Davie's headings, "The Boyhood Diary 1911-18," "The Lancing Diary 1919-21," and "The Twenties Diary 1924-28" show the diarist at his best, possibly because for most of this period he is not yet self-consciously thinking of an eventual self-portrait in prose. These diaries provide a more detailed, sometimes more candid picture of Waugh's schooldays than can be found in *A Little Learning*. Waugh enjoys the distinction of being the only modern writer of major consequence to keep day-by-day accounts of his school life as it happened. Besides revealing a surprisingly ambitious young man, the diaries for boyhood and for grammar school at Lancing cover the only phases of his existence Waugh never translated into fiction. Once the successful novelist and obstreperous public figure emerges, certainly by "The Thirties Diary 1930-39," one's general knowledge of Waugh's career and the constant use he made of it in his fiction preclude further surprises in "The Wartime Diary 1939-45," "The 1945-56 Diary," and the "Irregular Notes" Waugh jotted down between 1960-65.

Unfairly referred to by a Lancing contemporary as "that awful little tick Waugh," the grammar school boy exhibits few signs of the "consistent caddishness" his older self claims he possessed at age sixteen.[4] But the young aesthete and self-conscious dilettante has scant respect for the diurnal. Often an exemplary student and, on occasion, a taker of prizes, the seventeen-year-old Waugh finds his daily life "revolting," "depressing," "dull," "cheerless," "uneventful," and "infernal" (entries for 6-8 February 1920), an outlook very apparent in the antisecular satires against the modern world by the mature satirist.

Paul Pennyfeather declares that no British schoolboy will afterward consider imprisonment a hardship. Only occasionally does life at Lancing bear him out. Thanks to J. F. Roxburgh, a master who stresses good prose style, and Francis Crease, an unworldly artist in nearby Lychpole who teaches him lettering, Waugh develops strong aesthetic interests; he also grows increasingly skeptical of authority but rises to a position of leadership in his House.[5] By 1920 he is already courting success beyond the boundaries of his school: he begins illustrating book jackets for Chapman and Hall, where his father is managing editor.

In October of that same year Waugh decides "to do his first novel next holidays" (p. 107). As it proceeds, brother Alec is reportedly "apprehensive of a rival" (p. 108). Although nothing comes of this schoolboy effort, it betrays strong literary aspirations at an early age and explodes the impression, created by Waugh himself, that he was otherwise incompetent and fell into novel writing by accident.

Waugh wins the £100 Hertford Scholarship in December of 1921, an accomplishment that climaxes the early portions of the diary and allows him to leave Lancing for Oxford in glory: "I am sure I have left at the right time—as early as possible and with success" (p. 154). But ahead lies failure to take a university degree and the search, over nearly the rest of a decade, for a profession. The pattern of rise and fall adumbrated above is repeated regularly for Waugh: the success of *Decline and Fall* will be followed by the failure of his first marriage; annulment of his union with Evelyn Gardner in 1936 and marriage within a year to Laura Herbert takes place against a background filled with news of Mussolini and Hitler; the self-righteous entrance of England into World War II against Germany eventually allies her with the godless Communism of Tito and Stalin. But Waugh's entries are too preoccupied with names, dates, and places—and the impressions written over forty-four years of diary-keeping are too diffuse—for their author or the general reader to do more than sense, in the life being recorded, overarching themes discernible in the novels.

By the mid-1930s an uneasy Waugh is already heavily reliant on drink and on sleeping draughts, doping himself almost nightly, as he would continue to do until his death. The terse entry in "The Thirties Diary" for 18 April 1937—"Lovely day, lovely house, lovely wife, great happiness"—seems unintentionally ironic in light of imminent upheaval, the necessity to leave Piers Court for the duration, and nearly six years of frustrating military service that follow. The irony deepens when Waugh's account of martial misadventures in "The Wartime Diary," a depressing chronicle of boredom, futility, waste, and mismanagement, corroborates Crouchback's experiences in *Sword of Honour*, the novel for which Waugh's disillusionments in Laycock's Special Service Brigade (LAYFORCE) and his expulsion from Dubrovnik after angering Tito's partisans virtually provide a rough draft.

Waugh's finest hours during the wartime period take place far from battlefields. In 1944 he obtains special leave to write *Brideshead Revisited*. The romantic thesis of this novel, namely, that the hand of God still providentially pulls the strings, reflects the wartime surge of crusader's optimism in Waugh's thinking, a surge he must have realized was being discredited by daily events even as he wrote. In 1945 he appeals to his government and the Pope to halt the extinction of Christianity by the new regimes that were coming to power in Eastern Europe with support from the Allies. Waugh's essay, "Church and State in Liberated Croatia," which was sent, unsolicited, to the Foreign Office, is an excellent gesture and a prophecy. Along with *Brideshead Revisited* and the illegal maintenance of a diary when on active duty, this essay becomes one of only three decent pieces of war work during six years of service. A pidgin English description of aid raids, which Waugh overheard in Freetown-Gibraltar in 1940, can be used epigraphically to set the tone for the entire wartime diary: "Steam chicken top side drop plenty no good shit" (p. 483).

In the midst of disappointment with global war comes a rebirth in 1944 of creative energies: "Thank God I think I am beginning to acquire a style"; "I feel full of literary power" (pp. 558, 560). Entries in "The 1945-56 Diary" continue in this vein. Yet mounting artistic confidence cannot offset the conviction that life, after the war, has entered a postapocalyptic phase.

Announcing the collapse of Europe and dreading the advance of Russia and heathenism, Waugh hits upon a solution: catacombs. He prides himself on being "uncontemporary" (p. 627), like his own Scott-King. However, the acidity that once inspired him to characterize Noel Coward as "simple, friendly" but with "no brains" (p. 320) delightfully persists. In April of 1945 Waugh reports that he "chucked appointment to show London to insignificant Yank named Edmund Wilson, critic" (p. 625).

Waugh the ogre is much in evidence throughout the final 150 pages of the diaries. He confesses he can only look upon his children as "defective adults" (p. 640) and becomes inordinately fond of suing the newspapers for libel. Misanthropy, the bane of aging satirists, seems ever a distinct possibility. During the last nineteen years of his life Waugh makes only one major addition to his novelist's storehouse of experiences. Venturing to Hollywood in 1947 to discuss a film of *Brideshead Revisited*, which he knows will never be made, he finds, instead, the exploitable idiocy of Forest Lawn, "a deep mine of literary gold" (p. 675) and an obligatory target for a satirist resentful of the modern tendency to secularize everything, even Death.

By the mid-1950s Waugh's confidence in the Church as a "peculiar people bound by human and divine loyalties" gives place to the fear that it is really "a nondescript crowd with comings and goings hapzard" (p. 751), another worldly club not greatly superior to White's. Self-assessments, now indulged in more regularly, become harsh and unsparing. Waugh's dissatisfaction with changes in the Church's liturgy seems sufficiently bitter to become a statement universal in extent: "I shall not live to see things righted" (p. 789), he laments in 1965, the year before his death.

In view of so depressing a final prospect, the entry for 9 May 1962 can stand as the pivotal passage in the entire set of diaries. Waugh summarizes his final position under the heading *"Abjuring the realm.* To make an *interior* act of renunciation and to become a stranger in the world; to watch one's fellow-countrymen, as one used to watch foreigners . . . that is the secret of happiness in this century of the common man" (p. 783).

Waugh has no sympathy for the kind of century hailed by fellow convert G. K. Chesterton. The realm to be abjured, of course, is the temporal order. Observing it as a stranger would watch foreigners is to function as a satirist. Abjuration, recusancy, exile within one's own country and era, unconditional surrender of all hope for salvation or even sense within the secular world—these accumulated attitudes admit of retrospective application; they explain all of Waugh, not just *Sword of Honour*. This kind of contempt for the world pervades the Augustan poise of Waugh's earliest comedy and makes his satire and his Catholicism inseparable.

Pennyfeather retreats to Scone, Last vanishes into the Brazilian jungle, Crouchback abandons his crusade. None is particularly heroic or victorious, but each tries, although only Crouchback succeeds, to abjure the realm. An intrinsically religious impulse lies behind Waugh's finest satire, early and late: the urge not to chastize and reform, activities which seem hopeless anyway, but to renounce and repudiate.

One is tempted to repudiate some of the editorial principles at play throughout this seemingly endless edition. Excessively vigilant fastidiousness is one such faulty principle. As Davie notes, Waugh ripped out several entries from "The Lancing Diary" in October of 1919. They may have been about the undergraduate homosexual experiences mentioned by his official biographer. Waugh must have had a scare, real or imagined. His resolve in 1919 "to be wiser" (p. 26) in what he wrote from then on may have condemned him, at age sixteen, to the subsequent failures in candor that firmly exclude him from the select company of major diarists. Davie behaves as overprotectingly as Waugh. In addition to excisions made by the novelist, he deletes twenty-three allegedly libelous references and omits another twenty phrases on grounds of their pure offensiveness. To protect sensibilities Waugh often tried hard to outrage, Davie sometimes replaces names with dashes or, tantalizingly, supplies only initials. Seven supposedly brief cuts were made at the insistence of the Waugh Estate, which retained veto power over the project.

Suppressing what a man says in confidence to his diary, no matter how vulgar or unfair the observations, defeats the purpose of publishing so private a document in the first place. Printing someone's diary is an acute invasion of privacy. Famous people who compile personal records may be said to court the intrusion. Having committed the initial breach of decorum by electing to publish, Davie and the Waugh Estate might as well have told all. Their caution appears old-maidish, especially to American readers unfamiliar, as Waugh was not, with the minefield of English libel law.

Few of Waugh's friends ever knew he kept a diary. News that he did so must have caused considerable panic. Some no doubt feared the worst from Waugh's acerbic pen and his fondness for inventing mischievous fantasies about his acquaintances. A man who could pretend at length that Tito was actually a woman and keep up the joke even while serving as British liaison to anti-Nazi partisans in Yugoslavia was obviously not to be trusted. However, members of the extraordinarily large cast in Waugh's private pages have little about which to be seriously alarmed.

Consequently, further cuts, not of allegedly objectionable materials but of purely factual or repetitious entries, might have saved the reader from periodic attacks of boredom. Davie senses the danger. He abbreviates "The Lancing Diary" by about ten thousand words, which accounts in part for the superiority of this section. Elsewhere, only the occasional sentence has been canceled. Unintelligible words or phrases Davie sometimes relegates to his footnotes rather than guess at their meaning in the text. His policy, outside "The Lancing Diary," is editorial inclusiveness (rather than judicious cutting) on grounds that even tedious passages may interest someone. This position is difficult to refute but impossible to endorse with much enthusiasm. It presupposes a situation in which the statute of limitations never expires.

For example, whether Dudley Carew slept with a woman named Joyce in 1925—as Waugh's entry for 22 September charges but Carew, in a letter to the editor, disputes—seems to be, at this late date, of no earthly interest; yet one cannot be absolutely certain, and the diaries abound in more difficult, less ridiculous instances for their editor to resolve. The decision to publish in bulk and let posterity find what it needs is certainly safest. Still, one ought to speak up for the general reader. The original manuscript of the diaries remains available to scholars willing to travel to the Humanities Research Center, University of Texas (Austin). A shortened but more readable version might have been commercially and aesthetically advisable.

A poor speller, Waugh benefits throughout the diaries from Davie's silent corrections. The editor standardizes capitalization and adds some necessary punctuation, an aspect of style that Waugh often ignored in his diaries. Davie strives "to reproduce Waugh's own words as accurately as possible." His preface carefully describes the kind of loose sheets or notebook used for each diary. Starting in 1930, when Waugh became a celebrity and probably foresaw an autobiography, the quality of paper improves and the length of entries increases. Introductions Davie furnishes to the different diaries are uniformly brief but consistently serviceable.

It is as annotator that Davie's editorial practice appears most questionable. New relationships between Waugh's diaries and his fiction emerge at times on almost every page, but Davie's footnotes seldom venture beyond what is already established. Either he misses the rest or believes that editorial responsibilities and critical license must be kept separate. Perhaps they should remain distinct, but the decision to overburden the reader with notes and index meticulously identifying every personage Waugh encounters fosters tedium, while reluctance to lead critical opinion in new directions avoids controversy—and, of course, error—at the price of becoming editorially bland.

During the better part of the unsettled decade after Waugh leaves Oxford and searches for his true profession, life providentially supplies him with most of the material a beginning satirical novelist requires. Yet Davie includes no footnote on the similarity between Llanddulas, the location in Wales of Waugh's first teaching job, and Llanabba, where Pennyfeather toils. He identifies Young, whom Waugh calls a "monotonously pederastic" usher, as model for Grimes but neglects to comment on the remarkable similarity between Young's history of himself, delivered drunkenly to Waugh on 3

July 1925, and Grimes's seemingly far-fetched account of a checkered career three years later in *Decline and Fall.*

Footnoting is not only often remiss but frequently inconsistent. Davie can expend space to award a modicum of immortality to Enid Raphael for a remark worthy of Agatha Runcible: "I don't know why people talk about private parts. *Mine* aren't private" (p. 315). But his extended account of Waugh's preparations for a trip to Brazil draws none of the revealing parallels between this undertaking and Tony Last's journey in *A Handful of Dust.* Waugh seems to have left London for South America to forget his strong attachment to Baby Jungman,whom he believed his divorce and subsequent entrance into the church prevented him from marrying. In *A Handful of Dust* Tony bypasses Therese de Vitre and a pocket of sanity in Catholic Creole Trinidad to perish in the Brazilian jungle while pursuing a nonexistent Eldorado. Like Miss Vitre, Baby Jungman was Catholic. Her given name was Teresa. In the departure of a cuckolded Tony for insalubrious climes Waugh combines his own marital disappointments and his failure to investigate the possibility that, upon converting, he might have married again without impediment.

Entries from the diary suggest a resemblance between Dr. Roth, who offers to take Waugh "to the only place where unsophisticated Indians are still to be found" (p. 361), and Dr. Messinger, who conducts Tony to his death. Unlike Tony, Waugh knows that savages flourish everywhere in the modern world; he need not make a special trip to seek them out. Observations in the diary during March 1933 reveal that there really were Macushi Indians and even Piai (Pie-wie in *A Handful of Dust.*) On these and numerous other matters equally deserving of editorial attention, Davie remains silent.

As a result his edition of Waugh's diaries adds to the deficiencies of the diarist. The volume suffers from a fundamental lack of editorial direction: too long to be read generally, the diaries are too short on literary criticism and scholarly annotation to influence the state of Waugh studies directly. But they will doubtless remain a substitute for Waugh's unfinished autobiography and become a useful tool for essays in criticism by others.[6]

Notes

1. Sykes, *Evelyn Waugh: A Biography* (London: Collins, 1975). See my review in *Contemporary Literature*, 18 (Winter 1977), 98-109.

2. The secrecy surrounding rituals and relics at Debra Lebanos Monastery suddenly reveals to Waugh that "the classic basilica and open altar" of Western Christianity are "a great positive achievement." In Catholic Europe, "where Mass is said in a flood of light," the dark and hidden Church of the first century is gone forever. It evolved into a symbol for clarity and rationality. One can define its theology "as the science of simplification by which nebulous and elusive ideas are formalized and made intelligible and exact." This epiphany and Waugh's explication of it explain what the Catholic Church meant to him and why, upon entering it a short time before, he did so with quiet confidence rather than emotional fervor. See the excerpt from *Remote People* in *When the Going was Good* (Harmondsworth, England: Penguin Books, 1969), pp. 118-19.

3. Davie includes this passage as a footnote. It is taken from Waugh's "One Way to Immortality," *Daily Mail*, 28 June 1930, p. 8.

4. Waugh, *A Little Learning* (Boston: Little, Brown and Co., 1964), p. 127.

5. Waugh discusses his indebtedness to Roxburgh and Crease in "Two Mentors," Chapter 7 of *A Little Learning*.

6. Other works that shed light on Waugh's personality include David Pryce-Jones, *Evelyn Waugh and His World* (London: Weidenfeld and Nicholson, 1973); Frances Donaldson, *Evelyn Waugh: Portrait of a Country Neighbour* (London: Weidenfeld and Nicolson, 1967); John St. John, *To the War with Waugh* (London: Leo Cooper, 1974); and Alec Waugh, *My Brother Evelyn and Other Profiles* (New York: Farrar, Straus & Giroux, 1967).

The *Review* Association

Major funding for *Review* is provided by a grant from the Research Division and the College of Arts and Sciences at Virginia Polytechnic Institute and State University. Additional support is provided by The *Review* Association, a group of major universities which support the aims and purposes of the series. Member universities are as follows:

Columbia University
Duke University
University of Minnesota
Pennsylvania State
  University

Princeton University
University of Southern
  California
University of Virginia

Contributors

RICHARD D. ALTICK is Regents' Professor of English at Ohio State University.

N. F. BLAKE is Professor of English Language at the University of Sheffield.

JOHN C. BRODERICK, formerly Chief of the Manuscript Division at the Library of Congress, is now Assistant Librarian for Research Services.

PETER C. CARAFIOL is Assistant Professor of English at Temple University.

RONALD CHRIST is Professor of English at Livingston College, Rutgers University.

DON L. COOK is Professor of English at Indiana University and Chairman of the MLA Committee on Scholarly Editions.

RICHARD J. DUNN is Associate Professor of English at the University of Washington.

RICHARD J. FINNERAN is Professor of English at Newcomb College.

RALPH HANNA III is Associate Professor of English at the University of California, Riverside.

FRANCIS RUSSELL HART is Professor of English at the University of Massachusetts, Boston.

SAMUEL HYNES is Professor of English at Princeton University.

GERHARD JOSEPH is Professor of English at Herbert H. Lehman College, CUNY.

WAYNE R. KIME is Associate Professor of English at Fairmont State College.

WILLIAM MATHESON is Chief of the Rare Book and Special Collections Division, Library of Congress.

JEROME MECKIER is Professor of English at the University of Kentucky.

THOMAS L. McHANEY is Professor of English at Georgia State University.

JOHN H. MIDDENDORF is Professor of English at Columbia University and General Editor of the Yale Edition of the Works of Samuel Johnson.

HERSHEL PARKER is Professor of English at the University of Southern California.

JEAN F. PRESTON is Curator of Manuscripts at Princeton University Library.

DONALD H. REIMAN is Editor of *Shelley and his Circle* at The Carl H. Pforzheimer Library.

FLORENCE RIDLEY is Professor of English at UCLA.

ROSSELL HOPE ROBBINS is International Professor of English at the State University of New York at Albany.

G. THOMAS TANSELLE is Vice President of the John Simon Guggenheim Memorial Foundation.

WILLIAM B. TODD is Professor of English at the University of Texas at Austin and Editor of *Papers of the Bibliographical Society of America*.

STANLEY WEINTRAUB is Research Professor and Director of the Institute for the Arts and Humanistic Studies at Pennsylvania State University.

JAMES WELLS is Vice President of the Newberry Library and Custodian of the John M. Wing Foundation on the History of Printing.

WILLIAM P. WILLIAMS is Associate Professor of English at Northern Illinois University and Editor of *Analytical & Enumerative Bibliography*.

JOSEPH WITTREICH is Professor of English at the University of Maryland.